THE ART OF THE UNKNOWN

Quarto

First published in 2026 by Frances Lincoln,
an imprint of The Quarto Group.
One Triptych Place, London, SE1 9SH,
United Kingdom
T (0)20 7700 9000
www.Quarto.com

EEA Representation, WTS Tax d.o.o., Žanova ulica 3,
4000 Kranj, Slovenia
www.wts-tax.si

A catalogue record for this book is available from the British Library.

ISBN 978-1-80570-118-7
Ebook ISBN 978-1-80570-119-4

10 9 8 7 6 5 4 3 2 1

Design by Masumi Briozzo

Publisher: Philip Cooper
Editorial Director: Alice Graham
Managing Editor: Laura Bulbeck
Editorial Support: Róisín Duffy
Senior Designer: Isabel Eeles
Senior Production Controller: Rohana Yusof

Printed in Guangdong, China TT052026

FSC www.fsc.org MIX Paper | Supporting responsible forestry FSC® C016973

Front cover: *Dimensional Forest*, Linda Westin, 2019, photographic collage. © Linda Westin, 2019. Used by permission.

Back cover: *Phantasma*, Nona Limmen, 2023, photography. Model: Michele Delving; photograph © Nona Limmen.

Interior images copyright stated on p.239.

S. ELIZABETH

THE ART OF THE UNKNOWN

A VISUAL TREASURY OF THE ESOTERIC, UNCANNY AND UNEXPLAINED

FRANCES LINCOLN

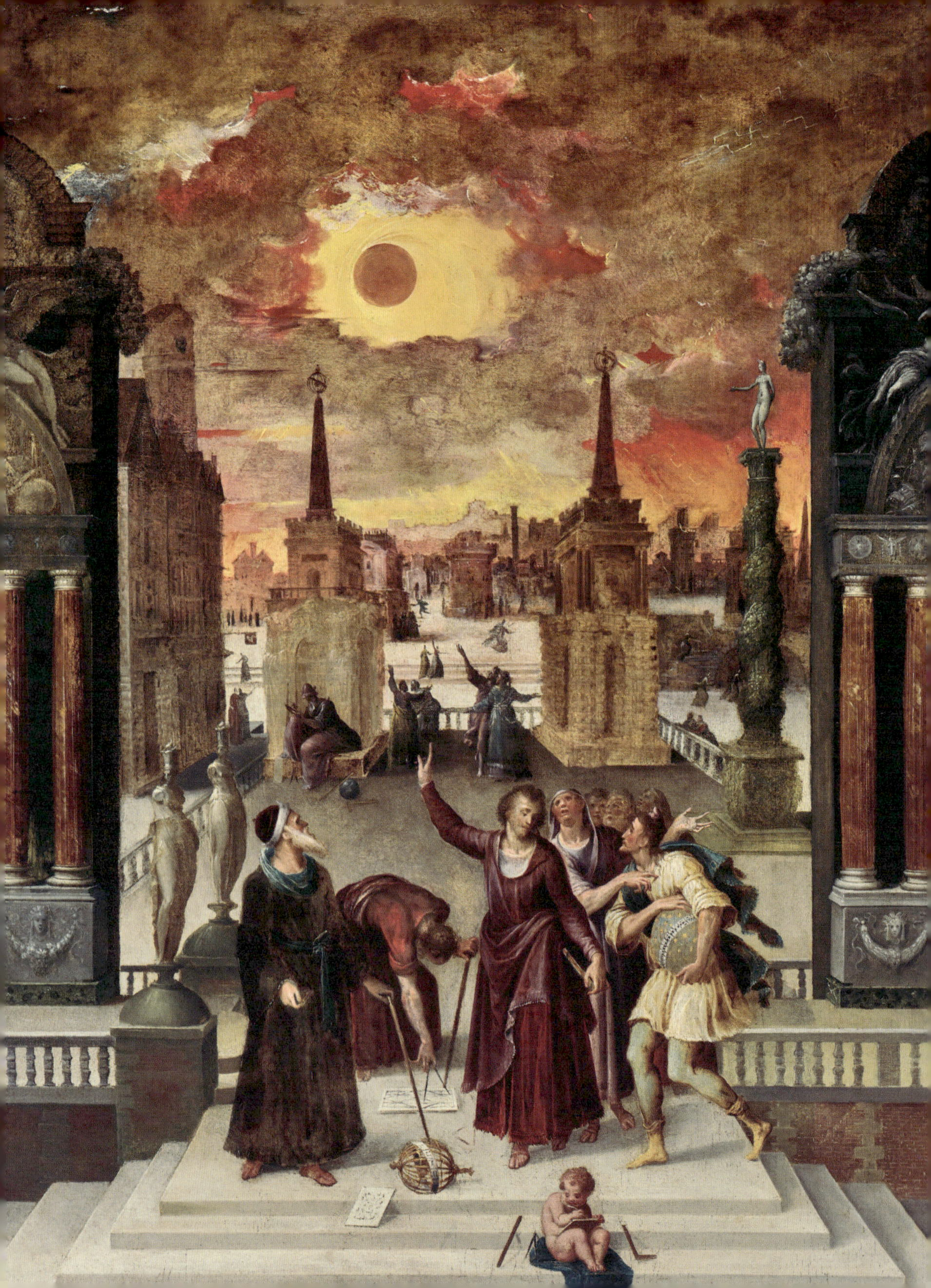

Introduction: The Mind Wobbles

In the 1980s, there was a wonderfully silly sketch comedy on Canadian TV called *You Can't Do That on Television*, where they would dump lurid green slime on anyone who said 'I don't know'. Great show, terrible lesson. An entire generation, including me, internalized the message to treat uncertainty like failure, instead of recognizing that the unknown is where all the best mysteries begin.

Three little words: I don't know. Why are they so hard to say? Whether we're asked about complex political issues or what happens after we die (no pressure!), we're often hesitant to admit when we don't have answers. Our brains actually hate uncertainty. Neurologically, not knowing can trigger the same threat response as physical danger. *Married... with Children*'s Kelly Bundy, the ditzy but lovable daughter from the irreverent American sitcom, accidentally nailed it, turning 'the mind boggles' into 'the mind wobbles', and that linguistic slip captured something true about how uncertainty affects us. That wobbling makes us rush to fill gaps in our knowledge, even with complete nonsense, just to alleviate the discomfort.

Ancient Greeks invented elaborate stories to explain why the sun moved across the sky. Medieval scholars populated their map margins with monsters that might as well have been labelled 'here be answers'. Victorian scientists envisioned an invisible 'aether' that filled all of space, like so much cosmic bubble wrap. Today, we have our own ways of filling the void: conspiracy theories, AI predictions and a culture that has embraced *The X-Files*' core principle that the truth is out there. This might seem contradictory, celebrating mystery while also championing the search for truth. But mystery is what makes truth-seeking necessary and worthwhile.

Throughout recorded time, we've been driven to explain the unexplainable, to find meaning in mystery, to illuminate the

Previous spread: Dionysius the Areopagite Converting the Pagan Philosophers, Antoine Caron, 1570s, oil on panel

Opposite: Chimères, Pascal Dagnan-Bouveret, *c.* 1899, oil on canvas

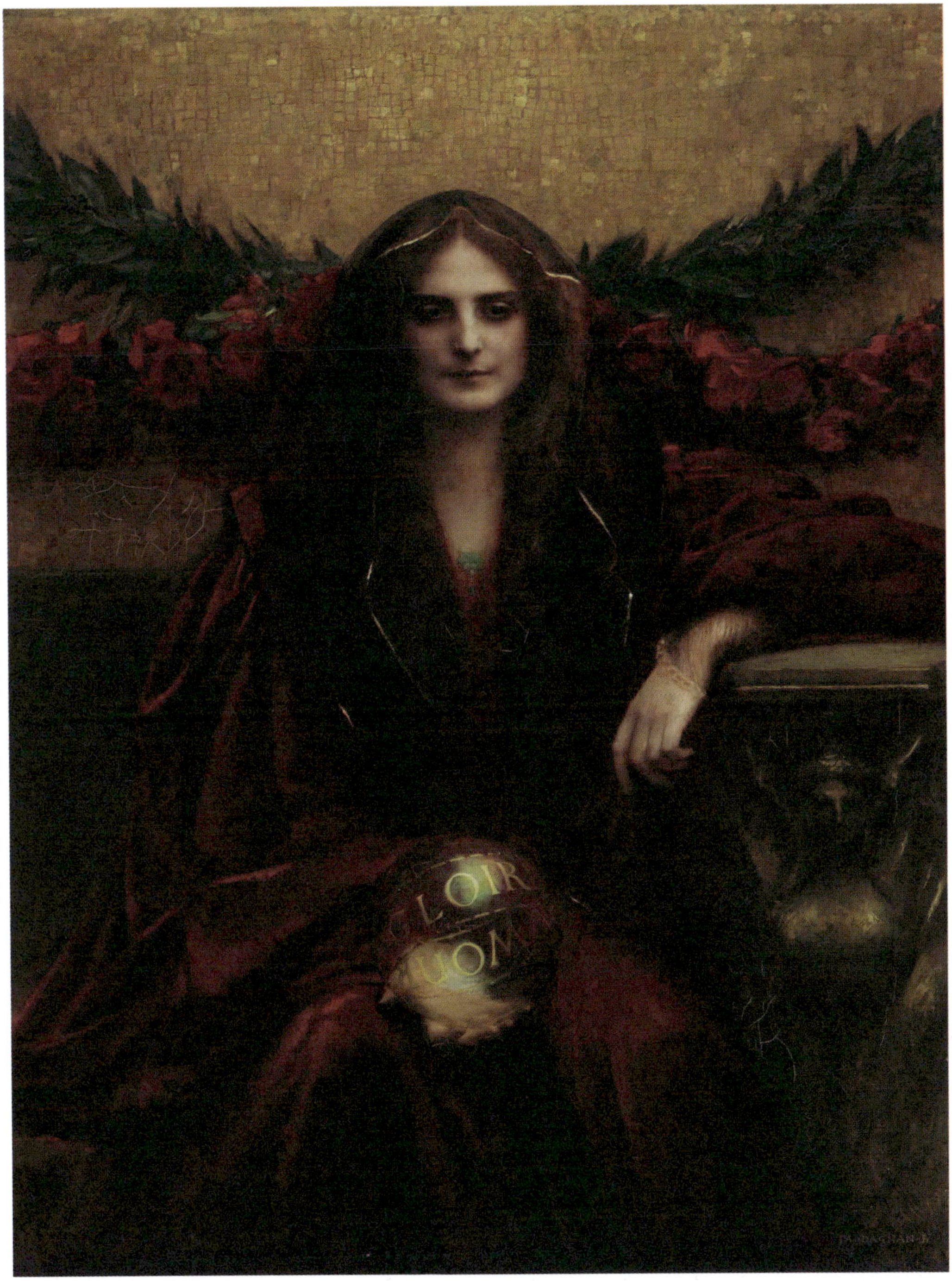
LOIR
UOM

darkness. When faced with phenomena we can't understand, we create stories, develop theories, seek solutions. When we acknowledge what we don't know, we make room for something new to emerge, whether that's knowledge, understanding or art that attempts to capture the very feeling of standing at the edge of the unknowable.

Like Charles Fort, the patron saint of 'I don't know', who spent his life collecting reports of unexplained phenomena (and whose name became synonymous with the unexplained itself!), artists approach mystery not necessarily with the goal of solving, but of exploring. They make art from the very thing the rest of us try to avoid. David Lynch, whose films left audiences simultaneously deeply disturbed and masterfully mesmerized, built an entire career exploring what couldn't be explained – without ever bothering to explain it!

Like any good Lynchian rabbit hole, this book will not provide answers. But when language fails us, when scientific instruments reach their limits, when religious doctrine raises

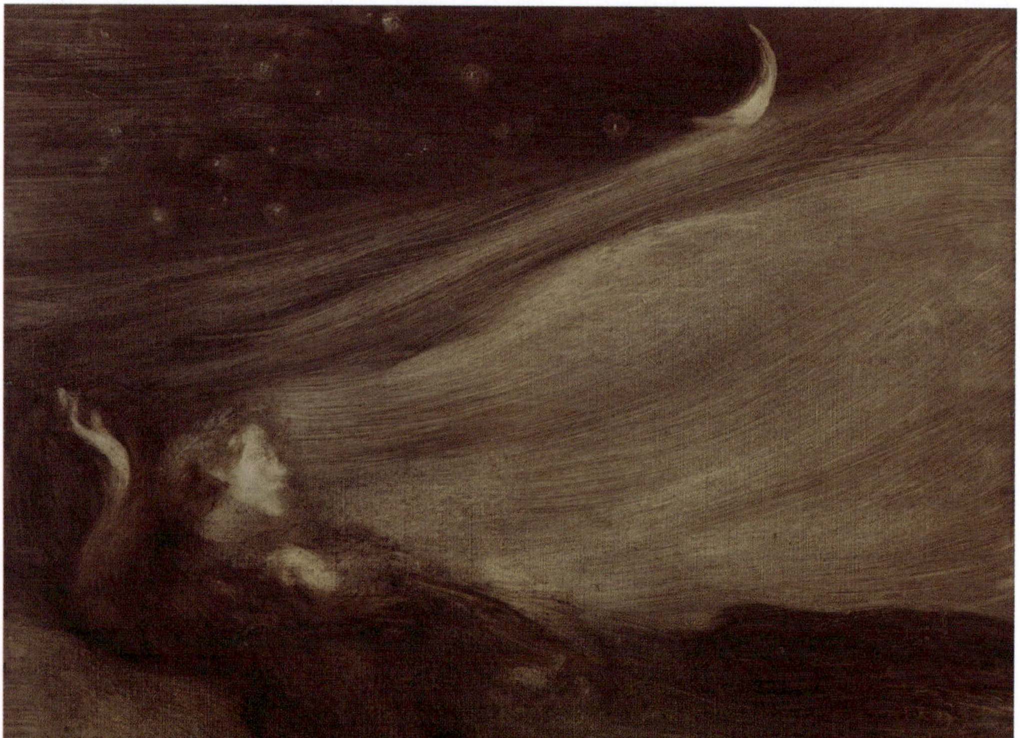

more questions than it settles, we turn to art. Artists throughout history have developed unique visual languages to document their encounters with the inexplicable, creating maps of unmappable territories, building bridges to unreachable realms, giving form to formless mysteries. Their work provides not explanations, but experiences; not certainty, but wonder. And wonder, that most precious of human responses, cannot be overrated. Writer, YouTube educator and champion of intellectual curiosity John Green once rated his own sense of wonder: 'Still, I am fond of my capacity for wonder. I give it three and a half stars.' (Why only 3.5? Perhaps that's what makes it trustworthy – I mean, who believes five-star self-reviews anyway?)

Ten-year-old cartoon wise guy/philosopher Bart Simpson once observed: '… what you don't know could fill a warehouse'. Consider this book your guided tour of that warehouse, but don't expect neat labels on these shelves. Like Lynch's dreamscapes or Bart Simpson's unwitting wisdom, what we don't know might just be the most interesting part of the journey.

These pages illuminate a path through the realms of mystery and wonder that artists have dared to explore. We begin by looking skywards, to cosmic forces and celestial powers that pulse through the universe, before venturing into twilight realms and parallel dimensions that exist alongside our own. We'll investigate curious remnants and inexplicable artefacts, from spirit photographs to forgotten symbols, from ghostly apparitions to ancient knowledge that hints at worlds beyond our grasp. Finally, we'll turn inwards to examine how humans have used art to navigate the mysteries of our own nature, from prophetic visions to sacred ceremonies, from altered states of consciousness to the eternal cycles that bind us to the unknown.

Step into this warehouse of wonders. Here in these shadowy aisles, between certainty and mystery, artists have left field notes from expeditions into the impossible. Some brought back photographs of ghosts; others drew maps of rooms that never existed, painted angels that arrived in midnight visions or captured portraits of their own doubles caught in endless mirrors. A few never returned at all, though you might glimpse their shadows flickering at the edges of unfinished canvases, still searching for ways to paint the unpaintable.

Their stories await. And in their wake, endless mysteries still unfold.

Opposite: The Contemplator, Eugène Carrière, 1901, oil on fabric

PART ONE

—

FORCES BEYOND

'When we try to pick out anything by itself, we find it hitched to everything else in the universe.'

– JOHN MUIR

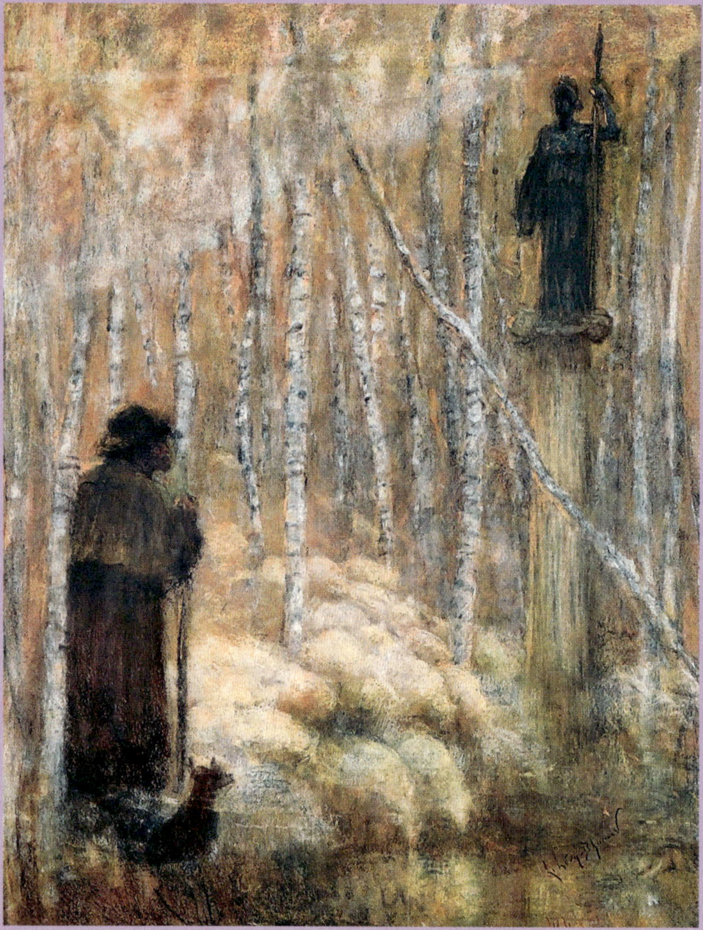

Greek Shepherd, Lucien Lévy-Dhurmer, date unknown, pastel on paper

Stand outside on a clear night, far from city lights. Let your eyes adjust until the Milky Way emerges like a river of light overhead. Now consider this: what you're seeing is already history. Those photons travelled hundreds, thousands, millions of years to reach your retina. Some of those stars are already dead, their light a ghost story written in radiation. Others harbour planets we'll never see, mysteries we'll never solve. And this faintly, flickeringly visible cosmos is but a fraction of what's out there! Dark matter and dark energy make up 95 per cent of the universe, yet remain fundamentally undetectable to our best instruments. We can't see them, touch them or measure them directly. We only know they're there because of how they bend space, move galaxies and shape everything we can see.

Look closer now, at your own hand silhouetted against the stars. Within each of your cells, energy transforms matter according to rules we barely understand. Consciousness itself – the part of you experiencing this moment – arises from neural firing patterns that defy complete explanation. Forces beyond comprehension stretch across light years while simultaneously flowing through our bodies, whispering in our dreams, inhabiting the shadowy territories between certainty and intuition. Artists across the ages have ventured into these nebulous realms armed with brushes, chisels, cameras and courage, returning with artefacts from their encounters with the infinite.

Medieval manuscript illuminators painted angels wrestling with cosmic spheres, their gold leaf alternately sharpening and softening candlelight like woozy stars swimming in and out of focus. Renaissance mystics mapped celestial hierarchies with mathematical precision, while Romantic painters tried to capture divine light breaking through storm clouds. The night sky has beckoned countless creative souls to its mysteries. Some braved sleepless nights translating constellations into vibrating watercolours; others sought desert refuges where celestial bodies burned with unfiltered brilliance, inspiring works in which cosmic energies crystallize into pigment and form.

From prehistoric cave paintings to immersive digital environments, humans have documented our curious awareness of unseen companions in the world around us. That disquieting shiver of being watched when no one is there has manifested across cultural traditions – Japanese prints alive with spectral yokai lurking at forest edges, Renaissance paintings where angels

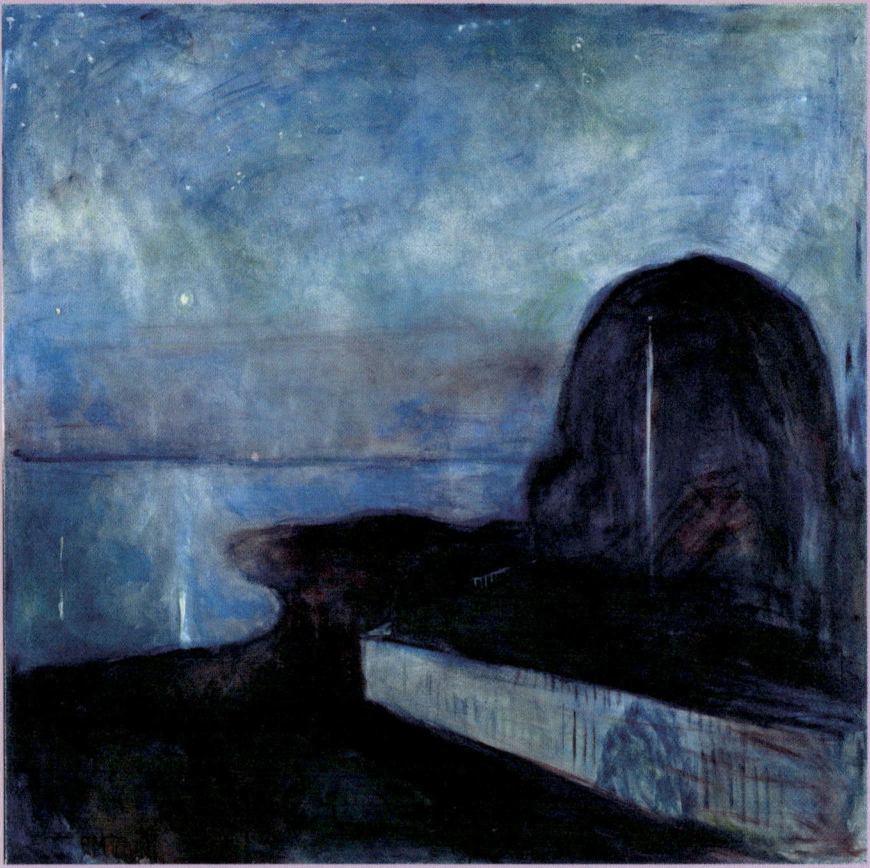

peer from behind clouds, contemporary installations where surveillance becomes a metaphor for cosmic attention. We create these otherworldly observers perhaps because we intuitively sense the universe as conscious presence – not an empty void but a living attention, holding everything in its gaze.

In studios ancient and modern, artists have pursued the mysteries of transformation with the fervour of alchemists – though thankfully with considerably less poisoning by mercury vapour. Today's artistic innovators transform paint through oxidation, coax metals to bloom into crystalline structures and transmute digital code into living patterns that seem to breathe with consciousness. Where scientists map the pathways of these transmutations, artists capture their poetry – the moment when liquid becomes solid, when organic matter ignites into flame, when consciousness flickers into being across neural networks of living tissue or silicon. They

Above: Starry Night, Edvard Munch, 1893, oil on canvas

document matter's journey through its endless incarnations: water to vapour to cloud to rain, seed to tree to paper to ash, stardust to human to art and back to stardust again.

From the infinite above to the ineffable within, wildly mind-bending realities pulse through our existence. Visual artists aren't alone in their fascination with these mysteries. As the modern era dawned, creators across disciplines developed new vocabularies for the ineffable – Italo Calvino imagining the birth of the universe through the eyes of a cosmic witness, Björk weaving ancient myths into electronic soundscapes about creation, Iris van Herpen crafting garments that transform like living organisms under impossible physics, Andrei Tarkovsky's cinematic meditations, where time itself becomes visible. These parallel explorations mirror what painters and sculptors have long pursued: how to capture the uncapturable, how to speak the unspeakable, how to give form to forces that exist at the edges of human comprehension.

As Carl Sagan reminded us, we are made of 'star-stuff', our very atoms forged in cosmic furnaces that died before Earth was born. When artists venture into these luminous mysteries, perhaps they are simply following an ancient calling: the universe, through our art, learning to see its own wonders, teaching itself to dream.

Below: Death of the Sun, Moon and Stars Falling, Cristoforo de Predis, *c.* 1476, illuminated miniature on parchment

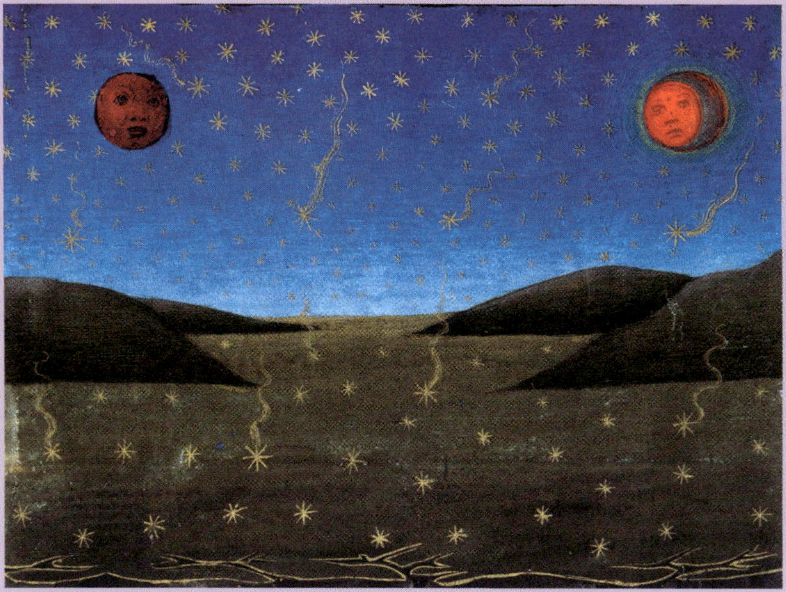

I

—

COSMIC MYSTERIES

'When you consider things like the stars, our affairs don't seem to matter very much, do they?'

– VIRGINIA WOOLF

Imagine standing beside Galileo on that January night in 1610, your breath visible in the cold air as you peer through his telescope. What appeared at first to be fixed stars are actually four moons circling Jupiter – and with that, the awkward realization that the universe doesn't actually revolve around us. Such moments of extraordinary (and humbling!) revelation have both expanded and confounded our cosmic comprehension throughout history, leaving us to grapple with perplexities and paradoxes that seem to multiply with each new discovery.

Throughout time, humans have gazed upwards and found themselves staggered by the vast unknowns above. Ancient astronomers traced patterns in the stars, medieval mystics sought divine whispers in celestial events, and contemporary scientists, for all their gleaming instruments and elegant equations, still fumble in the darkness to grasp dark matter – that invisible force that comprises most of our universe yet remains stubbornly, perhaps gloriously, unknowable. As America's first professional woman astronomer, Maria Mitchell knew something about reaching for the seemingly impossible. Looking up at the same stars we see today, she captured our shared sense of cosmic vertigo perfectly: 'The world of learning is so broad, and the human soul is so limited in power! We reach forth and strain every nerve, but we seize only a bit of the curtain that hides the infinite from us.'

This cosmic uncertainty extends even to the familiar canvas of our own skies, and throughout history, humans have documented unexplained celestial phenomena. Illuminators worked by candlelight in dimly lit medieval scriptoriums to capture the mysteries above, fingers stained with precious gold leaf and lapis lazuli, tracing cosmic diagrams that merged earthly observation with divine vision. Remarkable twelfth-century abbess Hildegard von Bingen reimagined the cosmos as a luminous egg cradling all of creation, its shell a resplendent aurora crackling with stars and radiantly ablaze with divine fire, a cosmic devilled egg with a filling of pure divinity. Meanwhile, Arab astronomers created star maps that married mathematical precision with such artistic finesse that celestial choreography looked like cartographic poetry.

Giovanni di Paolo's 1445 *Creation of the World* reimagined the universe as a dazzling cosmic mechanism, God whirling the wheel of creation like a gigantic over-engineered hula hoop.

William Blake, that glorious mystic-rebel, gave us *The Ancient of Days*, with his fierce cosmic architect leaning from the molten heart of a sun, through churning clouds of creation, golden compass poised to inscribe the boundaries of existence upon the void. Blake's creator, part divine geometer, part celestial tyrant, burns with sublime intensity as he imposes sacred geometry upon primordial darkness.

Below: God, Cosmos and Humanity, miniature from *Liber Scivias*, Hildegard von Bingen, *c.* 1175, watercolour on parchment

When Romantic painters turned their eyes to the heavens, they wrestled with the sublime terror and beauty of infinite space. Vincent van Gogh's stars pulse and swirl with almost desperate energy, as if capturing not just their light but their very essence. Caspar David Friedrich's moonwatchers stand at the edge of the world – solitary figures embodying our eternal awe before the great cosmic unknown. Later, visionary Albert Pinkham Ryder transformed his canvases into windows into primordial chaos, with waves that could be either ocean or cosmic matter, eternally churning under a moon that feels like an omnipotent, all-seeing (but hopefully nonjudgemental?) eye gazing back at us.

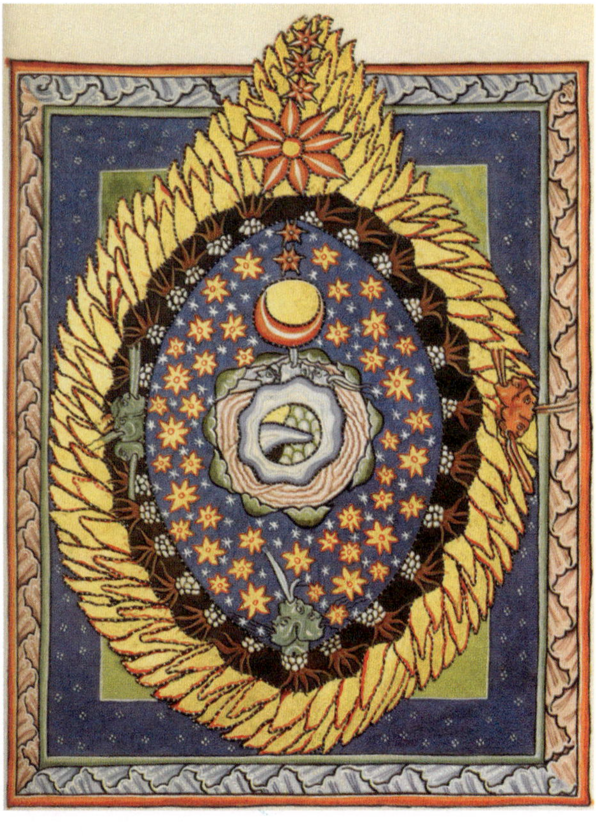

Today's artists are cosmic explorers with new tools in hand but ancient questions in heart. Step into one of James Turrell's viewing chambers at Roden Crater, and you'll find yourself sprawled beneath the heavens like our ancestors, only here, the sky's moods shift through impossible colours as your perception unravels and reconstructs itself. Tomás Saraceno suspends us in gossamer realms where we drift, weightless, through installations that mirror vast cosmic webs, while Sarah Sze, part magician, part curator of overlooked infinities, summons entire universes from the forgotten debris of everyday life.

Consider this cosmic irony: the more we learn about the universe, the more we realize just how much of it is literally invisible to us.

Right: The Creation of the World and the Expulsion from Paradise, Giovanni di Paolo, 1445, tempera and gold on wood

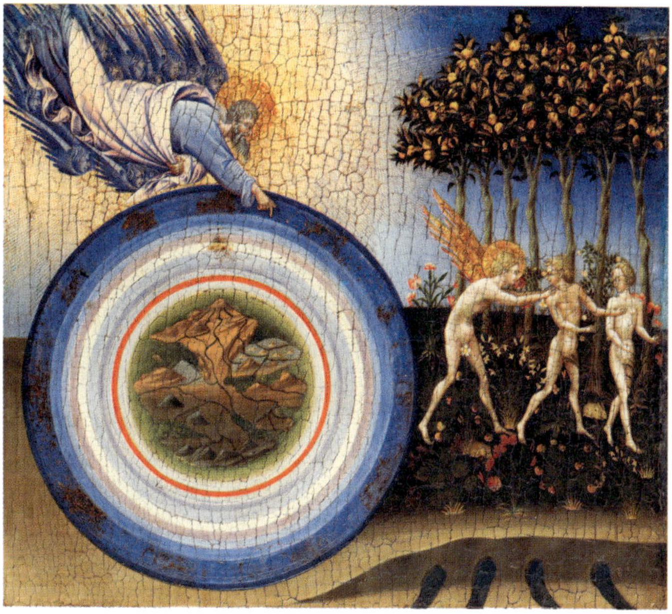

As astronomer Vera Rubin wryly noted, 'In a spiral galaxy, the ratio of dark-to-light matter is about a factor of ten. That's probably a good number for the ratio of our ignorance-to-knowledge.' The cosmos has a wicked sense of humour about keeping its secrets – revealing just enough to leave us perpetually humbled and hungry for more.

These explorations of cosmic mystery transcend artistic exercise and stand as scintillating invitations to wonder. Whether squinting through a primitive telescope, tracing fingers along gilded medieval star charts or wandering through glowing chambers where reality bends with the setting sun, we aren't just viewing art. We're gazing through windows of imagination, glimpsing impossibly distant realms, revelling in new pathways through the void. The mystery above us remains vast and largely untouchable, but perhaps that very unattainability is what keeps us looking up, night after night, century after century, asking questions beyond what language can answer and creating art that stretches our fingers towards the stars.

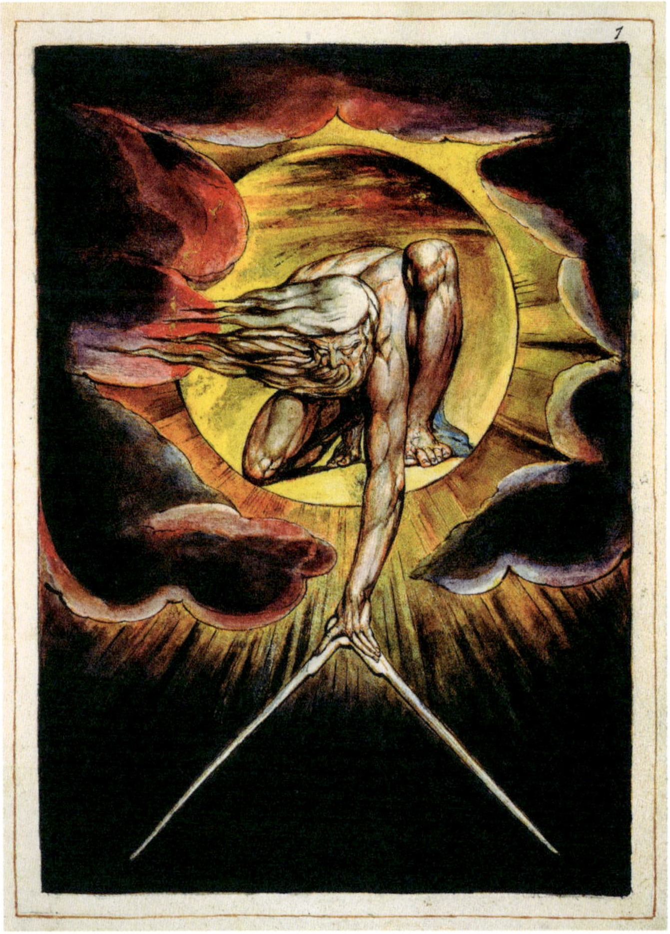

Left: The Ancient of Days, William Blake, 1794, etching with pen, ink and watercolour on paper

William Blake (1757–1827) gives us perhaps history's most magnificently unsettling vision of cosmic creation. A bearded figure crouches within a fiery sun, golden compasses stretching into darkness – not God but Urizen, Blake's reimagining of the creator as a complicated anti-hero who measures and constrains the universe with mathematical precision. Through his revolutionary relief etching technique, Blake captures the profound tension at the heart of creation – a figure simultaneously divine and terrifyingly human representing his lifelong struggle between reason's cold geometry and imagination's wildfire. In Urizen's hand, the compass becomes both instrument of cosmic order and symbol of our own beautiful, terrible need to measure infinity.

Opposite: The Creation of the Skies – The Separation of the Waters, from *De aetatibus mundi imagines*, Francisco de Holanda, between 1545 and 1573, brush, pen, pencil black, brown and brown ink, gouache and gold colours, on beige laid paper

In an era when most artists were painting muscular saints and classical heroes, Portuguese visionary Francisco de Holanda (1517–85) was doing something radically different. Though he studied with Michelangelo and moved in the highest artistic circles of the Renaissance, Holanda developed a unique visual language that seemed to predict artistic movements centuries ahead of its time. His masterwork *De aetatibus mundi imagines*, created over three decades, reimagines biblical creation through sacred geometry and mathematical mysticism – envisioning divine creation as an interaction of abstract forms rather than the typical powerful human figure reaching down from the heavens. This revolutionary approach remained largely unknown until his notebooks were discovered in Spain's National Library in the mid-twentieth century. Part architect, part mystic, part spy for the Portuguese crown, Holanda bridges the seemingly vast gap between Renaissance religious art and modern abstraction.

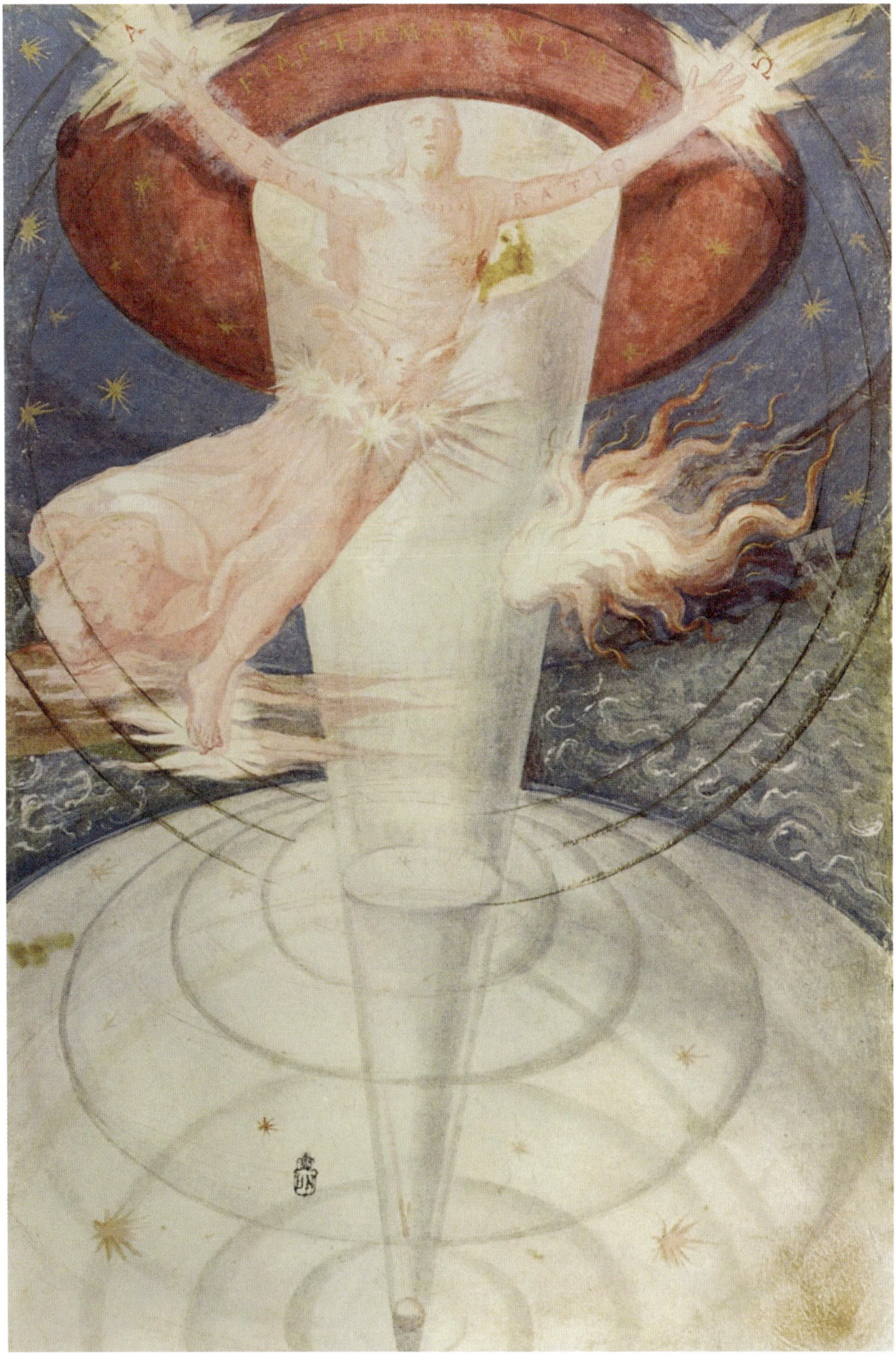
FIAT FIRMAMENTUM
PIETAS
RATIO
Ω

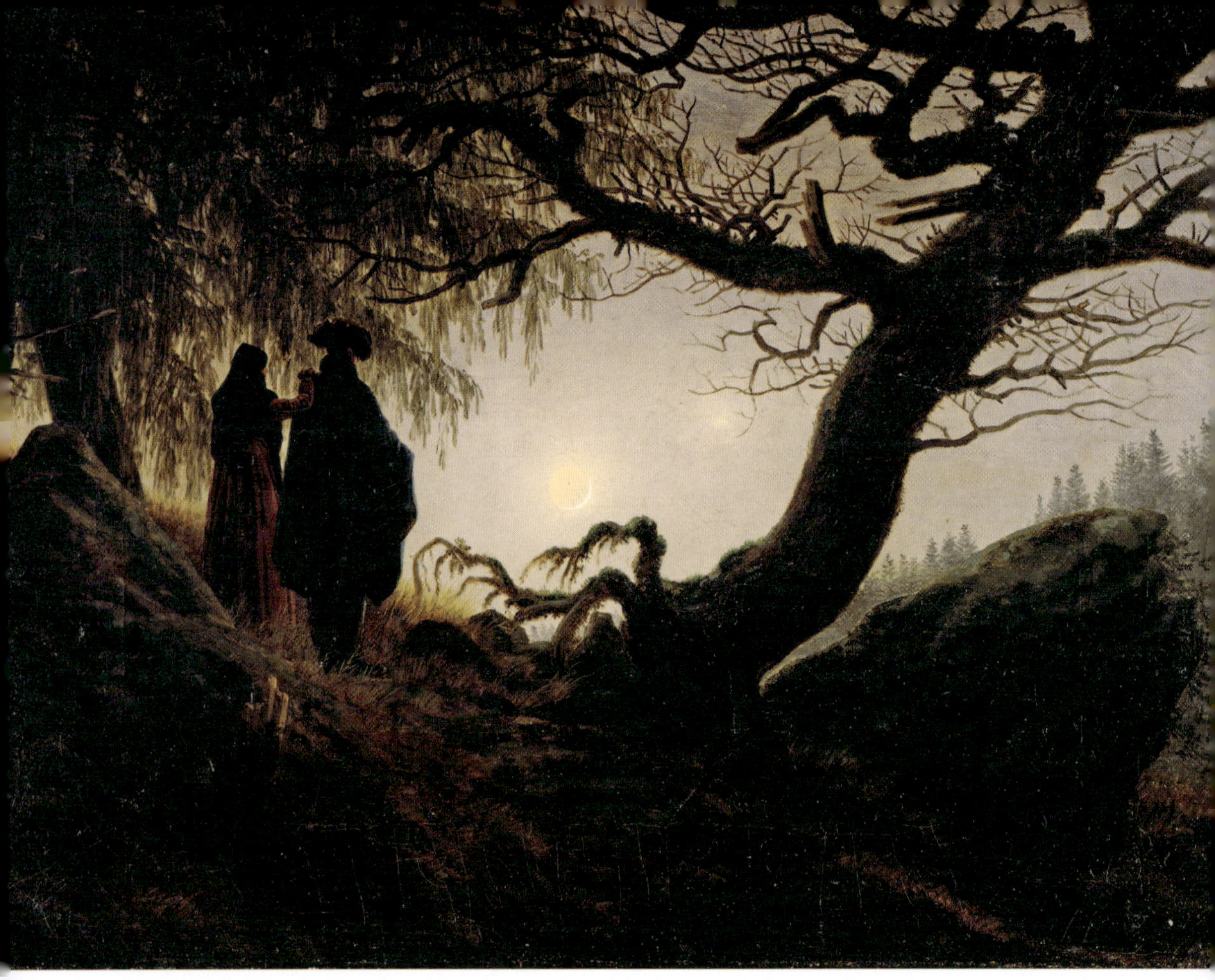

Man and Woman Contemplating the Moon, Caspar David Friedrich, *c*. 1824, oil on canvas

Few images distil Romanticism's essence as perfectly as Caspar David Friedrich's (1774–1840) moongazers. A couple stands on a rocky outcrop, backs turned – a signature Friedrich technique that makes us eavesdroppers on their cosmic communion. Before them hangs a waxing crescent moon in twilight splendour, framed by a dramatically uprooted oak whose gnarled form provides perfect counterpoint to celestial serenity. Friedrich's genius lies in the visual tension between jagged foreground and infinite beyond – humanity suspended between earthly constraints and cosmic aspiration. Years later, Samuel Beckett would gesture towards this painting and declare, 'This was the source of *Waiting for Godot*,' revealing how Friedrich's patient contemplation before the vast unknown continues to resonate. Though the artist died in obscurity in 1840, his silent watchers remain our stand-ins beneath indifferent skies, still searching for cosmic connection in the luminous beyond.

Star Gazer, Agnes Pelton, 1929, oil on canvas

Like a star-gazing Communion chalice offering viewers a taste of cosmic nectar, Agnes Pelton's (1881–1961) gleaming goblet glows with otherworldly light. Working in solitude in her converted windmill on Long Island, far from the clamour of the art world, Pelton conjured a mystical space where the earthly transforms into the celestial. This jewel-toned form rises against hills bathed in blazing twilight crimson, while an ethereal blossom unfurls towards a solitary star. With a patience bordering on devotion, she layered gossamer veils of translucent colour, a technique shared with Renaissance masters but directed towards her vision of cosmic interconnection, until her surfaces seem to pulse with starlight itself within their depths. In this early vision, we glimpse Pelton beginning to develop the unique visual language that would flourish when she later retreated to the California desert. There, beneath vast night skies, she spent three decades painting what she beautifully called 'the without seen from within' – the invisible currents of celestial energy flowing through all things, made momentarily visible through her reverent brush.

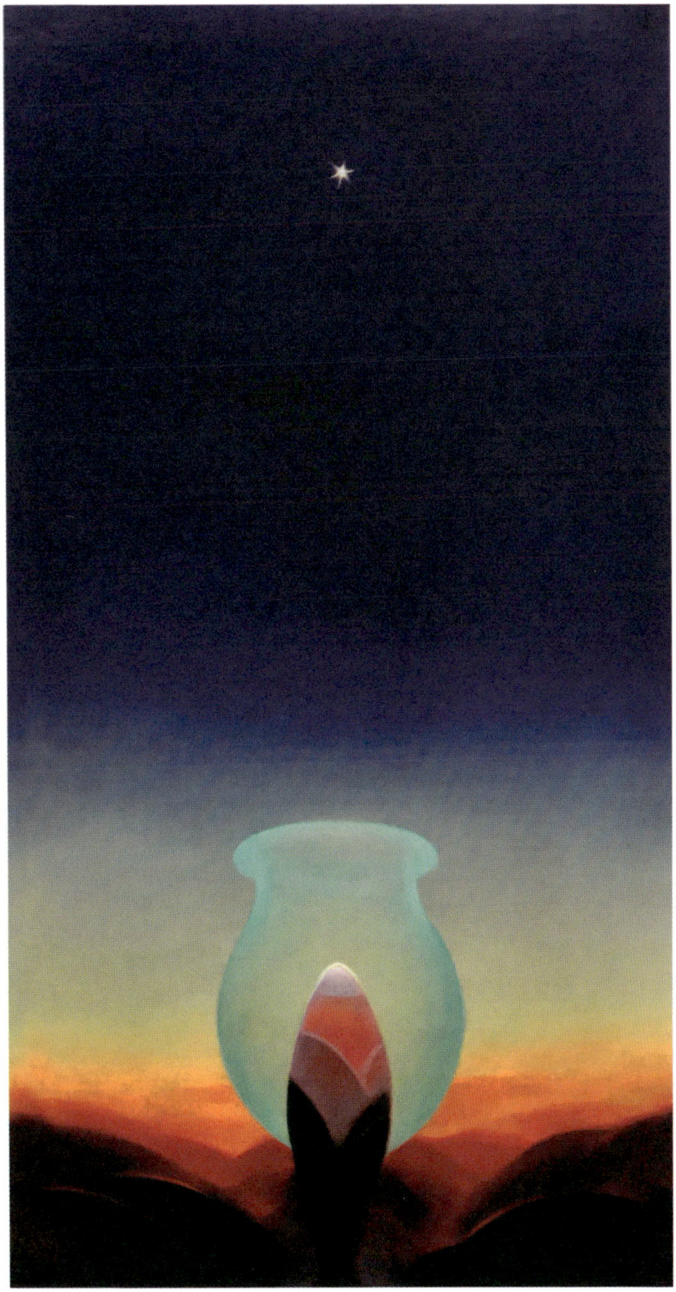

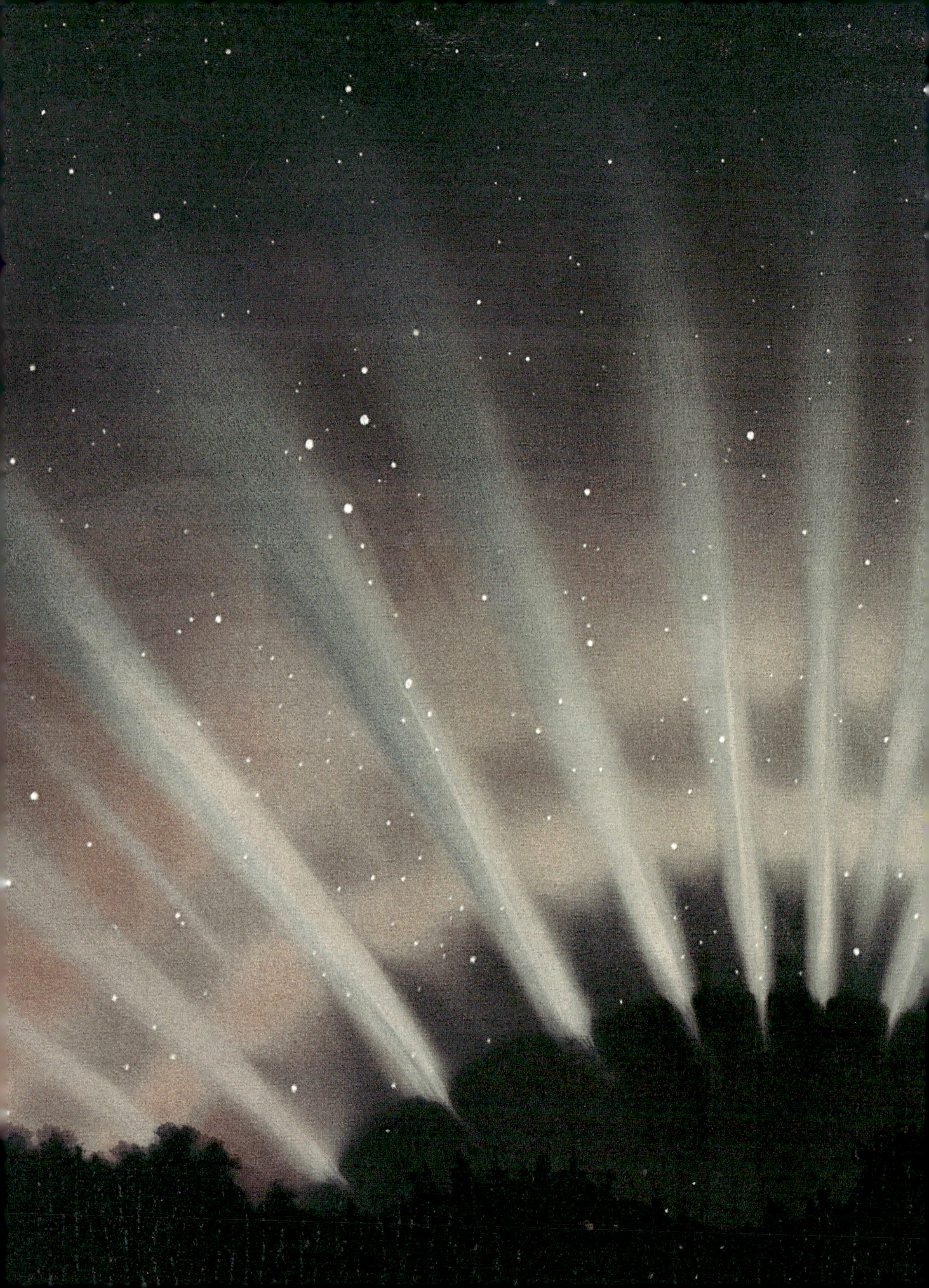

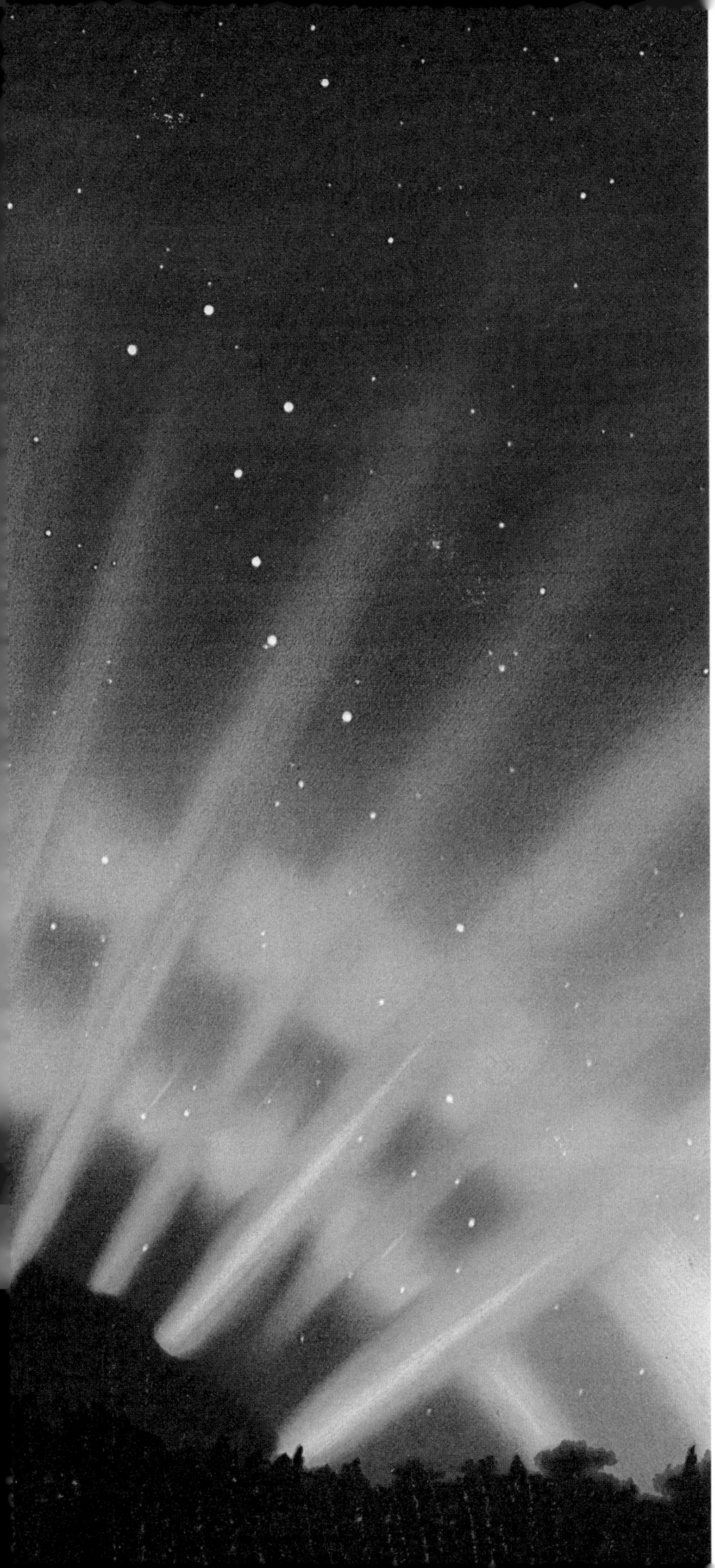

Aurora Borealis: As Observed March 1, 1872, at 9 h. 25 m. P.M., Étienne Léopold Trouvelot, 1881, chromolithograph print

French artist and astronomer Étienne Léopold Trouvelot (1827–95) is remembered for two things: creating some of the most exquisite astronomical illustrations ever made and accidentally unleashing the devastating gypsy moth onto North American soil. After that ecological disaster ended his entomological career, he turned his artistic eye to the heavens, creating over 7,000 astronomical drawings that caught the attention of Harvard Observatory. This stunning pastel study of the Aurora Borealis was one of 15 selected for his masterwork *The Trouvelot Astronomical Drawings* (1881). At a time when early astrophotography was producing blurry, indistinct images, Trouvelot argued for the superiority of the human eye and hand in capturing celestial wonders.

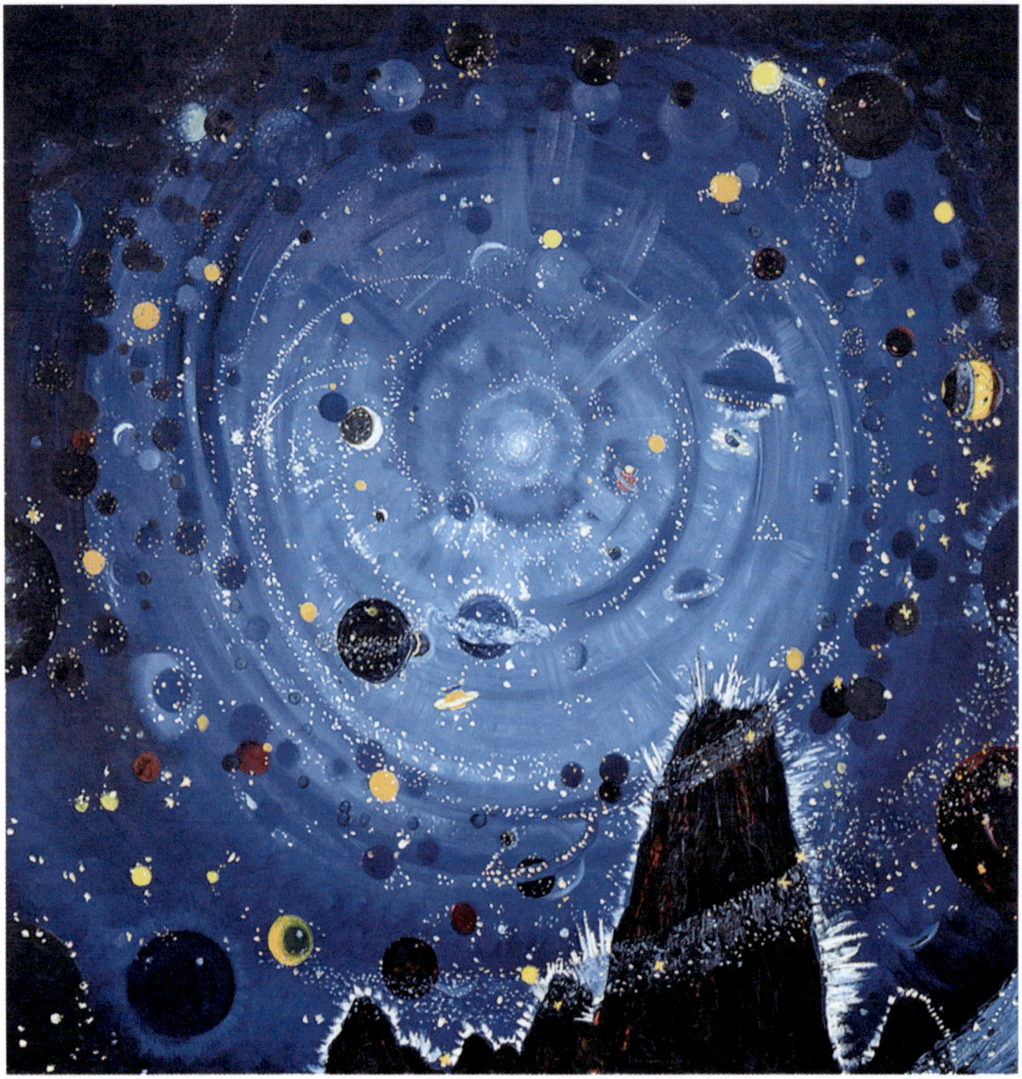

Starry Sky, Attempt, Wenzel Hablik, 1909, oil on canvas

What Wenzel Hablik (1881-1934) achieves in this magnificent artwork makes the word 'attempt' in his title seem almost comically modest. *In Starry Sky, Attempt* (1909), this visionary Czech artist transforms the cosmos into a pulsing, living thing. Planets hang at eye level, stars cluster and swarm like bees and the very fabric of space seems encrusted with crystalline light. This crystalline quality was no accident - a chance discovery of a crystal fragment in his childhood sparked Hablik's lifelong obsession with geometric forms and luminous patterns. Against a backdrop of deepest midnight, his celestial bodies pulse and throb with impossible colours. Crimson planets hang like ripe fruit, violet nebulae swirl like smoke, and countless stars burn in constellations of gold, azure and white. That Hablik called this a mere 'attempt' speaks volumes - as if this breathtaking cosmic vision were just a preliminary sketch rather than the universe reimagined in its full glory.

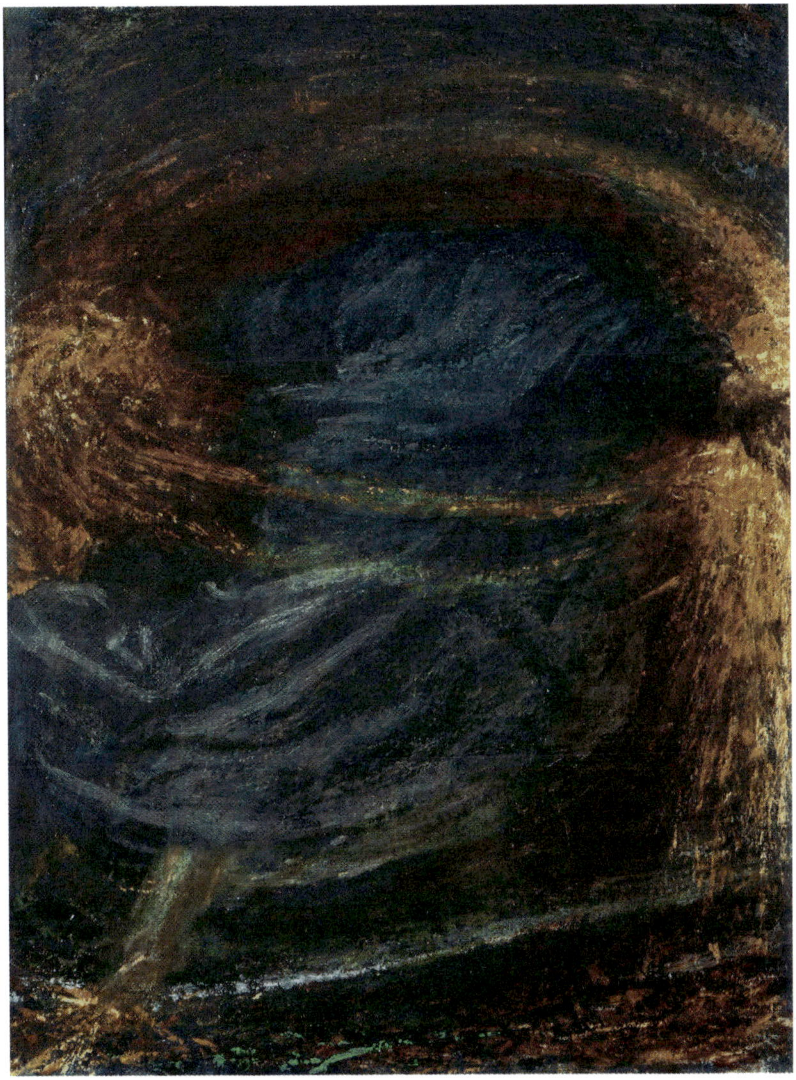

The Sower of Systems, George Frederic Watts, 1902, oil on canvas

When George Frederic Watts (1817–1904) painted *The Sower of Systems* in 1902, abstract art was barely a whisper on the horizon. Yet here was Victorian England's most revered painter, in his final years, conjuring a vision straight from cosmic dreams. Through billowing stellar mists, a mysterious figure strides with purpose, trailing seeds of light from outstretched arms like stars scattered across the primordial void. Shrouded in deepest midnight, this cosmic wanderer moves through space surrounded by luminous rings that echo Saturn's bands, which Watts had observed through a telescope, calling it 'a sight that dwarfed all others'. Watts pursued something profoundly ambitious: the visualization of cosmic forces typically hidden from human comprehension.

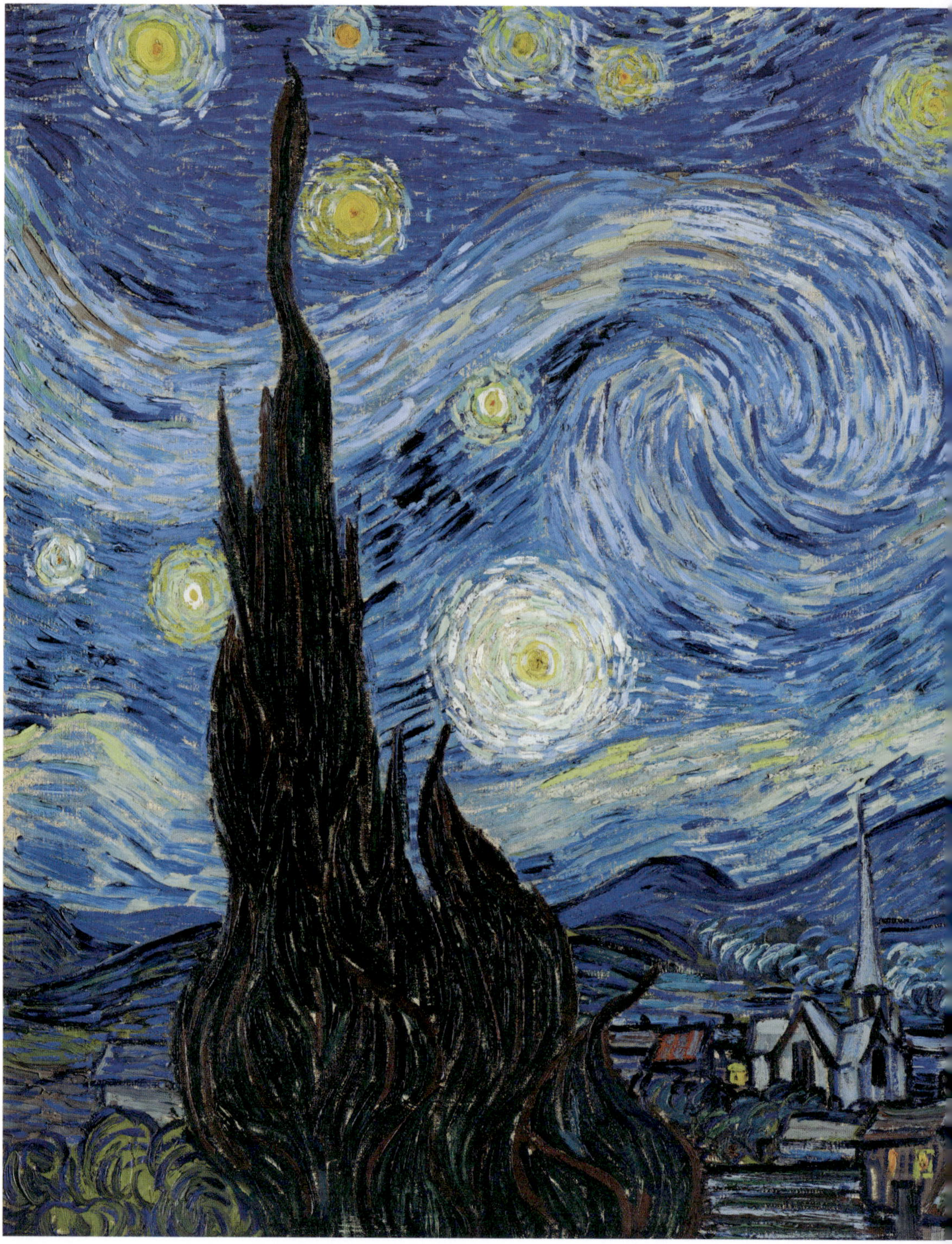

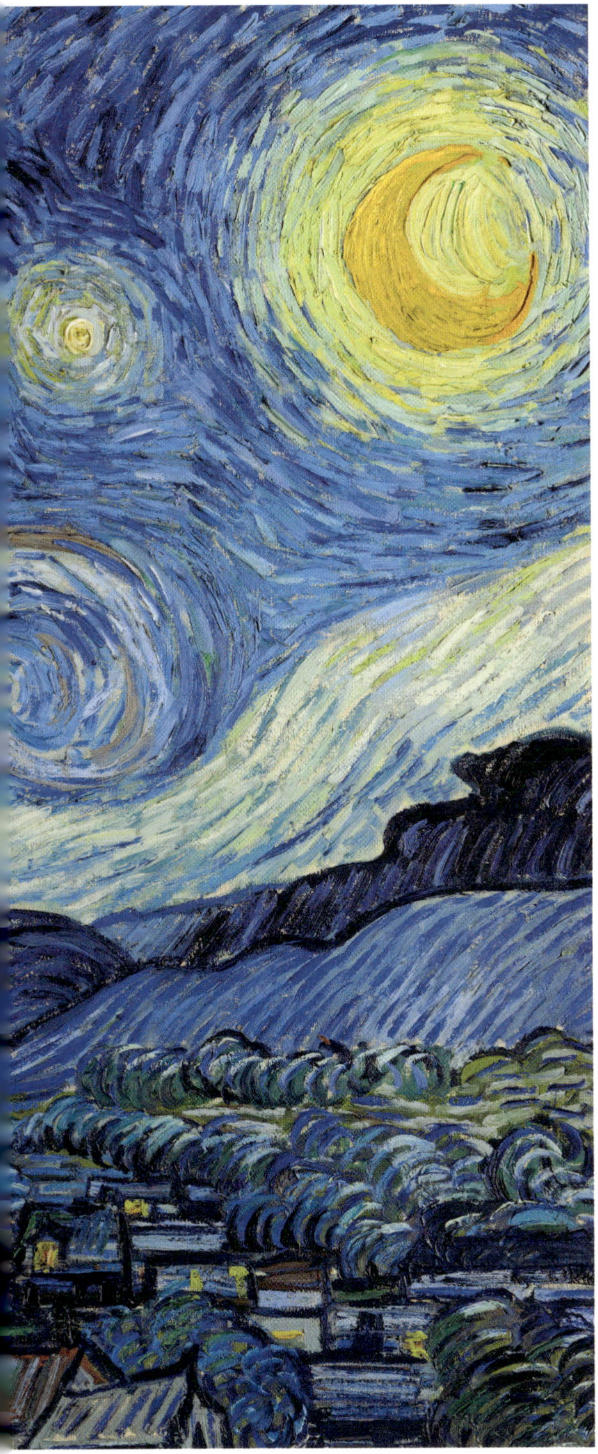

The Starry Night, Vincent van Gogh, 1889, oil on canvas

What can be said about this work that hasn't already been whispered by lovers, scrawled by poets or wept over by dreamers in countless dark nights? And yet, how can we fail to include it here? Vincent van Gogh (1853–90) painted *The Starry Night* in 1889 from his asylum window at Saint-Paul de Mausole in Saint-Rémy. During daylight hours, he worked to capture what he had witnessed in the depths of night: a sky where stars pulse like fevered hearts, each wrapped in rings of golden light, while a crescent moon burns through clouds that spiral and churn like celestial tide pools. The cypress tree rises like a black flame, bridging the quiet order of the sleeping village and the cosmic drama above. 'Looking at the stars always makes me dream,' he wrote to his brother Theo, and in this single canvas, Van Gogh captures the sort of dream state in which we feel simultaneously infinitesimal and infinite. The stars above Saint-Rémy aren't just astronomical bodies but beacons of wonder, each swirling brushstroke a testament to the universe's breathtaking, terrible beauty. Here is the cosmos, not as science charts it, but as the soul experiences it – alive, pulsing and calling to something equally vast within us.

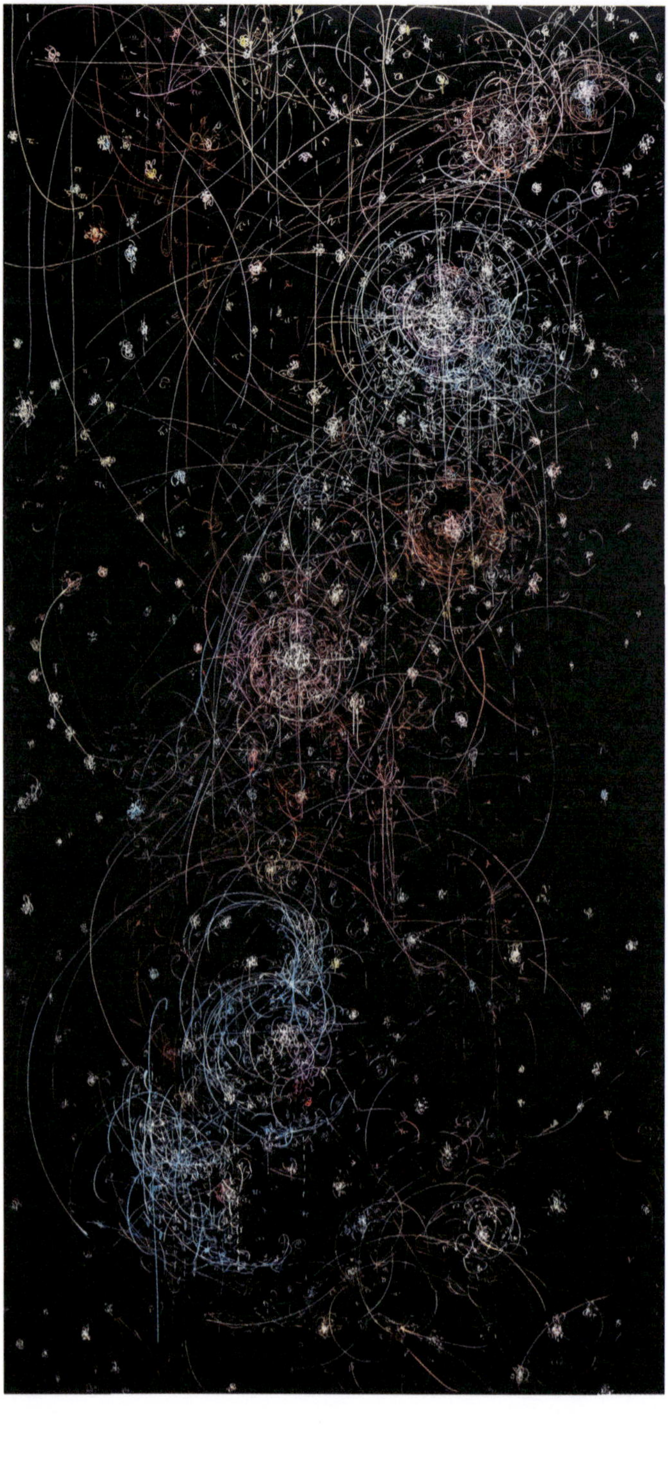

Blow up 319 – the long goodbye – (history of gold) – subatomic decay patterns and quantum particles distorting light from neutron star RX J1856, Kysa Johnson, 2017, ink on high gloss on board

Like fireworks frozen in deep space, Kysa Johnson's dazzling cosmogram bursts across its dark surface in brilliant streaks of magenta, yellow and violet. But these cosmic pyrotechnics hide the clever secret that each explosive arc is actually one of eleven subatomic decay patterns, each repeated and layered to build something greater than its parts. Johnson uses the hidden mathematics of particle physics as her artistic vocabulary, drawing with the equations that govern matter's most fundamental behaviours. Part of her 'Long Goodbye' series, this work visualizes neutron star RX J1856, emerging the same year that scientists confirmed a key astronomical discovery: that neutron star collisions generate many of our universe's heavy elements, including gold. Johnson's work beautifully connects the smallest processes in physics with grand astronomical events, revealing how decay patterns paradoxically enable creation itself. Her artwork visualizes this cosmic alchemy, showing how catastrophic stellar events forge the precious elements that eventually find their way to Earth.

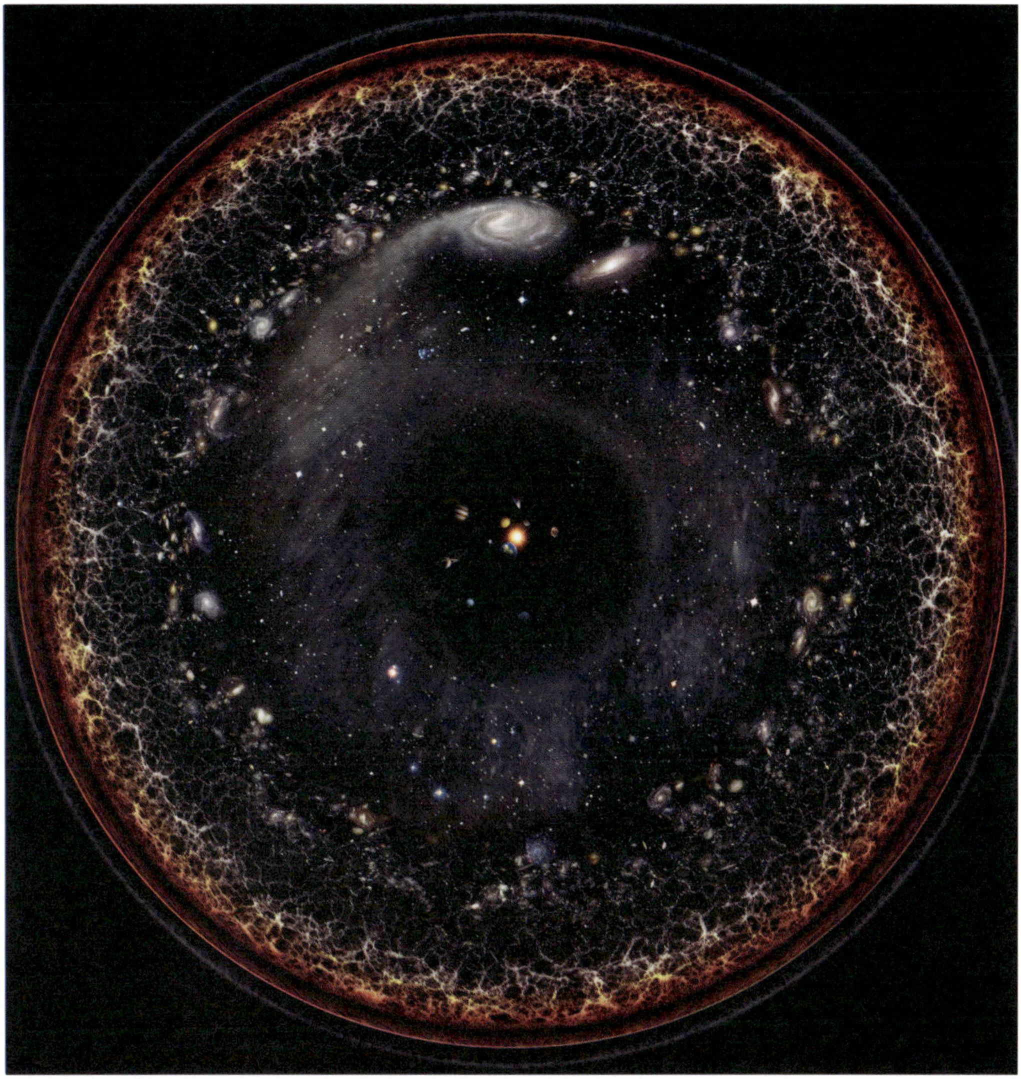

Observable Universe Logarithmic illustration, Pablo Carlos Budassi, 2016, digital art

Imagine trying to map everything that exists in a single kaleidoscopic image. That's exactly what Pablo Carlos Budassi achieved in this breathtaking visualization. Using a logarithmic scale that allows both subatomic particles and sprawling galaxies to coexist on the same intricate canvas, he places our tiny solar system at the centre of a hypnotic cosmic mandala. As the eye journeys outwards, each concentric ring represents vastly larger scales of space. Nearby stars surrender to glittering galactic clusters, and finally to the gossamer cosmic web itself, that intricate network of matter spanning billions of light years. What began as a father's humble experiment with paper models for his son's birthday has evolved into one of the most profound visualizations of our cosmic address, earning a revered place in planetariums and science museums worldwide. It captures that vertiginous moment when we glimpse our true place in the unfathomable infinite.

II

—

HIDDEN WATCHERS

'We saw to the edge of all there is –
So brutal and alive it seemed to comprehend us back.'

– TRACY K. SMITH

That electric prickle at the base of your neck. The weight of unseen eyes pressing against your skin. Shadows deepening in empty corners, though no clouds cross the sun. Even alone, we sense our clandestine audience. The urge to turn around seizes us although we know nothing, or no one, will be there. In empty rooms, on deserted streets, in seemingly vacant wilderness, humans have long sensed the presence of unseen observers. We build this awareness into our languages and folklore: 'Someone walked over my grave,' whisper the English. *Les murs ont des oreilles* – 'the walls have ears' – warns the old French proverb, speaking to our ancient understanding that we are never truly alone.

These hidden presences take many forms across cultures and time periods. Ancient peoples carved protective eyes into their doorways and painted vigilant spirits on their walls. Medieval Europeans reported encounters with angels and demons lurking at crossroads and hovering in church spires – watchers both divine and diabolical. Japanese folklore speaks of yokai watching from the shadows, while Indigenous peoples across the Americas have long spoken of star visitors and sky watchers observing from above – from the Hopi's star beings to the Cherokee's stellar watchers. Even today, eyes are painted on boats in Mediterranean harbours, a tradition stretching back millennia. The practice has evolved in unexpected ways – now we stick googly eyes on houseplants and vacuum cleaners, modern-day talismans that transform our mundane objects into oddly endearing guardians.

Open a medieval manuscript, and you'll find demons and angels treading the same ground as mortals, their presence as tangible as the aureate pigment and foil applied to their divine halos. When William Blake and Henry Fuseli took up their brushes in the Romantic era, these watchers began to shift and blur. Fuseli's nightmarish figures crouch at the edges of our vision, while Blake's angels burst through the boundaries between worlds, their wings trailing cosmic fire.

The Symbolists took things even further. Odilon Redon's eyes float free in darkened spaces, completely detached from faces or bodies or any earthly logic. They watch us watching them, existing in an unsettling territory where it's impossible to tell who's doing the observing and who's being observed.

We might have expected that, when photography arrived, with its power of mechanical truth, it would have banished these watchers back to the realm of imagination. Instead, something fascinating happened: the watchers simply adapted to the new medium. They learned to manifest in silver gelatin, to flare at the edges of long exposures, to flitter in and out of existence between the frames of early motion pictures. Even the Countess of Castiglione transformed herself into a watching entity, her singular eye in Pierre-Louis Pierson's lens gazing out across time with unsettling intensity.

When the aviator Kenneth Arnold spotted mysterious flying objects in 1947, he wasn't just reporting a UFO sighting, he was confirming what artists had long suspected about our invisible audience. The artistic response came in many forms. David Huggins documented what he claimed were direct encounters with extraterrestrial beings – large black eyes watching from spacecraft doorways or approaching through bedroom walls. But artists also explored many forms of hidden watchers beyond the extraterrestrial. Peter Birkhäuser's *The Observer* suggested an eternal witness to human experience, while Louise Bourgeois' anatomical voyeurs transformed the body itself into a surveillance network. Mark Rogers' enigmatic 'Observer' works and Tony Oursler's projected eyes that transform architecture into watching entities continued this exploration of unseen presences. Whether lurking in Gothic shadows or enchanted forests, wearing the faces of dolls or demons, angels or aristocrats, these watchers all share the peculiar quality of looking back at us looking at them, as if they've been waiting for us to notice them all along. They remind us that,

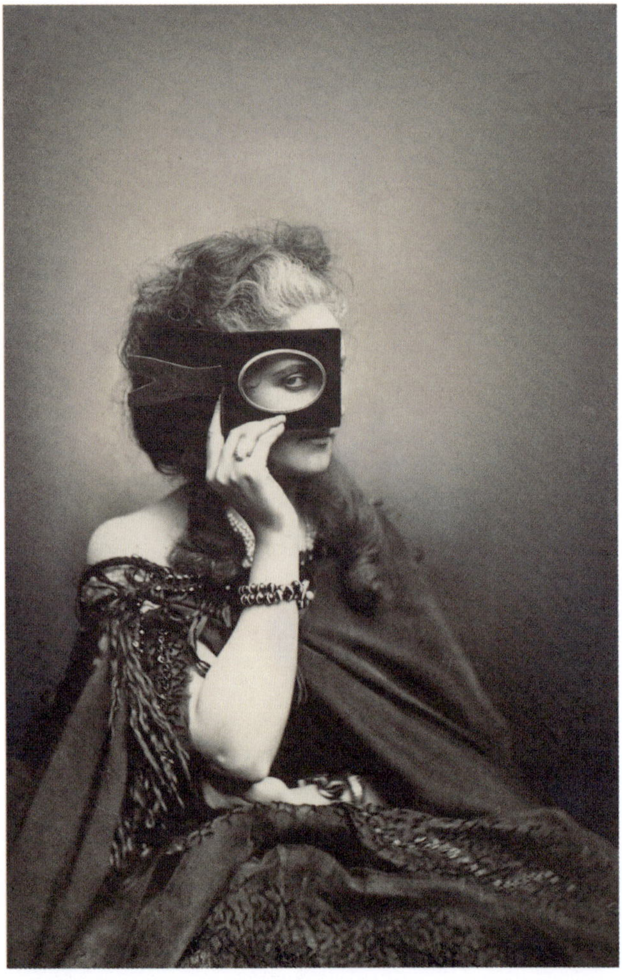

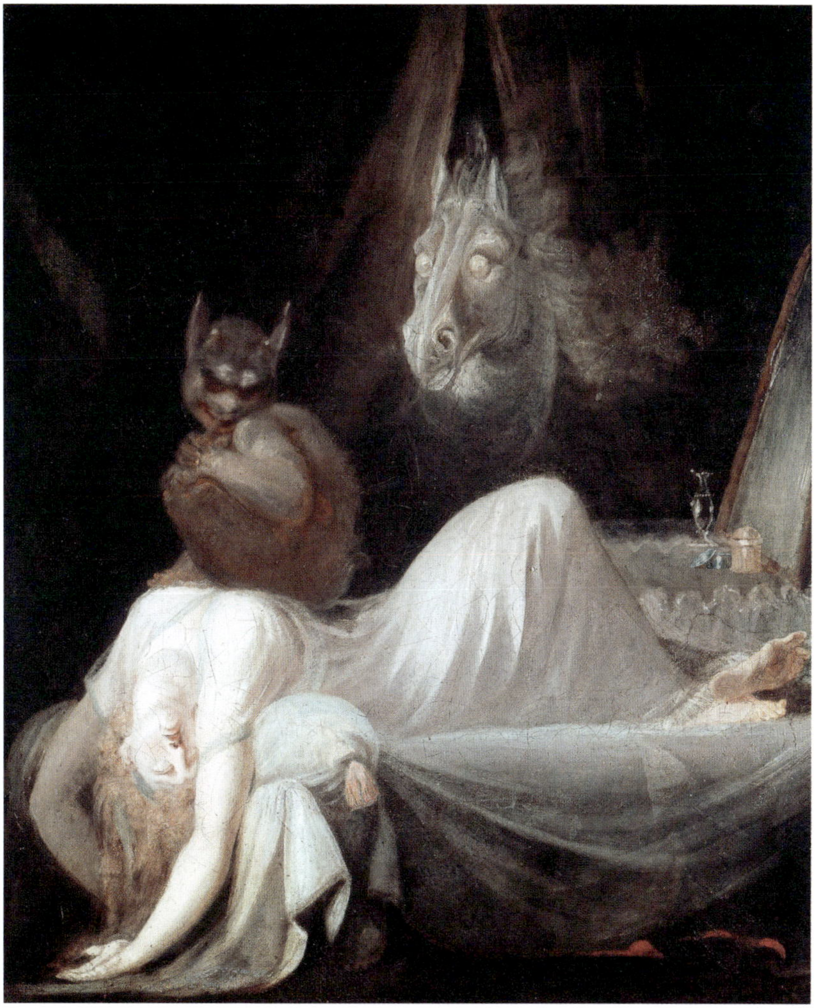

no matter how our tools for image-making evolve, the ancient sensation of being watched – that itchy, tickling certainty of unseen eyes – remains fundamentally unchanged.

What artists reveal in their attempts to document these watchers goes beyond mere paranoia or primitive instinct. They tap into something older than art itself: an inherited radar that keeps scanning the edges of comprehension, reminding us that observation is never a one-way street. Gaze too long at these works and the question shifts: while we've been observing the observers, what secrets have they been collecting from our stares?

Opposite: Joke of Madness (Countess of Castiglione), Pierre-Louis Pierson, *c.* 1865, photograph

Above: The Nightmare, Henry Fuseli, 1790–91, oil on canvas

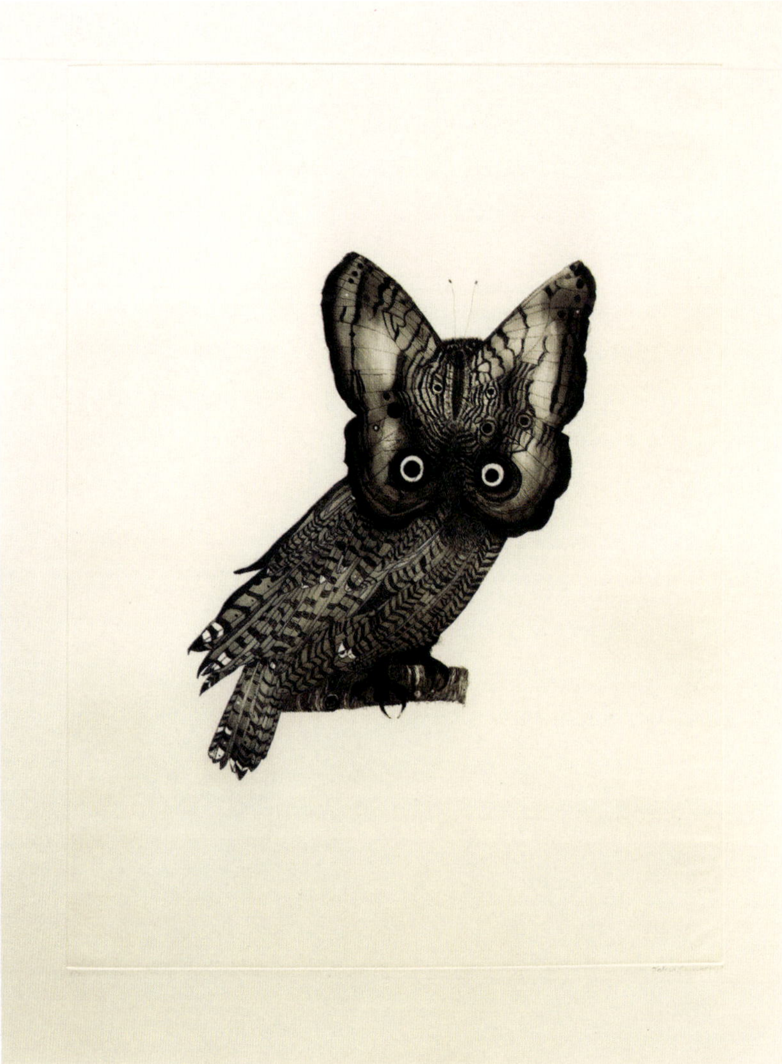

Owlmoth, Valerie Hammond, 2019, etching and aquatint on rag paper

Within this mesmerizing hybrid creature, an owl's powerful form hosts a large moth as its face, two legendary nocturnal watchers merged into a single entity through Valerie Hammond's masterful etching technique. Hammond, whose work consistently explores the permeable boundary between the physical and spiritual realms, here creates a strange sentinel embodying a disorienting duality: the owl, traditionally symbolizing wisdom and vigilance, now wears the face of its potential prey, creating a visual paradox whereby the observer and observed have fused into one consciousness. Moths themselves possess an ancient association with spiritual messengers and psychic awareness, their attraction to light representing humanity's pursuit of enlightenment, while owls have long been regarded as guardians of the unseen world. These qualities make this chimeric being a powerful representation of what Hammond describes as 'the indefinable boundary between presence and absence', a watcher that exists both within and beyond conventional perception.

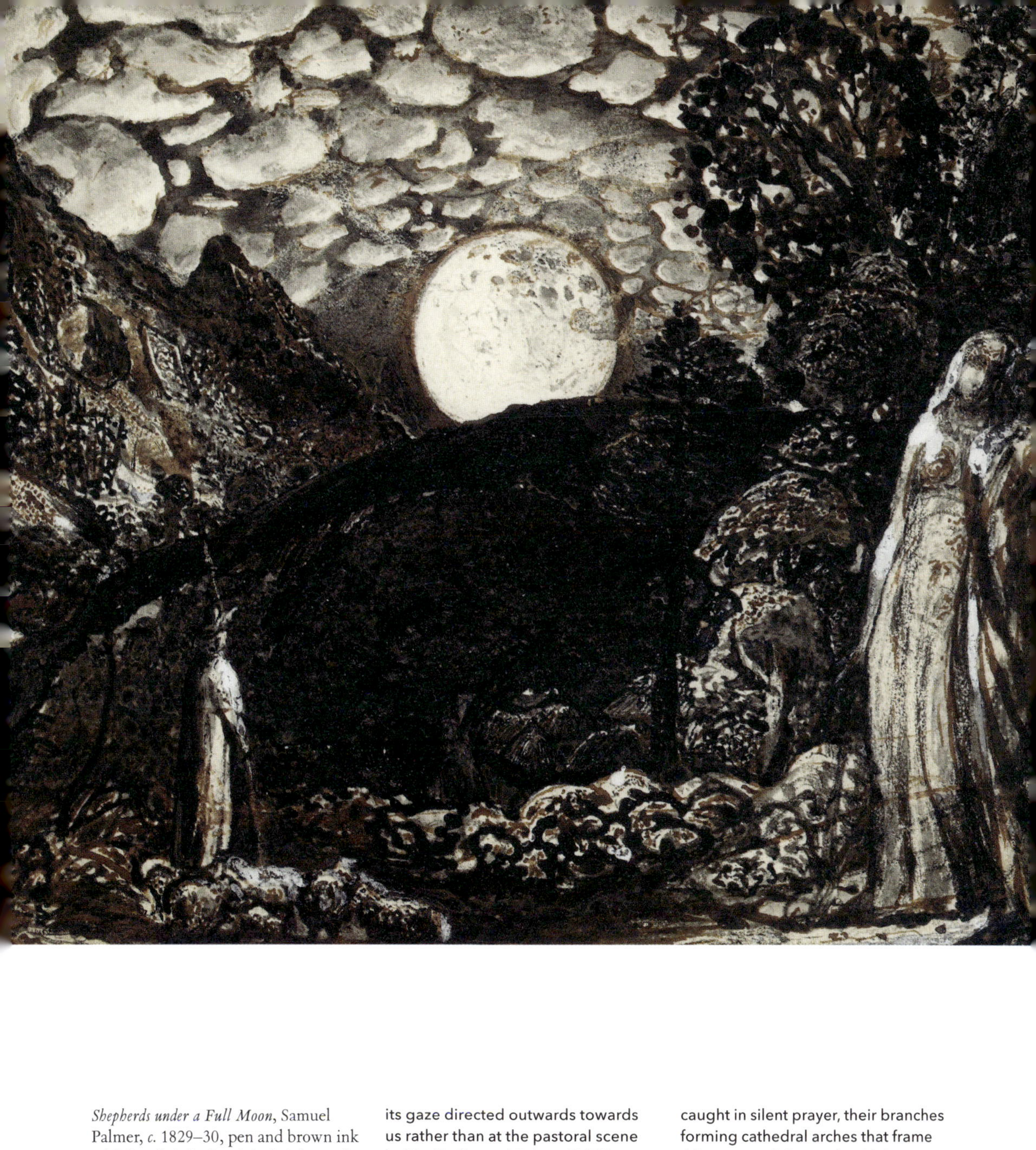

Shepherds under a Full Moon, Samuel Palmer, *c.* 1829–30, pen and brown ink with brush in Indian ink, heightened with bodycolour on white card

Beneath a moon pulsing with divine radiance, a lone shepherd huddles beside his flock while, in the foreground, a mysterious figure - neither fully human nor stone - stands partially concealed, its gaze directed outwards towards us rather than at the pastoral scene behind it. Samuel Palmer (1805-81), working during his mystical 'Shoreham period', transforms this Kent landscape into a living sanctuary where his unsettling watcher performs a visual sleight of hand, flipping our role from observer to the observed. The trees bend and bow like worshippers caught in silent prayer, their branches forming cathedral arches that frame this nocturnal theatre in which we suddenly find ourselves participants rather than audience. Palmer's enigmatic foreground figure executes the ultimate reversal: we who came to witness the pastoral scene discover too late that something ancient and knowing within the artwork has been tracking our movements all along.

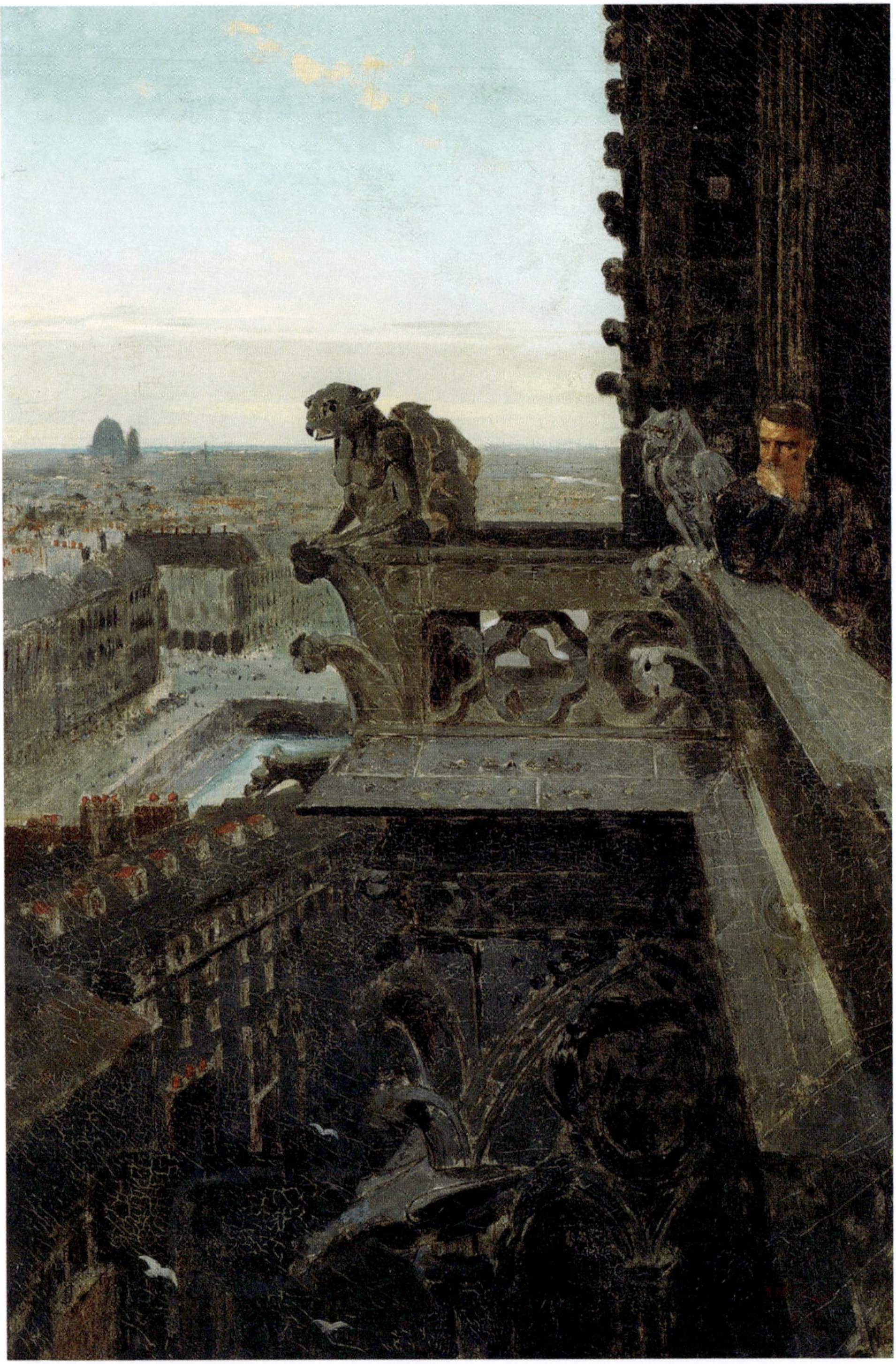

Right: Death and the Gravedigger, Carlos Schwabe, 1900, gouache, watercolour and pencil

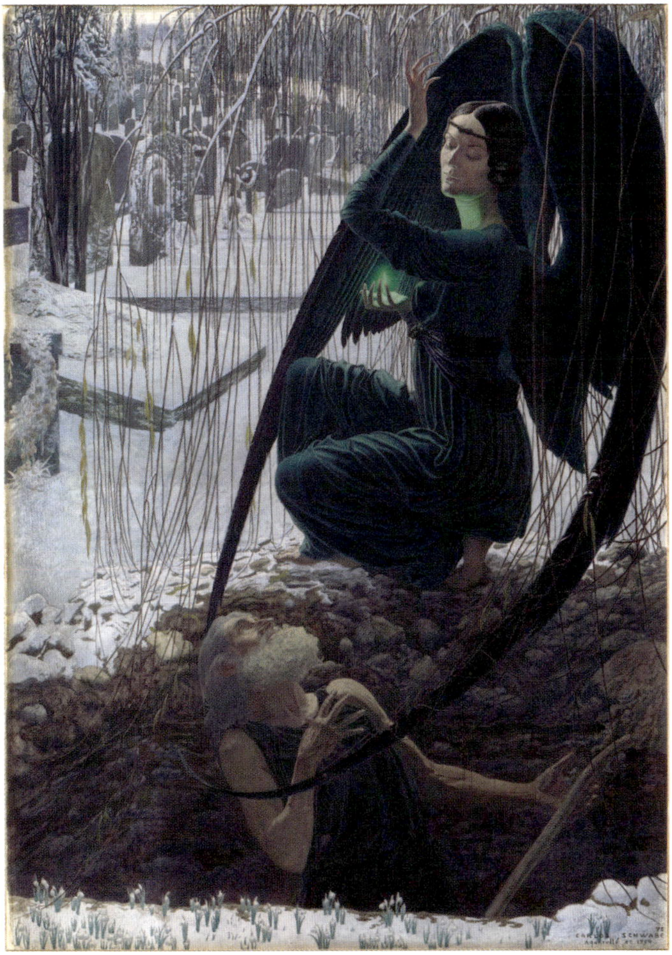

Dark wings spreading like velvet-tipped shadows against winter's stark white canvas and a tangle of trailing willow branches, Death arrives not as a skeletal harvester but as a solemn angel to claim the gravedigger caught in his own freshly dug pit. Carlos Schwabe (1866–1926), a Swiss-German Symbolist whose wife modelled for this haunting figure, transforms mortality into something both beautiful and terrible – an observer who has always been present, merely waiting for the right moment to reveal herself. The gravedigger's shocked face and clutched heart speak of sudden recognition, as though seeing for the first time what has been watching him throughout his career of burying others. This is surveillance at its most fundamental: the ultimate watcher who witnesses our most private moments, biding her time until she steps from shadow into our direct line of sight.

Opposite: Gargoyles at Notre Dame, Winslow Homer, 1867, oil on canvas

Most tourists crane their necks upwards, but Winslow Homer (1836–1910) went further – climbing the towers of Notre Dame to meet its stone guardians face to face during his Parisian sojourn. What he discovered were not merely architectural curiosities but psychological companions to his own artistic isolation, captured here in moody oil that reveals Homer's fascination with observers who exist outside society yet see everything. The gargoyles' brooding expressions mirror the artist's own growing desire for solitude, a yearning that would eventually lead him to the remote Maine coastline where he created his most profound work. These manufactured monsters embody an amusing paradox: they appear medieval yet are modern inventions, much like nostalgia itself. Homer recognized in these liminal creatures a powerful metaphor for the artist's role – perched between worlds, watching without participation, separate from the human drama below yet eternally vigilant and impossibly lonely in their stone imprisonment.

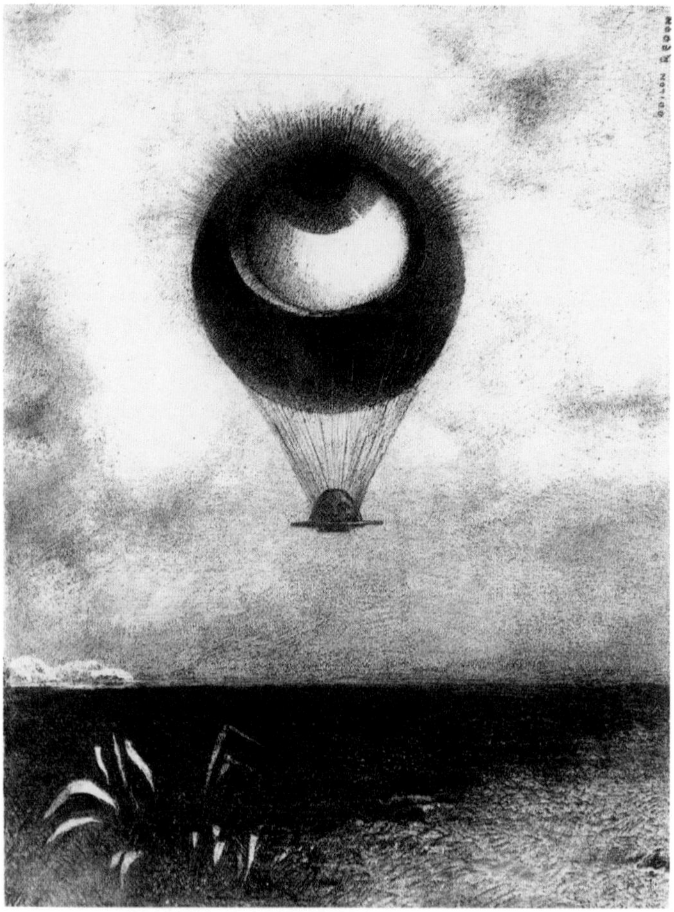

Left: The Eye, Like a Strange Balloon, Mounts Towards Infinity, Odilon Redon, *c.* 1882, lithograph

A gigantic disembodied eye drifts across a sombre landscape like a grotesque hot-air balloon, carrying what appears to be a human head in its basket towards unknown realms. Odilon Redon (1840–1916), master of the dark lithographic arts, created this unsettling image for his portfolio tribute to Edgar Allan Poe, whose fascination with eyes as spiritual vessels resonated with the French Symbolist's own obsessions. Rejecting realism for psychological truth, Redon sought to give life to improbable beings that followed their own mysterious logic. This floating eye becomes the ultimate watcher freed from bodily constraints, pursuing its relentless gaze beyond earthly limitations. The image suggests observation taken to metaphysical extremes, where the act of seeing becomes a form of flight itself, carrying consciousness into territories no earthbound vision could reach.

Opposite: The Ancestors, Luciana Lupe Vasconcelos, 2020, ink on paper

Four hooded figures stand in ceremonial formation behind an immense disembodied eye, their faces frozen in expressions of ancient vigilance while the cosmic pupil hovers before them like a portal between worlds. Luciana Lupe Vasconcelos, whose work explores the mythical, mystical and occult, employs stark black and white linework to conjure these ancestral watchers as primordial guardians of forbidden knowledge, their presence simultaneously protective and ominous. The floating eye serves as both collective vision and warning, suggesting that the dead never truly depart but instead transform into observers who bear witness across the veil, maintaining their eternal regard from beyond. Deeply influenced by occult traditions, Vasconcelos creates in this image a striking testament to the ancestral gaze – the sensation that those who came before us continue to track our movements through time.

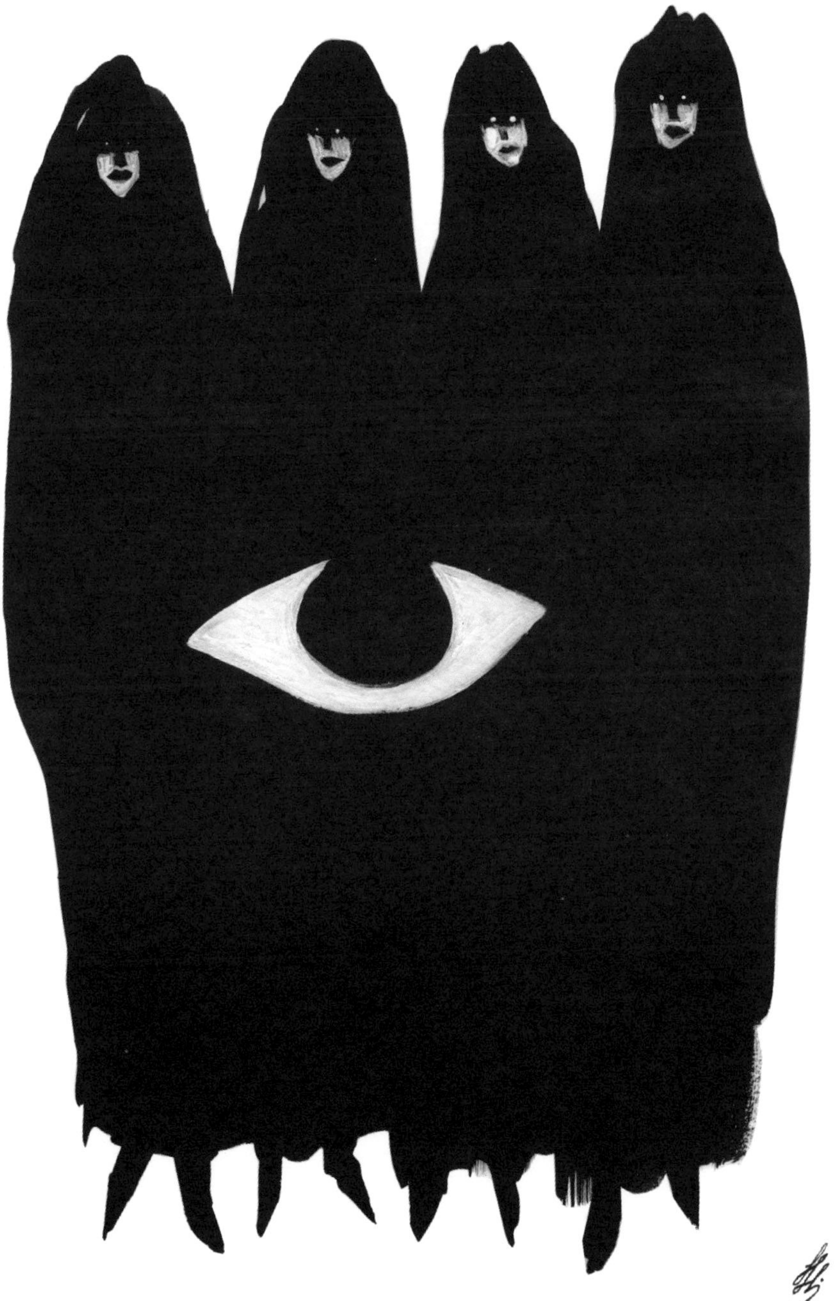

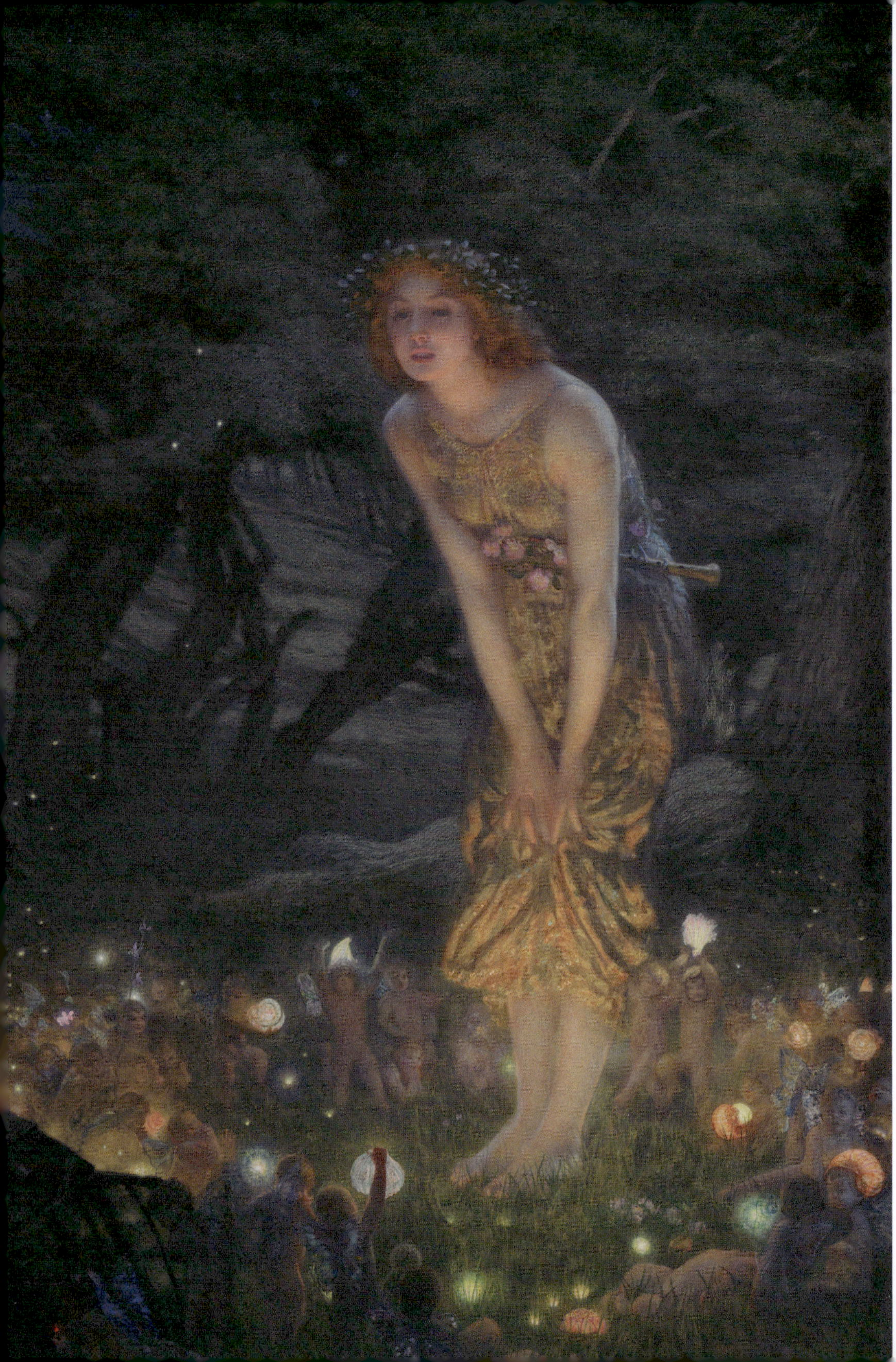

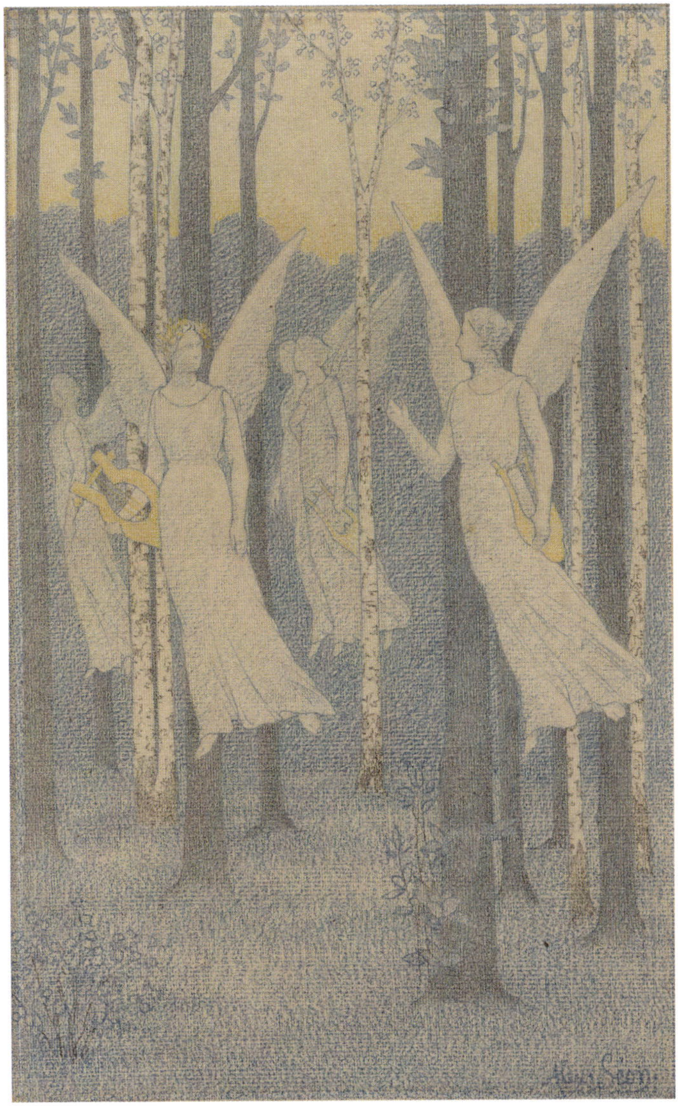

Right: Study for 'In the Woods, Evening', Alexandre Séon, 1892–94, coloured pencil on beige laid paper

The spiritual theories of colour that guided Alexandre Séon (1855–1917) infuse this drawing with mystical significance – white representing enlightenment, blue signifying melancholy – creating what appears to be a woodland waiting room for guardian angels on call. Séon's ethereal feminine figures hover in twilight limbo, their lyres silent and bodies motionless, captured through coloured pencils on textured paper – an unusual medium that deftly conjures the hazy boundary between physical and spiritual realms. Originally a study for a now-lost painting that captivated critics at the 1894 Société Nationale des Beaux-Arts, this drawing emerged from fairy tales surrounding Séon's rural French childhood. These vigilant sentinels exist in perfect stasis, suspended between arrival and departure, watching over the threshold between mundane reality and enchantment – embodiments of the belief that art can spiritually elevate viewers by revealing unseen presences in even the most seemingly empty woodland.

Opposite: Midsummer Eve, Edward Robert Hughes, *c.* 1908, watercolour on paper

In this enchanting watercolour, Edward Robert Hughes (1851–1914) transforms the ancient belief that supernatural barriers thin on midsummer nights into a visual symphony of observation. A young woman – perhaps a woodland nymph – stands illuminated at the centre, but the true subjects are the dozens of tiny fairy observers peering from every shadow and branch. These diminutive watchers, clutching glowing shells and flowers like primitive spotlights, form an audience for the human figure rather than the reverse. Hughes, trained by Pre-Raphaelite masters and influenced by Edward Burne-Jones, helped revolutionize Victorian fairy imagery from sinister to sublime through his dreamlike watercolour technique. Yet something subtly unnerving persists – the woman is completely surrounded, studied from every angle by countless miniature eyes.

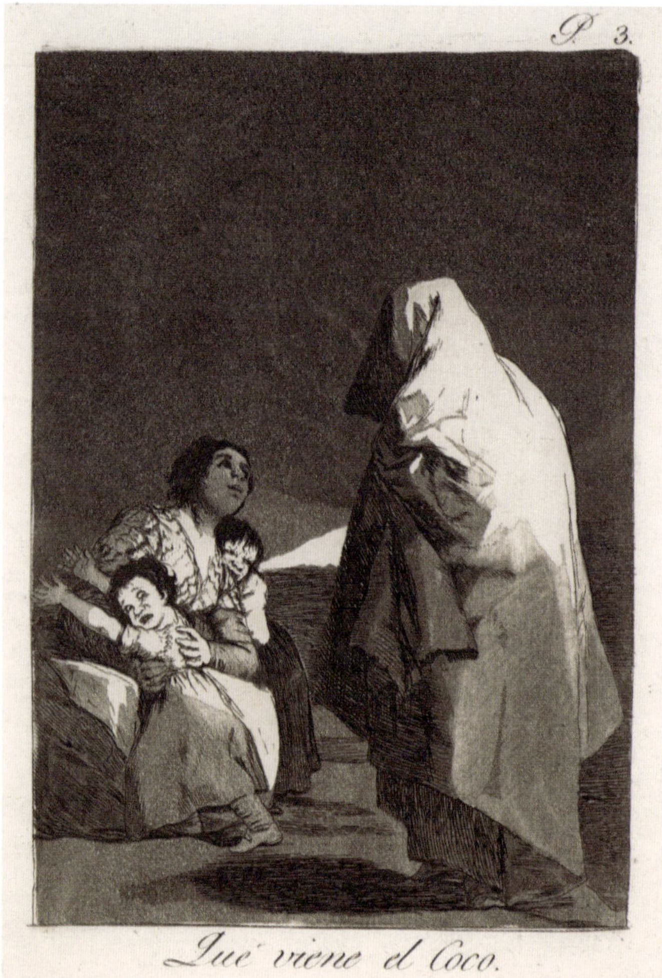

Left: Here Comes the Bogey-Man,
Francisco Goya, 1797–99, etching and burnished aquatint

In this haunting aquatint from his 'Los Caprichos' series, Goya reveals the power of unseen watchers in Spanish folklore. A mysterious hooded figure looms over a mother and her terrified children - the embodiment of 'el Coco', the bogeyman parents invoked to ensure good behaviour. Beyond critique of parental manipulation, Goya's shadowy observer speaks to deeper cultural anxieties. Created while Spain straddled superstition and Enlightenment, this image captures something universal: the strategic exploitation of fear. While today's parents might not threaten children with cloaked figures, Goya's Coco lives on as the nameless presence we've all sensed lurking just out of sight. The genius lies in what remains hidden; by concealing the figure entirely in shadow, Goya transforms a specific cultural bogeyman into something universally haunting. Three centuries later, his critique remains sharp. We still live with the uncomfortable suspicion that someone - or something - watches from just beyond our sight.

Opposite: Casquets Lighthouse,
Victor Hugo, 1866, pen and ink wash on paper

A solitary sentinel pierces the tempestuous darkness, its beacon sweeping across invisible waters like a Cyclops scanning for souls. The lighthouse stares back through storm and shadow, its lantern an unblinking eye that has witnessed countless maritime tragedies. Victor Hugo's (1802-85) rendering transforms the Casquets Lighthouse from passive beacon into active observer. The renowned French author - exiled on Guernsey for opposing Napoleon III's regime - created this haunting ink wash during the same period in which he penned his storm-wracked novel *The Man Who Laughs*. The lighthouse stands as a paradoxical lookout - designed to warn yet historically associated with disaster, meant to illuminate but shown here nearly consumed by darkness. Through his experimental technique, Hugo captures the essence of these coastal watchers: visible to all yet perpetually alone, their light illuminating darkness that holds its own secrets.

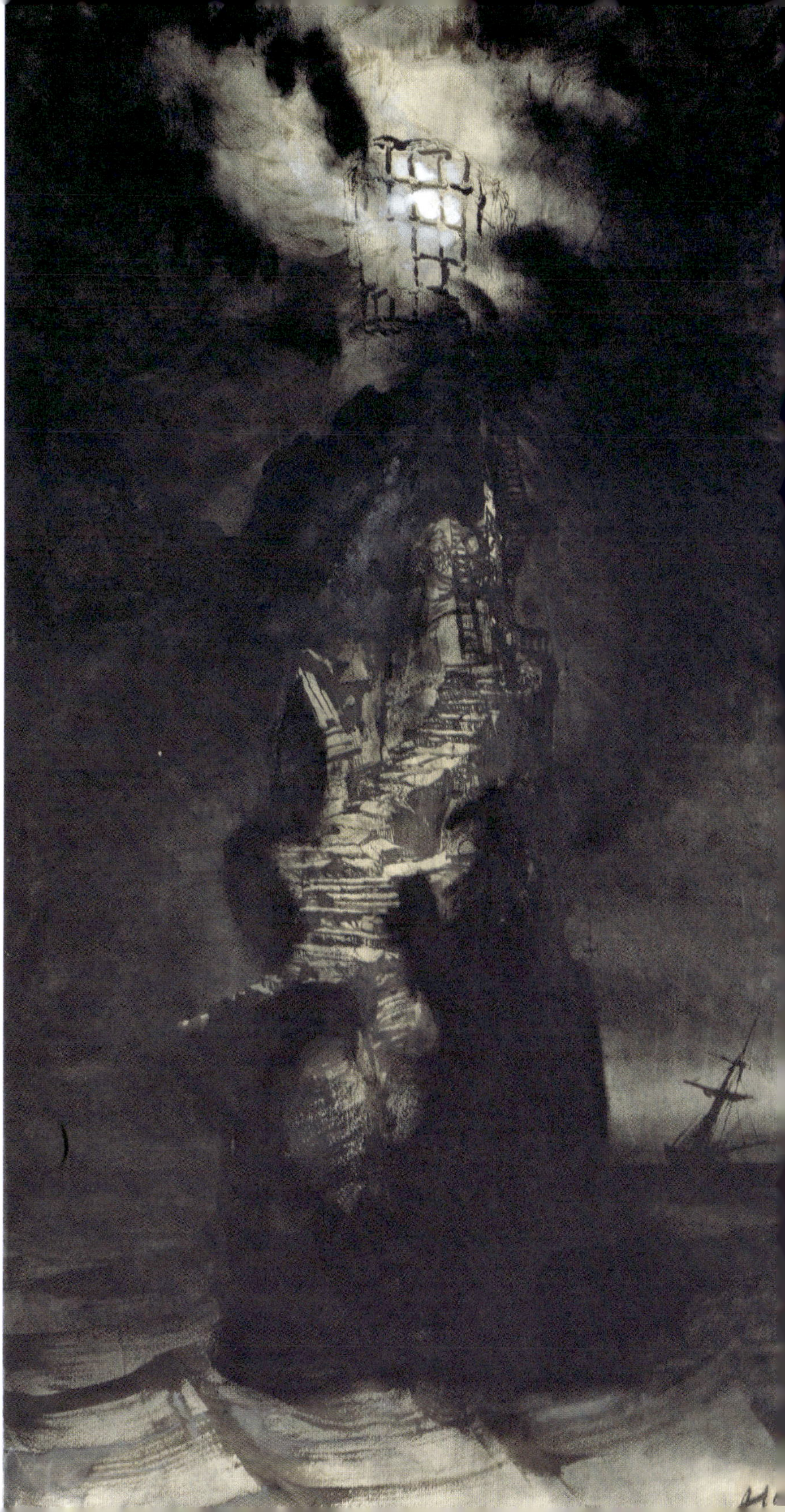

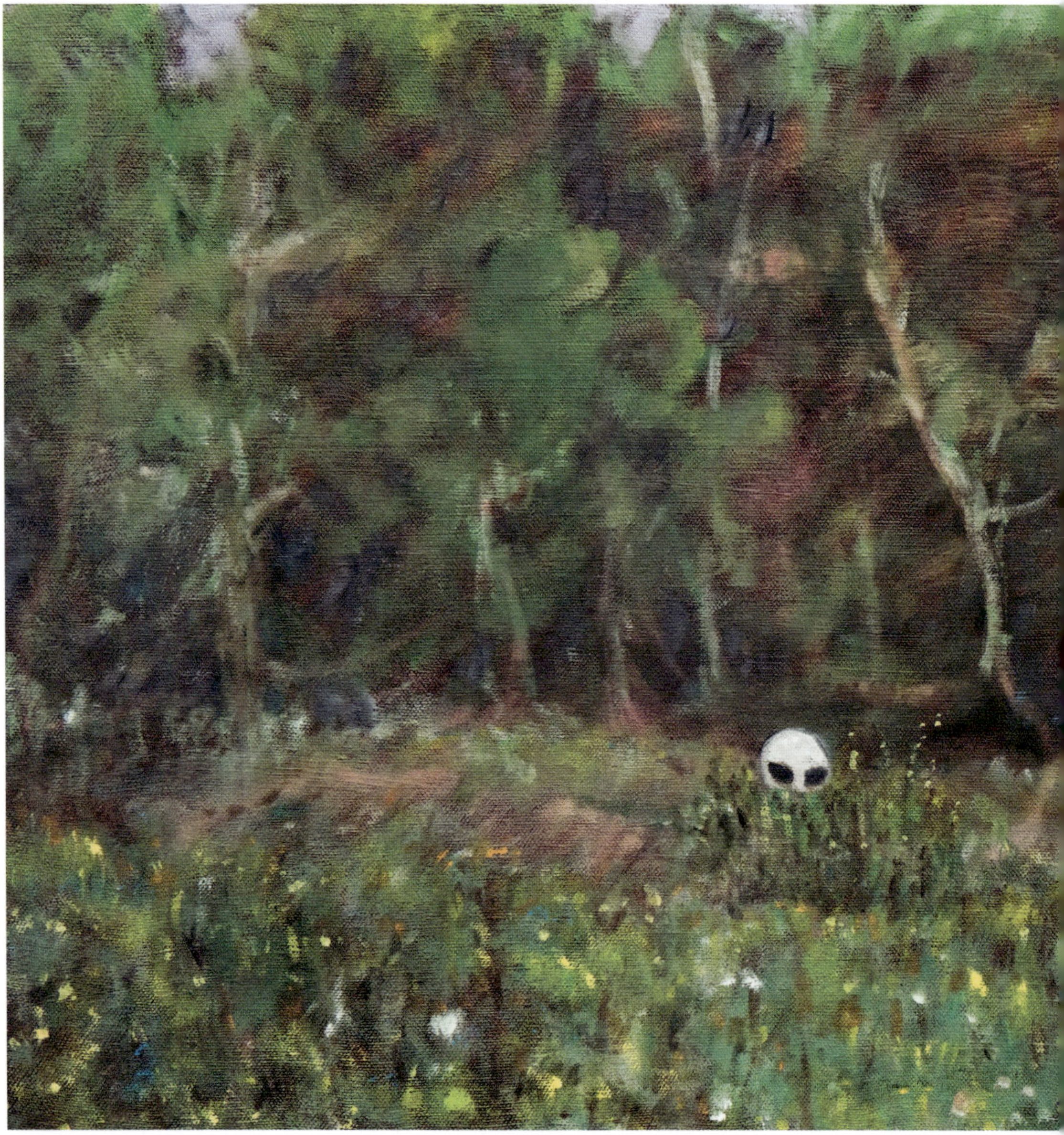

Walking Home, David Huggins, 2007, oil on canvas

In this startling pastoral scene, an ordinary countryside stroll becomes a moment of surveillance as the pale, oversized head of an alien observer peeks up from the tall grass like an unexpected game of wildflower meadow Whack-A-Mole. David Huggins (1940s–2019), who spent decades meticulously documenting what he claimed were lifelong encounters with extraterrestrial beings, created this autobiographical painting as part of his extensive visual record of interactions that allegedly began when he was just eight years old in rural Georgia. Huggins insisted his paintings were faithful reproductions of actual memories – visual testimony of beings that had been monitoring him since childhood. These beings often appear at the

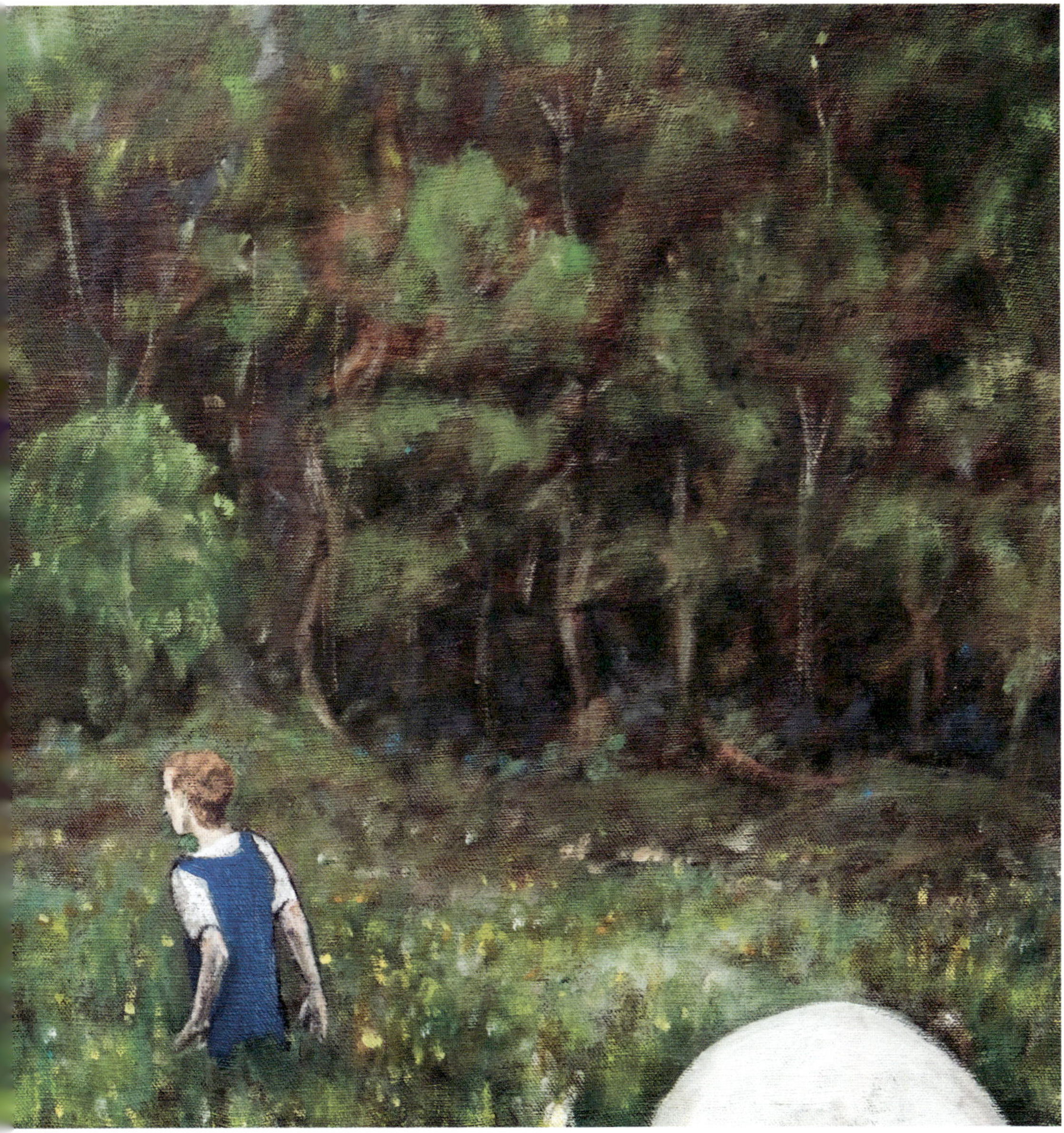

edges of ordinary settings where human and alien realms intersect, as if harvesting our unguarded moments in places we consider sanctuaries, collecting human experiences like botanists gathering specimens for study in gardens we mistakenly believe are ours alone.

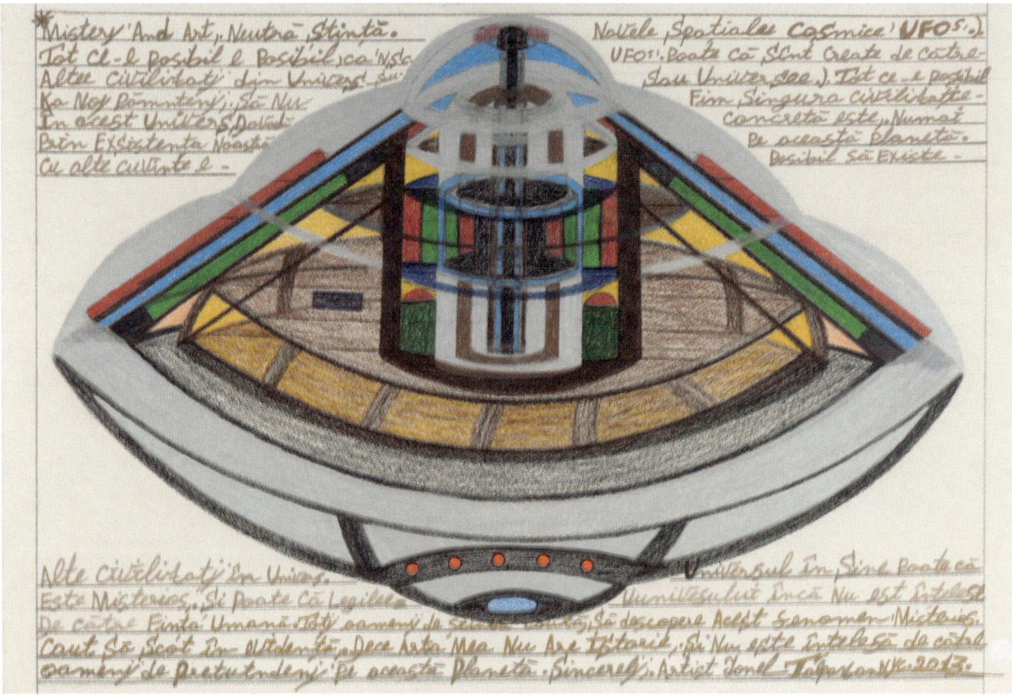

Untitled, Ionel Talpazan, date unknown, marker and pencil on paper

Within this feverish technospiritual blueprint, a classic flying saucer hovers between artistic vision and scientific diagram, its inner workings meticulously documented with coloured pencils, revealing a witness determined to share what conventional science cannot explain. Ionel Talpazan (1955–2015), a Romanian refugee who swam across the Danube to escape oppression, devoted his life to recording extraterrestrial craft after a childhood encounter with a mysterious blue light he believed came from another world. The handwritten Romanian annotations - part technical manual, part cosmic philosophy - suggest a mind grappling with profound questions of existence while attempting to articulate knowledge received through extraordinary channels. Unlike artists who merely imagine otherworldly visitors, Talpazan insisted his drawings held scientific value for NASA, portraying himself not as a passive observer but as an ambassador between worlds, documenting the presence of intelligent watchers waiting for us to evolve enough to understand their message.

I See You!!!, Louise Bourgeois, 2007, etching with hand additions

In this disorienting work of anatomical voyeurism, a disembodied torso floats against stark white space, its interior filled with a constellation of watching eyes, part human, part avian, part entirely uncategorizable, all fixed outwards in an unblinking collective stare. Louise Bourgeois (1911–2010), who spent her long career exploring psychological trauma through Surrealist-influenced imagery, created this etching towards the end of her life when she was confined largely to her New York brownstone, making the boundary-crossing surveillance even more distressing. Bourgeois transforms this figure into a living panopticon, not one central watcher but an entire anatomy of observation where organs have evolved into instruments of sight. The declaration of the title gleefully reverses the traditional gallery experience, transforming the passive viewer into the unwitting subject, turning the contemplative act of viewing inside out, so that we find ourselves caught in a discomforting web of mutual recognition.

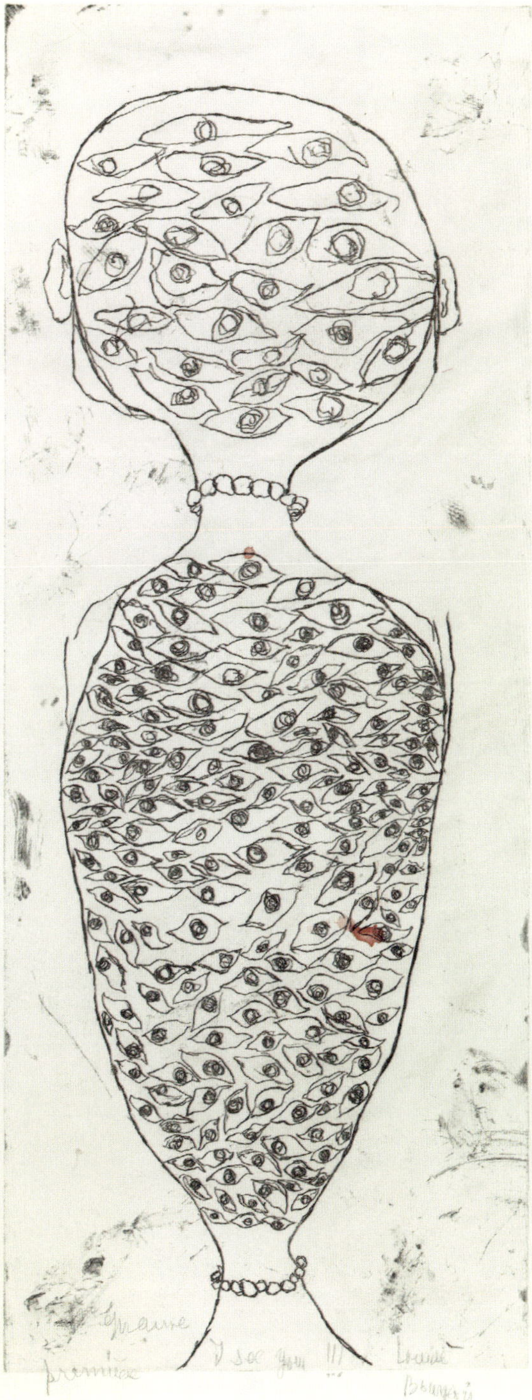

III

—

TRANSFORMATIVE POWERS

'Everything flows, nothing stands still.'

– HERACLITUS

A single drop of water hangs suspended in time, a perfect sphere of liquid crystal casting prismatic studies across space. For a fraction of a second, it exists as pure potential, an abstract composition awaiting metamorphosis, before piercing the pool's surface and reforming as a living canvas of sky and cloud. Watch a spark catch dry wood, and flames begin their hypnotic performance, transforming solid matter into a gallery of light and heat, leaving behind nothing but silvery ash, a monochrome meditation on impermanence. Deep in the Earth's dark belly, immense pressure transforms humble carbon into diamonds that trap light in their crystalline hearts. These elemental transformations have always carried a whiff of the divine, forces that speak to deeper mysteries of creation and change.

These phenomena captivated our ancestors so completely that they built entire cosmologies around them. The Greek philosopher Empedocles was so convinced of fire's sacred power that he allegedly jumped into Mount Etna to prove his oneness with the element, although one can't help but think there might have been less dramatic ways to demonstrate his enthusiasm for this theory. Yet his fiery exit aside, Empedocles' ideas about the sacred nature of elemental forces echoed across cultures. The Chinese Wuxing system saw the elements as forces in constant flux, each force flowing into the next, while twentieth-century philosopher Gaston Bachelard devoted entire books to poetic reveries about each element: water that dreams, fire that transforms, air that carries imagination.

The Fifth Treatise –The Dark Sun, artist unknown, from *Splendor Solis* by Salomon Trismosin, 1582, tempera, gold leaf and ink on vellum

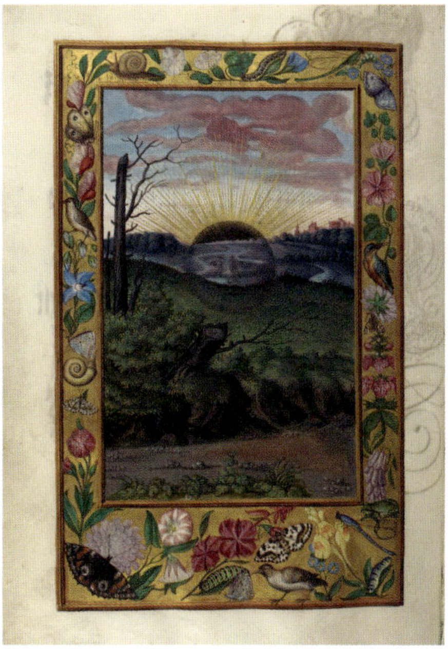

This marriage of material and mystical found its most dedicated practitioners in the alchemists, who saw their laboratories as temples where the mysteries of matter might reveal spiritual truths. Today's CERN laboratories, with their massive particle accelerators humming in underground caverns and their ethereal detection chambers, feel like modern temples to transformation. The white-coated priests of physics might bristle at the comparison to their alchemical ancestors, but when they speak in hushed tones about the 'God particle' or describe matter shifting between states like cosmic sleight-of-hand, the echoes of those ancient seekers ring through their words.

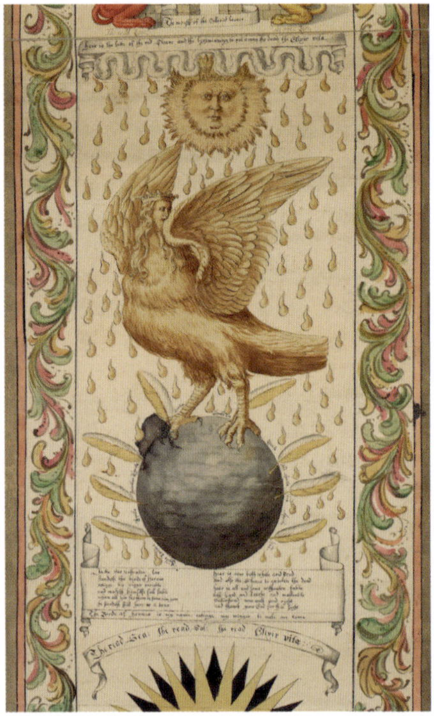

Some of history's most extraordinary manuscripts document this quest for transformation. The Ripley Scrolls are a perfect example of alchemical extravagance – a fantastical plethora of sun-swallowing dragons and feathered kings, a visual fever dream of sacred science. The *Splendor Solis* manuscripts take a similarly maximalist approach, their pages blazing with golden suns rising over crimson seas while mysterious figures emerge from flower-filled vessels. Each symbol was carefully chosen to convey specific aspects of transformation, but good luck getting a straight answer about their meanings from any self-respecting alchemist – 'the first rule of Alchemist Club' and all that, you understand.

This quest found its way onto canvas, where painters documented both the practical reality and mystical possibilities of alchemical pursuits. Pieter Bruegel's alchemists hunch over equipment in workshops crammed with glassware and furnaces, faces illuminated by mysterious flames. While Bruegel might have been poking fun at their obsessions, other artists approached the subject with earnest fascination. David Teniers the Younger filled his scenes with such precise detail that modern historians use them to reconstruct period laboratory practices. His 1649 painting *An Alchemist in His Workshop* reads like a catalogue of equipment, even as it captures the tension between scientific pursuit and mystical possibility.

Three centuries later, Leonora Carrington and Remedios Varo resurrected these alchemical workshops in their own mysterious paintings, although their laboratories operated according to decidedly stranger laws. Varo's delicate machines process starlight into a golden liquid, their intricate mechanisms resembling those of a mystic engineer. Carrington's kitchens double as workshops where meals become magical potions and everyday cooking tools perform cosmic operations. Both artists transformed the ancient iconography of alchemy into something uniquely modern yet timeless, revealing that the magic lies not in turning lead into gold, but in the extraordinary happening all around us, all the time.

Opposite: 'The Bird of Hermes' sequence, from *Rotulum hieroglyphicum G. Riplaei Equitis Aurati*, George Ripley, *c.* 1600, ink/gouache on vellum

Below: Tabulae Theosophicae Cabalisticae from *Amphitheatrum sapientiae aeternae*, Heinrich Khunrath, late sixteenth/early seventeenth century, manuscript

Today's painters continue this exploration of transformative forces, although their workshops look quite different. Massive canvases become alchemical experiments where lead oxidizes and straw blackens, the paintings themselves transforming over time. Figures caught in eternal metamorphosis flow across surfaces like liquid mercury, while vast abstract works map cosmic transmutations with layers of marks that seem to capture creation and dissolution in real time. Even our popular culture can't resist the allure of these transformative powers, from mystical arts in comics to intricate transmutation circles in anime, we keep reimagining these ancient forces through modern lenses.

We've spent centuries seeking to understand these elemental forces, building tools to measure them, creating languages to describe them. Yet the mystery remains as profound as a single drop of water hanging motionless in time. In that moment of perfect suspension, just before impact, everything is possible – matter and energy, form and formlessness, the one and the many all exist together. The search for understanding continues, but the mystery only deepens. We find not answers but an endless poetry, written in a language of constant change and eternal return.

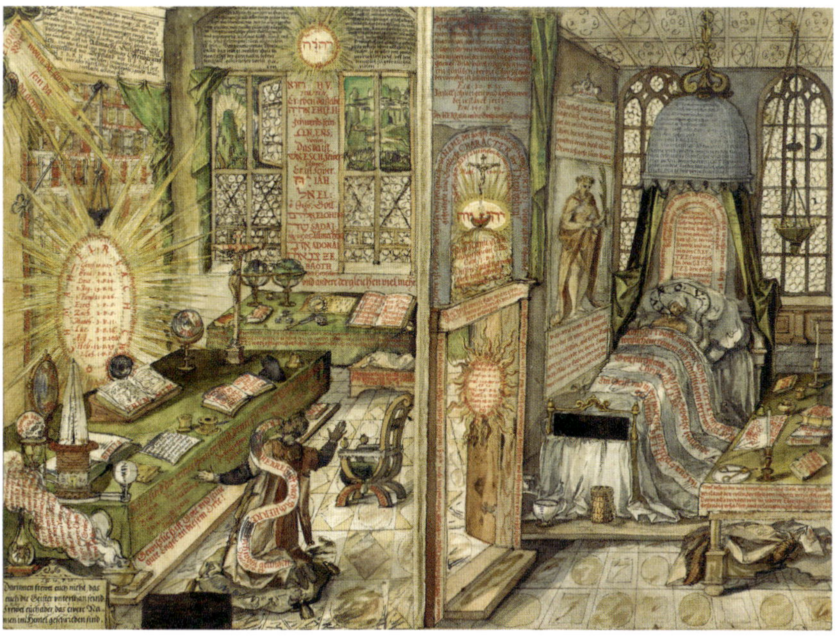

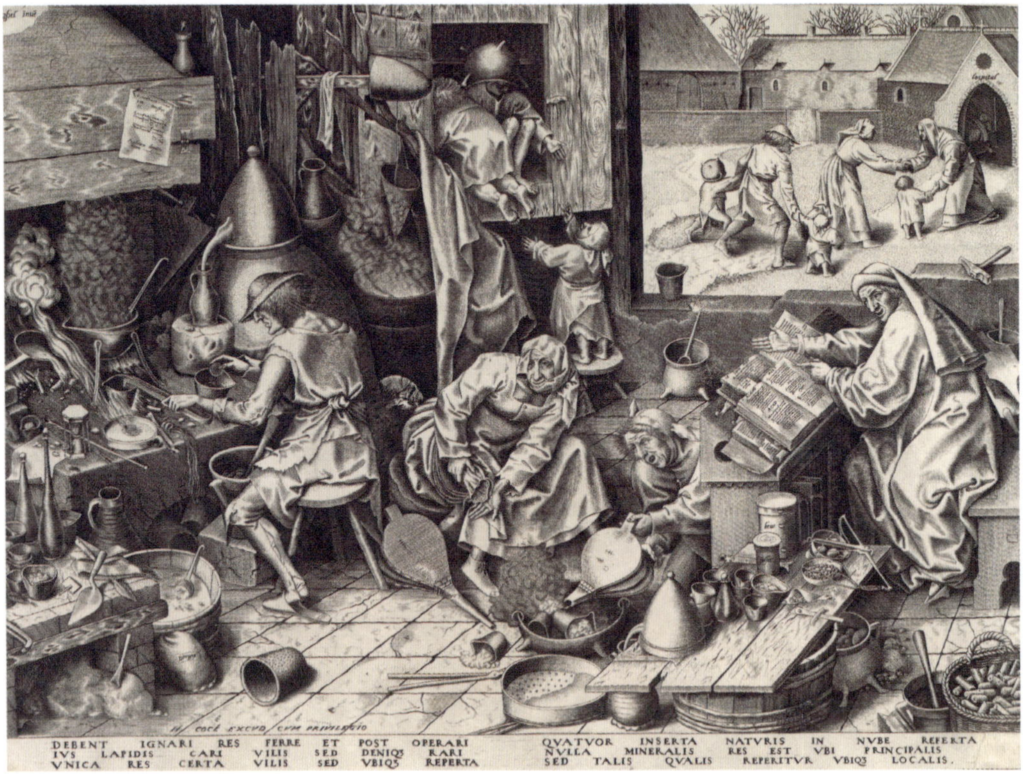

The Alchemist, Pieter Bruegel the Elder, after 1558, engraving

---

In this chaotic kitchen-turned-laboratory, Pieter Bruegel the Elder (c. 1525–69) stages a spectacular failed transmutation – not of lead into gold, but of wisdom into folly and prosperity into ruin. The desperate alchemist squanders his family's last coin while his hollow-cheeked wife shakes an empty purse, their starving children scavenging through barren cupboards (one little rascal wearing an upturned pot as a makeshift hat). Bruegel transforms everyday objects into symbols of alchemical delusion – kitchen pots repurposed for esoteric experiments, a bellows-pumping assistant wearing a fool's cap with ass ears, and a turbaned scholar pointing to a book titled *Alghe Mist* (a pun meaning both 'alchemist' and 'all is lost'). Through the window, the family's future selves approach a poorhouse, the final destination of their mystical journey. This biting satire strips away alchemy's spiritual pretensions to expose its material consequences, suggesting that the true philosopher's stone might simply be common sense – the most elusive element of all in the crucible of human ambition.

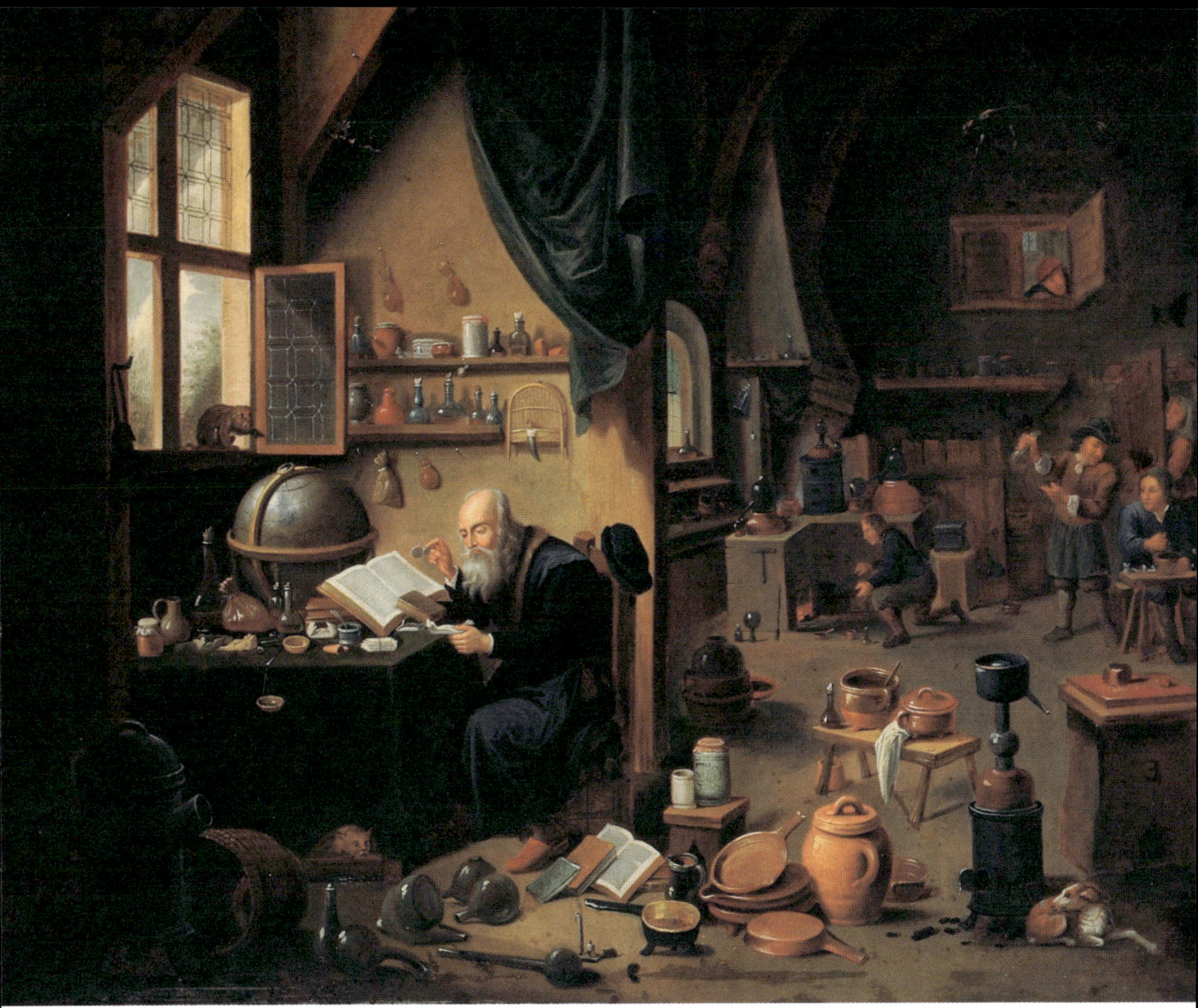

An Alchemist in His Workshop, David Teniers the Younger, seventeenth century, oil on canvas

Unlike Bruegel's scathing satire, David Teniers the Younger (1610–90) approaches the alchemist's laboratory with genuine reverence, transforming this candlelit workshop into a sanctuary where mundane materials might undergo spiritual elevation. The elderly practitioner, concentration etched into every line of his face, carefully directs oxygen into a small fire beneath a ceramic vessel, surrounded by beautiful experimental apparatus: glass flasks capturing light like liquid knowledge, earthenware crucibles awaiting their alchemical baptism and metal instruments gleaming with purpose. Teniers, who created over 350 alchemical scenes, depicts neither charlatan nor fool but a dedicated seeker navigating between ancient wisdom and emerging science. While Bruegel's alchemist sacrificed his family to futile pursuits, Teniers' dignified practitioner seems to embody something rather aspirational, perhaps the belief that true transformation happens not through turning lead into gold, but through the patient work of turning ignorance into understanding and observation into insight.

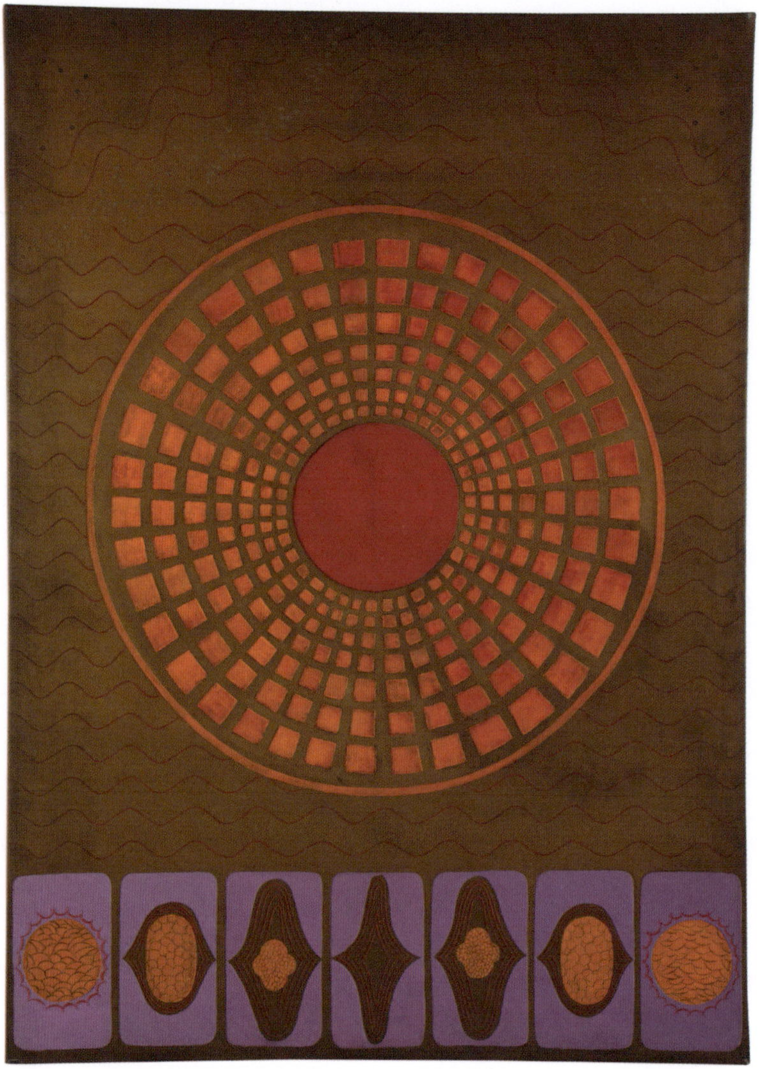

Structure of generative cores 1 and 2. Multiplicity, from the series 'Isolated Beta Being', Elda Cerrato, 1970, oil on canvas

Glowing with otherworldly exactitude, these geometric constellations reveal what Elda Cerrato (1930–2023) discovered after seeing a UFO in the hills of Tucumán: that transformation happens first in the invisible realms. Her 'Beta Beings' hover between states of becoming, their cellular structures and luminous pathways captured as energy crystallizes into form. Each node in these metaphysical diagrams pulses with generative potential, making visible what Cerrato called 'the inner vibrations of life'. A biochemist who also studied George Gurdjieff's esoteric teachings, Cerrato approaches cosmic transformation through both scientific observation and mystical experience – her paintings like field notes from experiments in awareness. These works invite viewers to witness the same transformative forces Cerrato encountered in her mystical practice, whereby the mathematics of creation becomes momentarily visible through the artist's heightened perception.

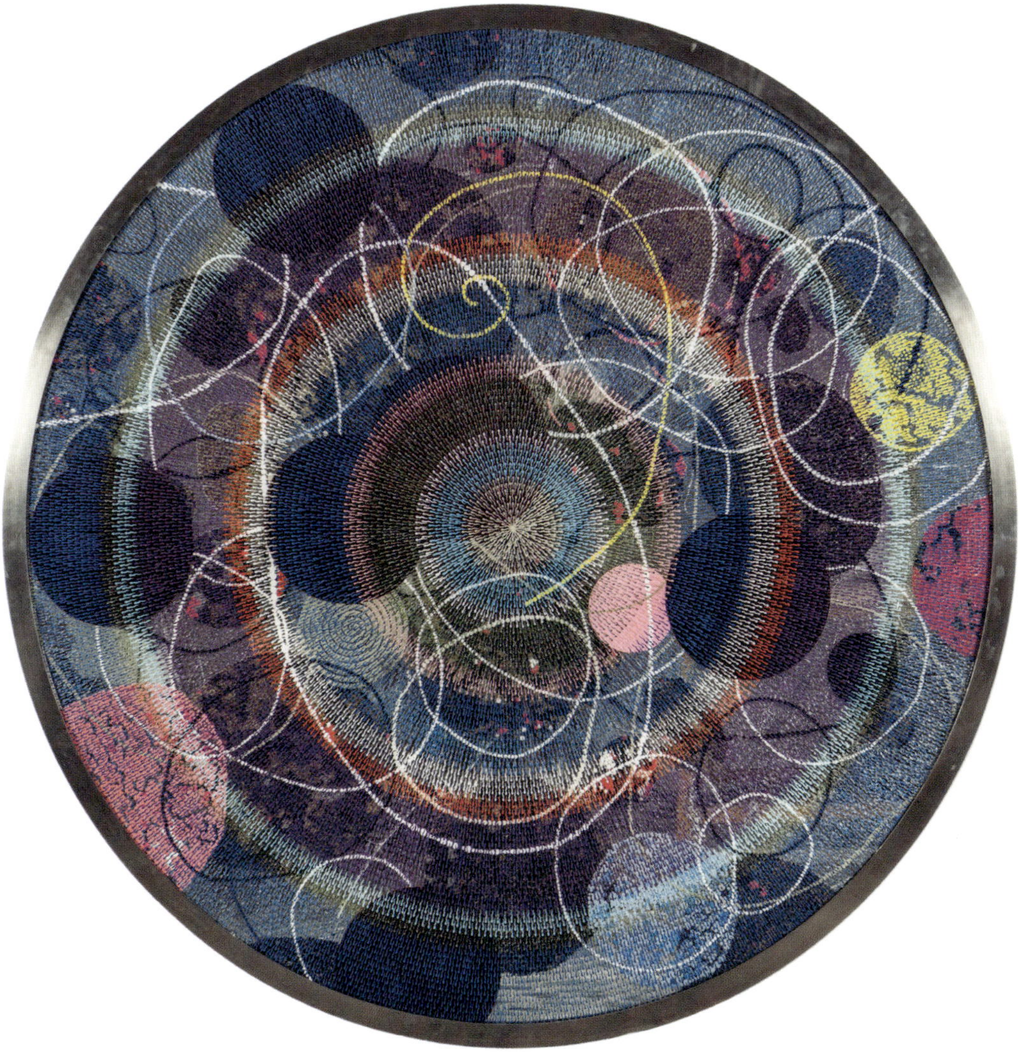

Algorithm that turns up your automatic response for sharp reflex and deep subliminal structuring, Bharti Kher, 2019, bindis on mirror

Thousands of tiny bindis swirl across mirrored glass like celestial bodies in an eternal dance as Bharti Kher performs a kind of material alchemy, transforming mass-produced dots into sources of mystical energy.

The British-Indian artist meticulously builds these spiralling patterns by hand, each humble bindi transmuted from everyday object into part of a larger cosmic force that draws viewers into its reflective field. Your reflection fragments and reconfigures through Kher's painstaking geometry, your consciousness momentarily captured by the elemental power she has conjured through rigorous repetition.

This mirror becomes an alchemical vessel, creating a dizzying conversation between material and spiritual worlds. The title itself reveals the work's true nature as activation rather than decoration, these patterns generating tangible energy that reaches through glass to awaken something within our perception, turning the mundane into magic through obsessive repetition and exquisite precision.

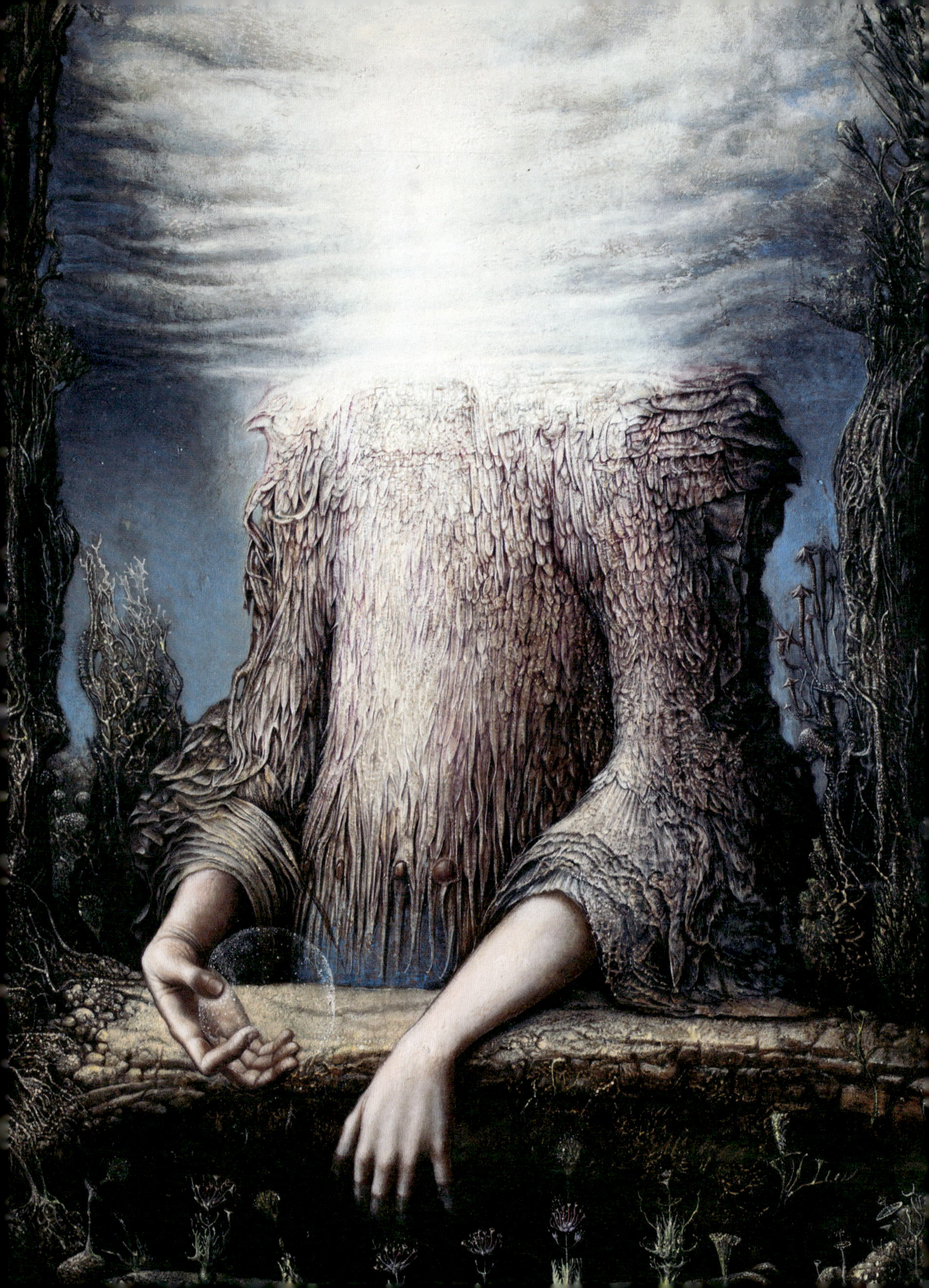

Right: Calaquichix Faerie flying across the Rainbow, Tino Rodríguez, 2022, gouache and pastel on paper

A a dreamy pastel spun-sugar sweet skeleton soars over a rainbow highway astride a spotted butterfly, dandelion wand raised in jubilant greeting! This playful dance with mortality explodes with the colour and joy that defines Tino Rodríguez's enchanted visual universes, where death wears flowers and flies on butterfly wings. Rodríguez infuses his work with the captivating allure of Catholic saints, European fairy tales and vibrant Mexican myths, creating visual poetry that transcends borders and language. This skeletal faerie, neither fearsome nor grim, invites us into a world where transformation is celebrated with gentle humour and a candy floss palette. Here we see how the macabre becomes magical and how profound metamorphosis, even death, can be a vibrant adventure. In this joyful vision of transformation, Rodríguez reveals that everything changes, nothing truly ends, and even our bones can sprout wings to carry us into brilliant new dimensions of being.

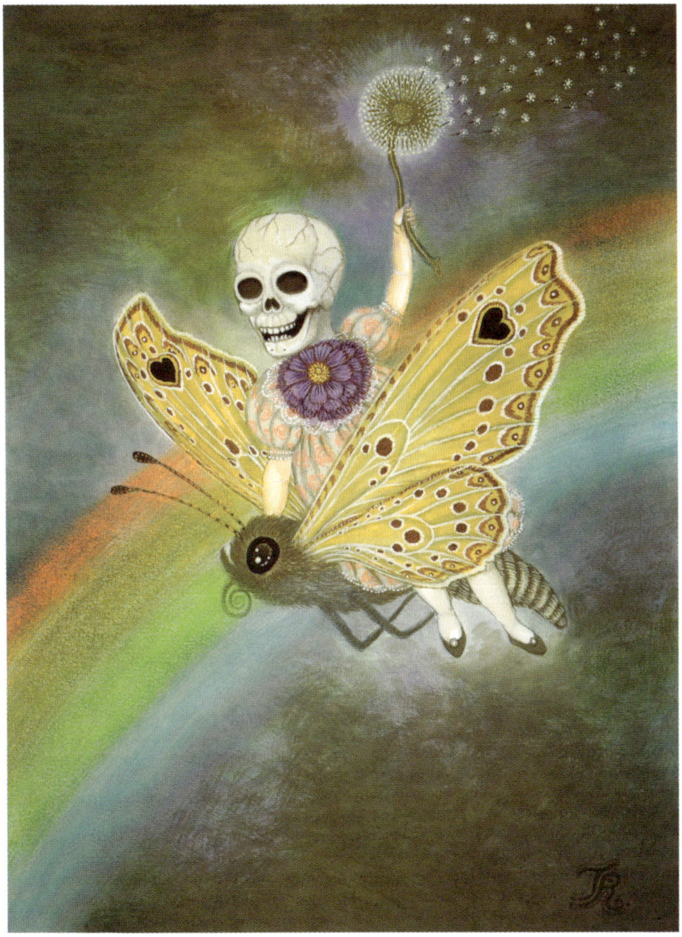

Opposite: L'Orbe, Agostino Arrivabene, 2018, oil on linen

At the threshold between states of being, a headless figure extends its perfect hands, the only remaining human elements, as mist dissolves what was once a face and bark-like integuments consume the flesh in their strange embrace. Agostino Arrivabene shows us transformation at its most uncanny point, where identity surrenders to metamorphosis, leaving only a transparent orb, an inscrutable pellucid offering. Working with ancient layering techniques that echo the alchemical processes he depicts, Arrivabene creates beings caught in perpetual becoming. The figure's elaborate cloak shifts between impossible states - simultaneously coral reef, tree bark and feathered plumage - while the ambiguous environment hovers between desert wasteland and oceanic depths, reinforcing this liminal existence. Through this haunting visual poetry, Arrivabene embodies what he describes as 'the medium that translates every dormant impulse' into revelation, revealing the strange territory where matter and spirit trade their essential properties.

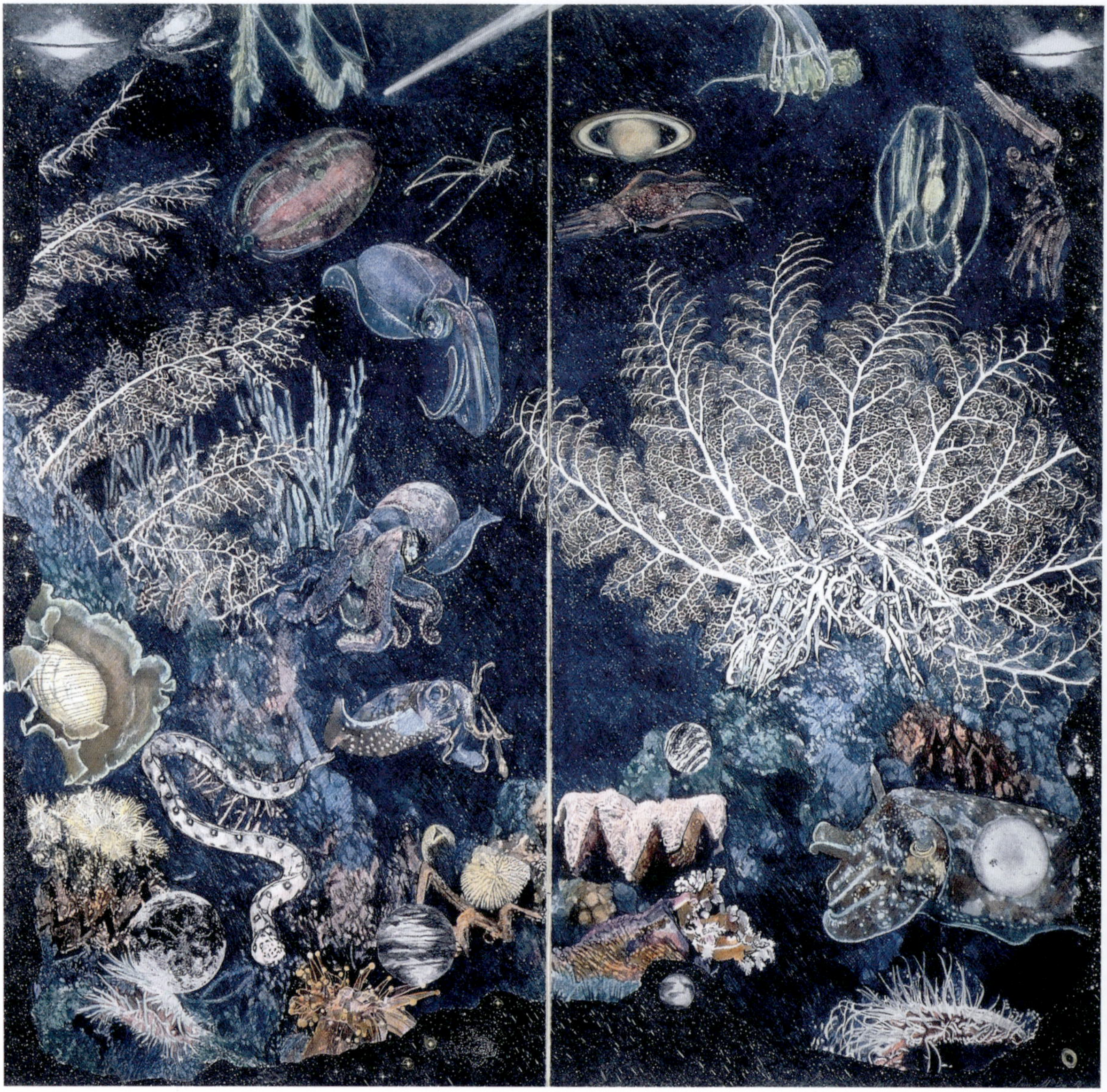

The Night Sea, Ann McCoy, 1978, lithograph, hand coloured with coloured pencil

In this cosmic ocean where galaxies and jellyfish intermingle, Ann McCoy transforms the aquatic depths into an alchemical vessel for psychological renewal. Following what Jung called 'the night sea journey' – the hero's descent into darkness before rebirth – McCoy renders bioluminescent creatures and celestial bodies with microscopic precision using thousands of tiny coloured pencil marks, creating a work of monumental scale that required months of meditative labour. Inspired by her actual night dives in Australia and a prophetic dream where 'sea turtles and scientists were guiding me through the waters showing me the beauty of the sea at night', McCoy crafts a visual meditation on the alchemical nigredo, the blackening phase where old forms break down before transmutation can occur. A longtime student of Jungian analysis, McCoy creates an underwater realm where the boundaries between cosmos and consciousness, matter and spirit, become hypnotically fluid.

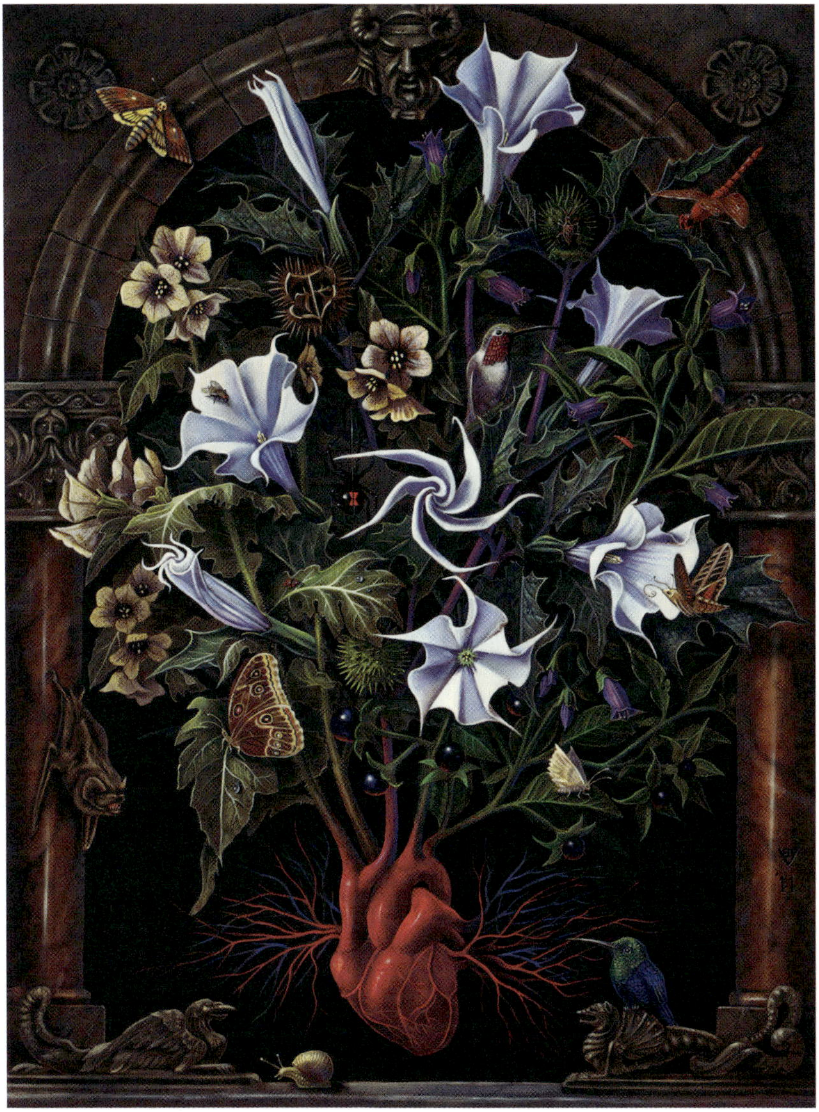

Sacred Heart, Benjamin A. Vierling, 2011, egg tempera and oil on panel

Genesis unfolds through an exposed heart in Benjamin A. Vierling's alchemical garden, where poisonous plants sprout directly from an aortic chamber to perform their enigmatic botanical magic. Working with Renaissance techniques that layer egg tempera beneath translucent oil glazes, Vierling creates a modern allegory where deadly nightshades - belladonna, jimsonweed and henbane - bloom with unexpected beauty. Like an anatomical manuscript illuminated by a phytological mystic, the painting reveals what Vierling calls 'the dynamic relationships that exist between flora and fauna, colour and form, spirit and matter'. Thirteen species of insects and small creatures inhabit this microcosm, each participating in the delicate exchange between poison and nourishment, death, and regeneration. The crimson organ serves as both reliquary and crucible, where baneful toxins become visionary insight through the beating, pulsing centre of all creation.

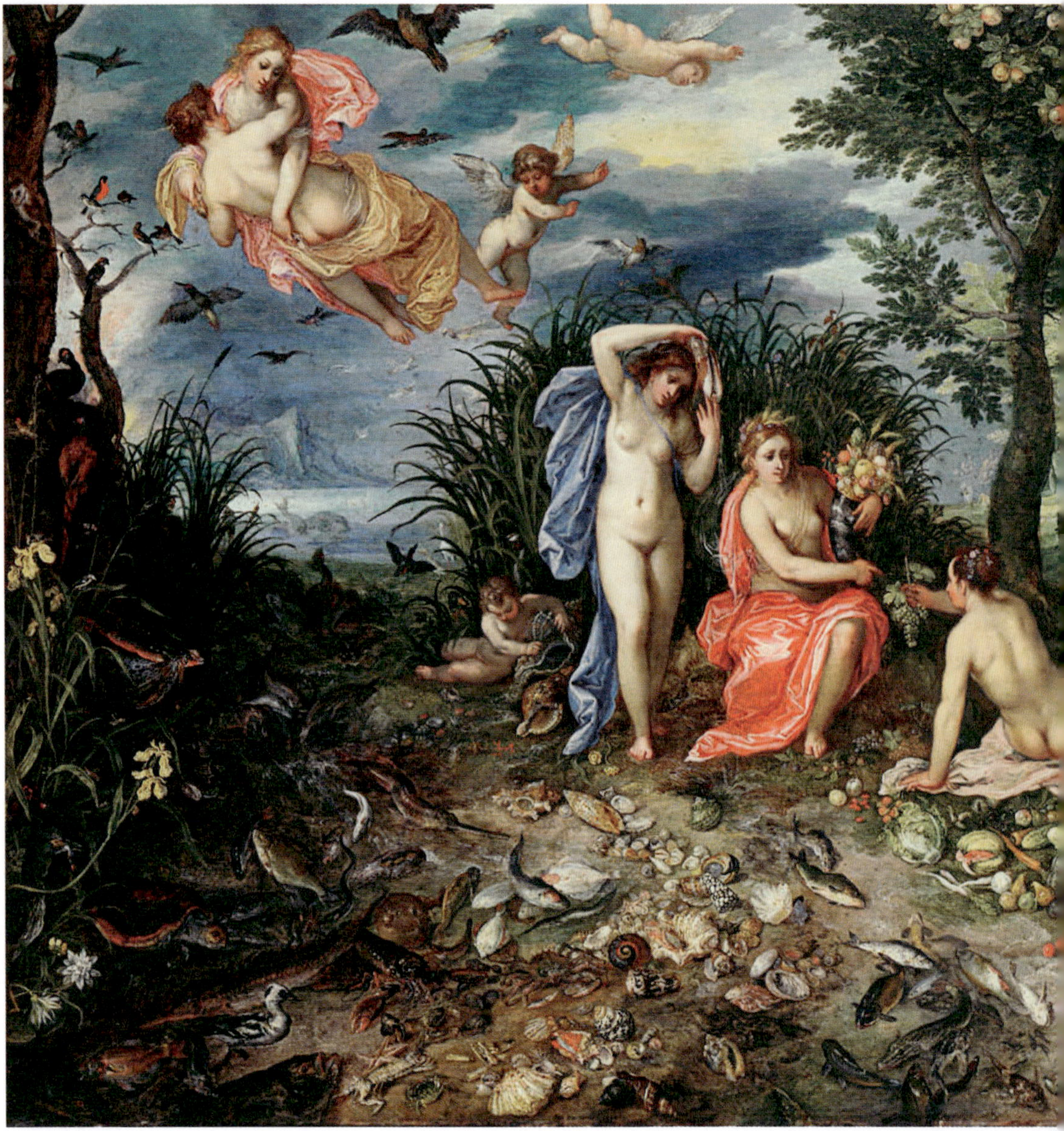

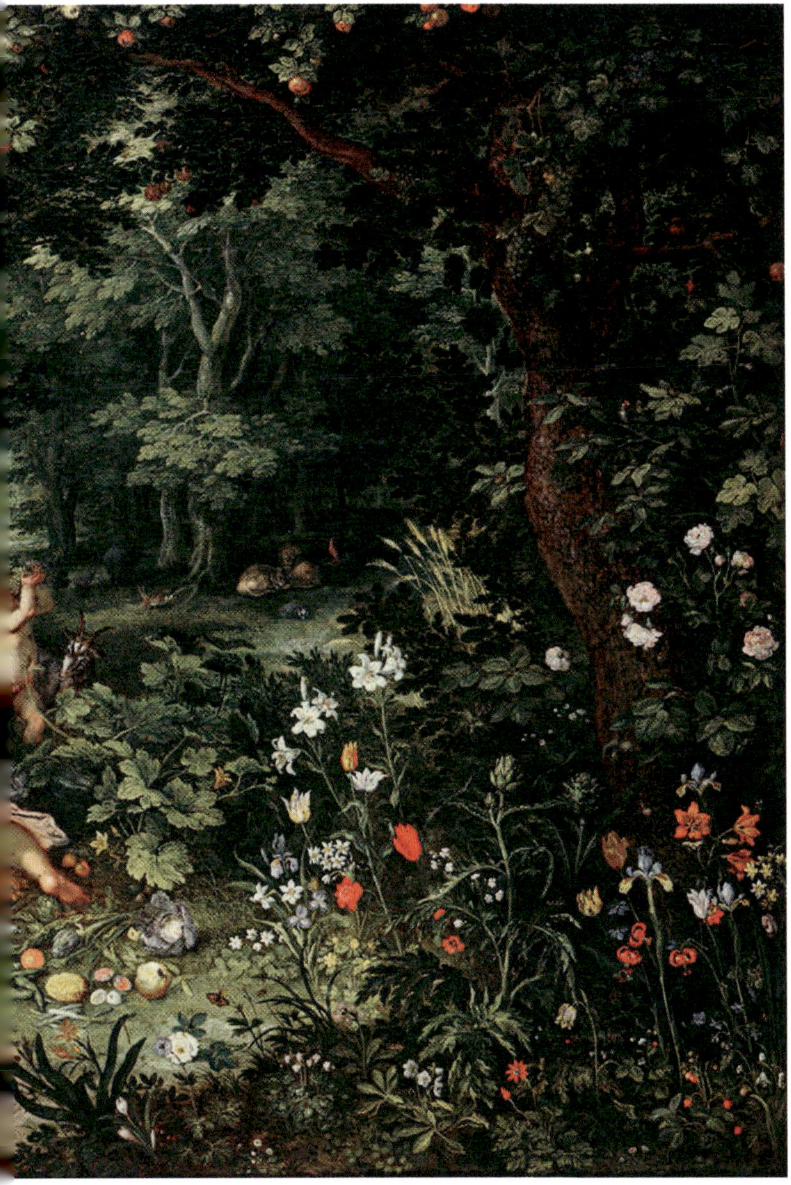

Ceres and the Four Elements,
Jan Brueghel the Elder, 1604,
oil painting on copper

In this lush allegorical tableau, Jan Brueghel the Elder (1568-1625) captures Earth's perpetual alchemy through mythic symbolism and careful natural observation. The goddess Ceres, adorned with wheat spikes and bearing her horn of plenty, presides over this botanical paradise, where every flower, fruit and creature seems to embody nature's transformative powers. Known as 'Velvet' Brueghel for his masterful rendering of textures, the artist turns oil paint into a vivid sensory experience. Each petal and leaf is precisely rendered while participating in the greater cycle of growth, decay and rebirth - where water becomes sap, seeds become fruits and sunlight becomes vital energy, through processes far more mysterious than those occurring in any alchemist's workshop. This celebration reveals what Brueghel seems to have understood: that miraculous transmutation has always been happening right in front of us, in the endless cycle in which elements combine and recombine with quiet, relentless creativity.

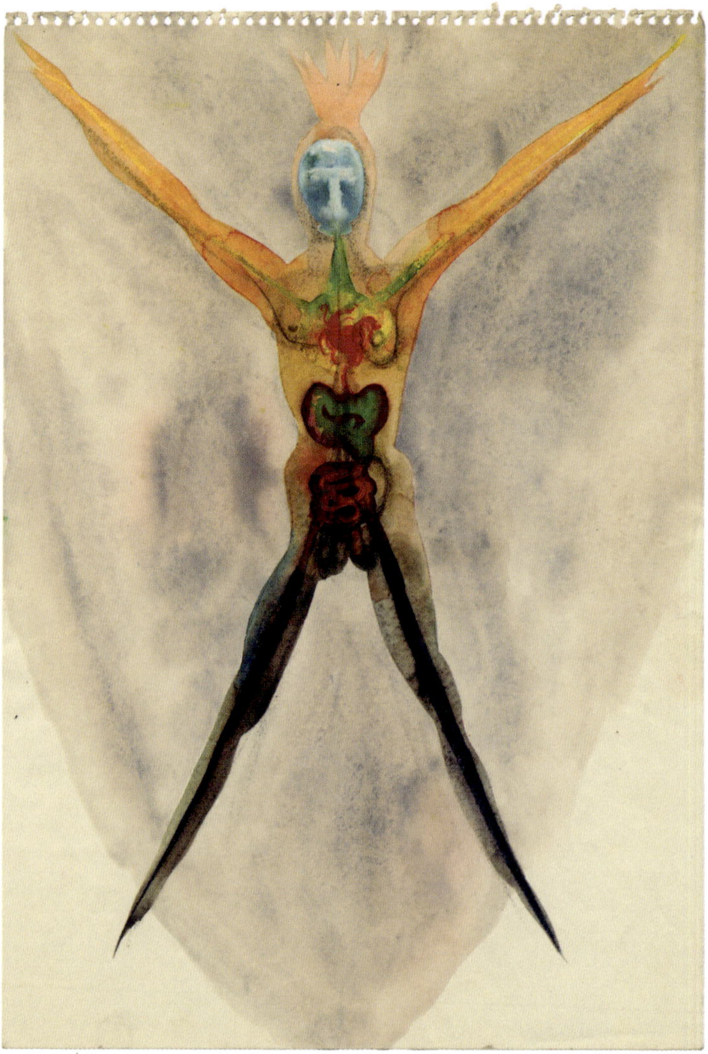

Alchemical Figure, Ithell Colquhoun, 1940, watercolour

A luminous androgynous figure stands sentinel against a pale backdrop, as Ithell Colquhoun's (1906–88) mystical vision brings forth a being that seems to exist at the nexus of realities. The British artist lived deeply within the world of magic, and her investigations shaped every aspect of her art – rendering her subject here like an otherworldly laboratory specimen viewed through enchanted glass, its body sectioned into glowing colour fields that map the hidden currents of energy that Colquhoun believed flowed through all existence. Each hue is carefully chosen according to esoteric colour theories, representing different mystical forces she encountered in her spiritual practice. Her lifelong quest to unite male and female, solid and fluid, visible and invisible flows through this alchemical body, where transformation happens through subtle energetic shifts. Colquhoun seems to propose that transformation works from the inside out – awakening the lively, kaleidoscopic forces already present within us through the artist's initiated vision.

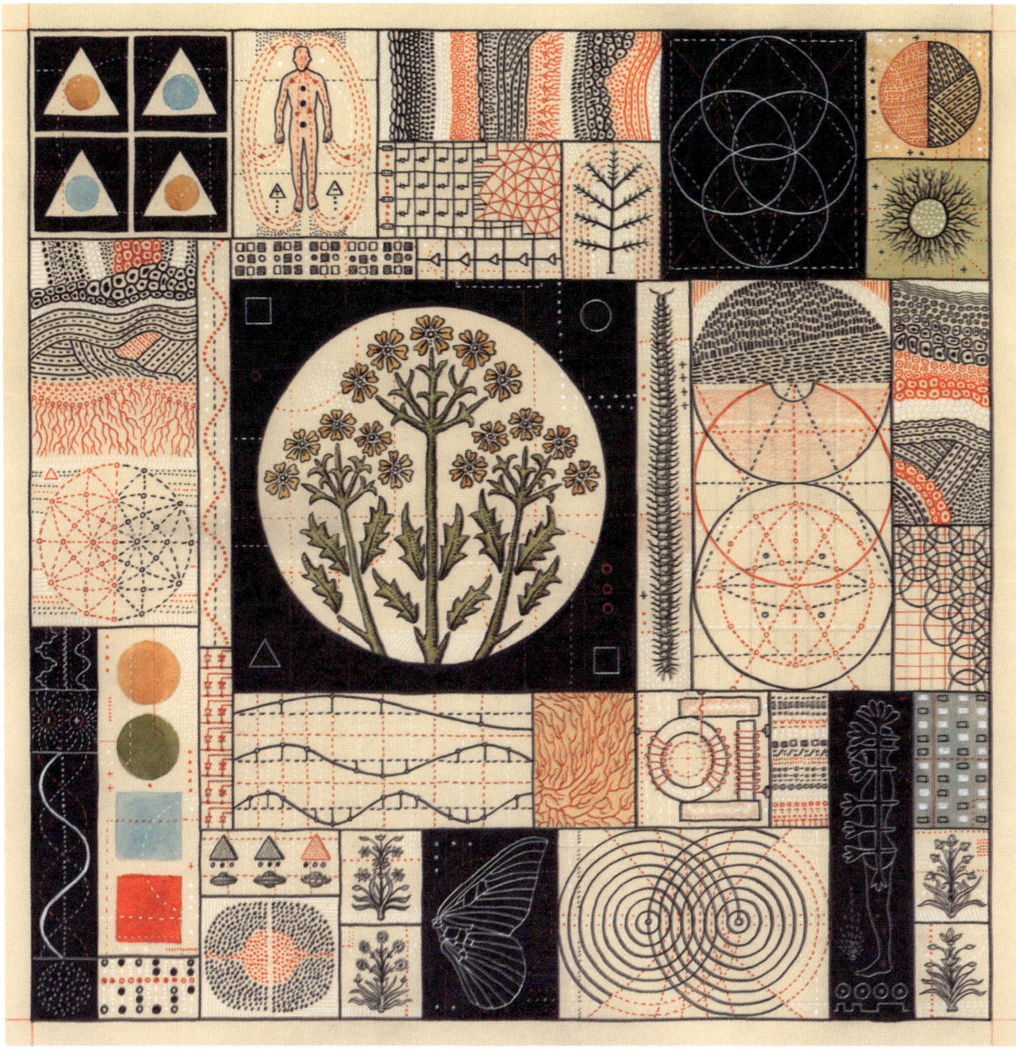

Transmutations, Daniel Martin Diaz, 2023, graphite, watercolour and ink on archival paper

Cellular biology meets cosmic geometry in this gridded meditation on transformation, in which Daniel Martin Diaz places a golden wildflower at the centre of what appears to be an alchemical instruction manual. A multitude of enigmatically illustrated panels surround it, containing mathematical formulas, architectural sketches and anatomical fragments, transforming a simple plant into something far more mysterious. Diaz, whose work explores what he calls 'the implications of technology on humanity's future', draws from scientific diagrams, ancient manuscripts and quantum physics to create what feels like a functional schematic rather than mere illustration. His meticulous lines seem to establish connections between realms - biological and technological, material and spiritual - suggesting that transformation requires understanding of both the minutest cellular detail and the vast mathematical patterns governing all matter. The encoded and intriguing grid pulses with hidden connections, inviting viewers to discover what secrets might be concealed within its rigorous geometry.

PART TWO

REALMS BETWEEN

'I have no idea where this will lead us, but I have a definite feeling it will be a place both wonderful and strange.'

– AGENT COOPER, *TWIN PEAKS*

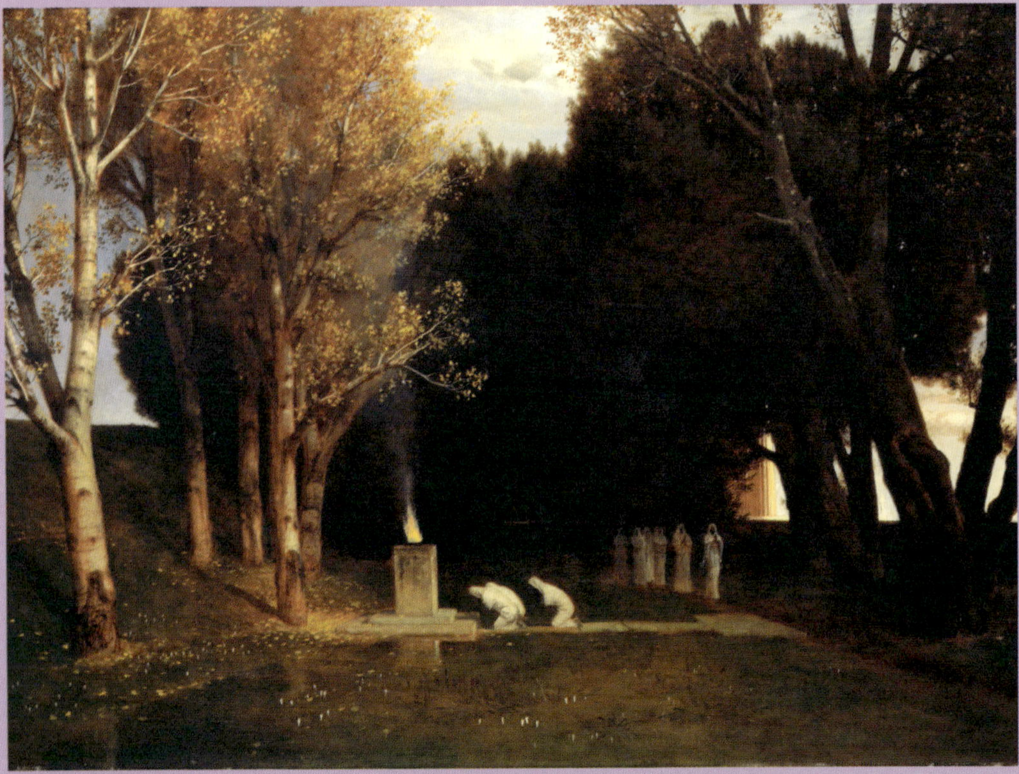

Quantum physicists tell us that the act of observation collapses infinite possibilities into a single reality. Until we look, a particle exists in all possible states simultaneously. Until we measure it, a cat is both alive and dead. But what happens in those spaces between observations? What exists in the margins of certainty, in the territories between 'is' and 'isn't'?

The Japanese have a word, *ma* (間), that describes the gap between things, the interval, the space between what was and what will be. But it's more than empty space; it's pregnant with possibility, alive with potential – like the pause between movements in a symphony, or the moment between stepping off one stone and landing on the next. In these intervals, anything might happen.

Every culture has mapped these alternate routes through reality. Chinese fox spirits slip between worlds through transformation and illusion, while Celtic travellers watch for fairy rings that could deposit them in the Land of the Ever-Young. Mississippi blues musicians speak of crossroads where Old Scratch waits with contracts written in blood. Even modern urban explorers report finding stairs in forests that lead nowhere, doorways in abandoned buildings that open onto impossible spaces, subway platforms that appear on no official maps. Physicists studying quantum tunnelling discover particles taking 'impossible' routes, passing through barriers as if they don't exist. Dark matter carves invisible highways through space that ordinary matter must follow. Even time might not flow in the straight line we imagine – some physicists propose it might loop, branch or fold back on itself like a Möbius strip.

What if those urban legends of disappeared explorers and folk tales of travellers stepping into other worlds aren't just stories but attempts to document something our limited perceptions can only glimpse indirectly? Whether through scientific instruments or artistic vision, humans have always tried to record evidence of these alternative routes through reality. The Victorians were particularly attuned to spaces where the familiar gives way to the impossible. Nineteenth-century painters found fairy realms in the English countryside, and poets wrote of markets that appeared only at twilight. Artists captured that daily reminder of transition, those moments when gaslight meets darkness and ordinary streets become stages for

Opposite: Sacred Grove, Arnold Böcklin, 1882, oil on canvas

the uncanny. Contemporary artists discover these threshold territories in the abandoned architecture of our recent past, in the moments when familiar spaces reveal their strange potential. These are the modern ruins where human intention has quietly withdrawn, leaving spaces that hover between what they were and what they might become.

Beneath the mundane reality of the mapped world lies a vast unmeasured wilderness. The soil beneath our feet, the caverns we've never explored, the ecosystems layered within what we think we've surveyed – all of it harbours chasms upon corridors upon catacombs of spatial marginalia we've failed to notice or chosen not to see. Underground networks threading through stone. Hidden valleys shrouded in perpetual mist. Subterranean chambers where light has never reached. What if the world we navigate daily is only the surface of something far stranger, the palest precipice of the proverbial iceberg, far more intricate, inscrutable (and, of course, extremely indifferent to our staggering ignorance)?

One wonders if the universe isn't hiding its secrets from us so much as operating according to rules our minds aren't equipped to comprehend. What if those Victorian schoolgirls at Hanging Rock didn't vanish but simply stepped into a dimension our eyes can't register? What if that tree you pass daily exists across multiple timelines simultaneously, its roots threading through centuries while its leaves rustle with futures we haven't yet imagined? What if every seemingly abandoned building actually teems with occupants… just not in the version of reality we happen to inhabit?

Artists who set up studios in the seams of these secret spaces surface as custodians and translators of uncomfortable answers. They return with evidence that challenges our understanding of what we think we know about time, space and consciousness itself. Their work suggests that reality isn't a solid thing at all, but rather a consensus we've agreed upon, one that could fold in on itself like eerie stop-motion origami in reverse the moment we look at it too closely. What they discover shows us that we inhabit only one layer of an infinite palimpsest, with countless other realities written over and under our own, occupying the same coordinates but different dimensions.

Sharing our space, but not our reality.

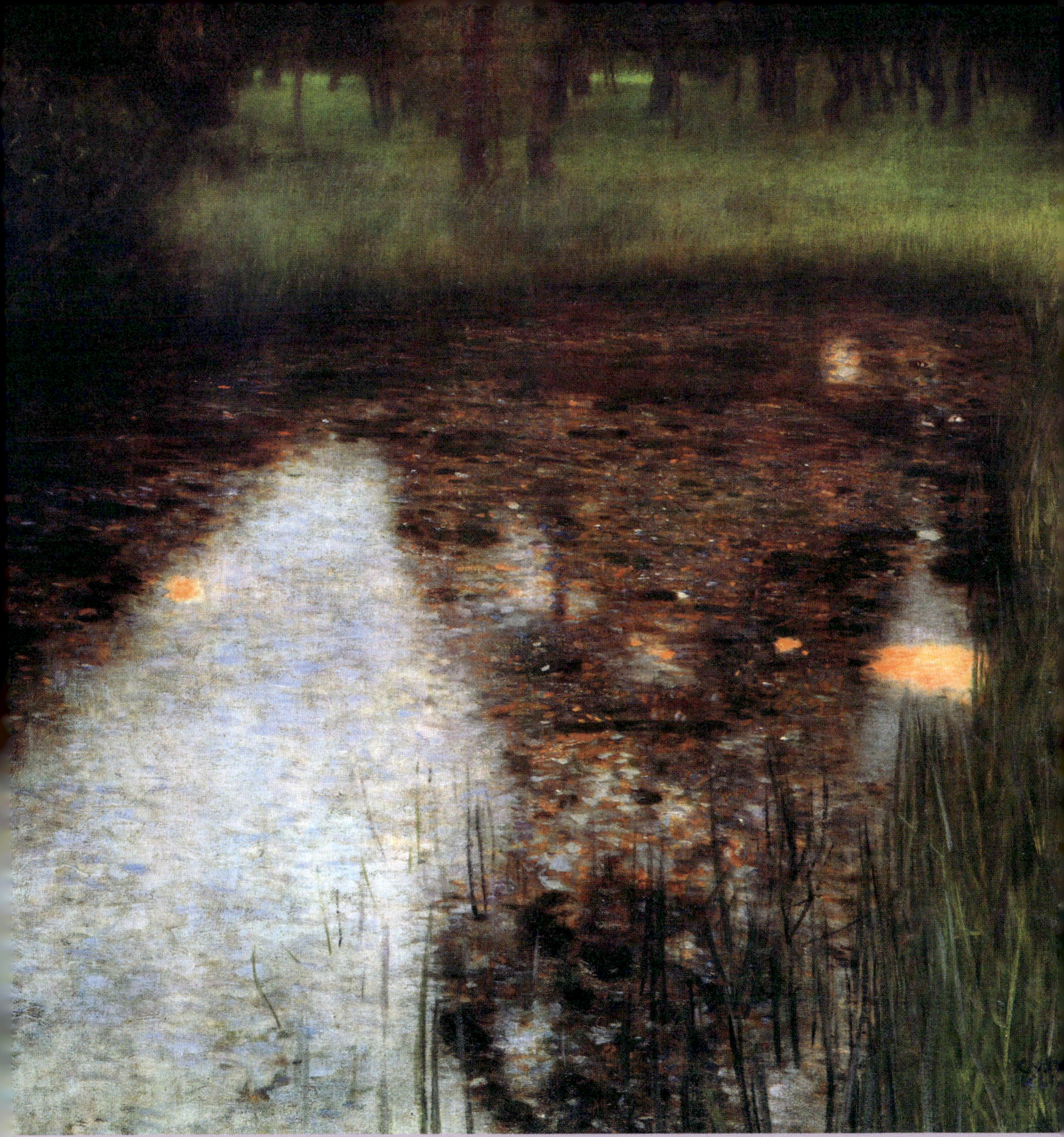

Calm Pond on the Kammer Castle Grounds, Gustav Klimt, 1899, oil on canvas

IV

—

PARALLEL WORLDS

'The people with whom we populate our universes are the shadows of whole other universes intersecting with our own.'

– DOUGLAS ADAMS

Picture a door where there shouldn't be one – not as metaphor or surrealistic composition, but an actual, literal door manifesting like a three-dimensional *trompe l'oeil*, its weathered wood gleaming with impossible morning dew at midnight. A study in contradictions: brass handle catching moonlight that isn't there, hinges creaking softly in a wind from nowhere.

Perchance you've glimpsed it in the corner of your eye, like an entrance to Studio Ghibli's spirit realm, where ancient forest spirits prowl and bathhouse steam carries the whispers of gods. Or perhaps you've sensed it in that transitive moment between sleeping and waking, when the world feels thin enough to tear, when reality might slip into *Silent Hill*'s rust-eaten otherworld of perpetual ash-fall, or into *Stranger Things*' Upside Down, where reality decays beneath blood-red skies and spores float like toxic snow. Possibly you've stumbled upon it in a still, silent grove, like C.S. Lewis's Wood Between the Worlds; or followed the instructions of the urban legend known as the Elevator Game, which takes you to the alternate world of the floor that doesn't exist; or possibly even found it waiting in that twilight space between dimensions that mystics call the astral plane. What lies beyond its threshold? According to folklore, quantum physics and countless artists' visions, the answer might be 'everything'.

'If the doors of perception were cleansed, everything would appear to man as it is, Infinite,' William Blake declared. Artists have long understood this, imagining the existence of other realms alongside our own. And of all these parallel domains, heaven and hell have commanded sustained artistic attention – perhaps because humans have spent so many centuries convinced they could map a route to either one. Sandro Botticelli's precisely rendered illustrations of Dante's cosmology and John Martin's vast apocalyptic canvases suggest vast realms of divine and demonic power whose very enormity threatens to swallow entire civilizations. From intricate historical engravings to Salvador Dalí's atomic interpretations of paradise, artists have repeatedly attempted to map these ultimate alternative realities. Heaven, it seems, must always be accessed by a staircase, because celestial elevators aren't a thing (and apparently nobody wants out-of-shape souls wheezing their way to paradise), while hell invariably lurks below like a 40-year-old stepson who won't move out of your basement.

Victorian artists became particularly entranced by the concept of parallel realms, especially the land of Faerie. John Anster Fitzgerald painted elaborate visions of this otherworld shimmering shiftily into ours, while painters like John Duncan reimagined Celtic legends as windows into a mythic alternative Britain. The Symbolists took this further, creating masterpieces that suggested entire shadow realms existing alongside our own, accessible through dreams and visions, consciousness shrouded in veils of metamorphosis and mystery. For the Surrealists, these adjacent realities weren't just artistic invention but psychological reality. Giorgio de Chirico's eerily empty piazzas evoke glimpses of an alternate Italy that exists in eternal afternoon, while René Magritte's parallel worlds often peek through in the form of impossible windows or mirrors that reflect what cannot be there.

Building on this inherited catalogue of portals, artists across generations have created entirely new ones. Some draw inspiration from quantum physics' many-worlds interpretation, creating works that attempt to visualize multiple timelines existing simultaneously. Others explore digital realms as modern parallel universes, creating spaces with their own gravitational pull and ecosystems of possibility. Through spiralling perspectives

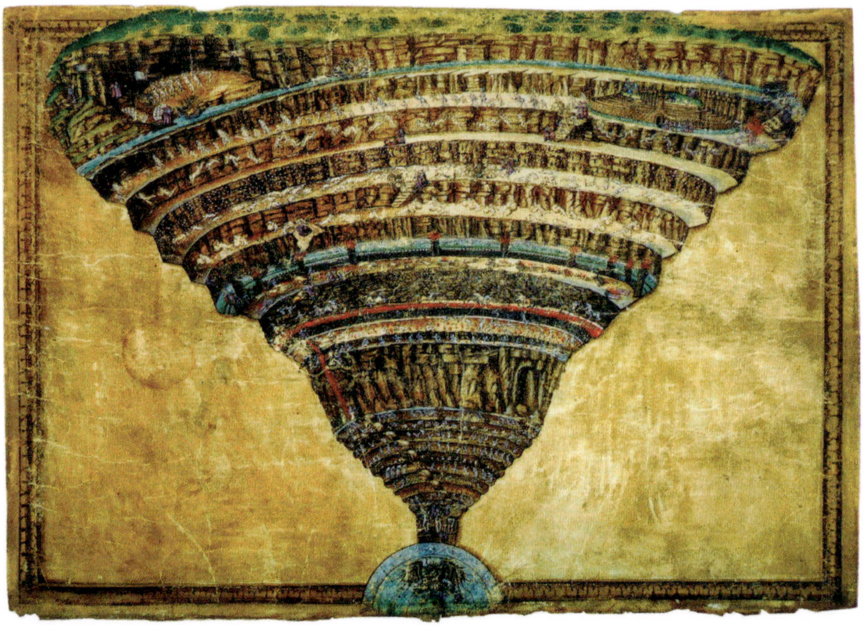

Opposite: Map of Hell, Sandro Botticelli, 1480–90, silverpoint and ink coloured with tempera

Right: Fairy Tale of the Kings, Mikalojus Konstantinas Čiurlionis, 1909, tempera on paper

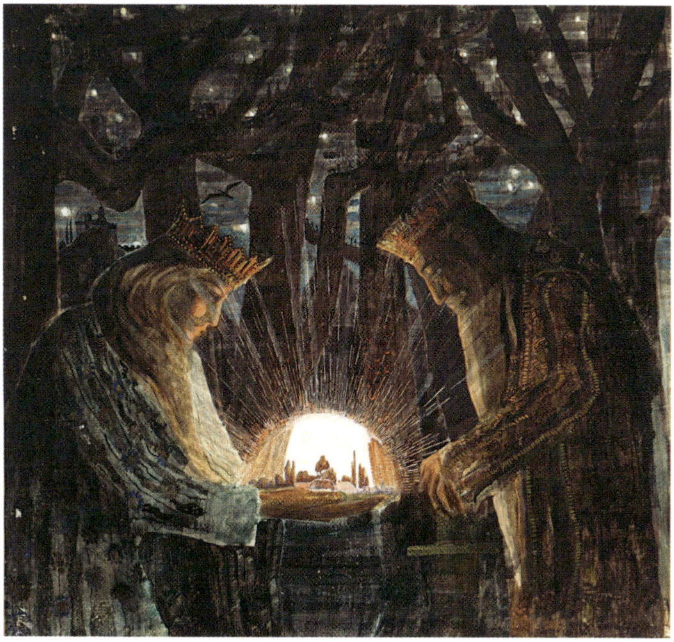

that destabilize equilibrium, through layered techniques and luminous imagery, artists craft dimensional breaches where natural and human worlds blur together in dreamlike alternate histories, capturing moments that seem to exist in some parallel version of memory.

Every generation of artists discover that they need their own doors to elsewhere. Medieval mystics built them from ultramarine depths and gilded surfaces, while Victorian painters hid them in fairy rings and flower gardens. The Surrealists discovered them in dreams, contemporary artists in quantum concepts about reality's multiplicity or constructed immersive virtual worlds. But they're all mapping the same truth: that reality is immeasurably larger than our daily perception of it. Countless worlds crowd the unrealized borders of what we think we know, pressing against the thin membrane of existence as we recognize it. So when you find a painting that stops you in your tracks, sends a shiver up your spine or a buzz to your brain, and pulls deep at your gut, take careful note – you're standing before a door. Every possible version of reality, every choice not taken, every world that could have been, is waiting just on the other side of that impossible door.

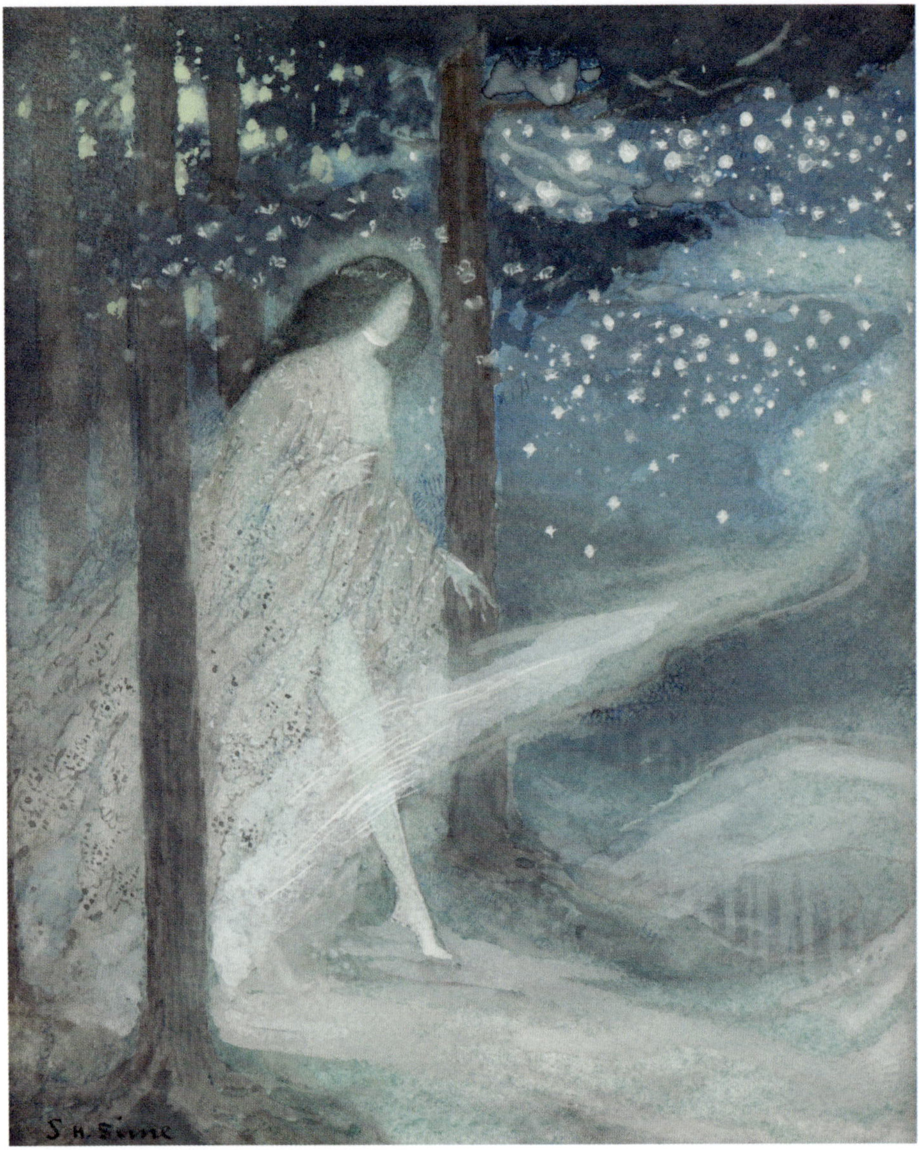

Moth Time, Sidney Sime, date unknown, watercolour

A phantom bride of the forest glides through Sidney Sime's (1865–1941) haunting *Moth Time*, her gossamer gown catching moonlight like the wings of her fluttering entourage. Preceded by a swarm of pearlescent moths that seem to herald her arrival, this spectral woman emerges from darkness as if summoned by their dance. Best known for breathing visual life into Lord Dunsany's fantasy realms, Sime's own transformation from poverty to artistic acclaim parallels his fascination with beings who exist between worlds. This twilight vision reveals that quintessential Sime magic – a parallel world flickering in your peripheral vision, always there but gone the moment you turn to look directly, where moths become messengers, guiding ghosts through the witching hour.

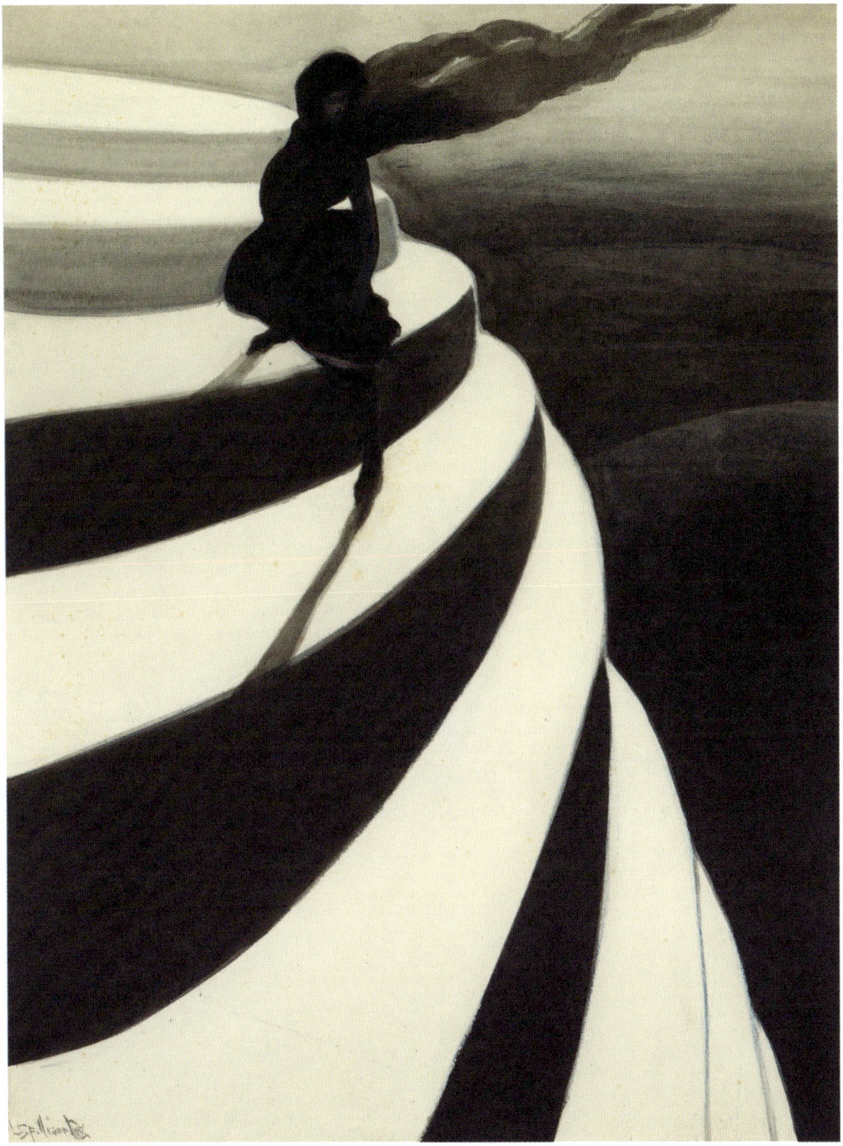

Vertigo, or The Magic Staircase, Léon Spilliaert, 1908, ink and pencil on paper

Plunge headlong into Léon Spilliaert's (1881–1946) spiralling staircase, where your inner ear and intrusive thoughts are in perfect, terrible agreement. The self-taught Belgian artist created this hypnotic ink and pencil drawing during his nocturnal wanderings through Ostend, a seaside town that transforms from bustling resort by day to desolate ghost town by night. A solitary female figure perches precariously on steps that seem to rotate into an abyss, her scarf and hair caught in an otherworldly wind as the sea dissolves into nothingness behind her. The composition tilts and twists, destabilizing all sense of equilibrium, yet the woman's body resists complete surrender, anchoring herself even as cosmic forces threaten to tear her into some adjacent reality. The exaggerated perspective creates a sickening pull, a dark, dizzying rush, your sense of self-preservation absolutely screaming at maximum bloody volume inside your heart.

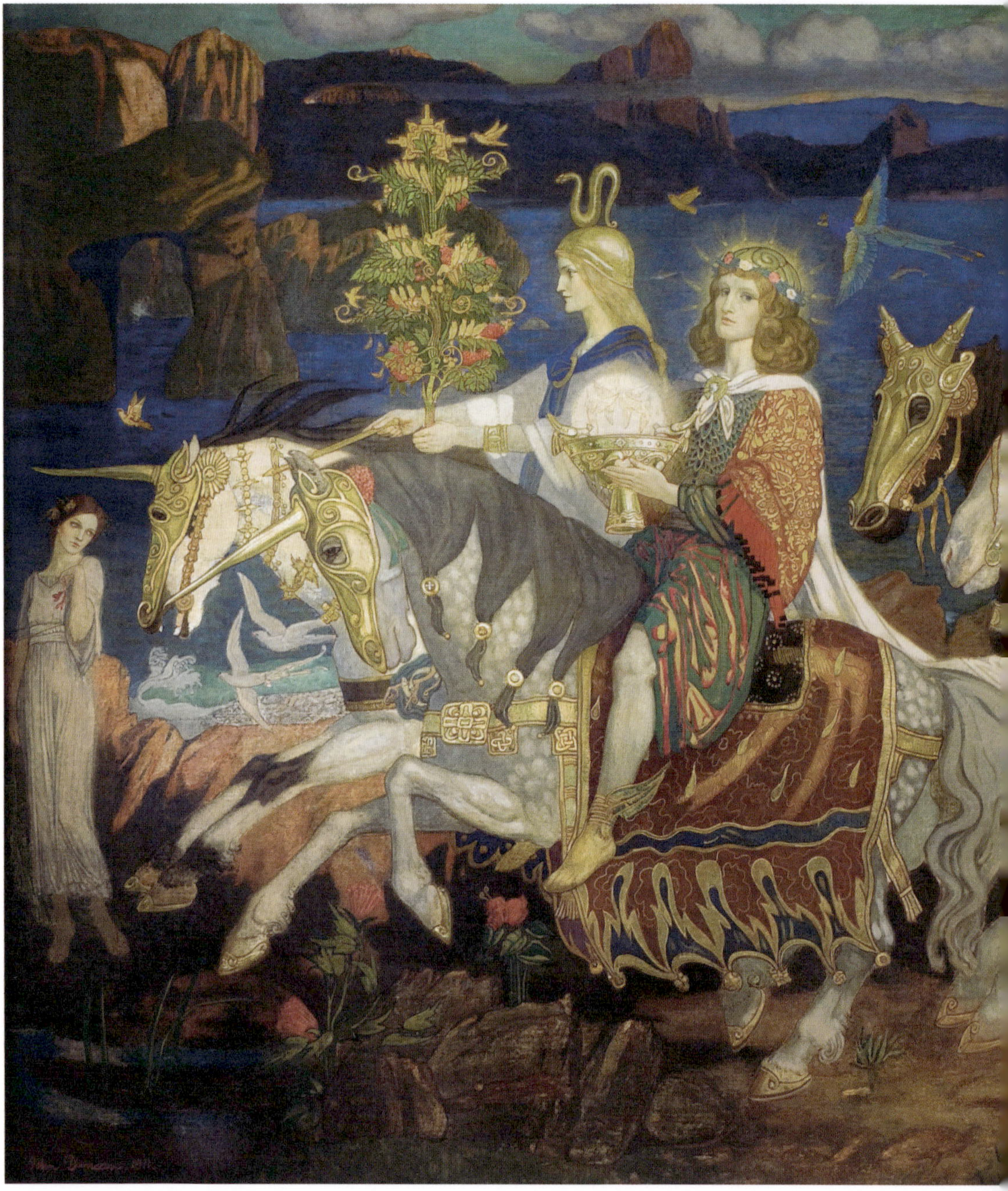

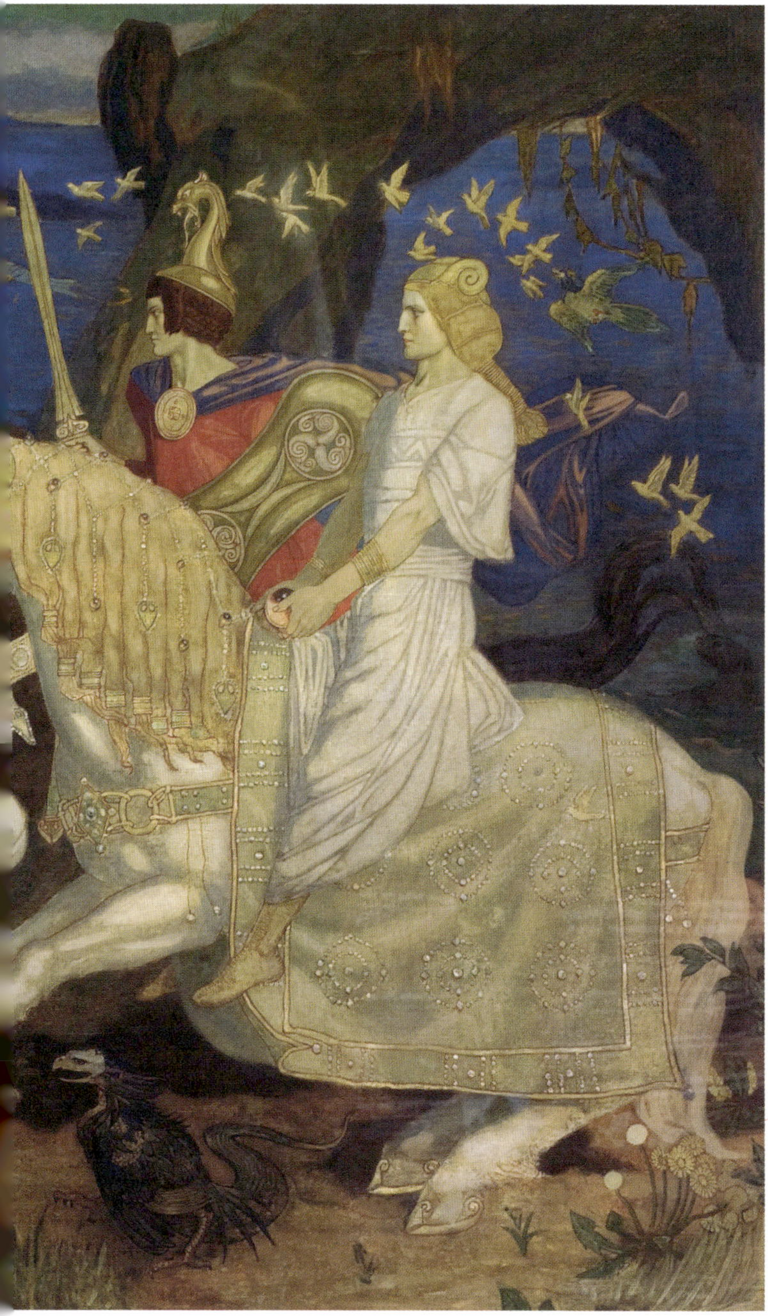

The Riders of the Sidhe, John Duncan, 1911, tempera on canvas

Galloping between dimensions on steeds adorned with ancient Celtic artefacts, John Duncan's (1866–1945) resplendent *Riders of the Sidhe* summons forth the divine fairy folk of Celtic legend. In this masterpiece – painted in egg tempera while the artist's family 'ate meringues for breakfast, lunch and dinner' – Duncan paints the Sidhe during their Beltane ride to initiate humans into their mysteries. Four ethereal figures emerge from twilight mists, their horses' ceremonial masks based on Iron Age relics Duncan studied in museum collections. Duncan's glowing colours and precisely rendered drapery reveal his devotion to Renaissance techniques, yet the subject pulses with Celtic mysticism, and each otherworldly rider bears a sacred object embodying cosmic principles. Like a half-remembered dream of ancestral memory, these figures exist in the gossamer border-realm where myth meets reality, where parallel worlds touch, and where, just for a moment, the veil between dimensions grows thin enough for mortals to glimpse the eternal riders on their endless journey.

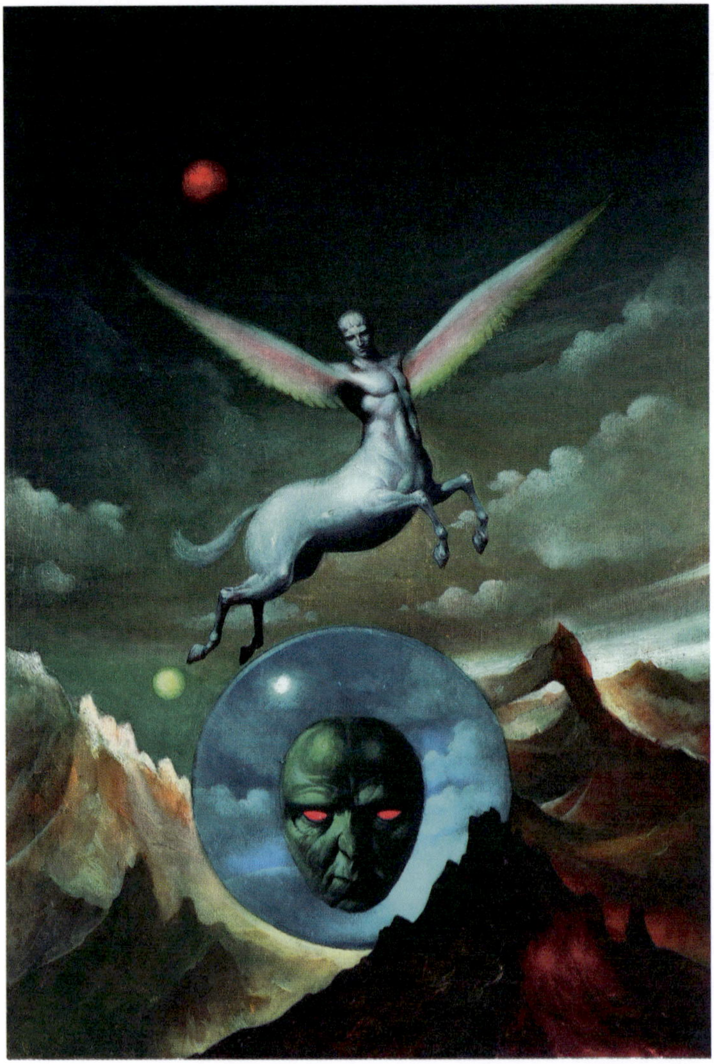

A Wrinkle in Time, Richard Bober, 1976, oil on panel

Pulsing with otherworldly luminescence, Richard Bober's (1945–2022) long-uncredited cover art for *A Wrinkle in Time* remains one of publishing's most memorable examples of gorgeous nightmare fuel. The notoriously reclusive artist conjures his vision of Madeleine L'Engle's cosmos, where supernatural forces shimmer with preternatural light and a red-eyed spectre floats with sinister purpose, while an improbable winged centaur soars through a viridescent alien sky. For generations of young readers, this cover served as their portal to L'Engle's multiverse, its beautiful horror burning into memory long after the book was closed. After decades of anonymity, Bober's identity was finally confirmed in 2023 through a collaborative investigation involving a stubborn blogger (that would be me!), passionate readers, genre enthusiasts, Reddit sleuths, art historians, persistent podcasters, and the artist's family. The rediscovery exemplifies how the most captivating artistic portals between dimensions sometimes conceal their own creators - the very hands that opened those cosmic doorways remaining hidden in plain sight for nearly half a century.

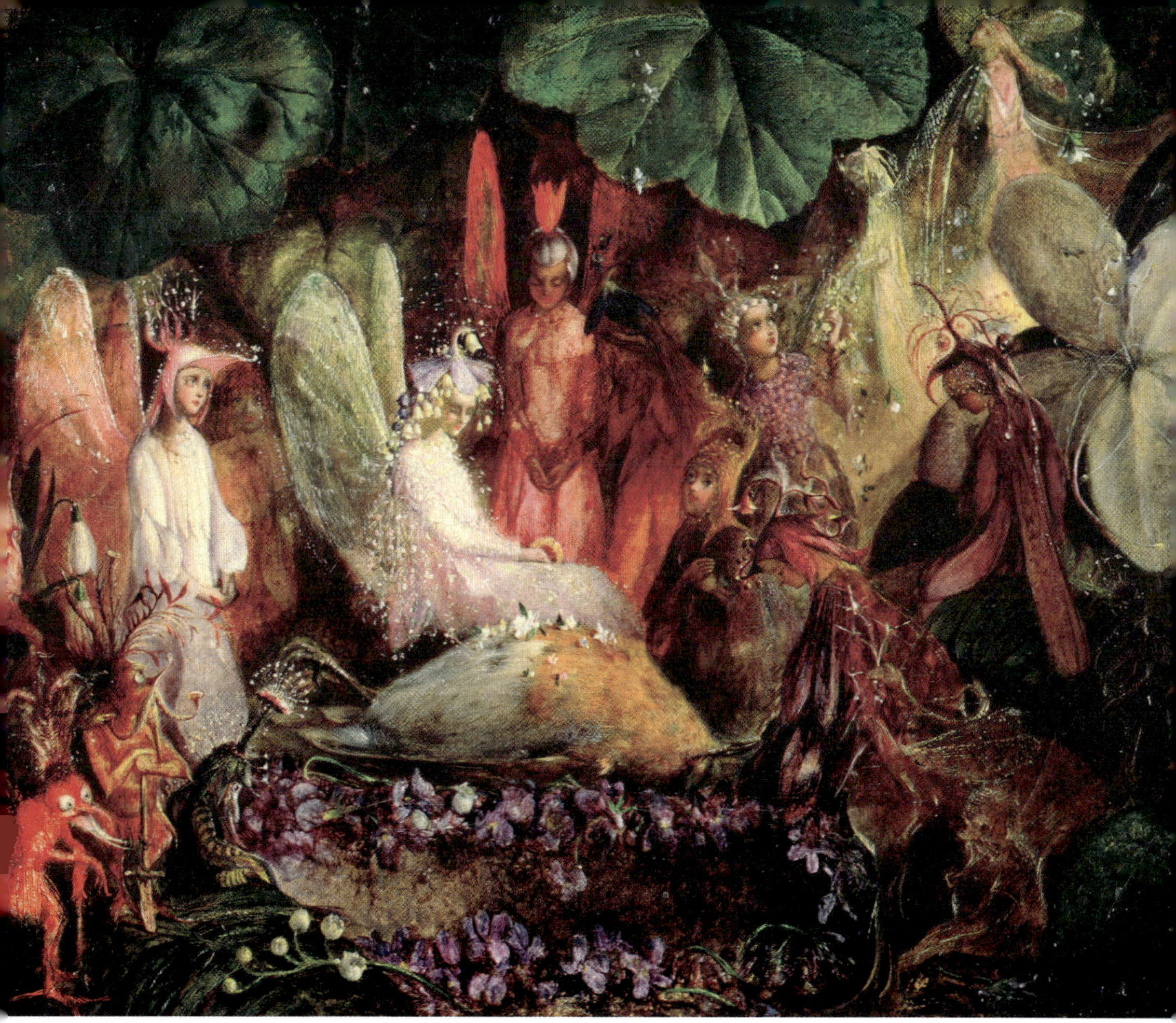

Who Killed Cock Robin?, John Anster Fitzgerald, *c.* 1860, oil on canvas

Murder most floral unfolds beneath apple blossoms in John Anster Fitzgerald's (c. 1819–1906) enchanting yet macabre *Who Killed Cock Robin?* The Victorian artist – nicknamed 'Fairy Fitzgerald' for his obsession with the fae realm – transforms the nursery rhyme into a supernatural crime scene in which tiny winged detectives examine their fallen feathered friend. Painted in lustrous colours with jewel-like precision, this miniature drama draws us into a parallel dimension where midnight mushroom circles and laudanum-laced dreams collide. The dead robin lies surrounded by fairy investigators with dragonfly wings and flower-petal clothing, some examining evidence, others consoling grieving companions. His fantastical vision offers a window into the Victorian fascination with parallel worlds, creating an alternative to the grim realities of industrialization and rigid social codes. Here in this blossom-strewn crime scene, we glimpse a magical realm – part ethereal wonderland, part eerie otherworld – where even murder inquests sparkle with mischievous enchantment.

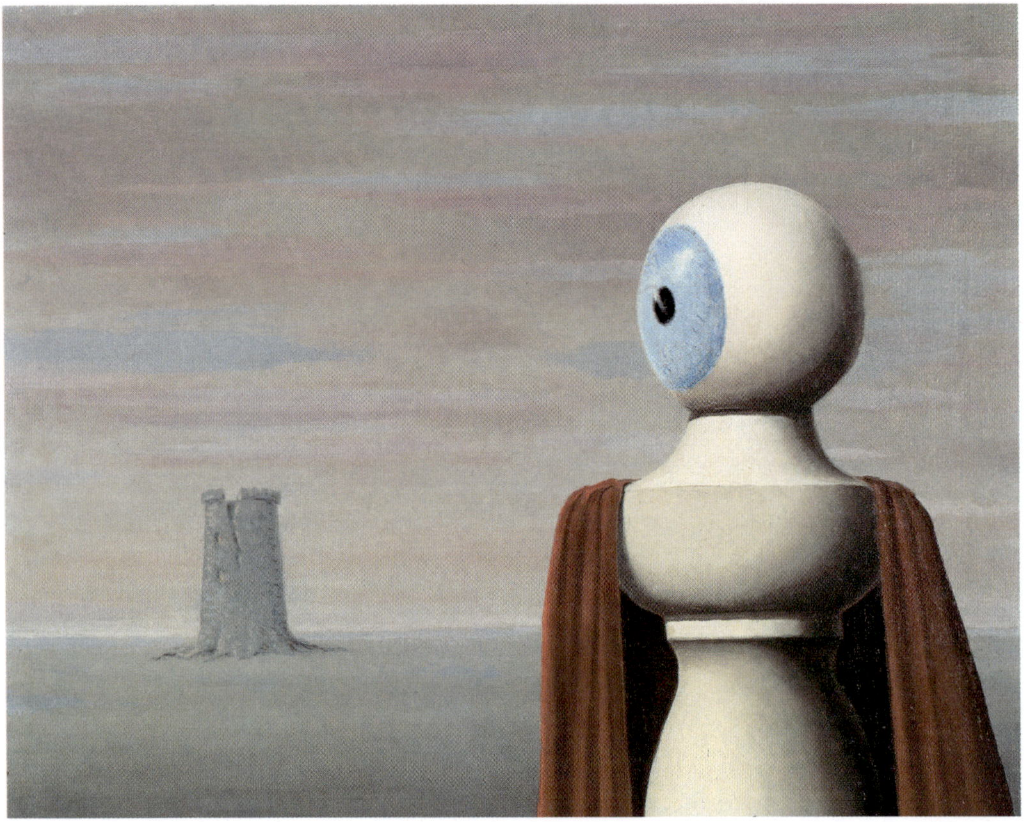

Above: La Belle Lurette, René Magritte, 1960, oil on canvas

In this enigmatic tableau from René Magritte (1898–1967), a wooden toy stands sentry in a barren landscape, elevated from nursery relic to interdimensional optician. A bilboquet (cup-and-ball toy) wears a theatrical cloak like some miniature wanderer between worlds, while its wooden 'head' has been replaced with an enormous disembodied eye that conducts business across realities and has clearly seen some stuff. The French expression *il y a belle lurette* means 'a long time ago', suggesting that this figure inhabits a realm where time flows differently. In the distance, appears one of Magritte's signature motifs: a crumbling tower with organic roots growing from its base, anchoring it to the earth while suggesting the possibility of metamorphosis. Magritte had a talent for making us look at everyday objects as if we'd never seen them before, writing: 'Everything we see hides another thing; we always want to see what is hidden by what we see.'

Right: The Egg and the Universe, Jan Konůpek, 1929, watercolour and gouache

As a founding member of the Prague Symbolist group Sursum, Czech architect Jan Konůpek (1883–1950) rejected realistic representation in favour of what he called 'cosmic architecture'. *The Egg and the Univérse* exemplifies his structural fantasies rendered in delicate washes of blue and violet. His background in structural engineering shows in the precise geometric relationships, yet these forms follow dream logic rather than physics. The composition centres on an enormous egg form surrounded by crystalline geometric structures that could be buildings, mountains or cosmic formations – Konůpek deliberately keeps us guessing. Through these spatial experiments, Konůpek painted alternative worlds where architecture wasn't bound by gravity, budgets or building codes, only by the limits of imagination rendered in ethereal pigment.

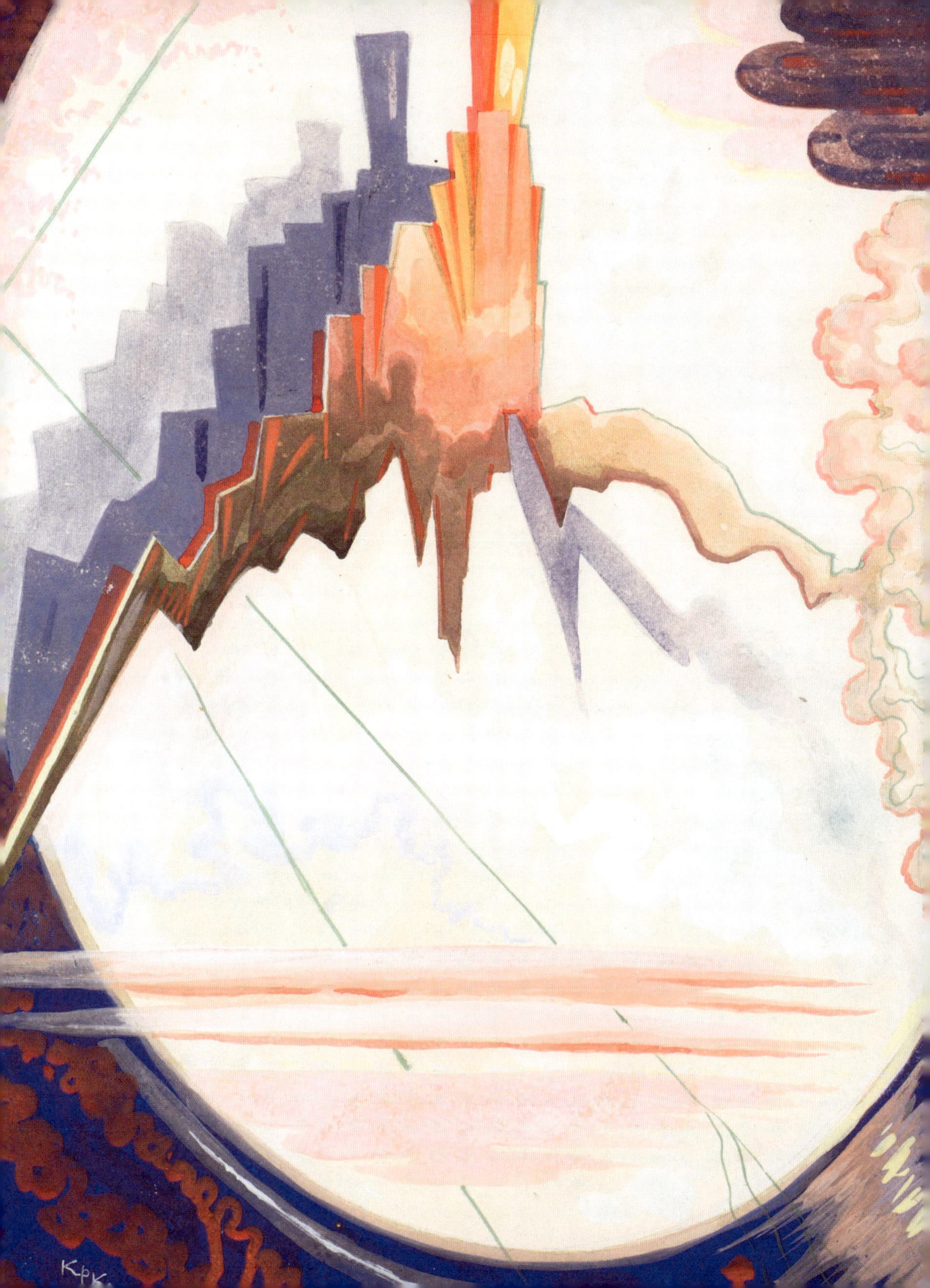

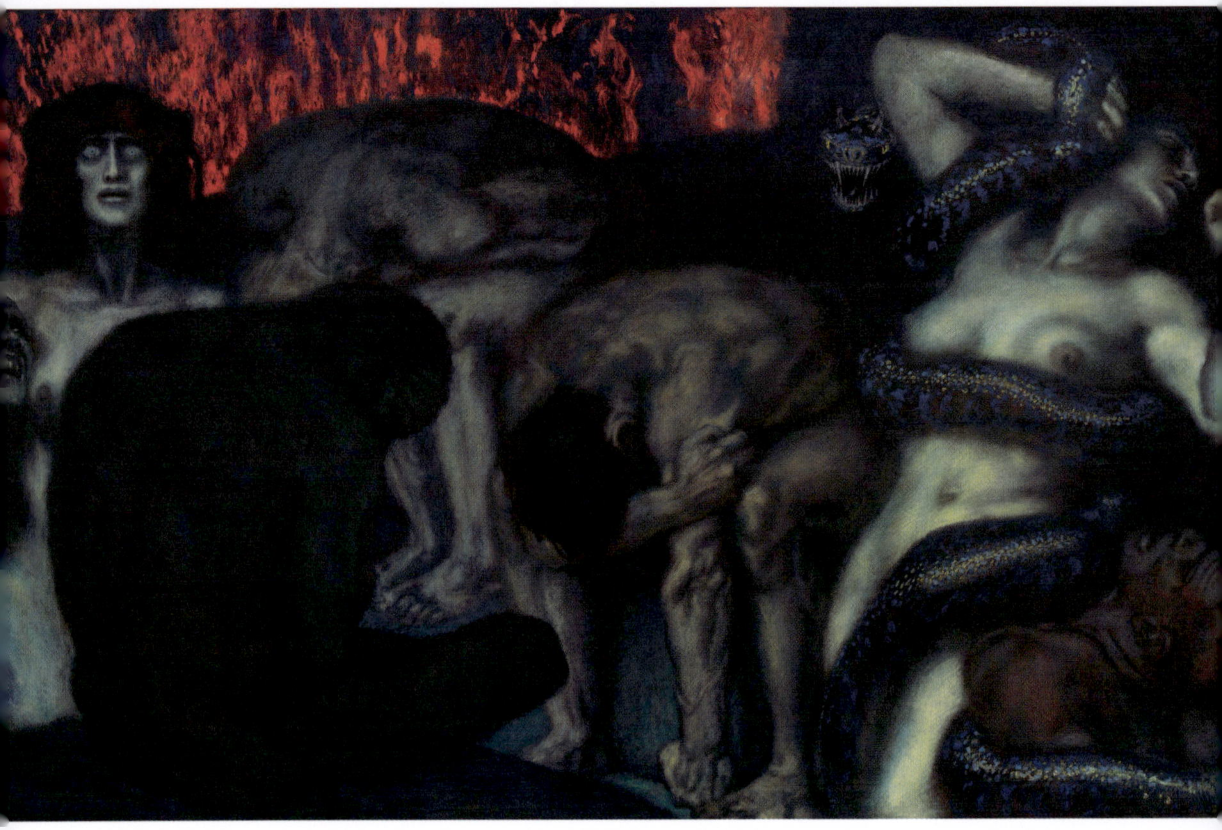

Inferno, Franz von Stuck, 1908, oil on canvas

German Symbolist Franz von Stuck (1863–1928) gives us a fevered glimpse into the underworld in this vision that both references Dante's medieval journey and reimagines hell for the early twentieth century. A mass of nude figures writhe in agonized communion, their bodies casting eerie shadows against sulphurous yellow light. The hell gate burns with hypnotic intensity, drawing viewers towards some deeper chamber mercifully hidden from view. When this painting debuted at The Met in 1909, critics praised its 'sovereign brutality' – an apt description for Stuck's ability to transform traditional underworld symbols into psychological space through dissonant colours and exaggerated poses. Here, hell exists not as a distant afterlife but as an adjacent reality separated from our own by nothing more than the fragile veneer of civilization – an ever-present neighbouring dimension that Stuck, unafraid to explore the darkest corners of the psyche, reveals with unflinching clarity.

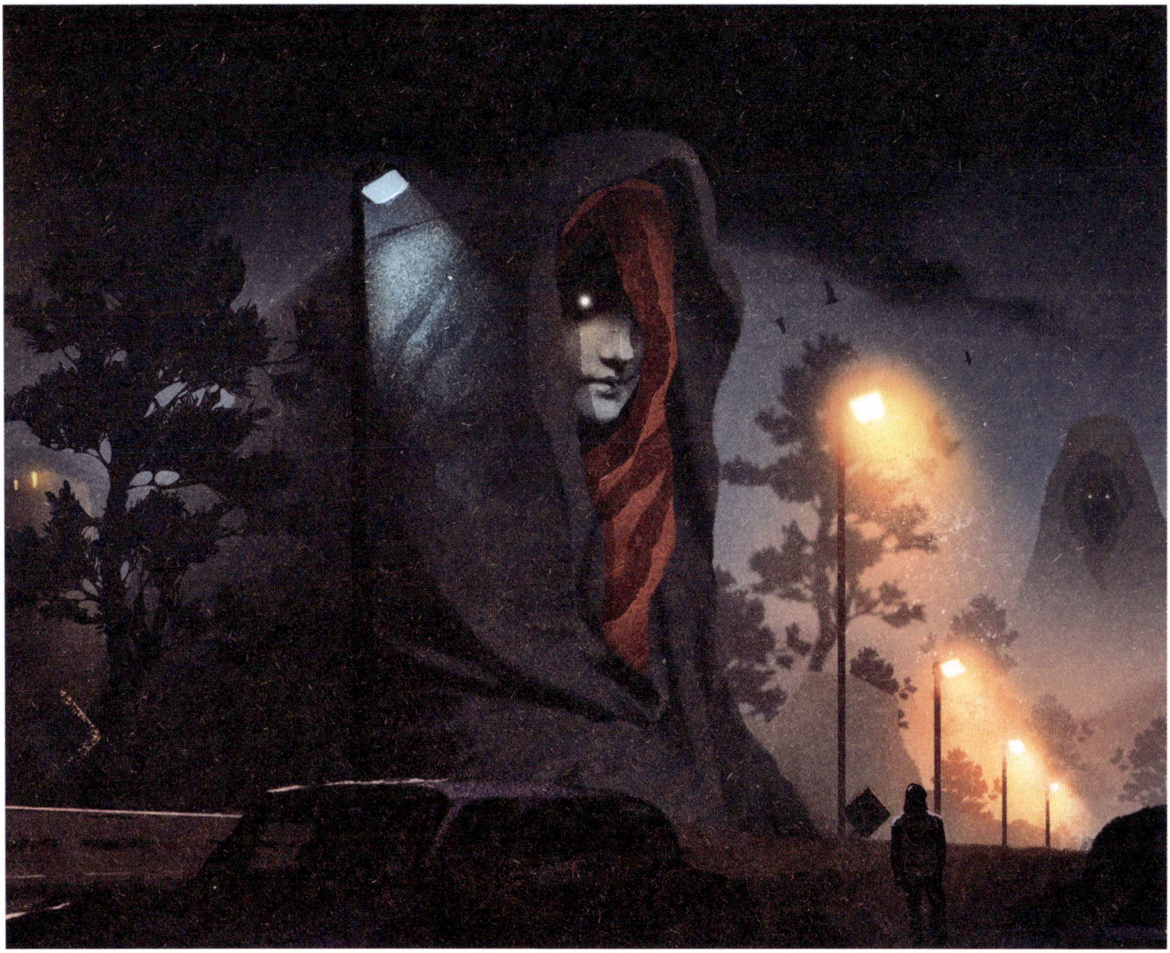

Foglights, Alex Eckman-Lawn, 2021, cut paper collage

Two massive cloaked figures materialize on an ordinary street in Alex Eckman-Lawn's *Foglights*, a recognizable night-time scene becoming the threshold where our local consensus hallucination briefly accommodates visitors from another reality. The artist achieves this dimensional overlap by hand-cutting multiple layers of paper to create collages with actual physical depth that mirror the overlapping worlds they depict. What emerges is both familiar and impossible – the towering visitors occupy both dimensions simultaneously, substantial yet incorporeal, while the human figure walks onwards, unaware that their familiar neighbourhood temporarily hosts beings that exist outside our agreed-upon version of reality. The street lamps create islands of visibility in darkness, illuminating just one small patch of what we mistake for the complete world. Here we glimpse this momentary breach – not a haunting or visitation, but a temporary alignment of multiple coexisting dimensions.

V

LIMINAL SPACES

'It isn't really anywhere! It's somewhere else instead!'

– A.A. MILNE

Three AM in an empty airport terminal, fluorescent lights humming against midnight-mirrored windows. A school corridor during summer break, chalk dust dancing in slanted sunbeams, paper scraps skittering across freshly waxed floors. The empty parking lot of an abandoned shopping centre at dusk, wind whistling through broken light poles whose bulbs burned out years ago. Every haunting frame of A24's dreamy, disquieting film *I Saw the TV Glow*, where suburban back gardens and teenage bedrooms feel like they belong to someone else's life, someone you never met, maybe who never even existed in the first place. These pockets of limbo feel wrong somehow, as if we're witnessing them in a state in which they were never meant to be seen, catching the world in an unguarded moment.

Ancient cultures took these weird places seriously; these strange way stations existing outside the routine traffic of the daily world. At crossroads where possibilities intersect, in twilight moments when reality thins, at thresholds where transformation occurs, boundaries, perception, and time get all wibbly wobbly and come unmoored. Shrines marked crossroads like spiritual warning signs. The Greeks and Romans saw these spaces as dangerous, haunted by beings who existed neither here nor there. Hecate ruled the crossroads, while Mercury himself served as psychopomp, guiding souls across the ultimate threshold between life and death.

'The threshold is the limit, the boundary, the frontier that distinguishes and opposes two worlds,' wrote Arnold van Gennep in his study of liminal spaces. Van Gennep probably never imagined that his scholarly description would one day be applied to everything from empty laundromats to after-hours car parks, but here we are – 'liminal' has become the internet's favourite word for atmospheric weirdness and a catch-all for any space that gives you the creeps. For real, though, nothing makes you appreciate a good, solid boundary quite like its absence. Artists have long been drawn to these uncomfortable spaces where nothing feels quite right, where your inner compass goes a bit wonky. Edward Hopper's works capture that all-American in-between: the diner at night, familiar yet estranged, simultaneously inviting and unsettling. Has anyone actually eaten in a Hopper diner? Or do they just stare moodily into coffee cups that never empty, waiting for a waitress who stepped out for a cigarette break sometime in 1926?

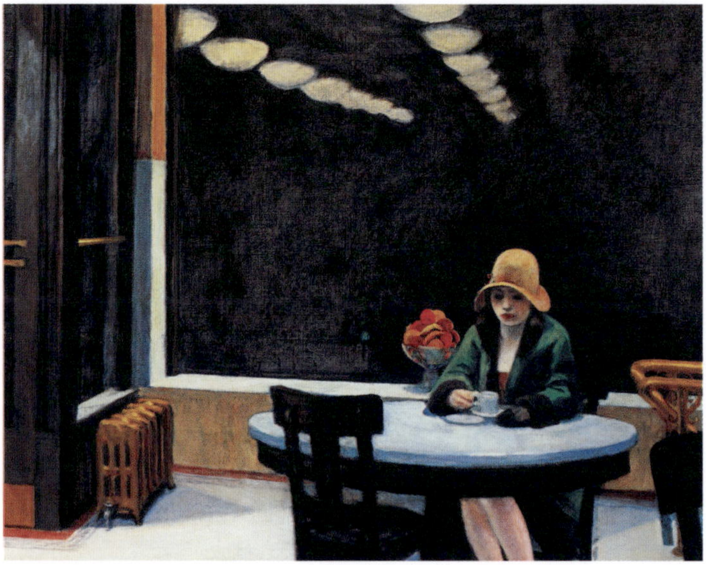

Victorian artists were particularly drawn to twilight – that daily reminder of fleeting liminal transformation across the horizon. John Atkinson Grimshaw made an entire career of painting urban dusks, his wet cobblestone streets reflecting gaslight in that contractually obligated handoff between day and dark. James Abbott McNeill Whistler captured similar moments – Chelsea's snow-covered streets turned dreamlike, familiar neighbourhoods suddenly foreign as moonscapes. The Romantics took this fascination even further. Caspar David Friedrich's abbey ruins and Viktor Vasnetsov's mythic crossroads suggest passages not just between times of day, but into other times, other places and other selves, where spatial, temporal and existential thresholds tangle and scatter.

In the twentieth century, photographers began documenting these liminal spaces with an almost obsessive focus. Louis Daguerre, at photography's very genesis, used his studio objects to capture that pivotal moment when reality transforms into permanent image. Later photographers like Todd Hido found echoes of this liminality in suburban neighbourhoods, where isolated homes glow with secrets behind fog-shrouded windows. Candida Höfer's empty theatres and institutions hold their breath, waiting for audiences that never come.

Contemporary artists have pushed this exploration into ever weirder territories, discovering liminal spaces in our everyday environments. Everyday objects caught mid-transformation, social spaces revealing hidden hierarchies and invisible barriers. Those abandoned shopping centres and office buildings that populate social media have become our modern ruins – spaces caught between purpose and abandonment, where one imagines muzak still plays faintly through disconnected speakers.

Opposite: Automat, Edward Hopper, 1927, oil on canvas

Below: A Moonlit Road, John Atkinson Grimshaw, 1881, oil on board

A playground at midnight, swings moving like they're being pushed by invisible children. That weird space behind every building that seems to exist solely to collect mysterious puddles and inexplicable chairs. These glimpses of in-between places catch our world with its trousers down, exposing the duct tape and safety pins holding everything together. Threshold moments make us realize how much of reality we just kind of shrug over and agree upon – pretending it all makes sense. Every empty corridor, every twilight pause, every space caught between purposes whispers the same secret: the world we've built sits atop something older and stranger that warps the places we've abandoned to the night.

Liminal spaces make us question what exactly we agreed to in the first place. Does this place actually exist? Are we really here?

Is any of this happening at all?

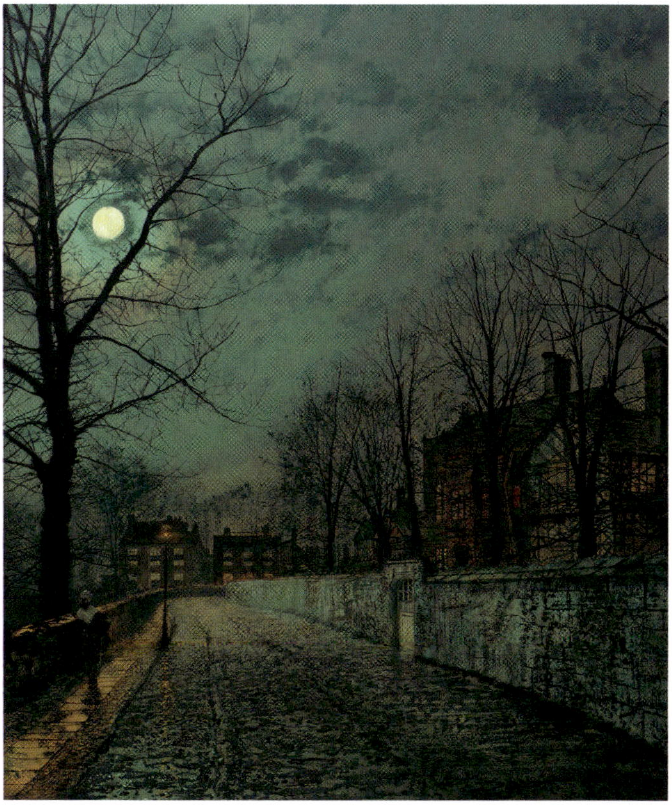

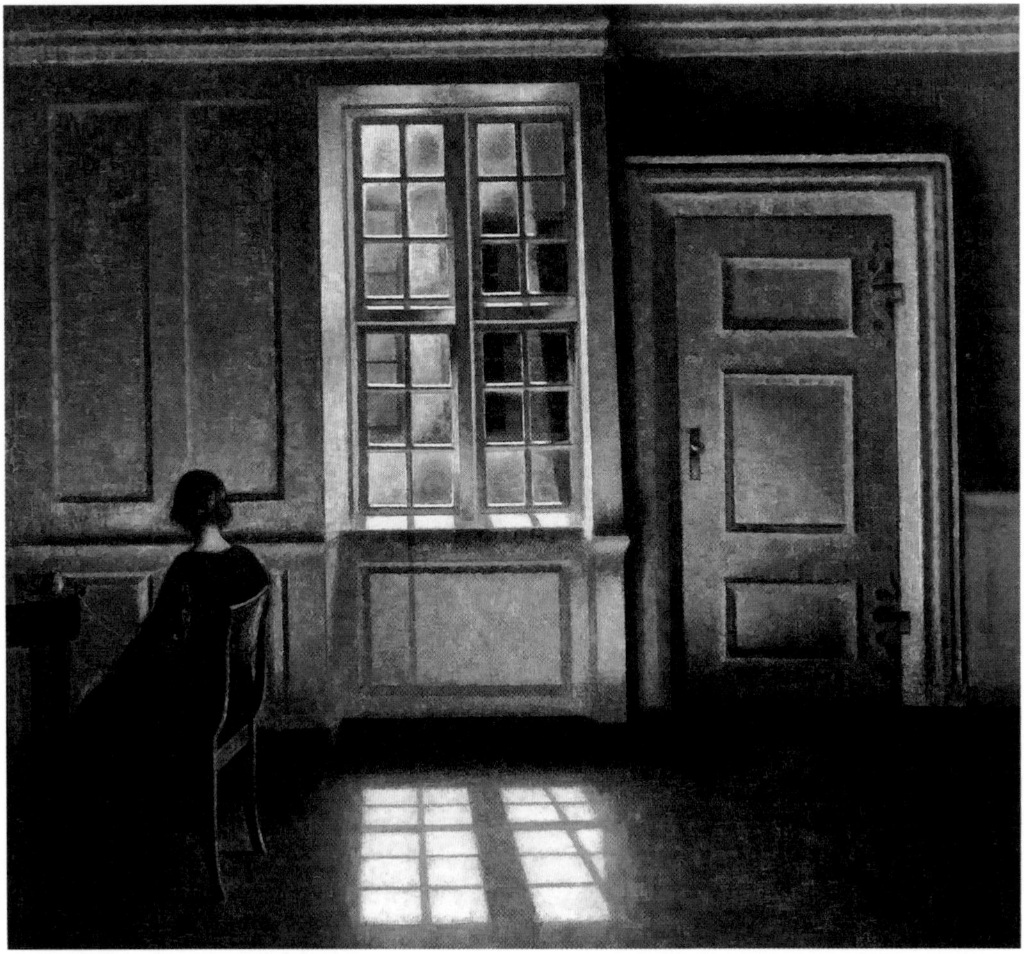

Interior, Strandgade 30, Vilhelm Hammershøi, 1909, oil on canvas

'Be patient toward all that is unsolved in your heart and try to love the questions themselves, like locked rooms and like books now written in a very foreign tongue,' wrote Rainer Maria Rilke, who greatly admired Danish painter Vilhelm Hammershøi (1864–1916). No artwork better embodies this sentiment than Hammershøi's hushed interior, where a solitary woman sits with her back to us in a space suspended between moments. Pale northern light filters through the high window, casting geometric shadows across bare floorboards, while the panelled door stands as a threshold to places unseen. Hammershøi strips away Victorian clutter, creating rooms of monastic simplicity in which muted greys and whites transform ordinary corners of his Copenhagen apartment into spaces of philosophical enquiry. The figure – his wife Ida, who appears in dozens of his paintings – becomes less a person than a presence occupying that liminal state between longing and fulfilment, between known and unknown.

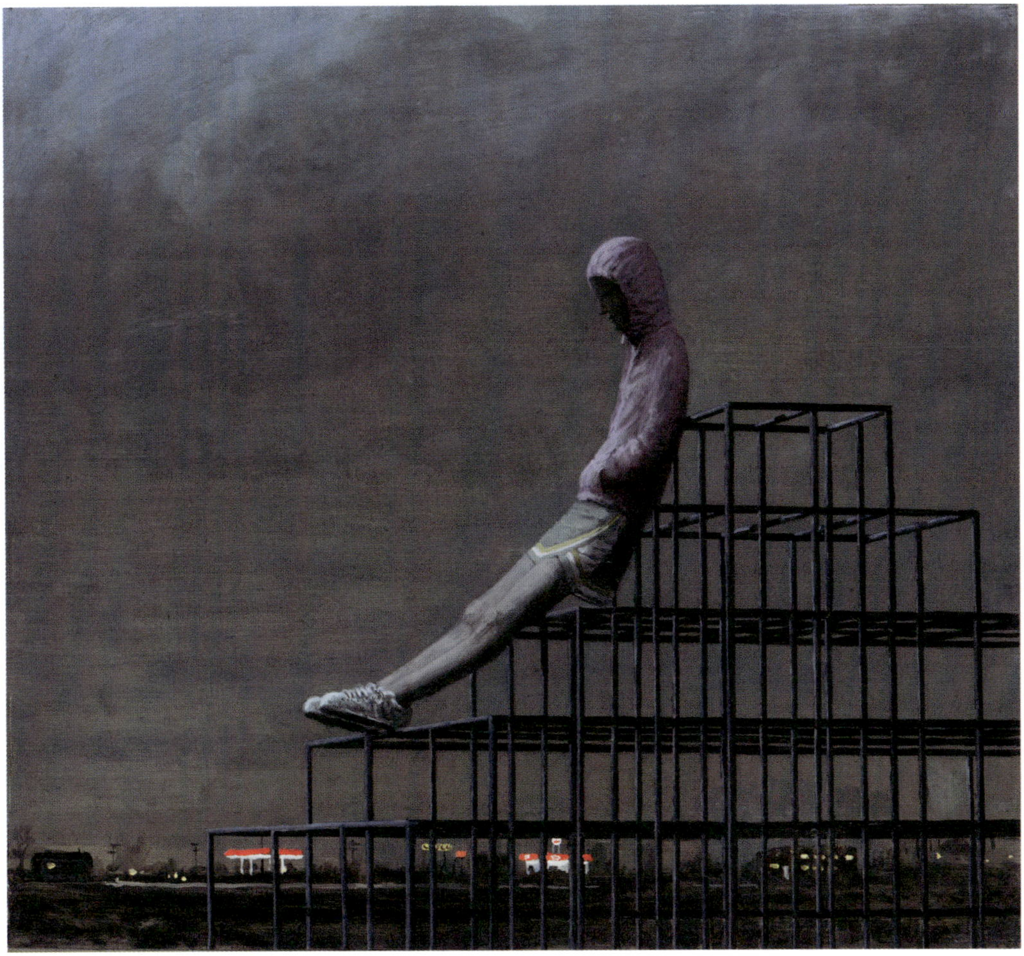

Playground, Aron Wiesenfeld, 2019, oil on panel

Twilight steals this playground's daytime purpose in Aron Wiesenfeld's haunting painting. The solitary figure in a pink hoodie stretches across a metal climbing frame, their body a curved crescent etched against the dusky sky – an upended bridge suspended between childhood and adulthood. Only the upper portion of the playground structure is visible, creating a disorienting perspective where familiar recreational equipment becomes something altar-like and strange. Distant buildings flicker with cold, artificial light across an ambiguous stretch of darkness, close enough to taunt but too far to reach. The playground exists in limbo, no longer serving its intended purpose but not yet fully abandoned to night. The hooded figure's face remains hidden, yet somehow we recognize this moment of solitary contemplation, when the world grows still enough for transformation. Wiesenfeld excels at creating these in-between spaces where ordinary suburban scenes slip into disquieting psychological territory.

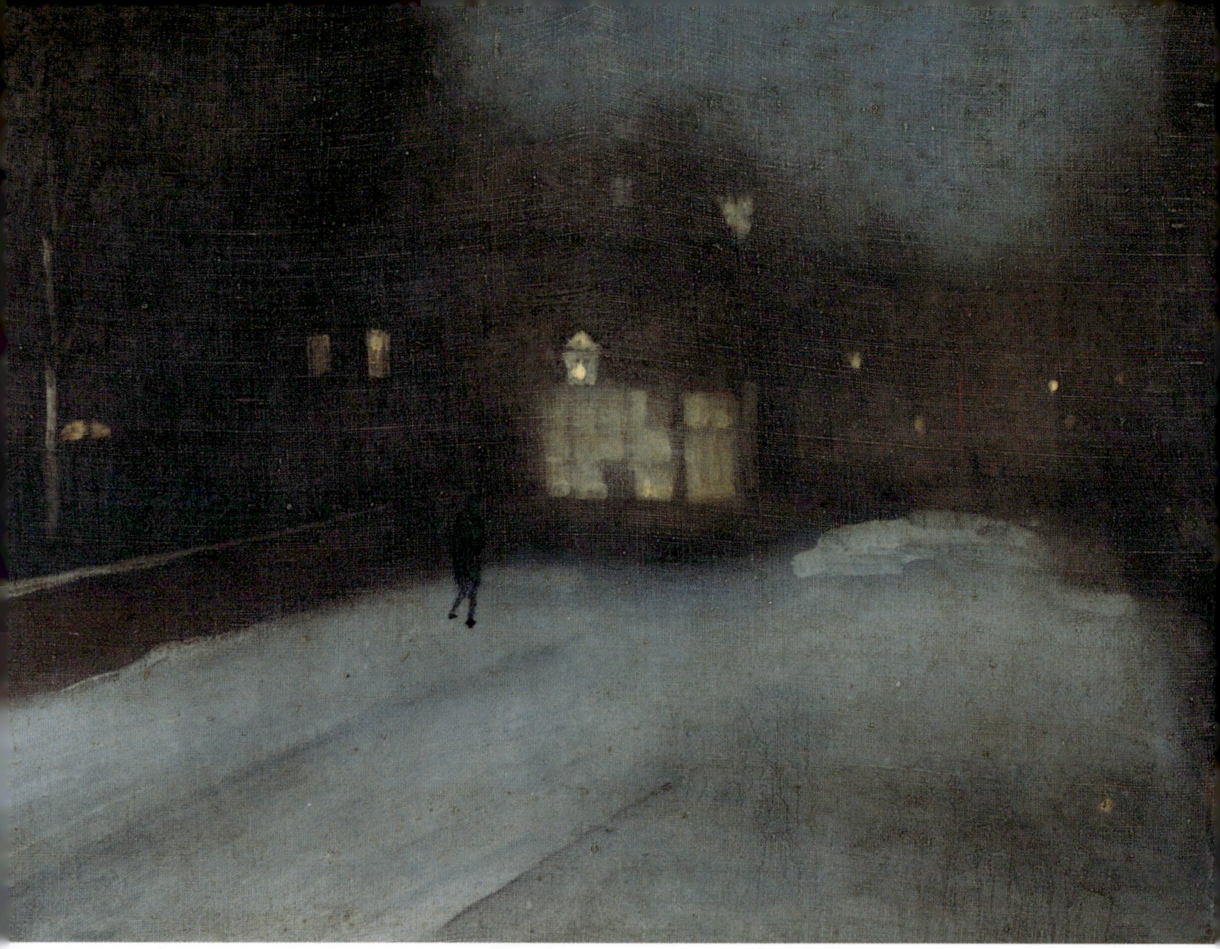

Nocturne in Grey and Gold: Chelsea Snow, James Abbott McNeill Whistler, 1876, oil on canvas

James Abbott McNeill Whistler (1834–1903) perfectly nails that peculiar sensation of walking down a street you've travelled countless times, only to find yourself suddenly, inexplicably lost. Snow has turned the familiar neighbourhood of Chelsea into an alien landscape, a liminal realm where nothing looks right anymore. The solitary figure stands nowhere and everywhere at once, surrounded by buildings that have become ghostly silhouettes.

Whistler's revolutionary technique – thin veils of paint applied in sweeping gestures – creates a world that seems to be actively dematerializing before our eyes. The few yellow windows offer faint beacons that fail to properly illuminate, their warmth unable to penetrate the enveloping snow-muffled silence. This scene exists in that threshold space between recognition and bewilderment, between 'I know exactly where I am' and 'I have never seen this place before' – a strange midnight moment when everything familiar suddenly feels foreign, and home itself becomes uncanny territory.

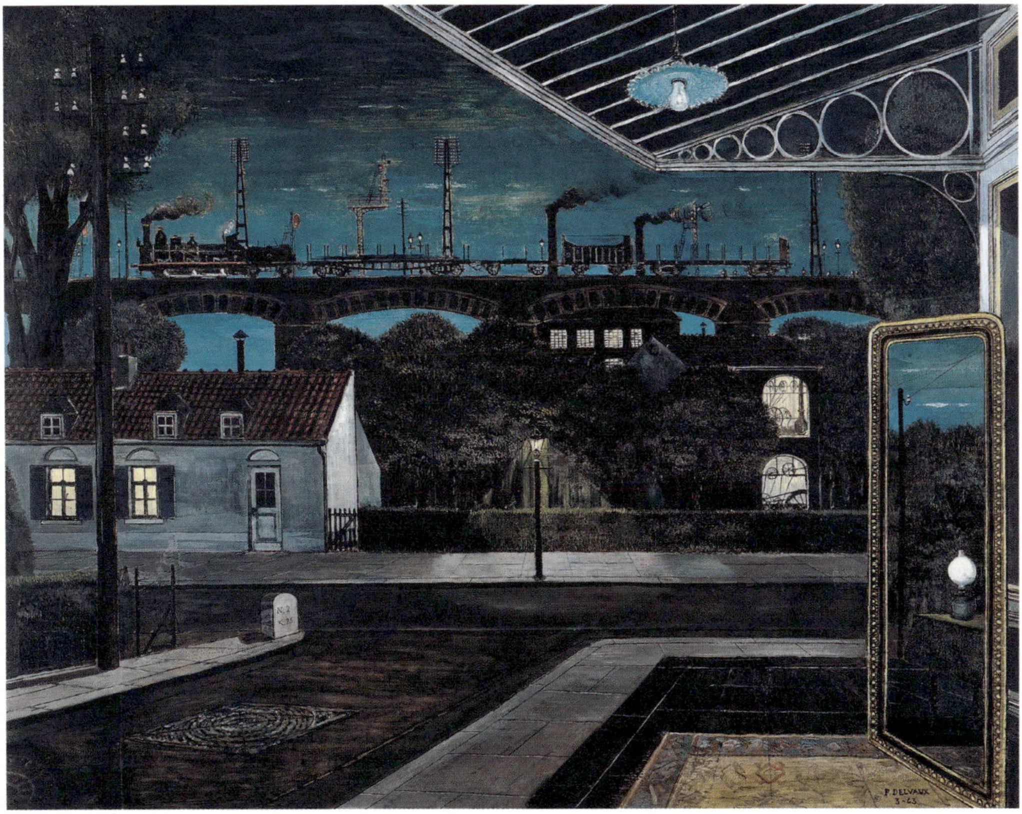

The Viaduct, Paul Delvaux ,1963, oil on canvas

Step to the edge of town, where Paul Delvaux's (1897–1994) viaduct looms like a bird of doom. The Belgian Surrealist builds a liminal zone where you'd be wise not to linger, a place steeped in quiet fatalism. This is where debts come due, where the ferryman waits, where humming wires and border fires mark the threshold where the reckoning happens. Every precisely rendered detail only deepens the dread – that floating mirror? It shows a lamp-lit table from nowhere. Those lit windows? Nobody's home. The phantom locomotive casts no reflection as it glides through a moment frozen between day and night. Delvaux's train station obsession becomes a visual ballad here, warning of boundaries that, once crossed, allow no return journey. The carefully structured unreality pulls you forwards like a gathering storm, even as your every instinct screams to run – a crossing we've all stood at before.

The Abbey in the Oakwood, Caspar David Friedrich, 1809–10, oil on canvas

Skeletal oak trees pierce a twilight sky above a snow-shrouded Gothic ruin in Caspar David Friedrich's (1774-1840) most unsettling vision. The abbey's facade has collapsed to a mere portal - a threshold leading nowhere yet beckoning entry. Through this graveyard of crooked tombstones and half-buried markers moves a procession of monks carrying a coffin, though such figures couldn't possibly inhabit this long-abandoned place. The scene exists in temporal suspension, neither past nor present, a place unstuck from time. The snow absorbs all sound, the fog dissolves all boundaries, and the faint crescent moon offers cold comfort to those crossing from life into whatever lies beyond. When Goethe first encountered this painting, he immediately recognized its power, describing it as embodying 'coldness, impetuousness, dying and despair'. Friedrich based the structure on Eldena Abbey, near his childhood home of Greifswald, turning it into a gateway between worlds - death as a doorway, rather than an ending.

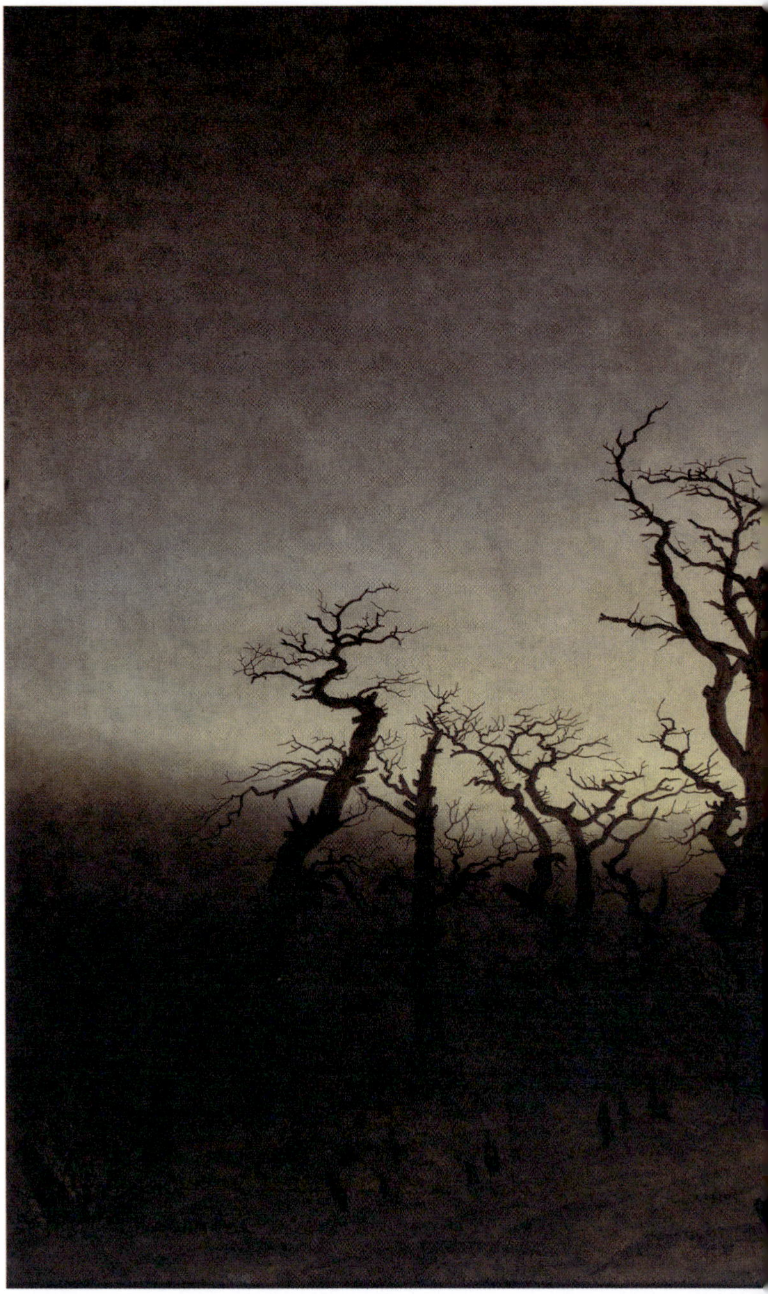

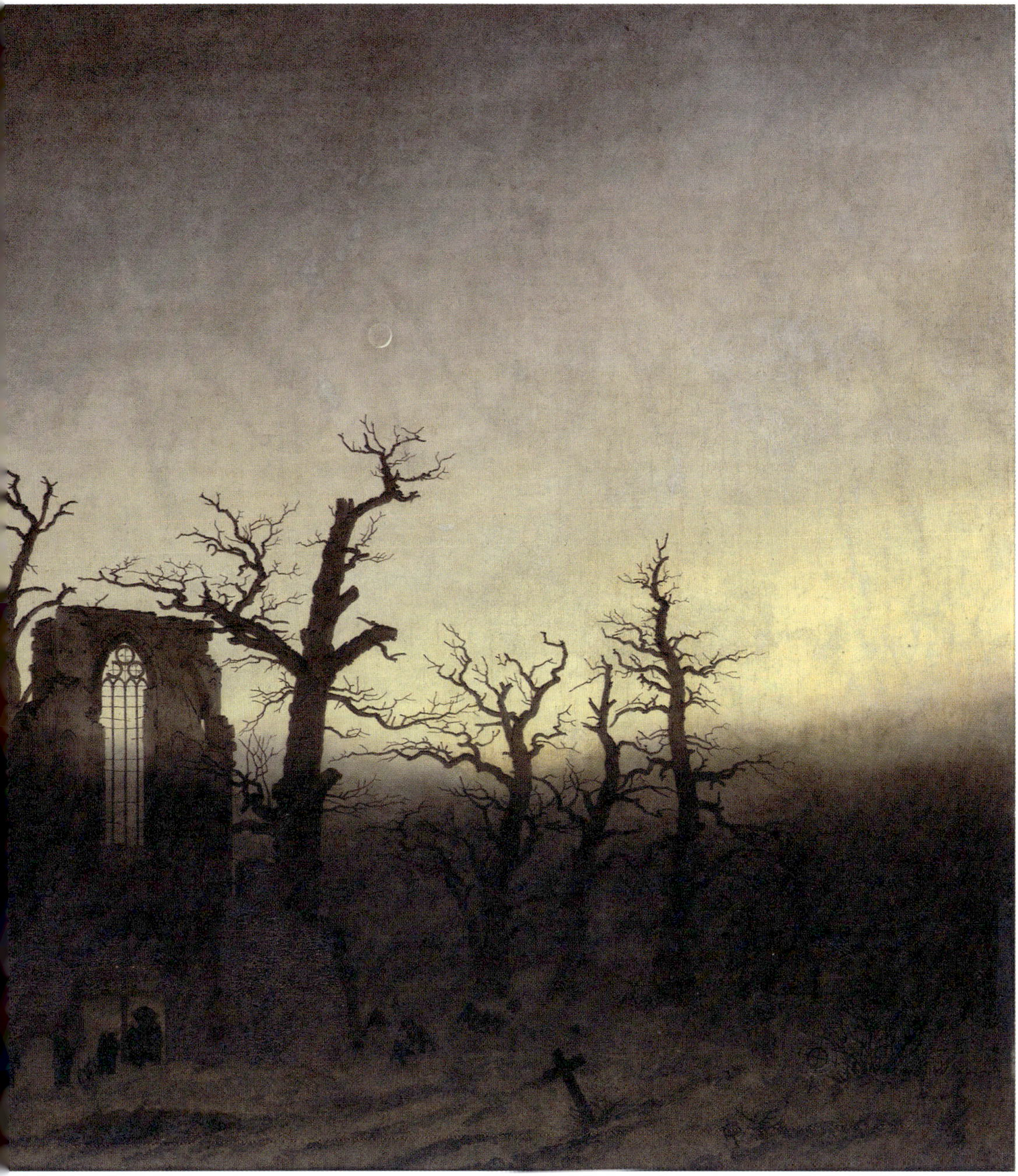

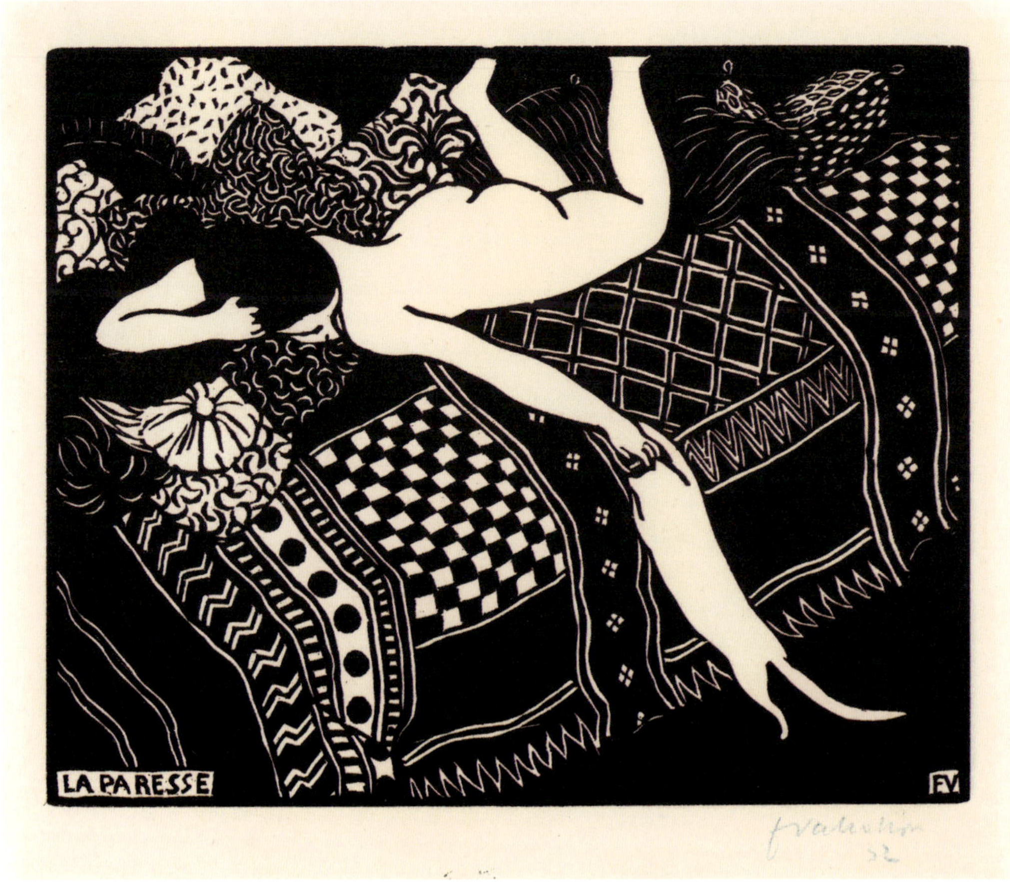

Laziness, Félix Vallotton, 1896, woodcut print on ivory wove paper

Look at this glorious ode to doing absolutely nothing! In this masterful woodcut, Swiss-French artist Félix Vallotton (1865–1925) celebrates that delicious suspended state between being awake and asleep, productive and utterly useless. A nude woman stretches across a patterned divan, reaching lazily to pet a cat that rises to meet her touch. Ancient Egyptians believed cats could travel between worlds, making this feline the perfect companion for sublime inertia. Vallotton's revolutionary black-and-white technique works its own magic here: the woman's pale form emerges from absolute darkness, floating in a pocket dimension of idleness where time stretches and ordinary constraints dissolve. These pauses between purpose and purposelessness aren't empty spaces but states worth savouring.

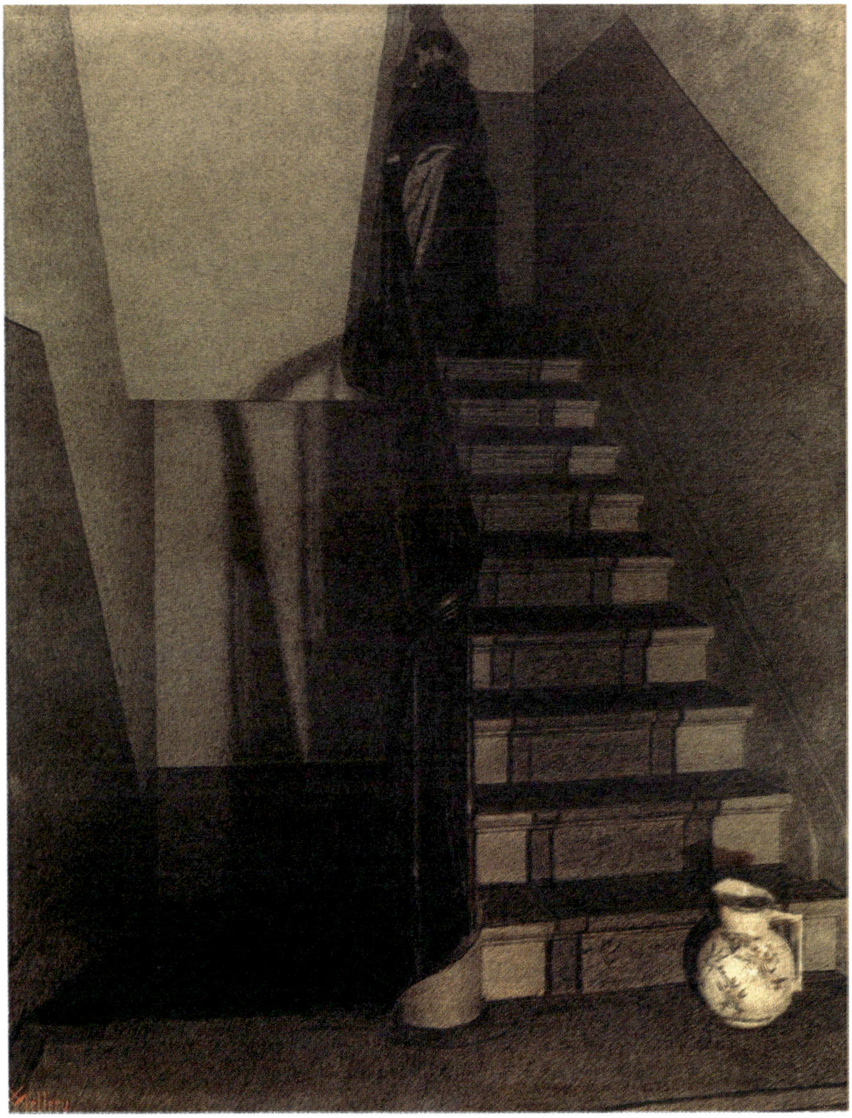

The Staircase, Xavier Mellery, 1889, red and black chalk on paper

Few spaces embody liminality more perfectly than a staircase – neither here nor there, neither up nor down, but perpetually in between. Belgian Symbolist Xavier Mellery (1845–1921) captures this threshold essence in his haunting charcoal drawing, in which the stairs rise from darkness into further darkness, with a shadowy figure hovering at the landing – not quite arriving, not quite departing, but suspended in transit. Mellery specialized in what he called 'the soul of things', believing that everyday spaces and objects possessed secret lives that emerged in stillness and shadow. This is precisely the kind of transitional space where conversations happen in whispers, where decisions crystallize, where one version of ourselves transforms into another with each step taken. In Mellery's vision, the staircase is a portal, where moving between floors might mean moving between selves.

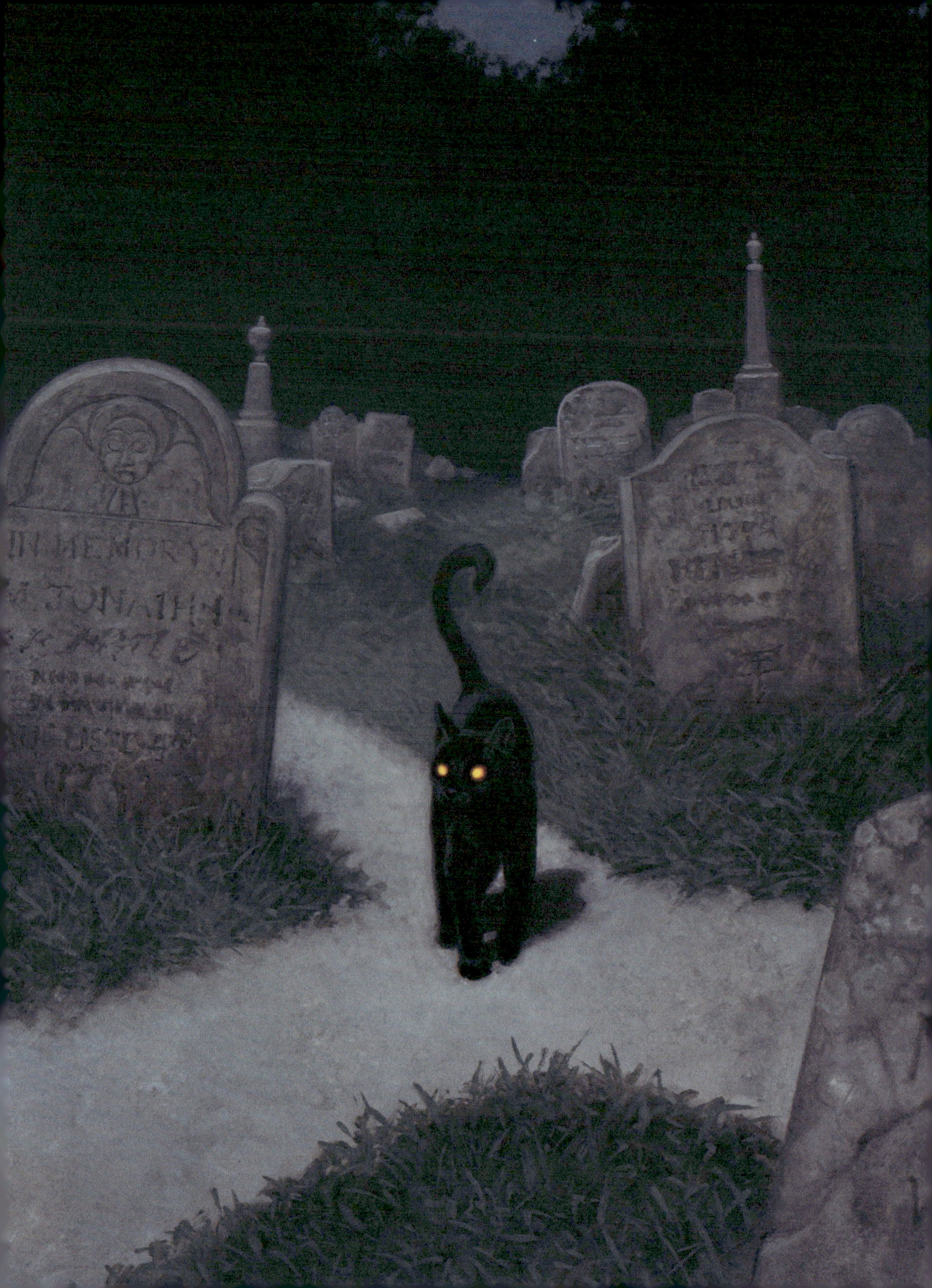
IN MEMORY

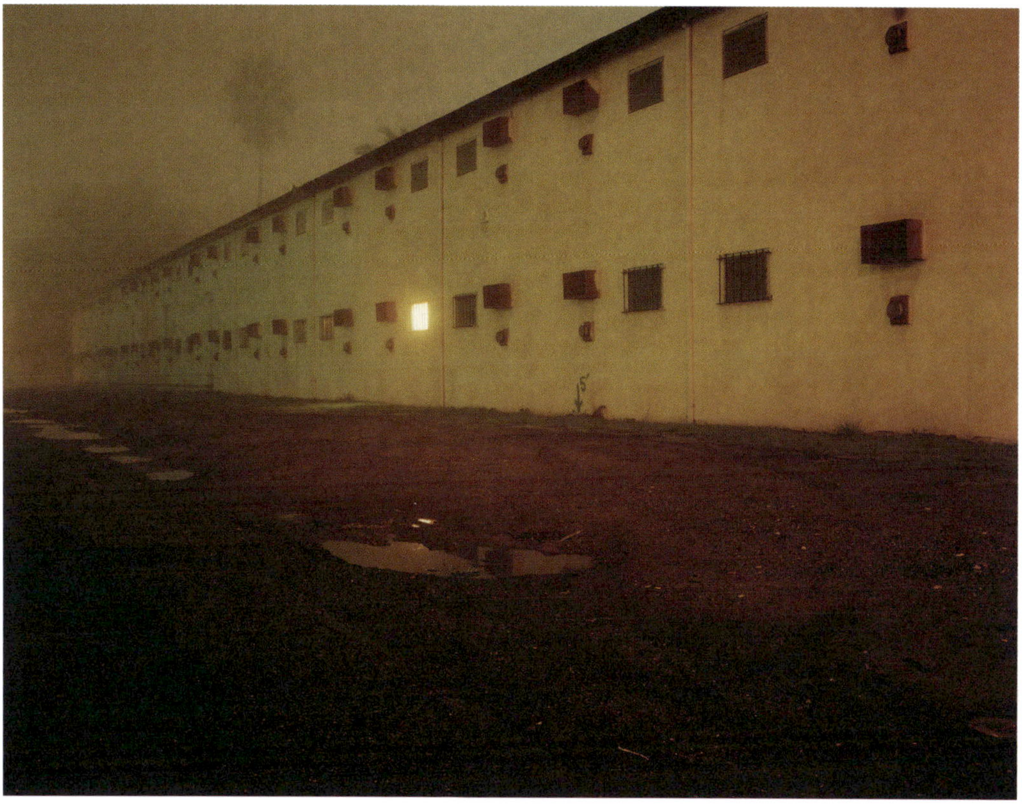

Opposite: Witch Way to Murder, Tristan Elwell, 2005, oil on board

In Tristan Elwell's deliriously eerie cover art for *Witch Way to Murder*, we're trespassing on a midnight cemetery that exists in suspended animation between day and night, life and death. Elwell, whose darkly whimsical visions have bewitched book covers and *Magic: The Gathering* cards alike, shows us a black cat - sleek as sin and twice as knowing - slinking along the path with unmistakable purpose, those amber eyes slyly beckoning, 'Follow me, if you dare.' The shaggy, unkempt grass exudes a damp chill you can almost feel against your ankles as it conspires with the shadows, whispering secrets only this furry patrolman comprehends. The cat's confident strut tells us everything: it's not lost, scared or confused - it's perfectly at home in this threshold space! This cemetery doubles as a waiting room, and our feline friend is clearly the appointed usher, padding silently between tombstones.

Above: #4022, from 'Homes at Night', Todd Hido, 2005, photography

A single illuminated window punctuates the fog-drenched facade of this anonymous two-storey building - neither fully present nor absent, occupied nor abandoned. The scattered puddles create distorted mirrors across the lot, doubling the scene with watery inversions, while the enveloping mist turns solid architecture into spectral remnants. Todd Hido, whose nocturnal teenage wanderings evolved into his acclaimed 'House Hunting' series, specializes in capturing these in-between moments when the infrastructure remains but the life drains out. The repetitive air-conditioning units and barred windows create a visual rhythm that feels both hypnotic and unsettling, streetlights humming and machines running for no one. That glowing window suggests life inside, but the fog and isolation make you question if anyone's really there, or if the lights just run automatically in this ghostly suburb.

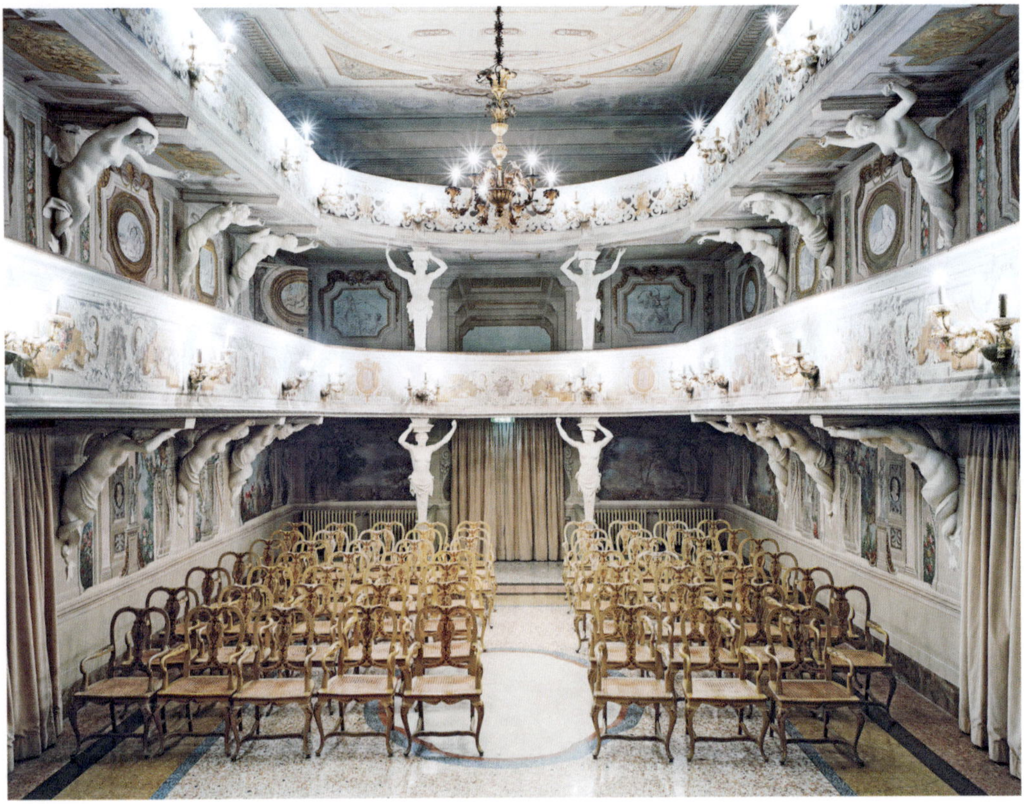

Teatro di Villa Mazzacurati di Bologna II 2006, Candida Höfer, 2006, photography

Ornate gilded angels gaze down from wooden balconies, their perpetual vigil unbroken by human presence in this mesmerizing Italian theatre captured by Candida Höfer. The space feels hypnotically unsettling - so meticulously designed for human congregation yet so eerily vacant. Those wooden chairs, arranged with military precision, seem almost accusatory in their emptiness. The elaborate ceiling frescoes and the imposing chandelier perform their splendour for absolutely no one, like actors continuing their roles long after the audience has gone home. Höfer specializes in this particular brand of beautiful abandonment - these grand cultural venues frozen in their moments between purpose. The theatre becomes a magnificent question mark: all this grandeur awaiting an audience that never arrives.

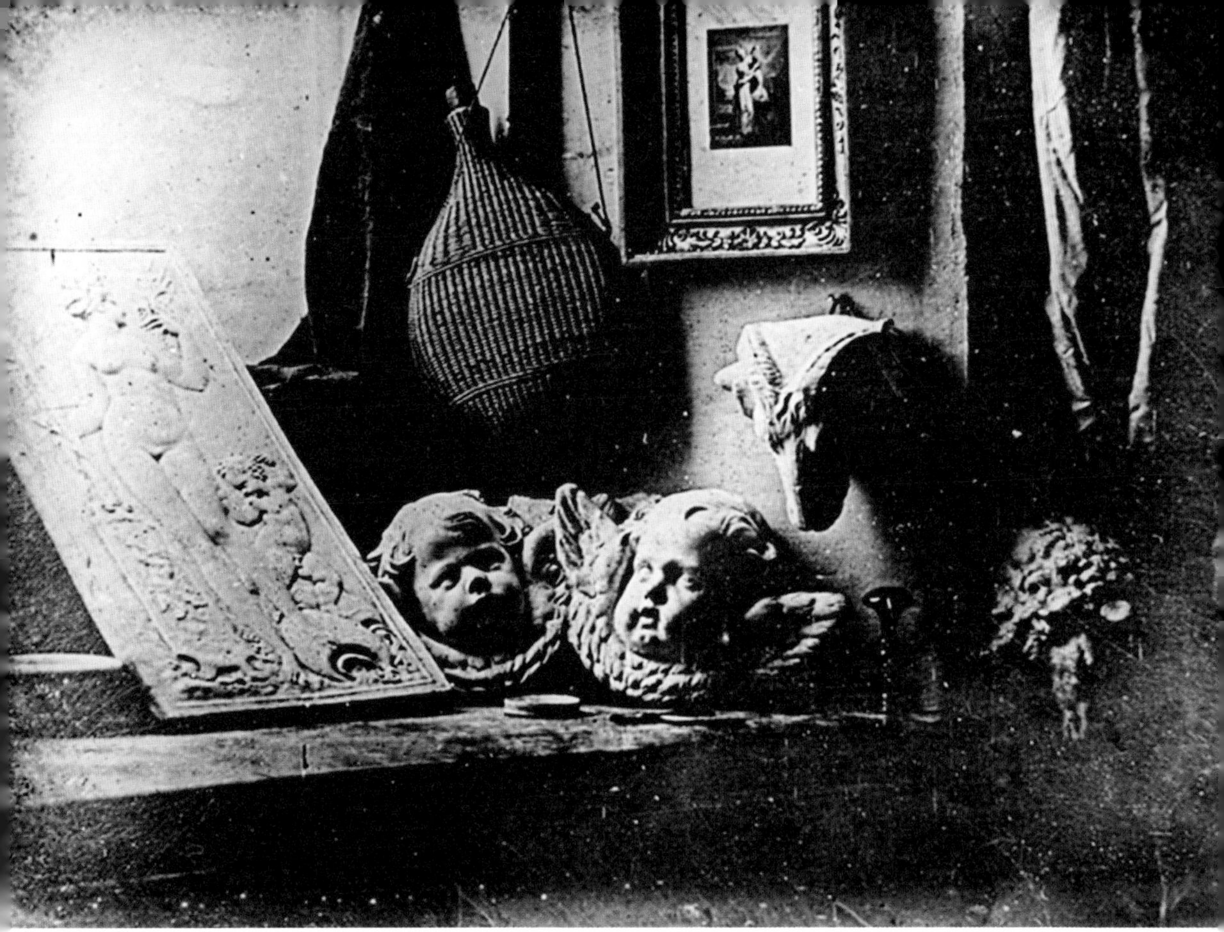

The Artist's Studio/Still Life with Plaster Casts, 1837, Louis Daguerre, daguerreotype

Louis Daguerre (1787–1851) captures light and freezes time itself in what many consider the oldest surviving photograph. Tucked into his Paris studio in 1837, Daguerre arranged this theatrical assembly of plaster casts – two cherubic heads with tiny wings, a carved relief panel, a ram's head and a wicker-covered bottle – then waited as silver and light conspired during the 15-minute exposure. What emerged on that polished copper plate was revolutionary: a bridge between perception and permanence. The inventor of the diorama (those immersive theatrical spectacles) understood liminal spaces intimately – after all, his entire career had been built on creating illusions that hovered between reality and fantasy. Daguerre stands at the point of photography's genesis, the last moment when the world remained unphotographed, and the first when it became eternally capturable.

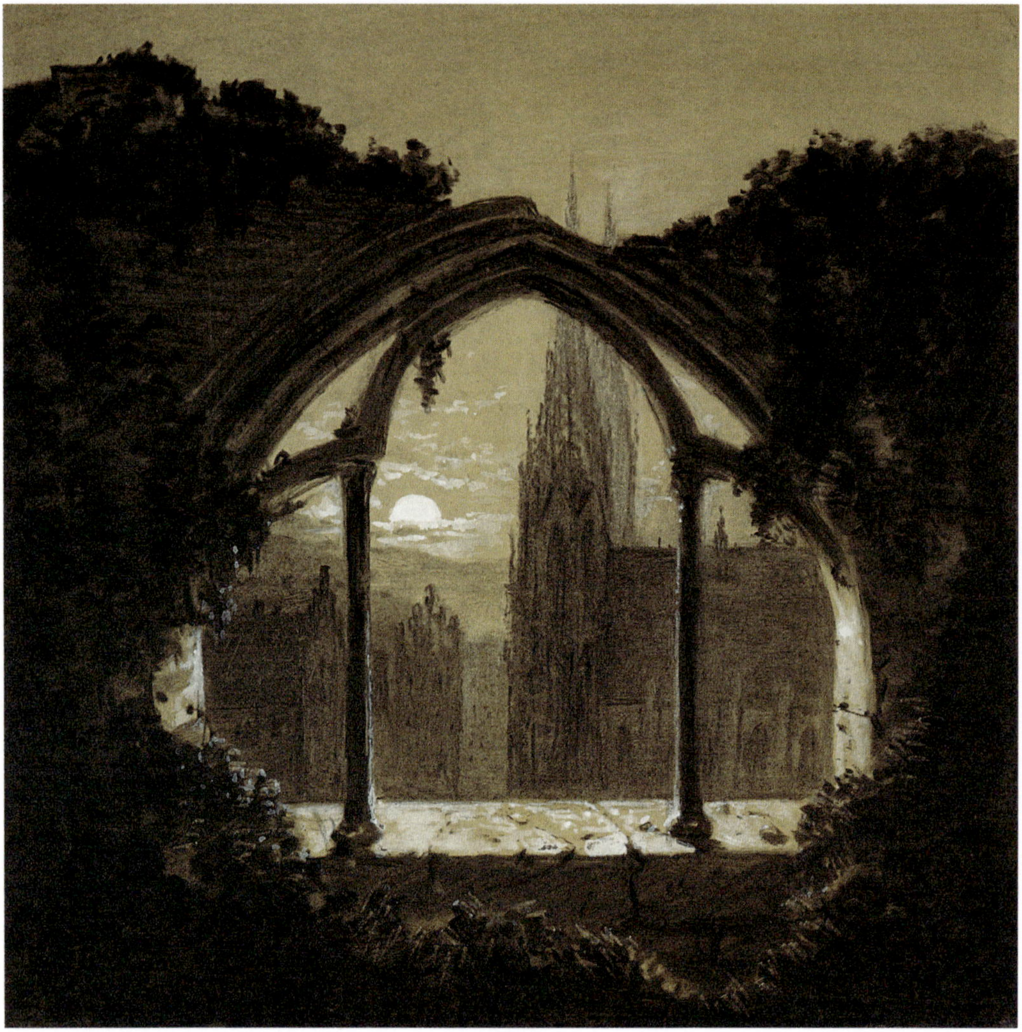

Gothic cathedral seen through ruins of a castle, Carl Gustav Carus, 1852, charcoal

Ancient arches frame a passage between worlds in Carl Gustav Carus's (1789–1869) haunting charcoal study – a peak threshold moment where ruins open onto revelation. A once-mighty castle's skeletal remains leave you neither within nor without, at no fixed point in time. Through this architectural aperture, a vast cathedral rises against a misty sunset, impossibly distant yet perfectly centred. Carus, a fascinating polymath who moved with equal confidence through medicine, philosophy and art, understood in-between spaces in ways his contemporaries couldn't match. While his friend Caspar David Friedrich painted direct confrontations with the sublime, Carus was drawn to these neither-nor states: the borderland between consciousness and unconsciousness (he pioneered early psychology), the mysterious boundary separating life and death (as a physician). Vegetation creeps over ancient stones, suspended between destruction and reclamation, while the Gothic cathedral stands as both monument and memory.

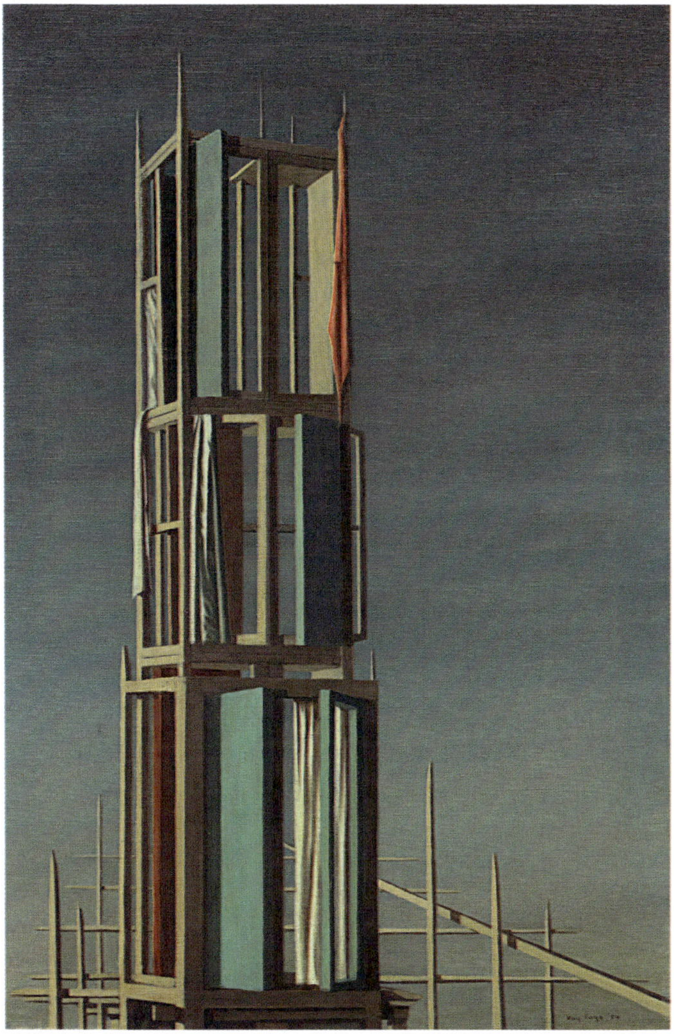

Hyphen, Kay Sage, 1954, oil on canvas

Kay Sage (1898–1963) builds impossible architecture from unrefined in-betweenness in *Hyphen*, a masterwork of suspended reality. Rising against a twilight-blue void, her latticed tower seems caught mid-transformation – part construction site, part ruin, part alien signal tower. Like the grammatical mark it's named for, this painting connects worlds without fully committing to either side. Sage knew something about living between states. She wandered Europe with her mother as a child, suffocated her creativity in an aristocratic marriage and only unleashed her artistic voice at 39 when she abandoned everything for Paris and Surrealism. Her disciplined, architectural approach stands in stark contrast to her Surrealist colleagues' biomorphic fantasies. While they explored the organic unconscious, Sage built precise labyrinths of transition and possibility.

VI

—

TERRA INCOGNITA

'Art will never come except from some small disregarded corner where an isolated and inspired man is studying the mysteries of nature.'

– JEAN-FRANÇOIS MILLET

Ancient cartographers marked uncharted territories with the warning *terra incognita* ('unknown land') and decorated these blank spaces with dragons and sea monsters. When we can't map something, we imagine what might lurk there. Today we fill the gaps with data points and grid coordinates and convince ourselves the blank spaces no longer exist. But despite our satellites and sensors, our geological surveys and classifications, Earth still guards her secrets. Miles beneath our feet, vast cave systems like Vietnam's Hang Son Doong harbour underground rivers and forests, their chambers so massive they generate their own weather. In ocean trenches deeper than Mount Everest is tall, bioluminescent creatures float through eternal darkness, their bodies transformed into living light. When the tide retreats from certain coastlines, it reveals ancient forests preserved in peat for millennia – nature's boreal memento mori unearthed from mineral-stained sand.

Some secrets reveal themselves only to the patient observer. Desert landscapes transform during rare flowering events that happen once a decade, turning barren plains into riots of colour before vanishing again. Certain mountaintops emerge from cloud cover only on specific days, and islands appear and disappear with tidal rhythms. Some geographic enigmas, like the Bermuda Triangle or Turkmenistan's 'Door to Hell' are legendary, but even the mundane and familiar conceal mysteries. A handful of garden soil contains microscopic worlds as alien as any science fiction landscape, while moss colonies viewed through magnification reveal architectural structures worthy of lost civilizations. And everywhere, nature patiently reclaims what humans abandoned – ivy threading through stained glass, tree roots lifting cathedral floors, desert sands flowing like water over forgotten cities.

'The same paths that lead us out can lead us in,' writes Robert Macfarlane in *The Old Ways*. Artists who venture into these territories understand this paradox intimately. The German Romantics found numinous presence in twisted trees and misty mountains. Caspar David Friedrich's moonlit shores pulse with invitation and warning, while Ivan Shishkin's solitary pine stands guard at the very edge of the mapped world. Georgia O'Keeffe discovered landscapes that were also revelations – sun-bleached bones and twisted rocks speaking an ancient language of wind and time, each painting a window into processes usually hidden from human eyes.

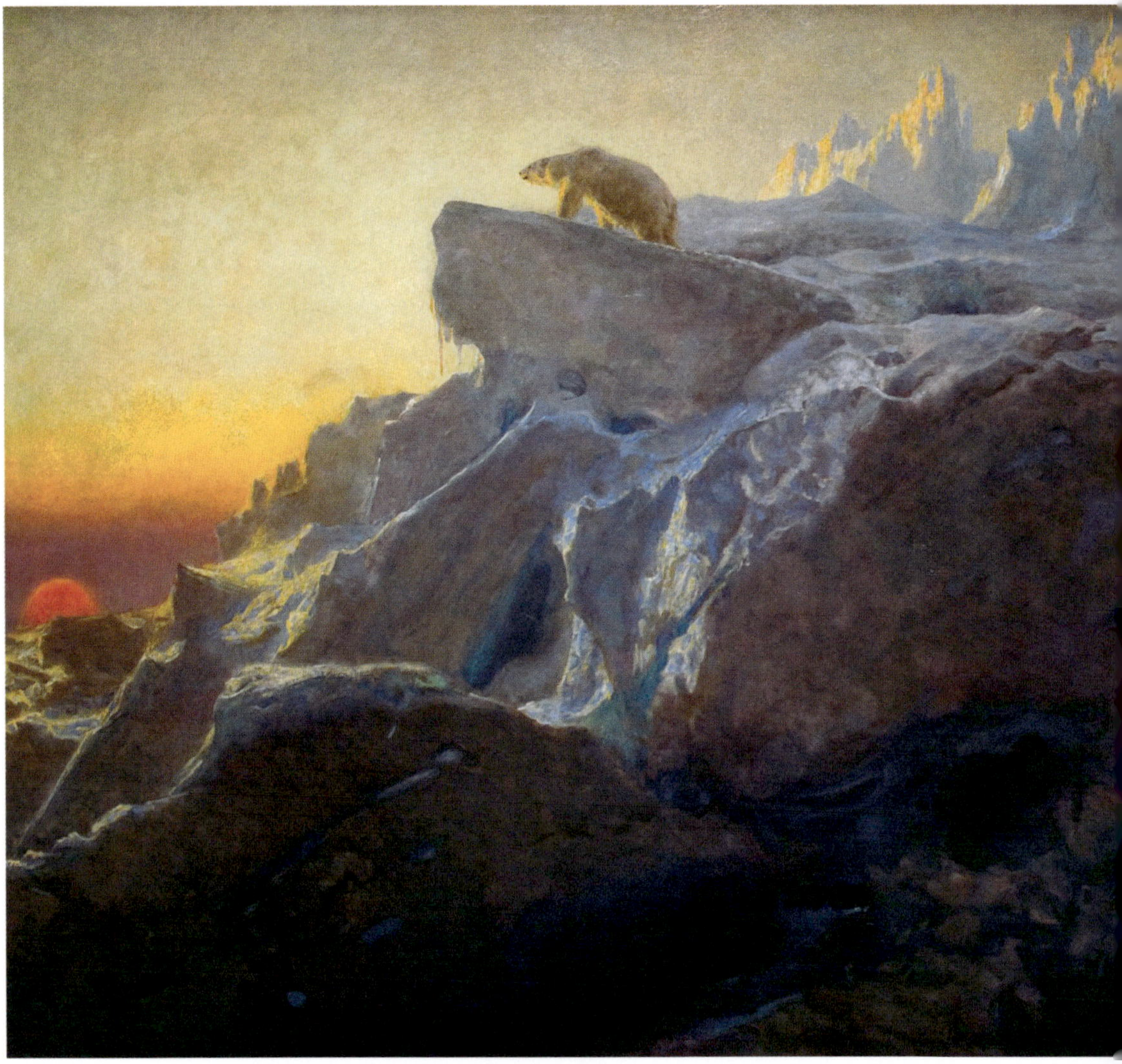

The forest holds particular power in this regard. Werner Herzog, in his typically cheerful way, once described the Amazon as a place where the birds don't sing, 'they just screech in pain'. But artists have long understood both the terror and beauty of wild places, whether deep woodland or stark desert. Thomas Moran's Grand Canyon vistas unveiled territories that once seemed so fantastical Eastern politicians dismissed them as imaginary, while Charles Burchfield's woodlands vibrate with an almost visible energy, as if he'd caught the forest in the middle

Beyond Man's Footsteps, Briton Rivière, *c.* 1894, oil on canvas

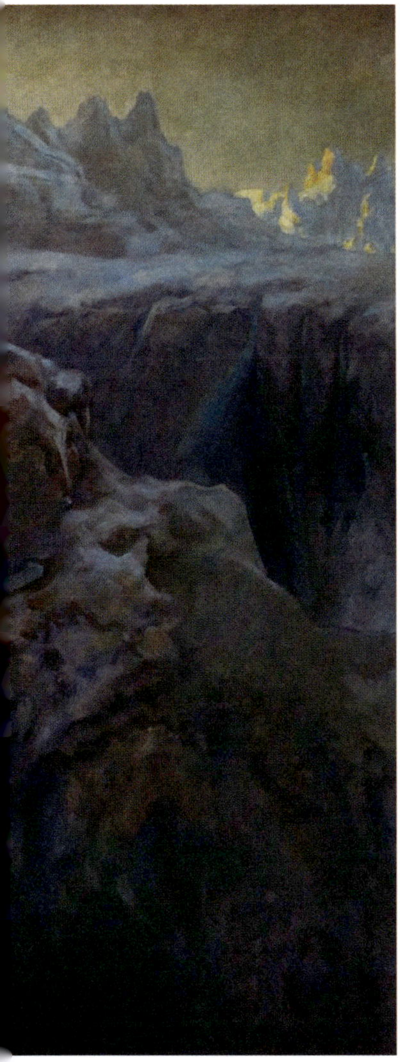

of an urgent conversation we weren't meant to hear. In the mountains, artists found different kinds of mystery: Nicholas Roerich's mystical Himalayas marking thresholds between physical and spiritual realms; Albert Bierstadt's Sierra Nevadas wreathed in otherworldly light.

Contemporary artists approach these mysteries with new tools but similar reverence. Roxy Paine's meticulous metal trees expose the malleable boundary between authentic and constructed wilderness, while Andy Goldsworthy's ephemeral ice sculptures melt back into the lakes from which he created them. These artists find nature's mysteries everywhere – tenacious plants claiming territory through pavement cracks, wildflowers turning abandoned lots into meadows, stubborn seabirds establishing their own micro-nations in beach car parks. Nature writes its own story over ours, patient and relentless.

Time moves differently in these works – mountain-slow, river-patient. Centuries pass like seasons, making our hurried human schedules seem almost quaint. Here, decay becomes a creative partner, carving its slow signature into stone and soil. Spiralling mine tunnels photograph as alien fossils. Haunting tintypes document landscapes where America's violent history has literally seeped into the soil. Some artists possess double vision – combining scientific precision with dreamlike perception – revealing what hides in forests, what colours exist beyond human sight, what patterns and relationships become visible only when someone takes the time to truly see what's already there.

'The land knows you, even when you are lost,' observes Robin Wall Kimmerer in *Braiding Sweetgrass: Indigenous Wisdom, Scientific Knowledge, and the Teachings of Plants*. Artists have long understood this strange reciprocal awareness, painting landscapes and sculpting forms that seem to gaze back at them with ancient, knowing eyes. Their work reveals nature as the real protagonist in these encounters, witnessing both our wonder and our destruction with quiet, enduring presence. They've figured out something the rest of us rush past: there's a difference between what we can wrench from the earth and what she'll willingly share. If you linger long and slow and patient, if you remain receptive enough to let her know you – footsteps, breath, heartbeat and all – the sharing becomes mutual.

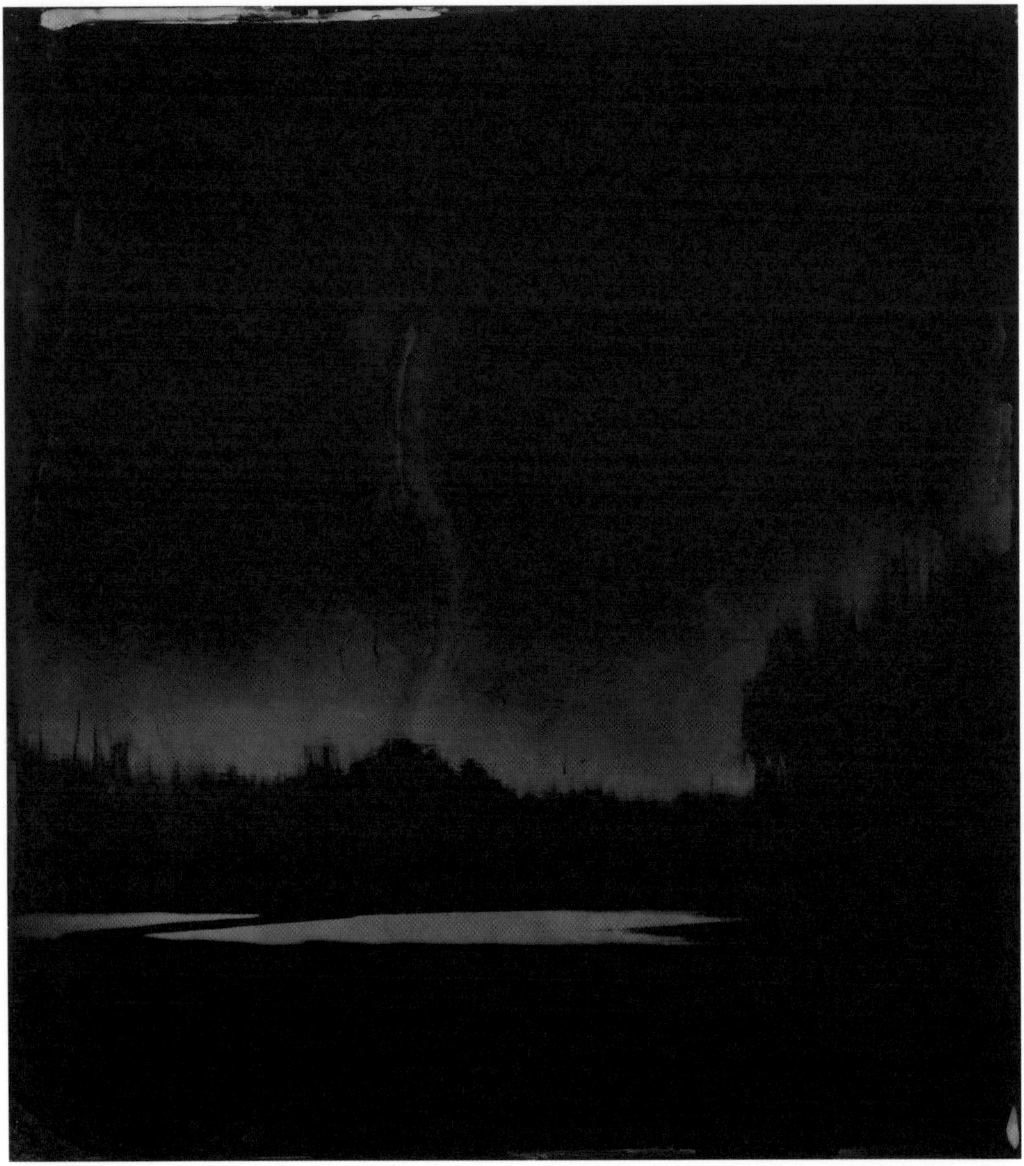

Blackwater 9, Sally Mann, 2008–12, tintype

Brooding darkness and reflective water create a sombre memorial in this 2008 tintype by Sally Mann. Using the same photographic process popular during the Civil War era, Mann documents Virginia's Great Dismal Swamp after devastating wildfires consumed thousands of acres. This land harbours dark secrets: it once provided refuge for escaped slaves who preferred its venomous snakes, predators and impenetrable terrain to the horrors of bondage. Mann deliberately chose the antiquated tintype technique, whose chemical imperfections, flares and distortions merge perfectly with the scarred landscape, creating what she calls 'a testament and reminder' that even fire cannot erase memory. By documenting this place where soil itself burned for years, Mann reveals a hidden territory most Americans never see – one where past violence refuses to stay buried and instead rises like smoke through history's thin surface.

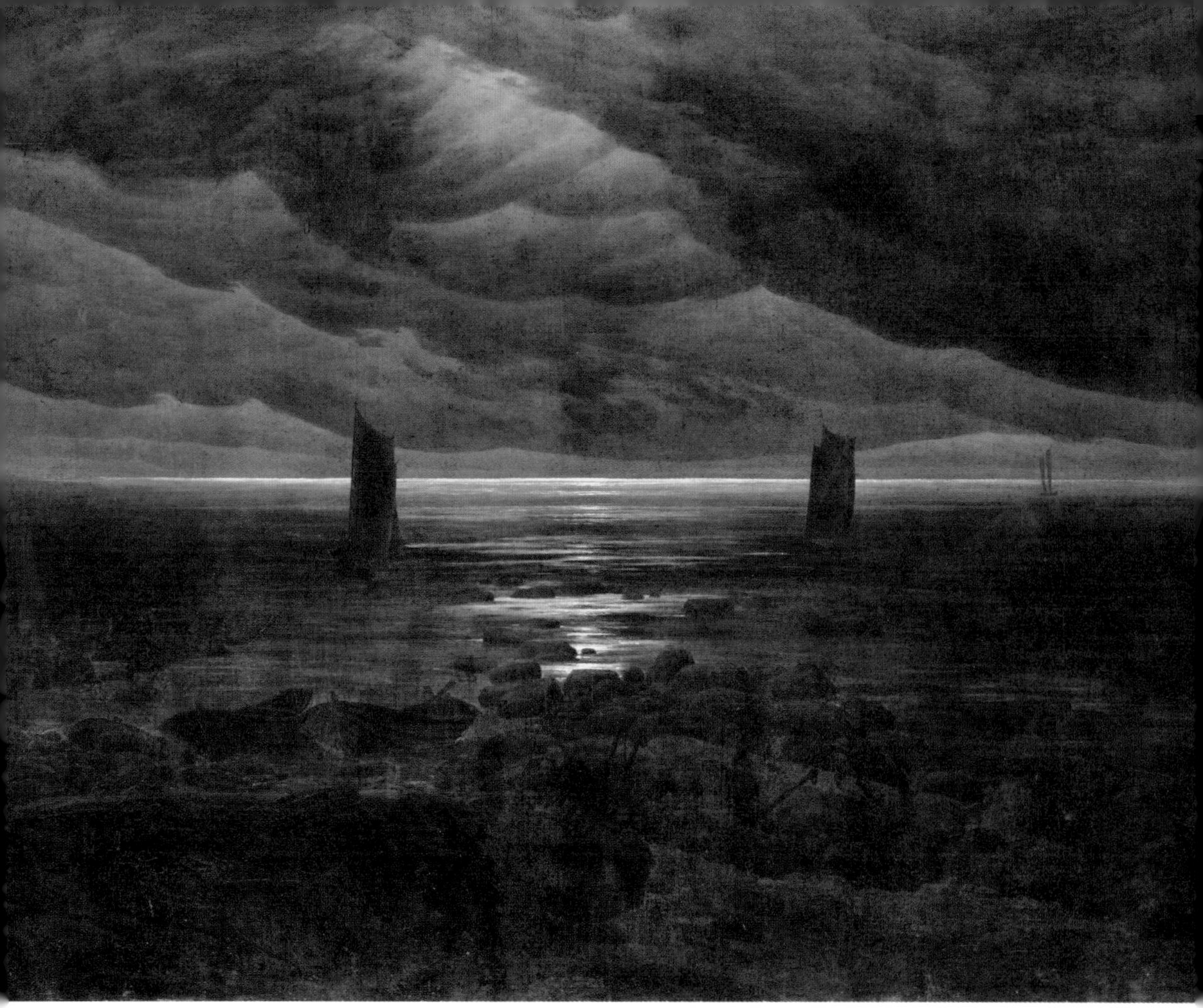

Sea Shore in Moonlight, Caspar David Friedrich, 1835–36, oil on canvas

A cold finger of moonlight reaches across black waters towards vessels, or what might be the wreckage of vessels – rendered indistinguishable by distance and darkness, they exist only as silhouettes, dark benedictions. Caspar David Friedrich (1774–1840), who was well acquainted with death from childhood – his mother, brother and two sisters all claimed before he reached adulthood – painted this work as his own body began to fail him, after a stroke left his limbs partially paralysed. The brooding coastal scene abandons his signature human figures, leaving us alone to face the decision: remain on solid ground or venture across that treacherous silver path stretching towards the unknown. Clouds mass overhead like gathering thoughts, their swirling forms echoing the invisible currents lurking beneath the water's deceptively calm surface. This is a landscape of silent invitation and quiet warning, where familiar shores no longer offer comfort and the distant horizon holds only darkness.

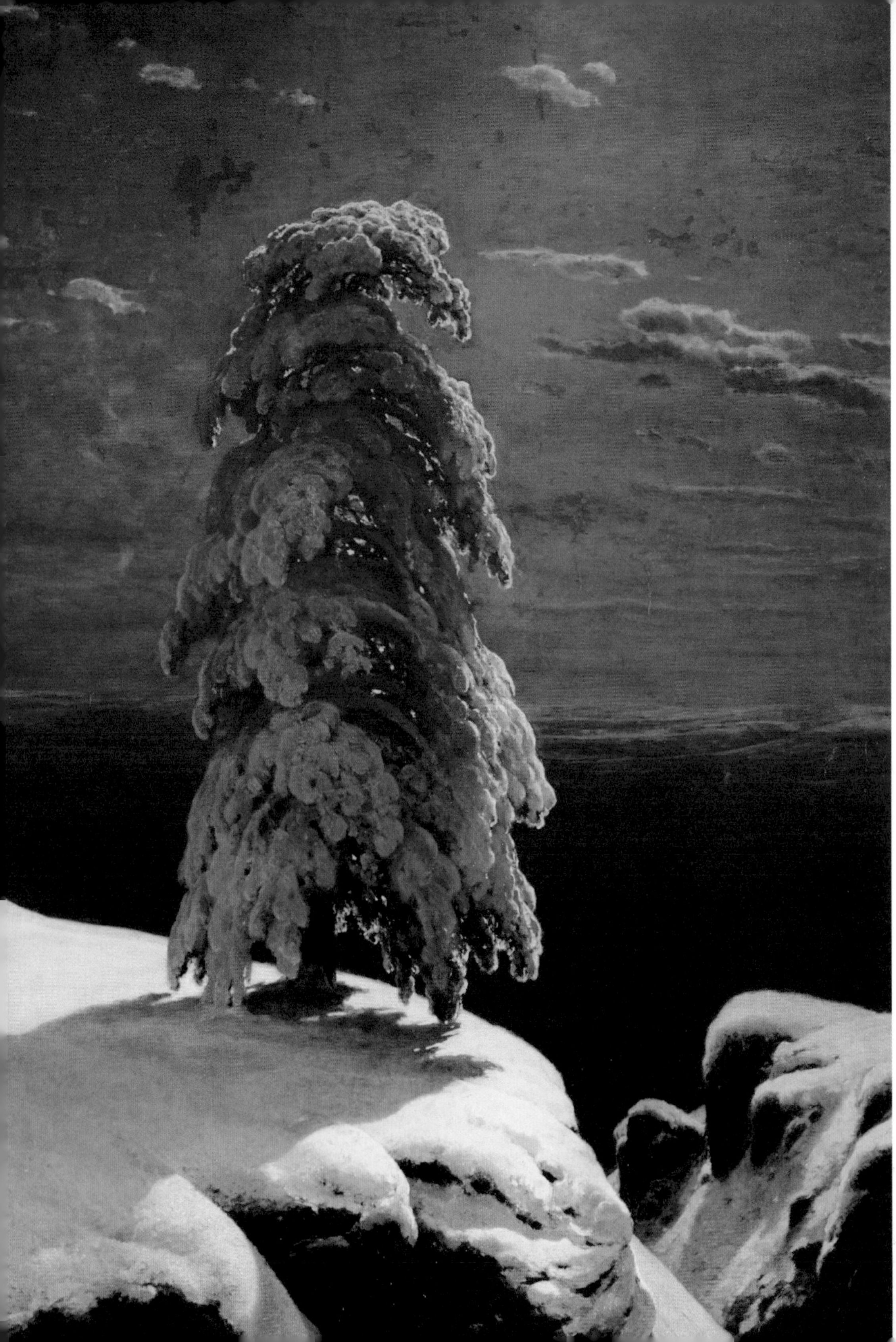

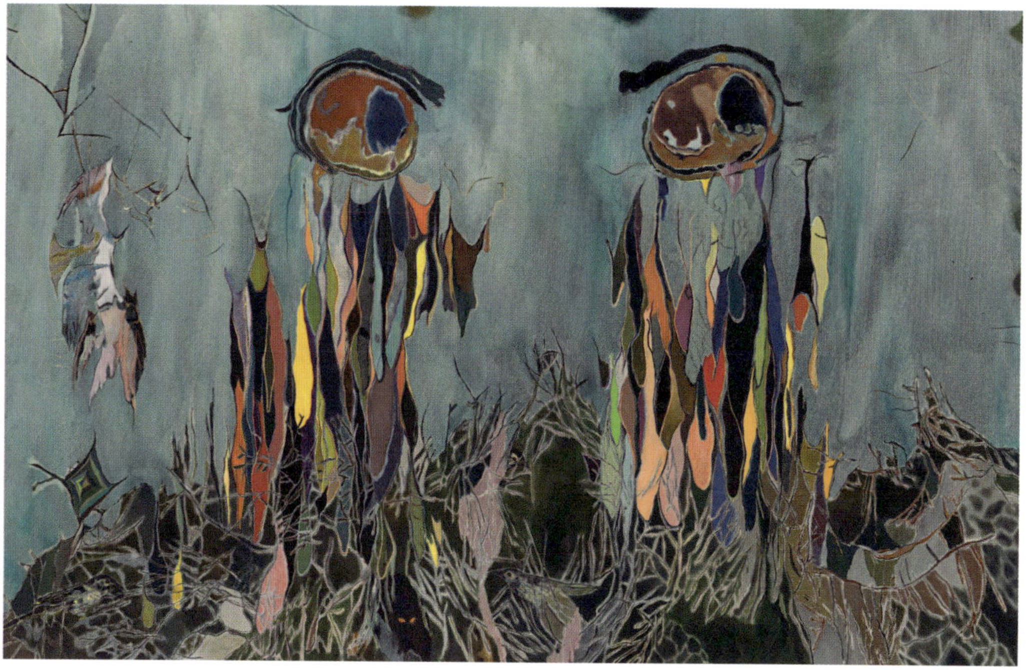

Opposite: In the Wild North,
Ivan Shishkin, 1891, oil on canvas

Perched at the edge of everything mappable, Ivan Shishkin's (1832–98) solitary pine stands sentinel on a precipice, its snow-laden branches reaching towards an inscrutable horizon, while its roots cling to the final outpost of solid ground. Shishkin, Russia's 'Tsar of the Forest', typically celebrated the dense woodland interiors of his homeland, but here he paints the very frontier of the mapped world. The tree commands the foreground with crystalline clarity, while beyond stretches an abyss of deepening shadows and half-glimpsed contours that dissolve into unmeasurable, soul-crushing nothingness. Shishkin's training at the Moscow School of Painting equipped him with extraordinary technical precision, yet this composition draws its power from what stays hidden – the vast territory that disappears into darkness below, distant mountains barely articulated against the night sky, worlds that exist beyond human reach.

Above: ʘJʘ, Adam Lee, 2024, oil and synthetic polymer paint on canvas

Something is gazing pointedly out of Adam Lee's watchful canvas: enormous eyes inspired by the granny moths native to his Australian studio. Below these watchful orbs, a chaotic thicket conceals critically endangered regent honeyeaters – birds rapidly disappearing from the Macedon Ranges where Lee works. Streams of vibrant pigment cascade downwards like psychedelic rainfall, inspired by marble paving Lee discovered in a Renaissance 'Annunciation' painting. The title uses an ancient glyph resembling paired eyes, while the painting itself was inspired by Bulgaria's Prohodna cave, known as 'God's Eyes' for the two ceiling openings that allow light to penetrate its depths. Lee's distinctive style merges scientific observation with ancestral memory, celebrating the wild places that persist despite shrinking with each passing season.

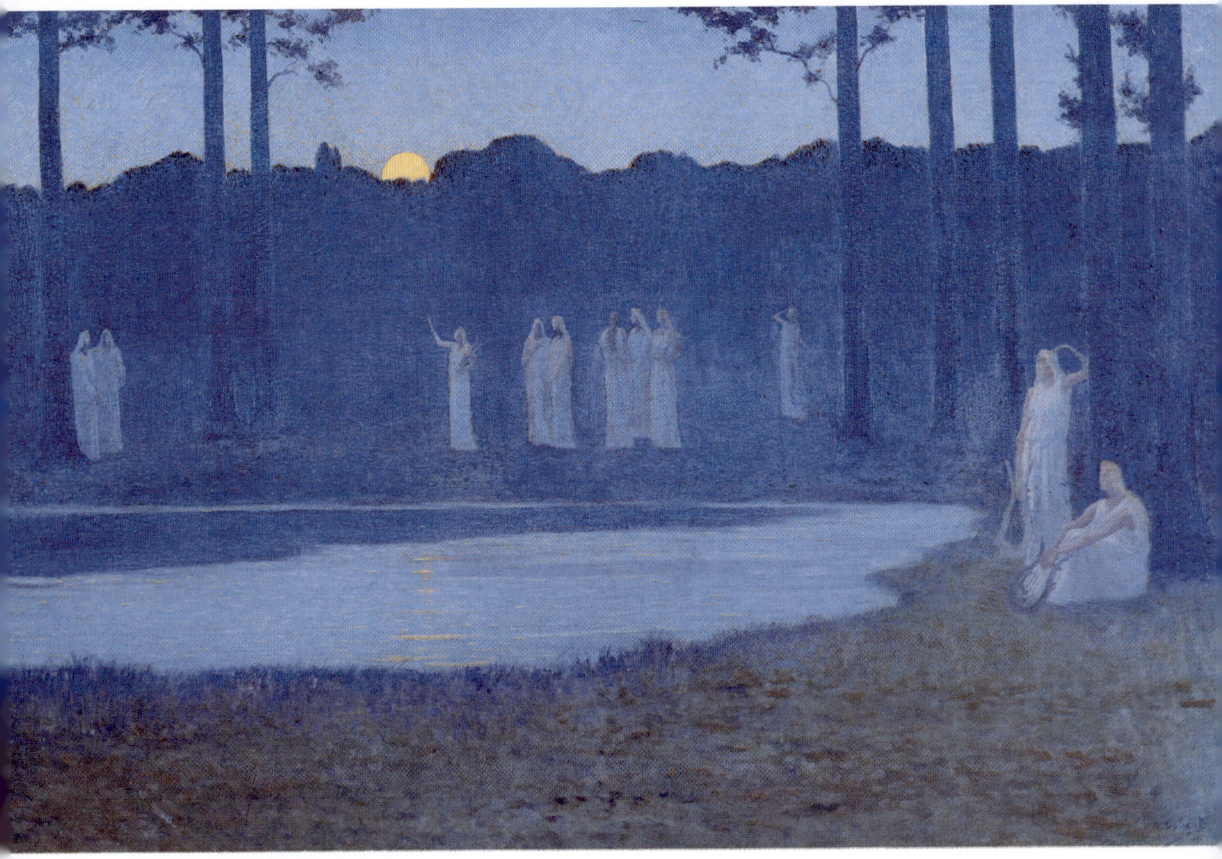

The Songs of the Night, Alphonse Osbert, 1896, oil on canvas

In this ethereal nocturne, Alphonse Osbert (1857–1939) bathes his composition in the distinctive 'Osbert blue' that became his hallmark – a colour so uniquely his that it practically glows with otherworldly intent. White-robed figures gather in ritualistic formation beside still waters, their ghostly silhouettes performing what appears to be a moonlit ceremony in this secluded forest clearing. Osbert believed twilight was the moment when nature's secret places dropped their daytime masks, when sacred knowledge could be accessed through ritual and contemplation. The misty atmosphere deliberately obscures specific details, preserving the mystery of this concealed location and whatever ancient practices unfold there under cover of darkness. The mysterious celebrants – perhaps priestesses or initiates – have sought out this hidden sanctuary deep within the forest, far from civilization's prying eyes and awkward questions.

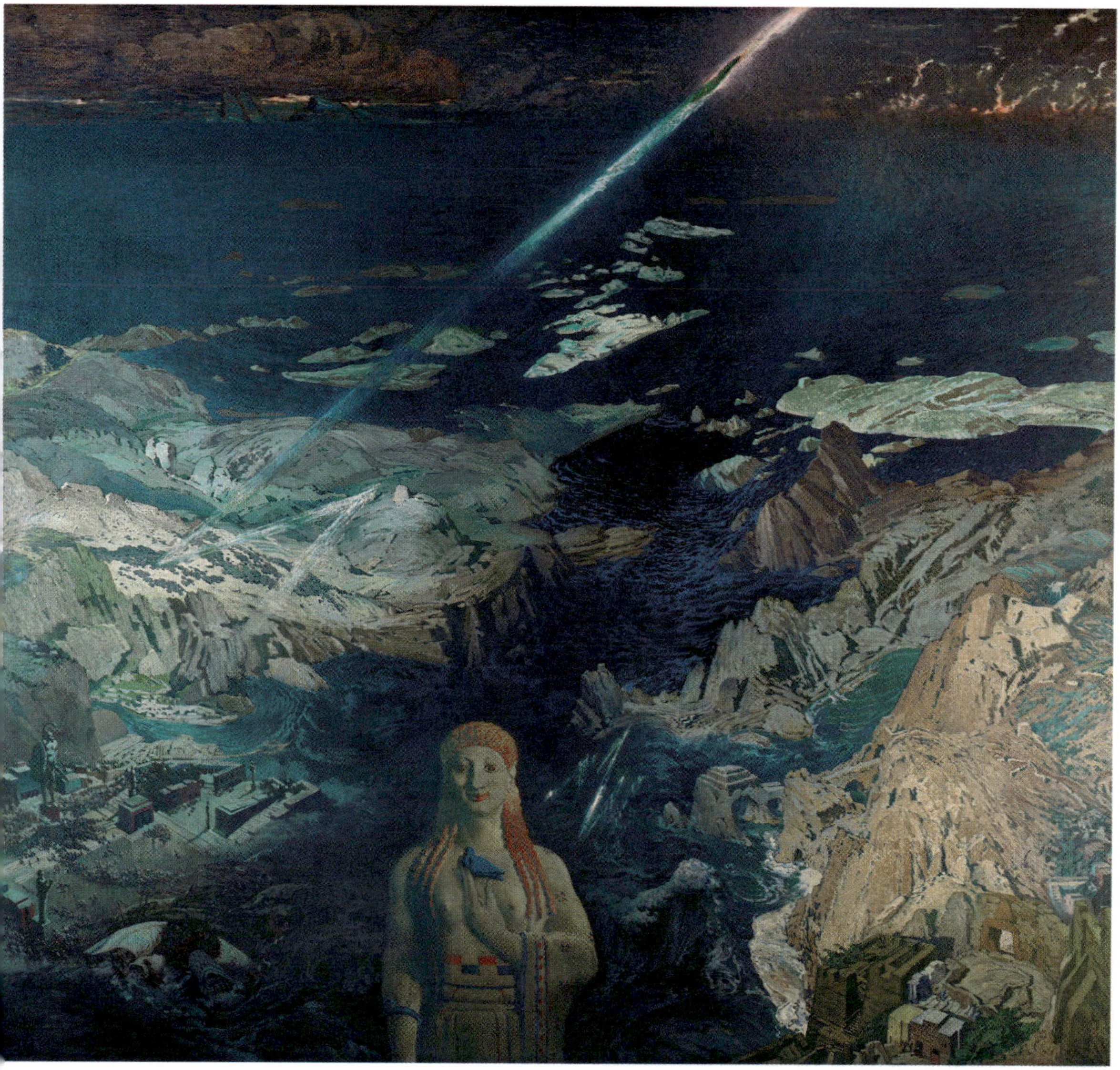

Terror Antiquus, Léon Bakst, 1908, oil on canvas

A serene marble maiden presides over apocalypse in Léon Bakst's (1866–1924) devastating 1908 masterpiece. A year earlier, with fellow painter Valentin Serov, the Russian-born artist had visited Greece, where ancient monuments and Mediterranean landscapes had ignited his imagination. Standing high above the chaos, an archaic kore figure watches calmly as cataclysm engulfs recognizable structures like the Lion Gate at Mycenae and the Athenian Acropolis. Archaeologists might wince at such romantic catastrophism, but Bakst knew his audience: the Victorian and Edwardian eras were obsessed with tales of lost civilizations and dramatic endings. His vision won gold at the 1910 Exposition Universelle in Brussels, proving that people have always loved watching the world end from a safe distance.

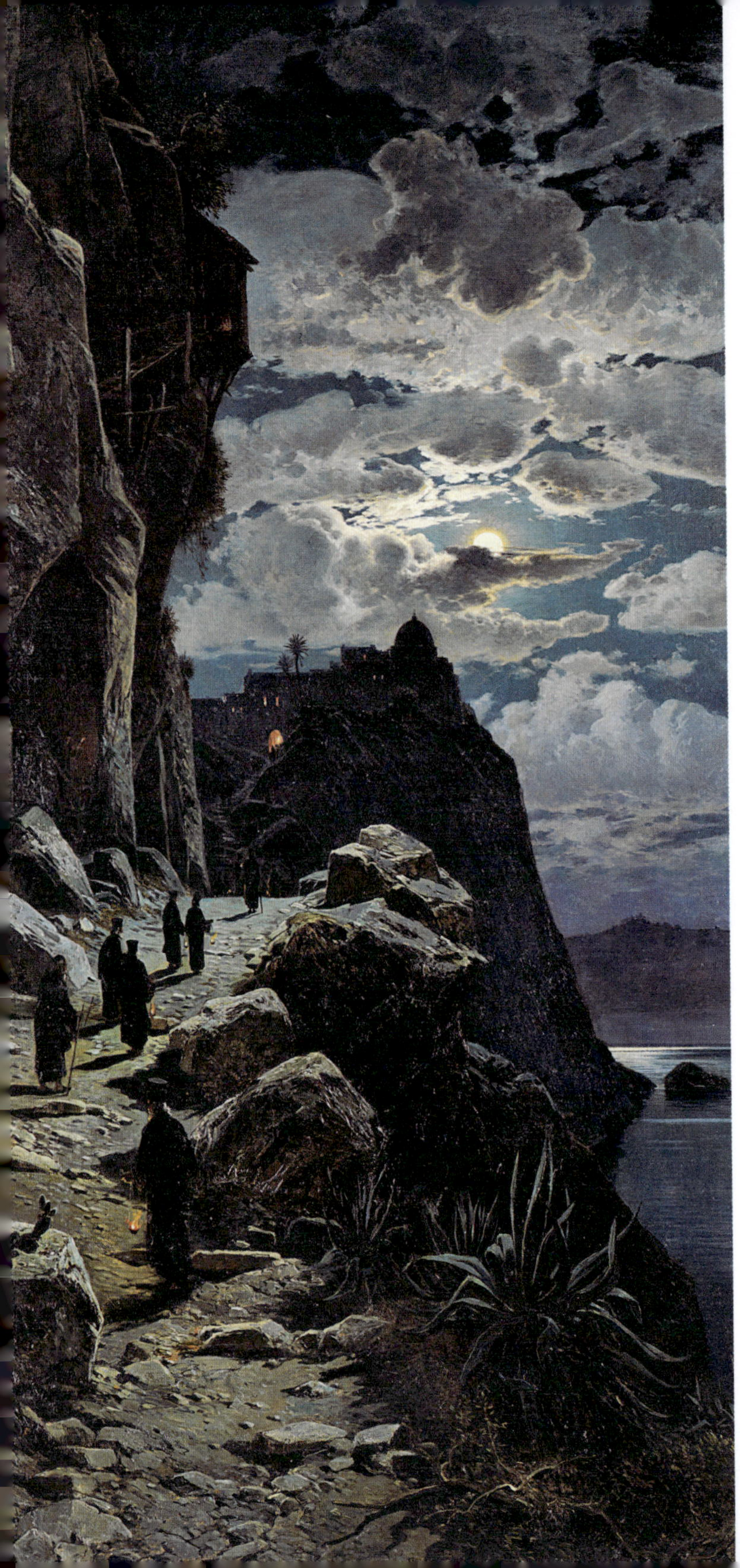

Walk of the Monks to Mount Athos Monastery, Hermann David Salomon Corrodi, 1905, oil on canvas

Darkness envelops all but that which moonlight pierces in this dramatic nocturne by Hermann David Salomon Corrodi (1844–1905). Robed monks navigate a treacherous cliffside path by lantern light, their small flames dwarfed by Mount Athos's imposing mass. This 1905 work, completed in the final year of Corrodi's life, reveals a hidden world few outsiders would witness: a sacred peninsula where monasteries cling to precipitous cliffs, accessible only by the most perilous routes. The Italian painter, friend to European royalty including Queen Victoria, renders the scene with theatrical intensity. The moon breaking through turbulent clouds casts an unearthly silver glow, while the distant monastery glimmers with golden promise. Here is one of Earth's most secluded sanctuaries, where monks have maintained their isolation for over a millennium, their nightly processions unchanged since Byzantine times, traversing paths where a single misstep means certain death.

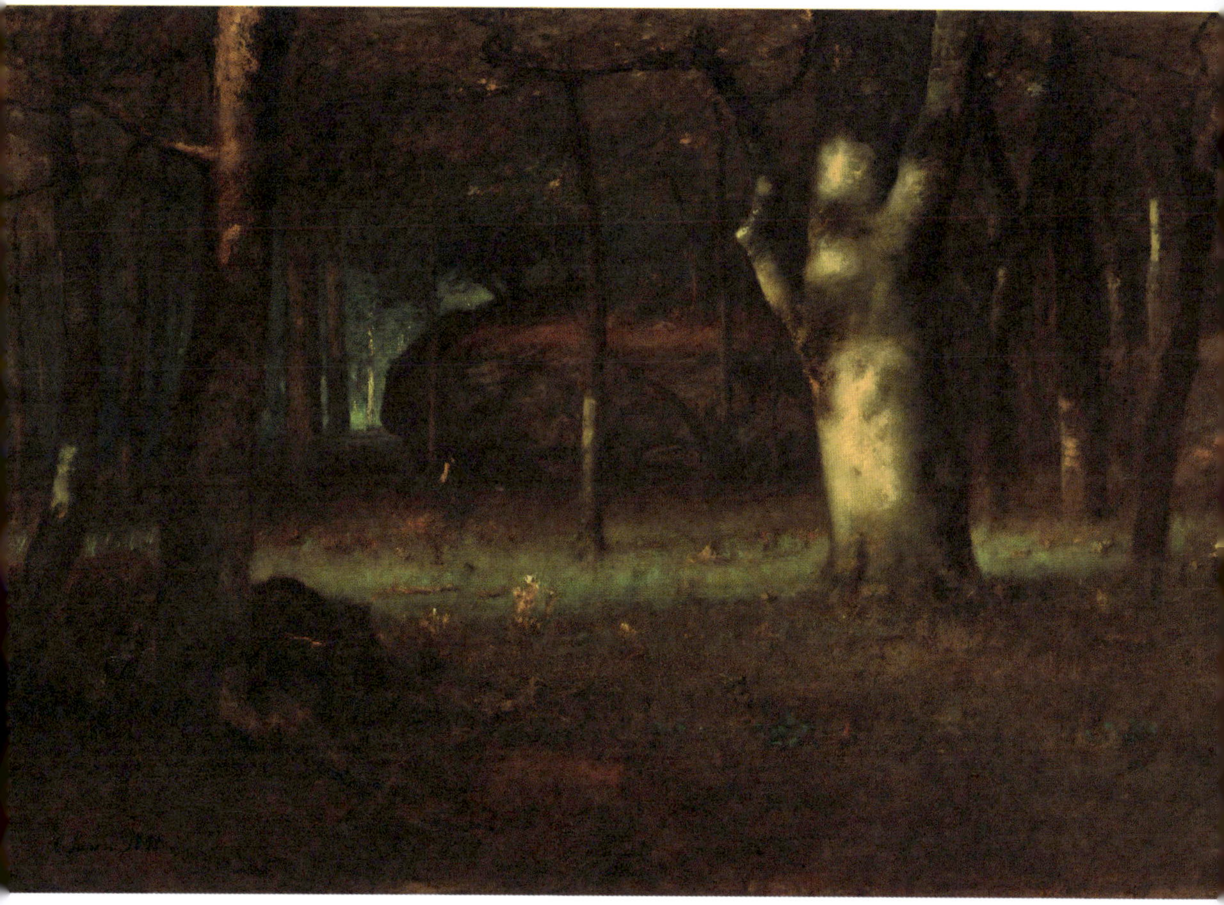

Sunset in the Woods, George Inness, 1891, oil on canvas

Light pierces the forest canopy in this meditative exploration of woodland depths by George Inness (1825–94), who waited years for the vision that would capture his initial encounter with this secluded grove. Here Inness abandons topographical accuracy for spiritual essence, creating a forest interior where time seems suspended in the gathering twilight. A solitary beech tree catches the last rays of sunset, its illuminated trunk serving as a beacon in territory that suddenly feels ancient and alive. The surrounding woodland recedes into quiet stillness in which solid forms soften into shadow and suggestion. Influenced by Emanuel Swedenborg's mystical philosophy, Inness sought to paint landscapes where the physical world reveals its hidden dimensions, and his mature technique of softened edges and atmospheric colour, rather than detail, evokes that contemplative moment when the woods we thought we knew reveal their hidden consciousness.

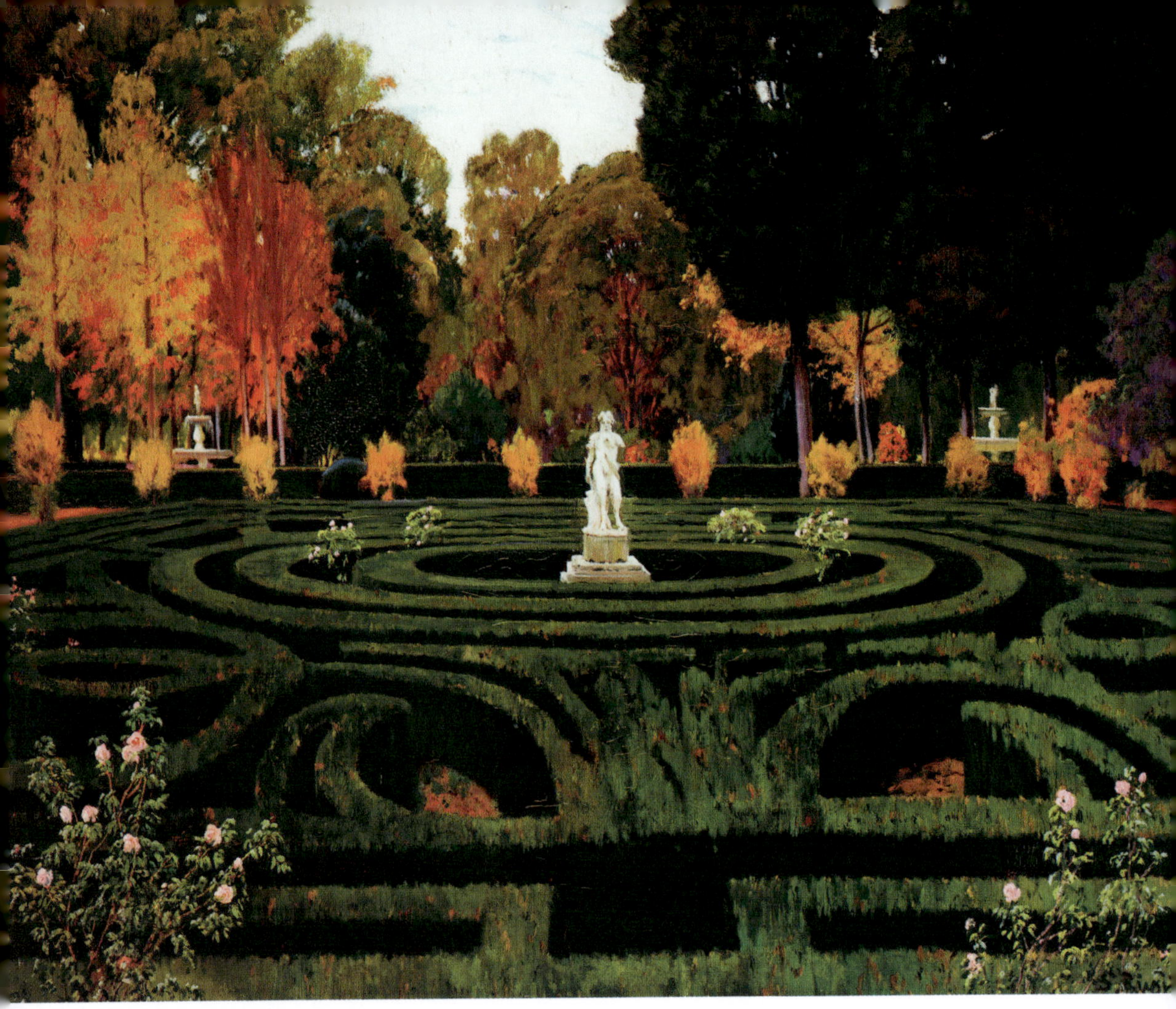

Old Faun (The Parterres of Aranjuez series), Santiago Rusiñol, 1911, oil on canvas

Santiago Rusiñol (1861–1931) captures one of his most beloved subjects in this 1911 oil painting. The Catalan Modernist became so captivated by the royal gardens at Aranjuez that King Alfonso XIII appointed him honorary chief gardener, ensuring his unrestricted access to this living puzzle. This particular garden labyrinth represents the perfect paradox: paths that invite you forwards only to lead you astray, all rendered in autumn's golden hour. Unlike wild forests that conceal through chaos, this garden deliberately obscures through perfect order – its precisely trimmed hedges creating a maze where even the most detailed map proves useless. What royal secrets might these pathways protect? What whispered conspiracies once unfolded in these hidden corners, where even palace guards couldn't observe? This labyrinth represents humanity's deliberate attempt to design disorientation, a place where getting lost becomes the entire point and every turn promises new mysteries.

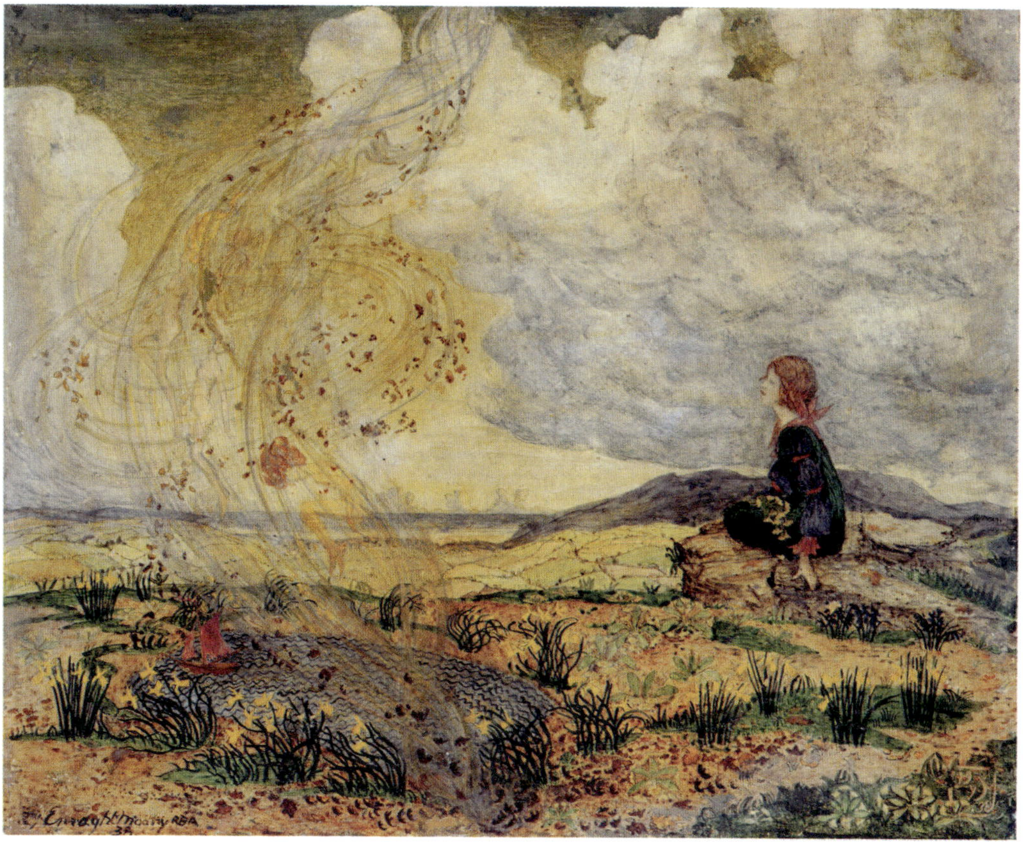

Wind Fairies, Robert James Enraght Moony, 1938, oil on linen laid on board

Leaf-like spirits spiral through the air while a lone figure sits among wildflowers, witnessing the hidden face of the breeze. Robert James Enraght Moony (1879–1946), influenced by Symbolists and Pre-Raphaelites, believed the natural world harboured invisible forces that revealed themselves only to patient observers. Magic doesn't require remote wilderness; sometimes it's waiting for someone willing to sit still and really look. His 1938 oil painting is essentially about how the world is constantly doing amazing things right in front of us, but we're all too busy scrolling on our phones to notice. (Well, they didn't have phones in 1938, but you get the idea.) We've all experienced this: you're sitting in some random place when, suddenly, the air feels electric, like the world just reminded you that it's a miracle, that you're a miracle, that this ordinary day in 1938, or right now, is actually the most extraordinary thing that's ever happened.

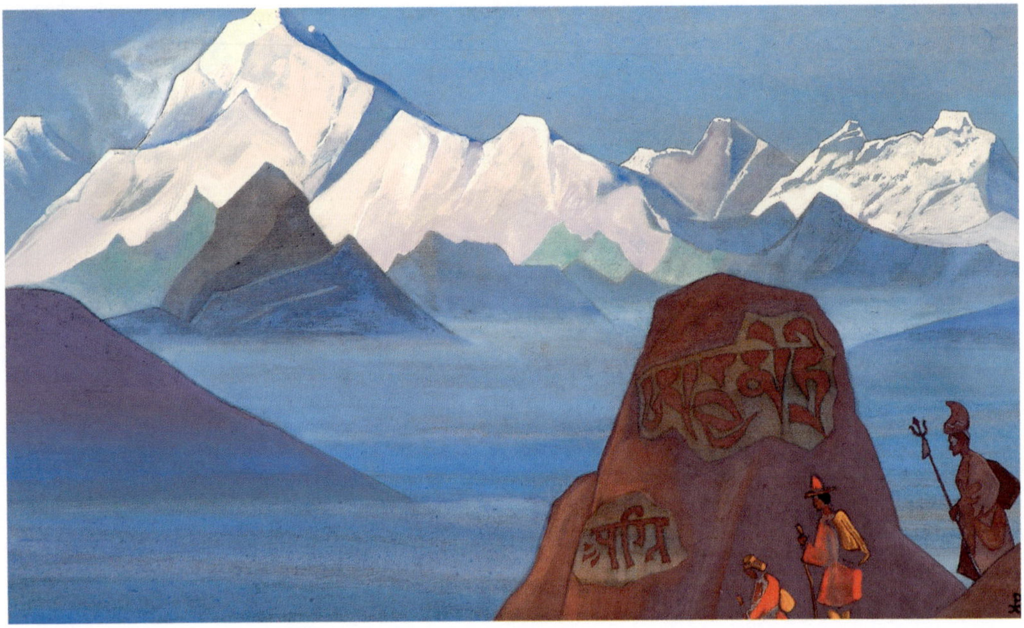

Path to Kailas, Nicholas Roerich, 1932, tempera on paper

Mount Kailash, suffused with light, rises in splendour in Nicholas Roerich's (1874–1947) 1932 vision of this deeply sacred peak. Four major religions converge on this remote Himalayan mountain, each claiming it as their spiritual centre: Buddhists know it as Demchog's palace of supreme bliss, Hindus see Lord Shiva's meditation seat, Jains recognize their first prophet's liberation site and Bon practitioners consider it their cosmic axis. The Russian mystic-explorer painted this scene during his five-year Central Asian expedition, capturing the inscribed stone in the foreground that marks the boundary between ordinary and sacred space. Never climbed by mountaineers, Kailash exists beyond geographical conquest. Its power lies not in its elevation, but in its ability to draw pilgrims across vast distances towards what they believe is the centre of the universe, a place where Roerich's azure peaks can simultaneously embody four different versions of paradise to four different faiths.

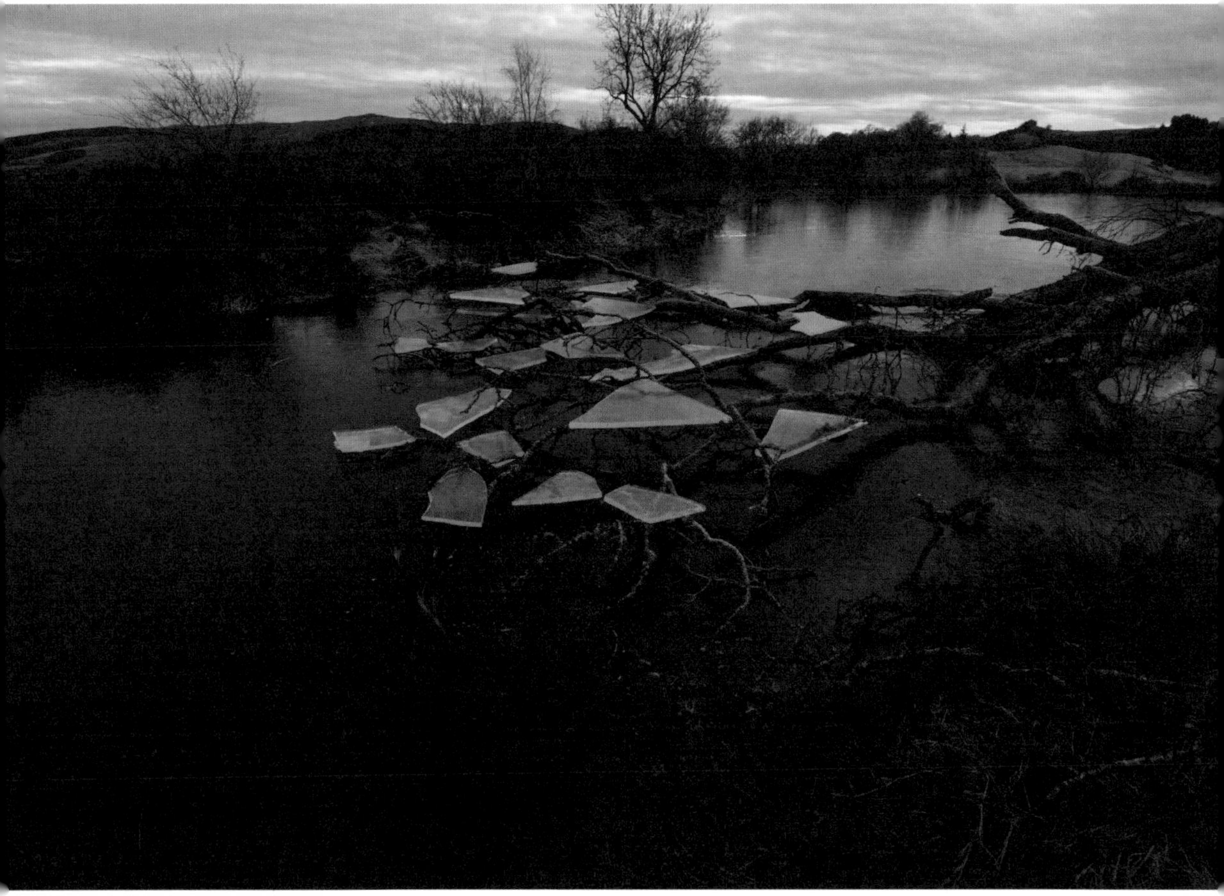

Ice laid on fallen oak. Dumfriesshire, Scotland. 6 December 2023, Andy Goldsworthy, 2023, photography

This sculpture existed temporarily before melting back into the water where Andy Goldsworthy found the ice. The British artist has built a career making ephemeral sculptures using only materials found on site. He harvested these sheets of ice from the small lake into which the oak bough had fallen and carefully arranged them along its branches, working in freezing temperatures and knowing his creation would vanish. Goldsworthy works in overlooked spaces where, for instance, trees have collapsed and begun their slow return to earth - forgotten corners in familiar landscapes. This photograph captures a moment in his collaboration between artist and elements, revealing the graceful architecture of these branches as they exist between living and dead. The work shows us how much beauty already exists in the ordinary wreckage around us, waiting to be noticed.

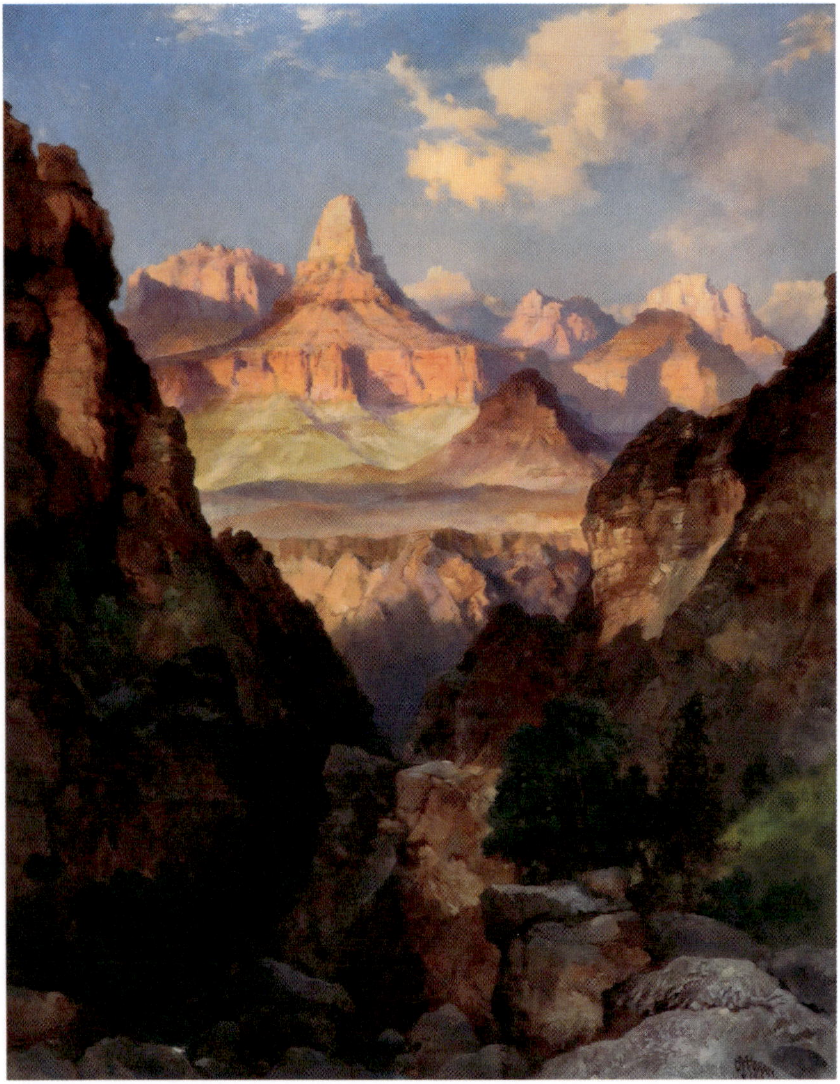

Zoroaster Temple at Sunset, Thomas Moran, 1916, oil on canvas

At 79, Thomas Moran (1837–1926) still painted the Grand Canyon with the enthusiasm of someone discovering it for the first time. Here is Zoroaster Temple, its russet spire catching the day's last light while shadows deepen in the labyrinth below. Moran brilliantly compresses impossible distances into a single frame, drawing viewers into a landscape that Eastern politicians once dismissed as fantasy, until his paintings proved otherwise. His compositions helped convince Congress to protect these territories, making his art a powerful conservation weapon. The genius lies in his selective revelation – showing just enough foreground detail to ground the eye before launching it towards that magnificent central peak, while strategically concealing challenging terrain that would confront any actual visitor. Moran used colour and composition to make Americans value places they might never personally explore; his bold signature choice – 'TYM' for 'Thomas "Yellowstone" Moran' – reveals his confidence as America's premier painter of impossible landscapes.

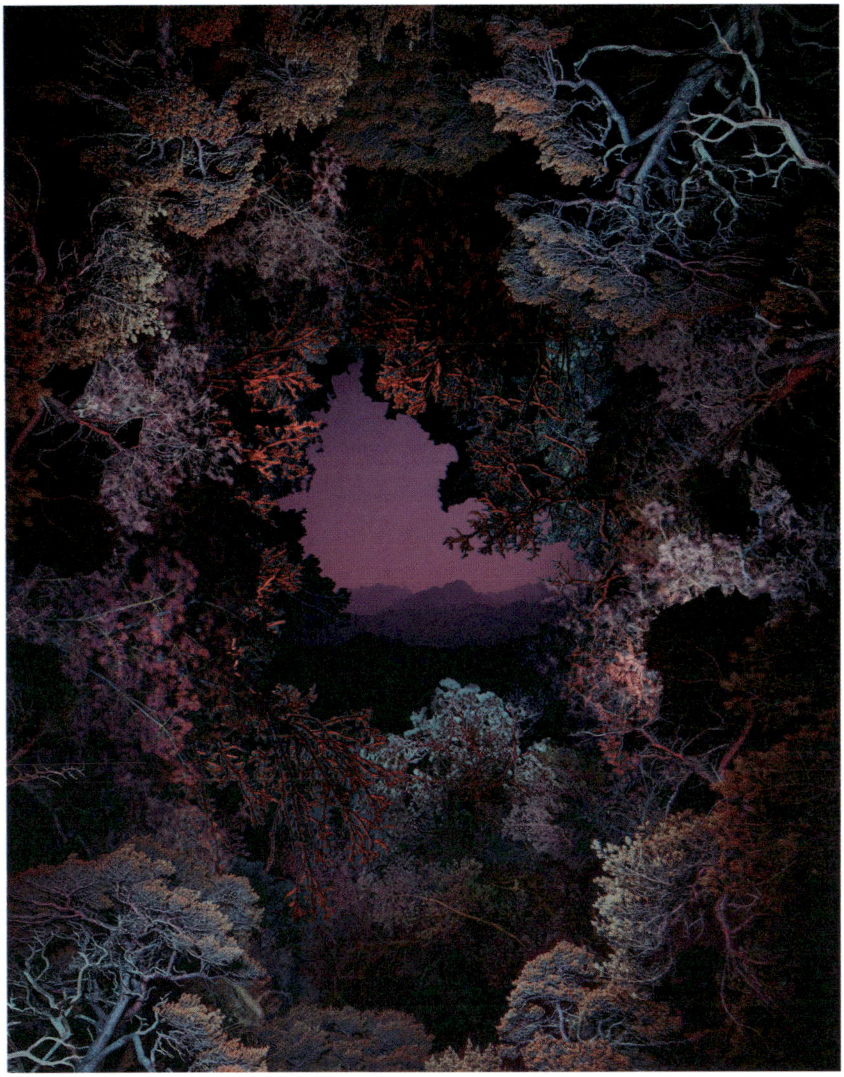

Dimensional Forest, Linda Westin, 2019, photographic collage

Linda Westin stumbled upon magic deep in a shadowy Swedish forest and had both the vision and technical skill to capture it. The Stockholm artist – who left photography to earn a PhD in neuroscience before the camera called her back – found the exact spot where tree branches create this perfect oculus framing distant mountains. Her scientific background isn't separate from her art but fundamental to it; she lights these woods using techniques borrowed from her days illuminating brain cells under microscopes. The otherworldly teals, magentas and burnt oranges aren't Photoshop tricks but infrared photography revealing colours that actually exist beyond human sight. The forest created an extraordinary window here, but only Westin, through her unique double vision as half scientist, half dreamer, found the one spot where you can gaze through it. Through this lens, we see a forest that reveals its secrets only to those who know how to look.

PART THREE

—

REMNANTS, RELICS & REVELATIONS

'Tell me something that only I will ever know, was perhaps what she wanted to ask him, or, What will you give me to remember you by?'

– SHIRLEY JACKSON, *THE HAUNTING OF HILL HOUSE*

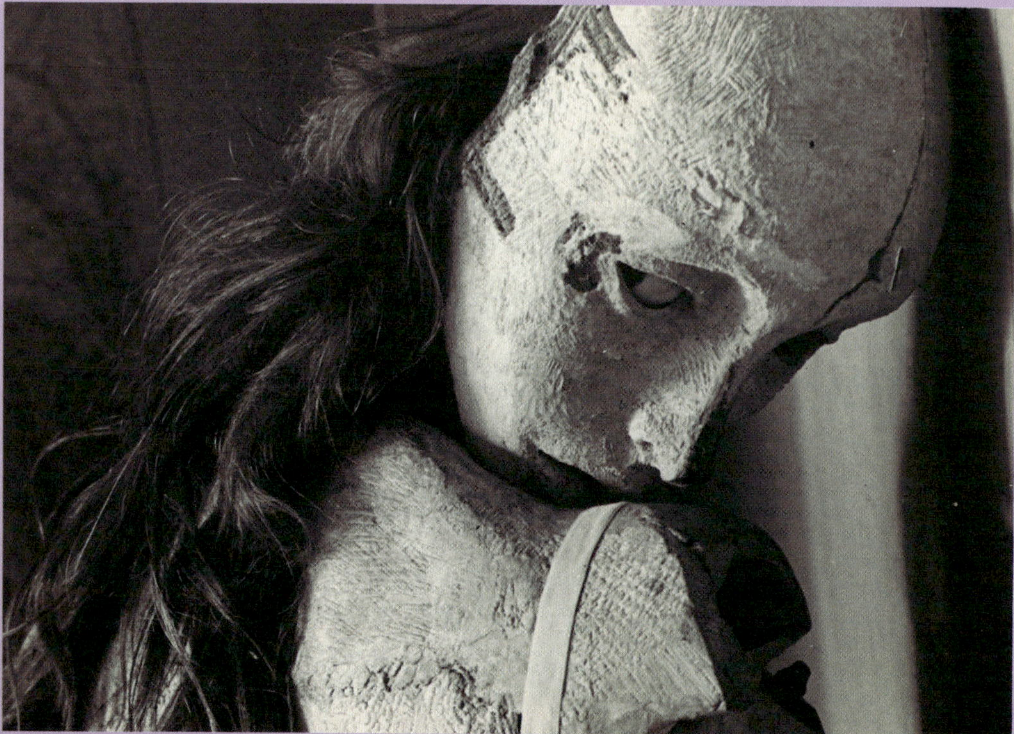

What will remain of us? What traces persist, what memories manifest, what evidence endures? A water-stained photograph between floorboards. A tarnished mirror that belonged to someone long dead. A cloth-bound book written in a script no one remembers how to read. Even IKEA instruction manuals, with their wordless hieroglyphic language, remind us that meaning can slip away the moment we need it most. Such objects turn up in cobwebbed attics, in climate-controlled museum storerooms, in muddy archaeological digs – puzzling bits of debris that resist our attempts to decode them.

These fragments share a curious power: they make the past present again in ways we can't fully explain. Like a haunting that lingers still, a reflection that murmurs secrets, a text whose slippery meaning eludes our understanding yet appears in dreams, these traces whisper that reality has more rooms than we've explored. They preserve what should be lost, persist when they should have vanished, reveal what should remain hidden.

'The past is never dead,' Faulkner reminds us. 'It's not even past.' Perhaps this says less about supernatural forces and more about humans being remarkably bad at letting things go. Consider what this inability to let go has produced: what remains of people haunts us – the restless dead who refuse proper departure, spirits that loiter in familiar spaces, apparitions that materialize in mirrors and darkened windows. The fragments of our own fractured selves trail in our wake: wayward reflections that betray us, unwelcome doubles that challenge our claim to uniqueness, endless eerie repetitions that drain meaning from the familiar. And always, the vast mysteries of what remains of entire civilizations still mock our certainty after centuries.

Even our most recent past becomes incomprehensible with startling speed. VHS tapes already look like ancient artefacts to anyone born after 2000, while floppy discs have achieved the mystique once reserved for stone tablets. We live surrounded by digital ghosts: old URLs that lead nowhere, defunct social media profiles that haunt search results like cyber-poltergeists, email accounts abandoned in the great AOL diaspora of the early 2000s.

Whether etched into cave walls or haunting search results, these mysteries and manifestations have always found their witness in artists. From shamanic visions to forgotten scripts to the digital ghosts we live with now, artists have been the ones compelled to see, and then compelled to tell. Victorian

Opposite: The Doll,
Hans Bellmer, *c.* 1934,
gelatin silver print

artists surrounded themselves with spectral creatures in their self-portraits, documenting visitors only they could see. Some painted mirrors that showed impossible places; others photographed themselves endlessly until their own faces became strangers. Renaissance painters captured melancholic figures amid tools that offered no comfort, while modern artists turned everyday objects into relics behind glass. Each developed visual languages for encounters in the twilight zones where those old standards – logic and reason, understanding and certainty – prove utterly useless guides.

Contemporary artists continue this exploration of encoded meaning and mysterious objects. Installation artists create rooms where memories take physical form. Photographers capture moments when familiar faces become suddenly alien. Digital artists construct encyclopedias for worlds that don't exist, complete with scripts that foil all translation attempts. They venture into spaces where past and present knot themselves together, where what was lost insists on being found, where what was forgotten demands to be remembered.

'What will you give me to remember you by?' Eleanor longs to ask in *The Haunting of Hill House*, but never does. Perhaps this unspoken question echoes through other stories of persistence: from Rebecca's pervasive presence haunting Manderley, to the cursed videotape in *Ringu* demanding to be viewed; from Wilde's rotting portrait of Dorian Gray recording what its subject tries to forget, to the baleful walls of Hill House itself, absorbing the psychic impressions of all who pass within. What do we leave behind that proves we were here? What traces persist beyond our presence? What fragments of ourselves might surface generations later, insisting on their own significance? These aren't just questions about memory or mortality; they're questions about how certain things refuse to relinquish their grip, choosing instead to linger in maddening ways that confound our understanding of time, presence and reality itself.

Throughout centuries and across cultures, artists have documented these attempts to persist beyond the boundaries of time. Their work reveals something profound: what we think of as uncanny or mysterious might simply be the evidence of human longing – every haunted object, every strange reflection, every indecipherable message a different expression of our desperate desire to remain.

Opposite: The Appearance, Karl Wilhelm Diefenbach, *c.* 1890, oil on wood

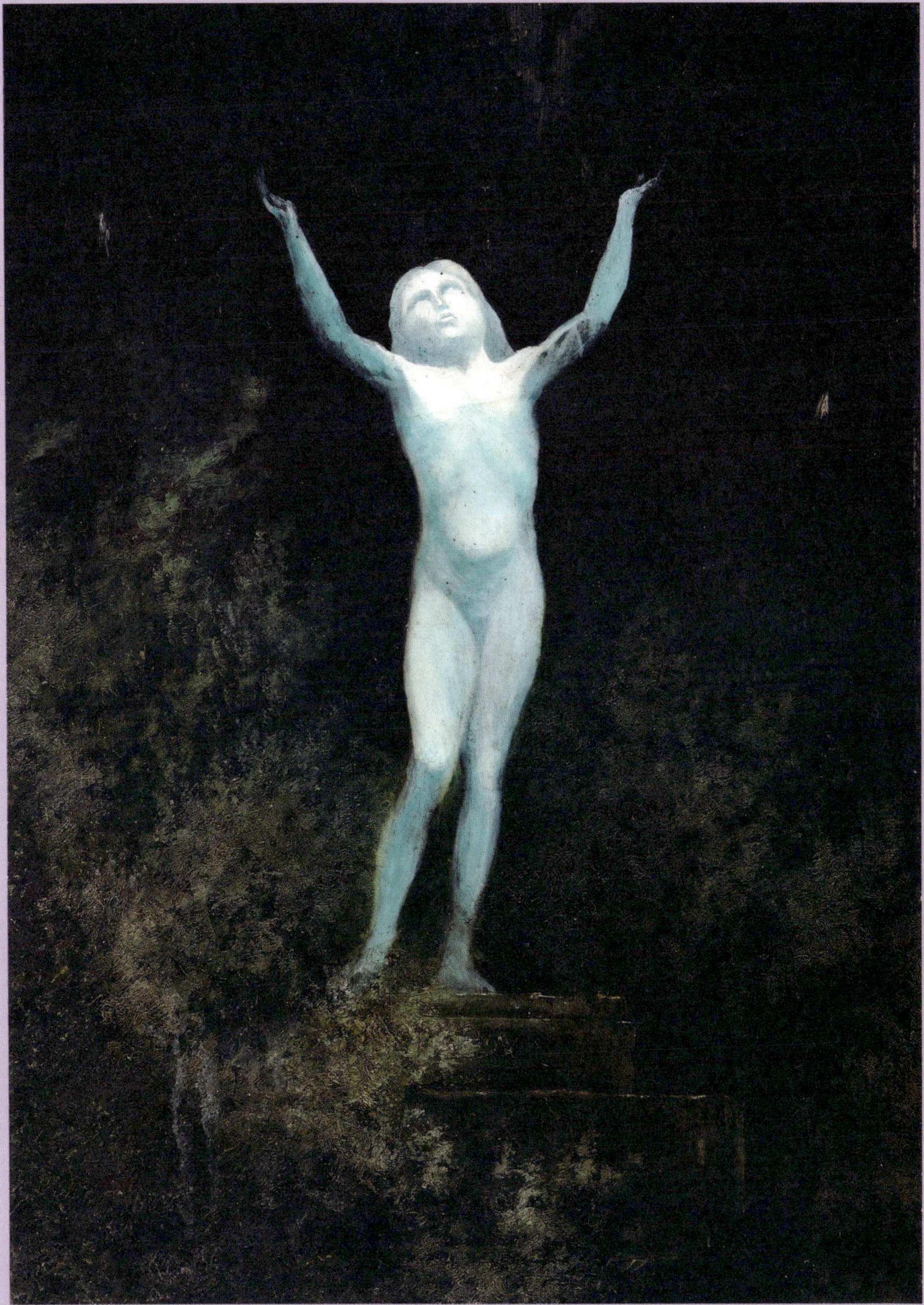

VII

—

RESTLESS SOULS & SPIRIT ENCOUNTERS

'Surely something resides in this heart that is not perishable – and life is more than a dream.'

– MARY WOLLSTONECRAFT

A figure on the staircase that shouldn't exist, visible only when you don't look directly at it. Day after day, returning to the same spot, persistent absence taking up space. Its non-presence somehow more palpable, more insistent than any living visitor. You dread climbing those stairs, knowing it waits there, knowing it has no intention of leaving – but the word intention implies that it is more than it is; it is something that should not possess resolve at all. We've all experienced these moments when there's something present where there should be nothing, something that, ostensibly, ought to have remained safely buried and silent. These aren't just universal fears but universal experiences, surfacing in every culture that's ever entombed its dead and wondered if that's truly the end of the story.

We are then faced with the eerie question of what could all these dead guys possibly want? They wait for us in mirrors and darkened windows. They stand at the foot of our beds while we lie paralysed between waking and sleep. The dead, or something wearing their faces, seem determined to make themselves known, to insist upon their continued existence, to refuse the finality we try to impose upon them. Perhaps they've been waiting all along, not for exorcism but for acknowledgement, for someone to beckon them rather than banish them.

Artists have always been the primary analysts and chroniclers of the dead's persistence, each culture developing distinct visual languages for these encounters. Though perhaps artists aren't just witnessing these encounters – maybe they're summoning them. (Plot twist: artists are part of the problem! The haunting is coming from inside the studio! The real ghost was the artist all along!) The Victorians elevated these ghostly pursuits to cultural obsession. Death pervaded their society, with mortality rates ensuring that the dead outnumbered the living in most families' memories. Their post-mortem photography posed corpses among the living, creating portraits in which death was simply another guest. Soon the dead began appearing uninvited, faces emerging on photographic plates in backgrounds where no one had posed. An entire industry of spirit photography emerged, with mediums producing images of ghostly figures draped in ectoplasm during séances. This fascination influenced countless Victorian artists – from Charles Altamont Doyle's swarms of spectral creatures to Philip Burne-Jones's uncanny wilderness encounters to Richard

Doyle's phantasmal houseguests, each developing their own eerie artistic vocabulary for capturing encounters with the unseen.

The Spiritualist movement reimagined drawing rooms as portals to the beyond. In velvet-curtained parlours, mediums worked in darkness, yet produced detailed spirit drawings with uncanny precision. William Blake claimed to receive visions like the *Ghost of a Flea*, a muscled nightmare with a bowl for drinking blood, while Victorian photographers like William Hope produced spirit photographs with ghostly messages unfurling around their sitters. Pre-Raphaelite artists and illustrators, including John Everett Millais and Elizabeth Eleanor Siddal, crafted haunting scenes in which the dead return with piercing clarity, each contributing to a distinctly Victorian visual language of loss and longing.

This fascination rippled across artistic movements, as Symbolists like Odilon Redon and Francisco Goya explored the shadowlands where nightmares and spirits blur together. Surrealists later expanded these territories. René Magritte and Remedios Varo depicted encounters with apparitions that follow dream logic rather than ghostly convention, while Leonora Carrington populated her canvases with spectral figures caught mid-ritual. Japanese master Katsuhika Hokusai transformed mundane objects into vessels for vengeful spirits, creating a distinctly non-Western approach to manifesting the dead. As photography evolved from silver plates to digital sensors, our obsession with capturing the uncanny remained unchanged. Contemporary artists inherit this legacy. Penny Slinger curates supernatural encounters with her own body as both haunter and haunted. Nona Limmen creates a visual archive of midnight otherworlds, analogue techniques rendering the supernatural as evidence of the eldritch and ethereal. Enigmatic artist Benz and Chang paints watercolours that resemble forgotten antique spirit photographs, leaving viewers holding their breath, listening for ghostly rustles and sighs from beyond the frame.

Perhaps what draws us to these spectral encounters isn't merely curiosity but a profound recognition that death's finality has always been the most suspect of our certainties. We sense this in our collective narratives, from ancient folklore to modern literature, where characters like Toni Morrison's Beloved and the spectral presence in Emily Brontë's *Wuthering Heights* demonstrate how the dead refuse clean departures. Just as Catherine's ghost insists to Lockwood, 'I'm come home,' so Morrison reminds us, 'Some things go. Pass on. Some things just stay.' Artists continue exploring these encounters not to prove the existence of spirits, but to speak to fundamentally human experiences: our relationship with absence, our navigation of loss, our certainty that a space can be simultaneously empty and full. These works reveal that ghost stories were never really about the dead at all. They're about the living – how we process mystery, how we hold memory, how we learn to live with the remnants of presence that persist long after form has vanished. That man on the stairs, you just gotta live with him, I guess.

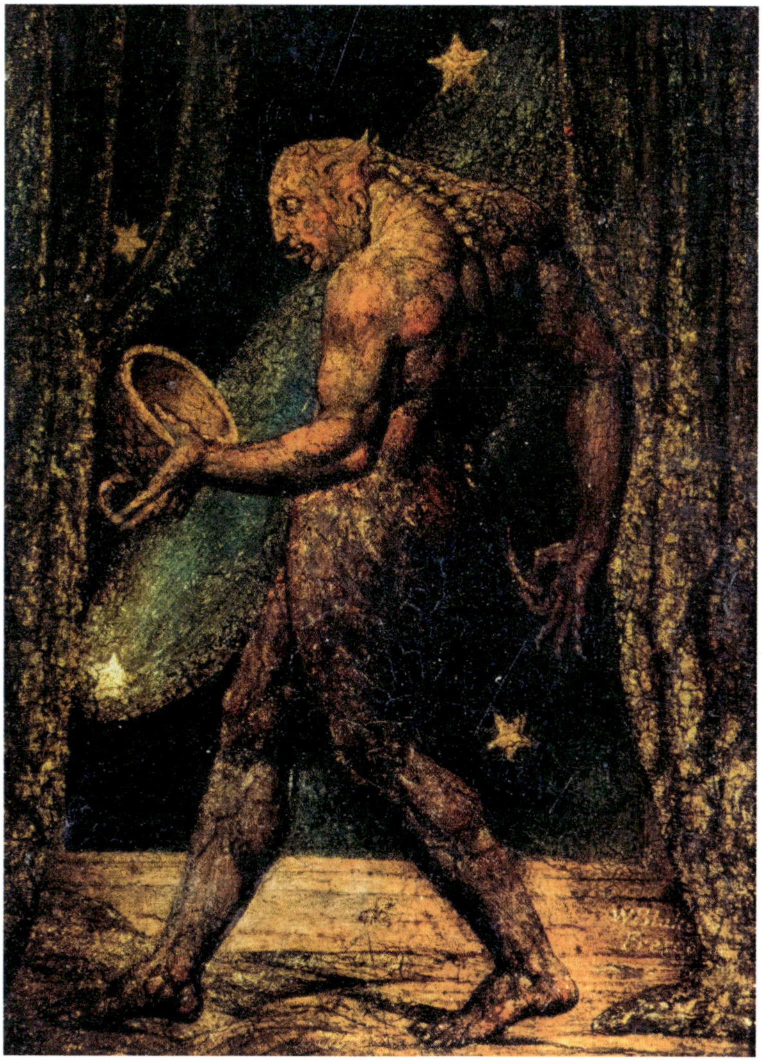

The Ghost of a Flea, William Blake, *c.* 1819–20, tempera and gold on mahogany

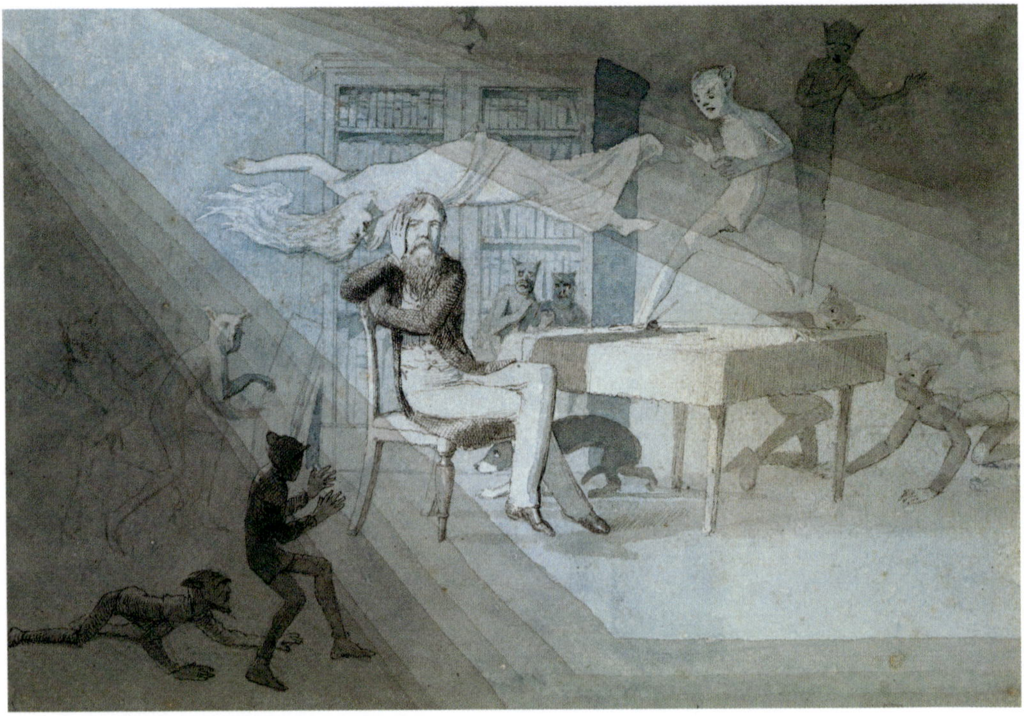

Meditation, Self-portrait, Charles Altamont Doyle, 1885–93, watercolour on paper

Exhaustion weighs on Charles Altamont Doyle (1832–93) as he slumps at his desk, but it's hard to get any rest when your studio doubles as a boarding house for the deceased. Institutionalized for what authorities deemed insanity, the father of Sherlock Holmes creator Arthur Conan Doyle produced this extraordinary self-portrait during his confinement years. Part human and part animal, the spectral creatures writhe and cavort through his study with unsettling familiarity. His weary posture, head supported by one hand amid the chaotic apparitions, creates a startling paradox: it's precisely his exhausted stillness that amplifies the frenetic energy surrounding him. The packed bookshelf suggests a lifetime of learning, perhaps overtaken by visions that his Victorian contemporaries could neither validate nor dismiss. Doyle's meticulous watercolour technique lends these phantoms disturbing credibility, as though he were cataloguing actual visitations rather than conjuring fantasies.

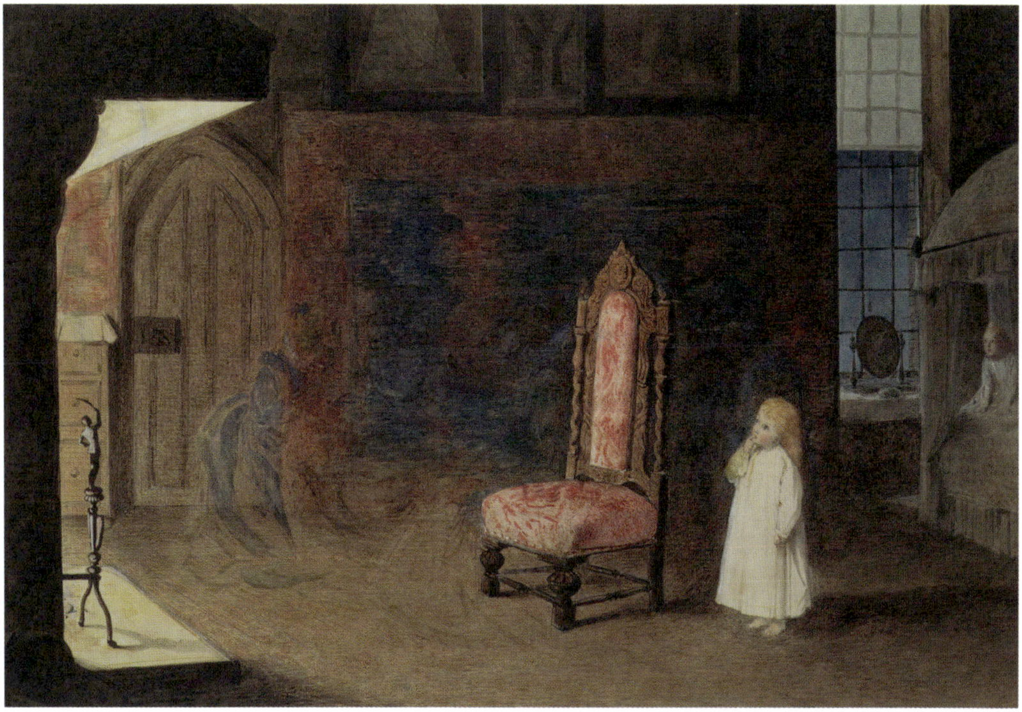

Ooh Ghosties, Richard Doyle, nineteenth century, oil on canvas

A phantasmal houseguest drops by in Richard 'Dickie' Doyle's (1824–83) whimsical illustration, in which a small girl in her nightgown greets her luminous visitor with more curiosity than terror, while her uncertain sibling hangs back in bed, content to leave the paranormal investigation in someone else's hands. The ghost, all wispy edges and translucent drapery, hovers in the doorway's shadow, caught between worlds, like a neighbour who's popped round to borrow sugar rather than rattle chains or prophesy doom. Moonlight streams through leaded windows, casting dramatic shadows across tapestried walls as the children show different reactions to the supernatural: one paralysed with fascination; the other displaying irrepressible curiosity. Doyle, the artistic uncle of Sherlock Holmes creator Arthur Conan Doyle, brings his signature whimsy to what should be terrifying but instead feels delightfully domestic. After years illustrating Dickens's Christmas tales and designing *Punch* magazine's iconic cover, Doyle knew exactly how to make the uncanny feel almost cosy.

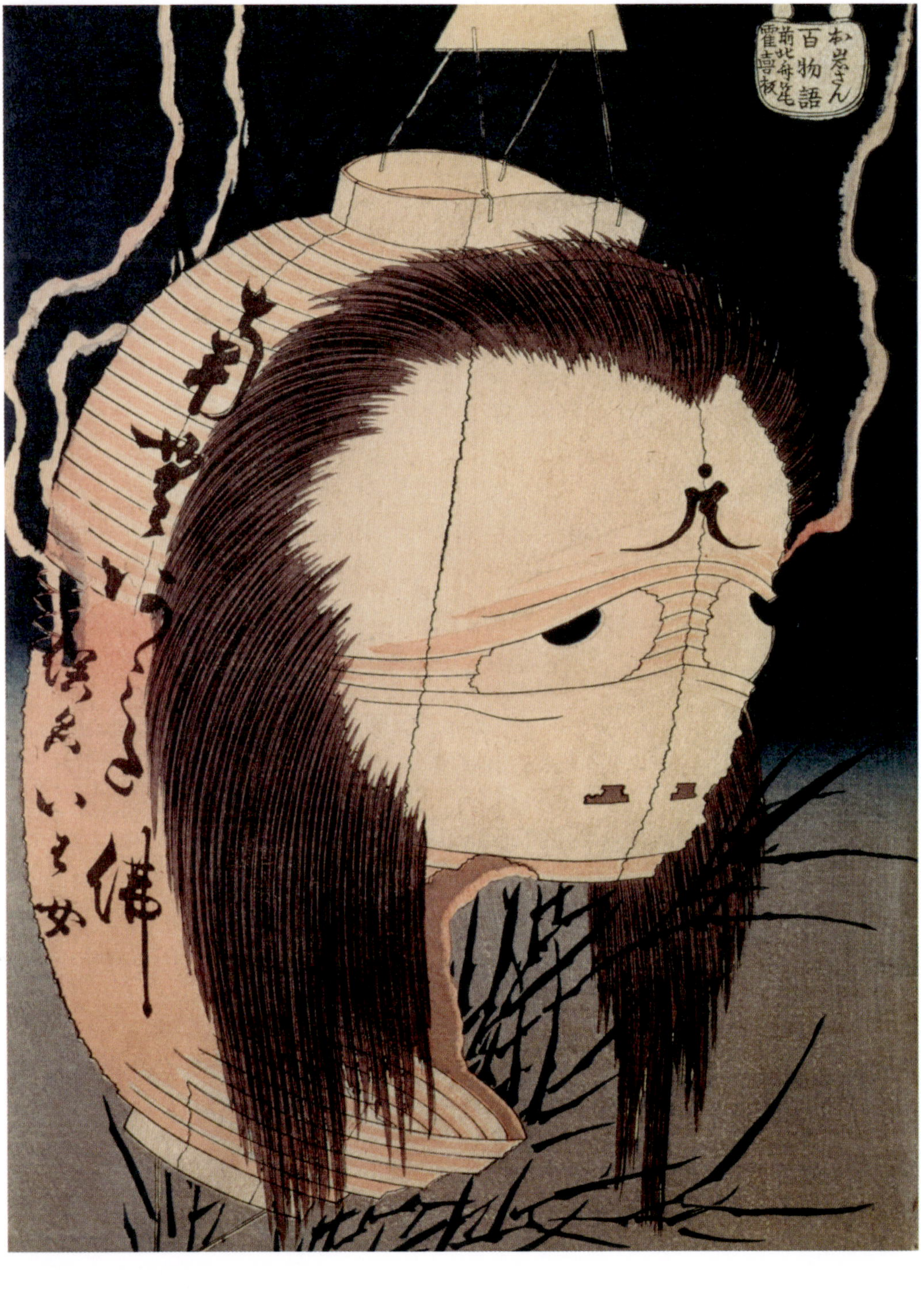
お岩さん
百物語

Right: A Ghostly Vision, Francisco Goya, 1801, oil on canvas

Francisco Goya (1746-1828) wrestled this nocturnal apparition onto canvas in under half an hour, working with such urgency that he skipped preliminary sketching entirely. Rediscovered in 2016 after vanishing for 90 years, this small painting emerged from Goya's post-illness period, when deafness had turned him towards darker visions. The horned spectre draped in darkness, face barely suggested, hovers menacingly before human witnesses rendered in nothing more than quick strokes against ochre darkness. Two centuries before death metal or dungeon synth existed, Goya had already painted the perfect album cover. Art historian Arturo Ansón Navarro declared it unlike anything else from its era, a raw transmission rather than a considered composition. Was this Goya's private demon made manifest? A hallucination born from illness? Or something he actually witnessed during sickness, when strange things become visible to those suffering?

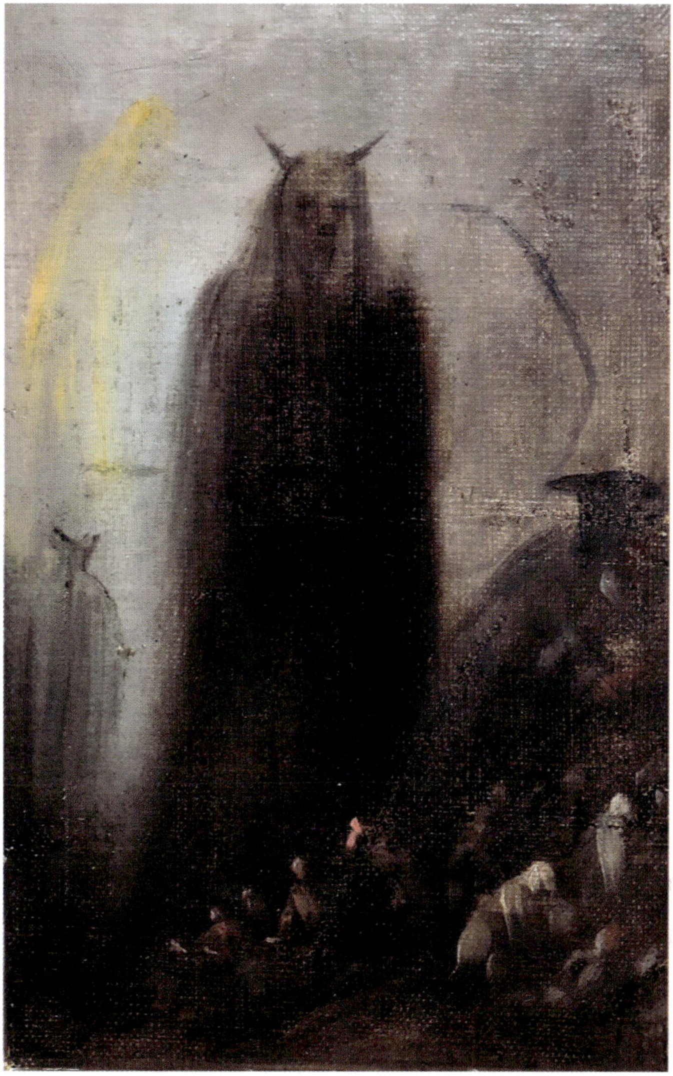

Opposite: The Ghost of Oiwa, Katsushika Hokusai, *c.* 1831–32, woodblock print

The paper lantern in Katsushika Hokusai's (1760-1849) woodblock shines with something other than oil or candlelight. The renowned master of waves and supernatural subjects creates an unsettling posession in which household objects quietly reveal they've become refuge for the wronged. Within the lantern's illuminated surface, a woman's disfigured features materialize. This is Oiwa, the betrayed wife whose story of poisoning and revenge is legendary in Japanese theatre. Her drooping eye and dishevelled hair bear the marks of the toxic 'beauty cream' that destroyed her beauty and her life. The distinctive Berlin blue suffusing the image creates an otherworldly radiance that Hokusai's contemporaries would have immediately recognized as spectral territory. His genius lies in restraint - just enough detail to trigger recognition, while leaving the imagination to fill in darker possibilities. For some souls, eternity means being trapped within the very objects that witnessed their suffering, forever fused with their final agony.

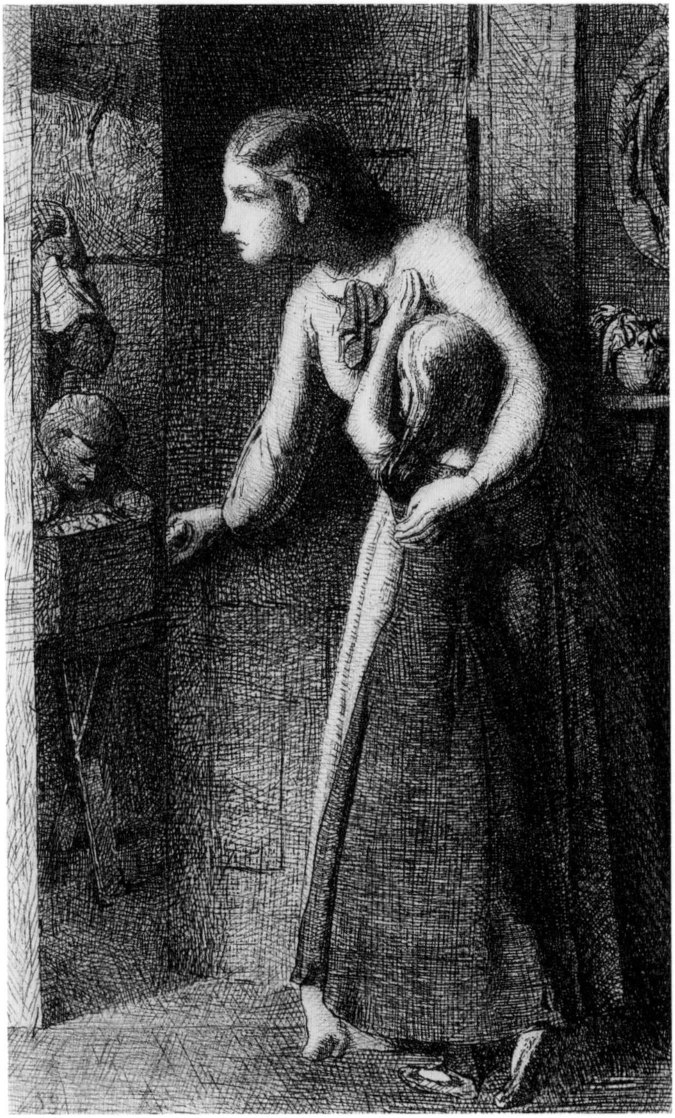

Left: The Haunted House, Simeon Solomon, 1855, etching on ivory wove paper, laid down on ivory wove paper

A doorway frames a haunting revelation in Simeon Solomon's (1840–1905) etching, in which a woman and child peer into a room where mourners gather around a coffin. Created when the artist was just 15, the work captures a terrible moment of discovery, as his figures stand frozen at what they've found. Solomon's dense cross-hatching builds shadows upon shadows, creating an atmosphere where grief thickens the very air. The woman's protective arm encircles the child clinging to her side, both paralysed between the urge to flee and the magnetic pull of witnessing mortality. This forgotten masterpiece hints at the visionary talent that would later be eclipsed by personal scandal and societal prejudice, leaving one of Victorian art's dreamiest artists buried in history's silence, still waiting for the world to remember what it lost.

Opposite: Phantasma, Nona Limmen, 2023, photography

Candlelight illuminates a spectral presence in Nona Limmen's eerie composition, in which a figure completely enshrouded in diaphanous white fabric stands frozen on a staircase landing, five flickering flames held aloft like beacons summoning lost souls. The Dutch photographer subverts the classic Gothic novel setup, but perhaps there's a wickedly unsettling twist here? What if the phantom pursuing the heroine through darkened hallways is actually her own ghost, returned from some future demise? Limmen's analogue techniques contribute a distinctive grainy texture that makes this manifestation feel like genuine evidence rather than artistic creation, as though something otherworldly has impressed itself directly onto film. The figure's deliberate pose creates unbearable tension, a held breath that can never be released. The usual Gothic narrative assumes we're watching someone else's nightmare, but Limmen suggests something far more disturbing: we might be witnessing our own spectral future.

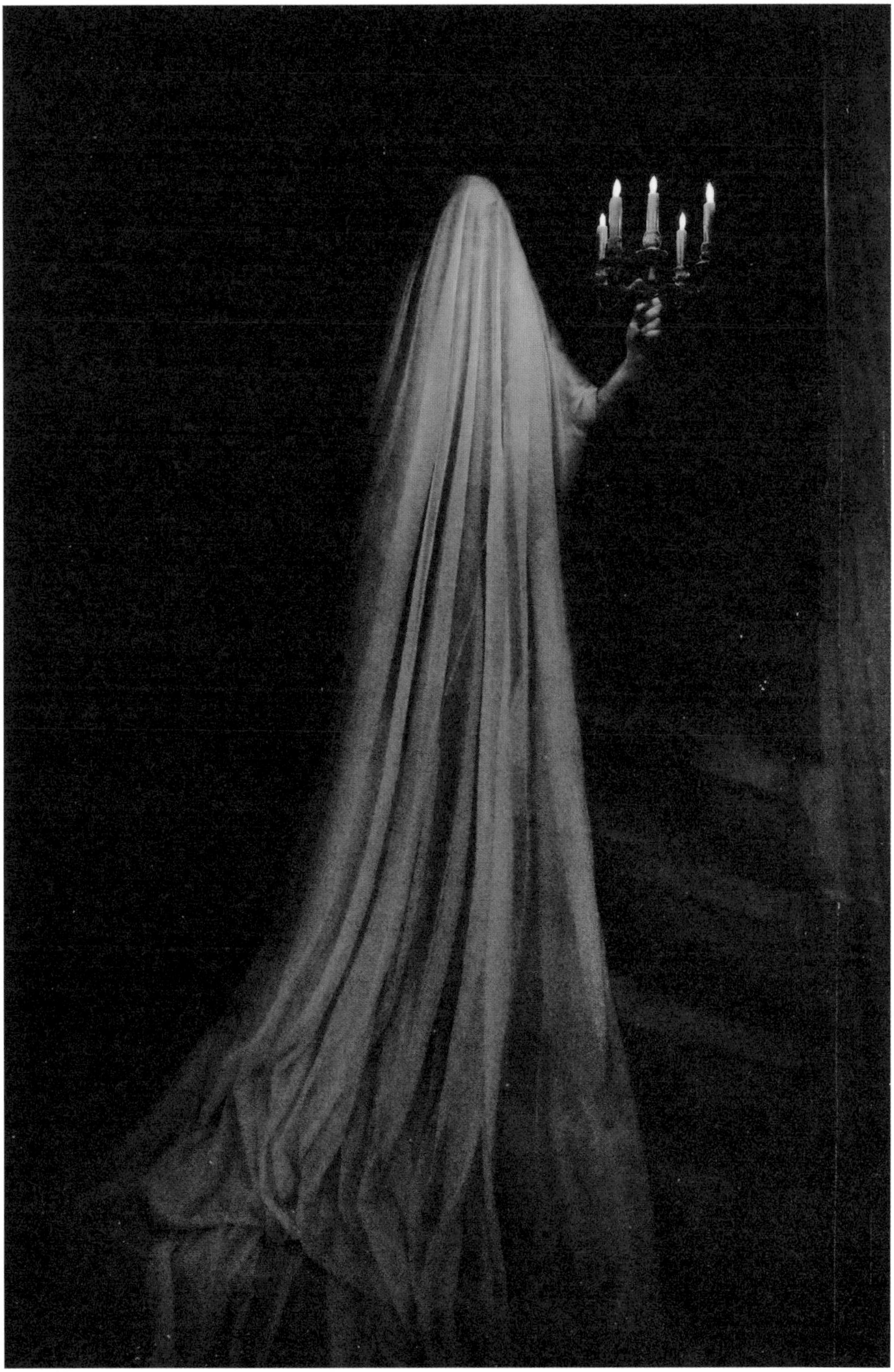

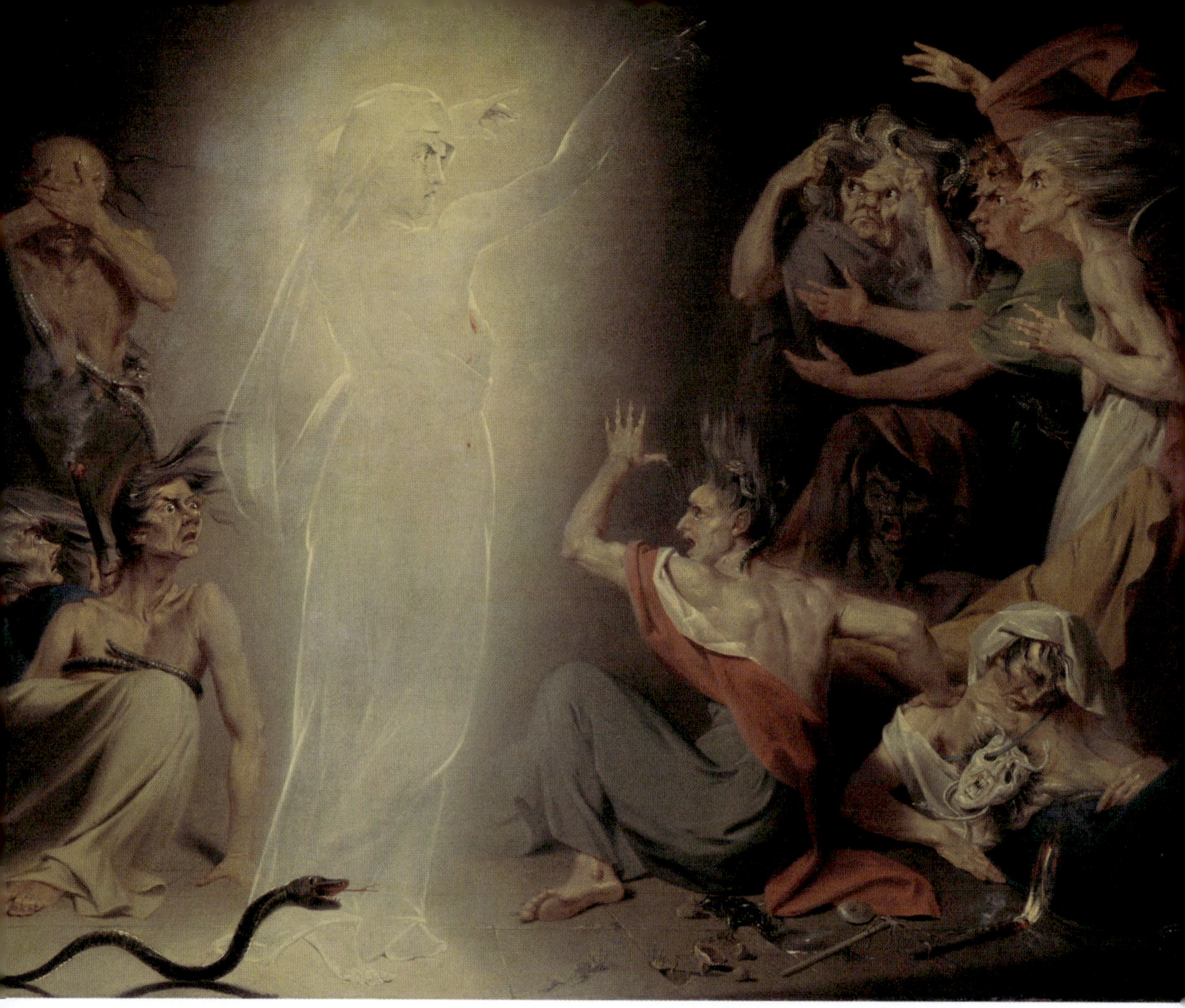

The Ghost of Clytemnestra Awakening the Furies, John Downman, 1781, oil on panel

John Downman (1750–1824) abandoned painting pretty society ladies to create this nightmare of maternal fury, and Georgian audiences never forgave him for it. Clytemnestra's ghost rises from the underworld with imperious authority, summoning the snake-haired Furies to pursue her son Orestes, who killed her after she murdered his father. Downman's expressionistic approach shocked viewers accustomed to his polished portraits of aristocratic children. Here, faces contort beyond all decorum, bodies twist into unnatural postures, and vengeance spreads like infection between worlds. The dead woman's grievances poison the living, turning family bonds into supernatural prosecution. Horace Walpole recoiled in disgust, and critics warned that Downman had 'lost himself' beyond his talents, but the artist had discovered something far more interesting than flattering the wealthy. This broken family drama plays out in a cosmic court, where a mother calls down divine justice against her own son – family dysfunction on a truly mythic scale.

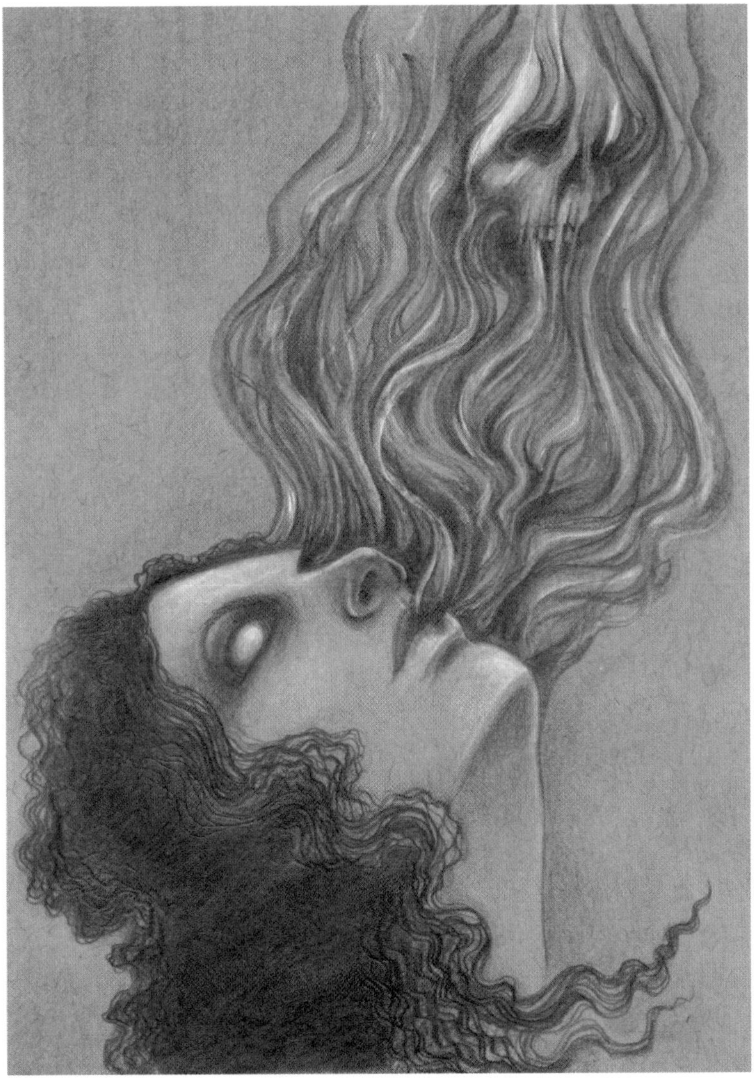

Death Smoke, Becky Munich, 2016, graphite and coloured pencils on toned paper

In Becky Munich's haunting illustration, giving up the ghost becomes an actual physical process, with ectoplasmic tendrils pouring from parted lips to coil upwards into spectral form. The contemporary artist renders this supernatural emanation with delicate lines and a subdued palette of soft greys, blues and whispers of pink against a dreamlike atmosphere. The subject's head tilts backwards in serene release, her pale face captured in profile, hair cascading in midnight waves, her eyes blank, unseeing. Munich's work merges beauty with horror, creating figures who command their darkness rather than fall victim to it, who relish their ghostly encounters and otherworldly dealings. The expression suggests not fear but willing partnership with the supernatural forces passing through mortal flesh. What emerges appears to be ancestral knowledge or buried secrets finally taking vaporous form, claiming a separate existence as it unfurls into the ether.

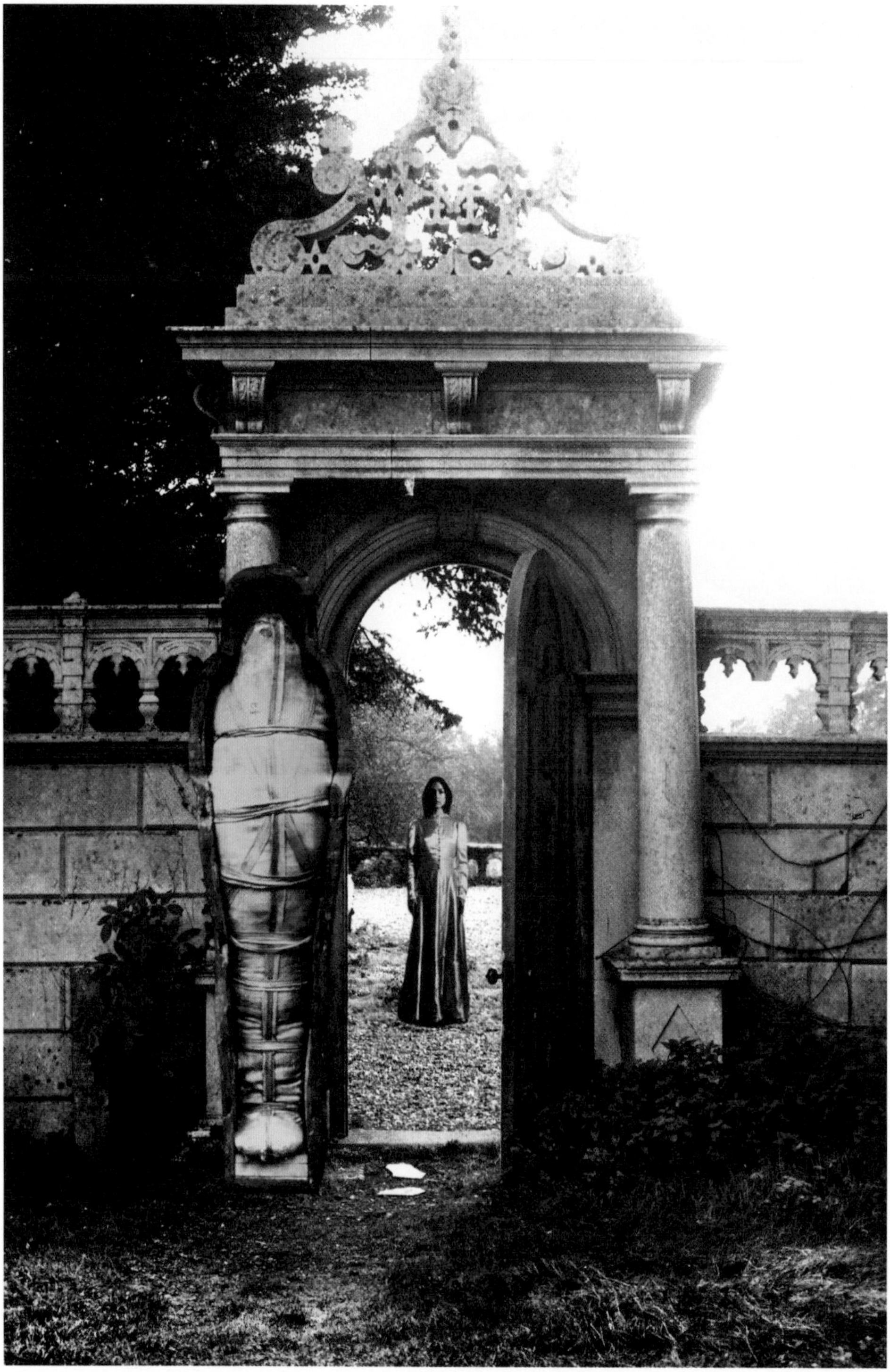

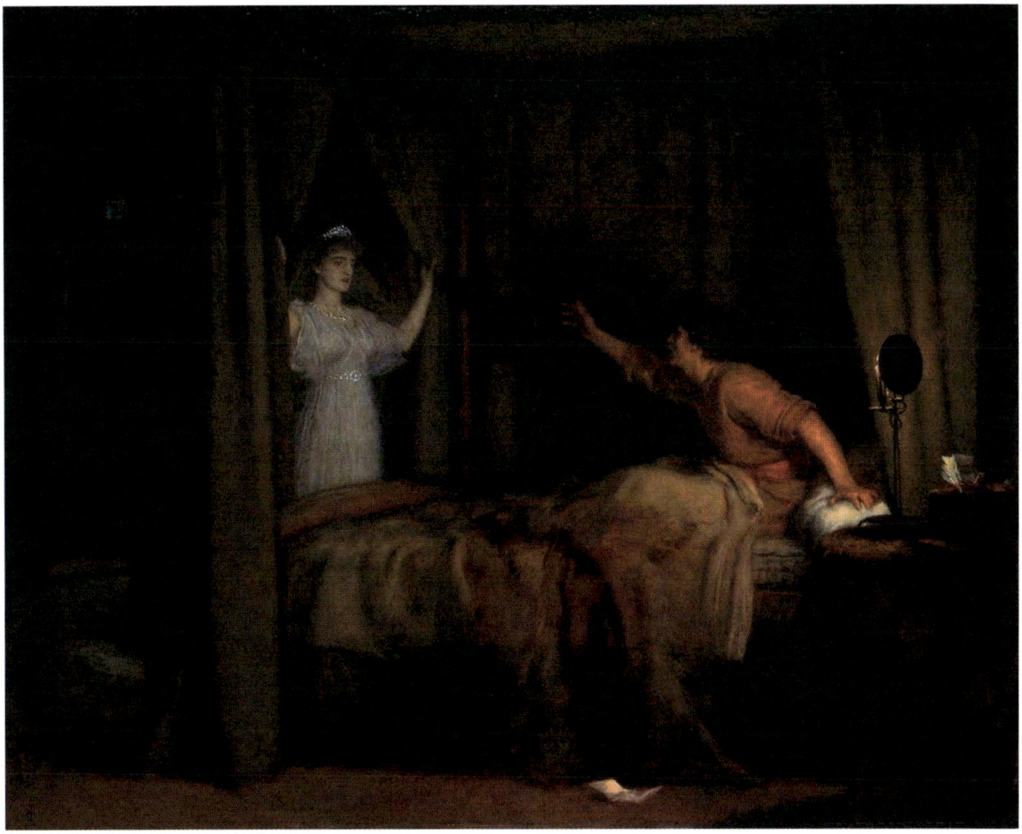

Opposite: Self Preservation,
Penny Slinger, 1970–77,
photo collage on card

A threshold beckons the dead in Penny Slinger's haunting photo-collage *Self Preservation*, in which a figure in flowing white hovers beyond an ornate doorway, while a stone sarcophagus stands open to its left. Created during Slinger's seven-year 'An Exorcism' series (1970-77), this blue-toned dreamscape transforms an abandoned English mansion into a stage for supernatural theatre. The feminist Surrealist uses her own photographed body as both artistic material and psychological subject, creating a ghost story in which she stars as both haunter and haunted. Unlike Victorian spirit photography that positioned women as passive mediums, Slinger becomes the active architect of her own supernatural encounter. The open sarcophagus reveals its shrouded occupant, raising questions about whether we're witnessing a departure or an arrival. The ambiguity feels deliberate, suggesting Slinger's interest not in resolving mysteries but in staging them, using the supernatural as a lens for exploring the psychology of transformation.

Above: Speak! Speak!, John Everett
Millais, 1895, oil on canvas

A spectral bride glows with impossible brilliance in John Everett Millais' (1829-96) dramatically Victorian ghost story rendered in oil. A young man bolts upright in his bed, arm flung forwards in a gesture hovering between terror and desperate longing, while his dead lover stands resplendent in wedding finery at the foot of his bed. Love letters scattered across his nightstand suggest he summoned her through obsessive remembrance, a midnight séance of the heart. When asked whether she was a genuine ghost or a living woman, Millais gave his best answer: 'I don't know either... nor does he,' pointing to his painted protagonist. This late-career masterpiece was scorned by some critics but adored by the public, who recognized the universal fantasy Millais had captured: the possibility that grief might break the laws of nature and bring back our beloved dead, if only for one impossible conversation.

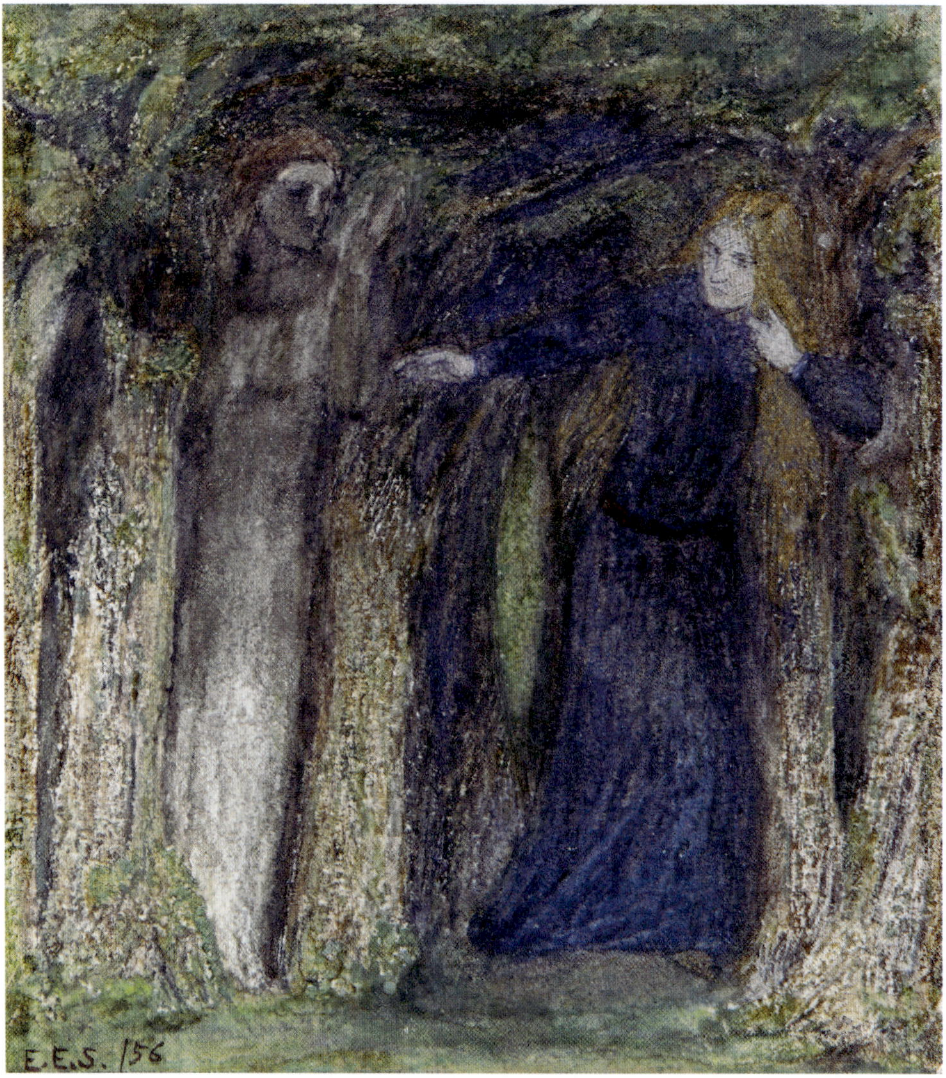

The Haunted Wood, Elizabeth Eleanor Siddal, 1856, gouache on paper

A ghostly manifestation emerges among twisted trees in Elizabeth Eleanor Siddal's (1829–62) haunting gouache, in which a red-haired woman confronts an apparition of herself within the darkened forest While history tends to remember Siddal as a Pre-Raphaelite muse and Rossetti's doomed wife, this work suggests her considerable artistic talent and distinctive vision. Siddal's stylized approach, influenced by her study of medieval manuscripts and early Italian art, creates an otherworldly atmosphere perfectly suited for this supernatural meeting. Her own poem 'A Silent Wood' provides eerie accompaniment: 'Frozen like a thing of stone / I sit in thy shadow but not alone.'
Perhaps this work reveals Siddal's understanding of Victorian supernatural anxieties, or maybe it foreshadows her own artistic fate as the ghost in the Pre-Raphaelite attic, her creative spirit overshadowed by her role as model and muse.

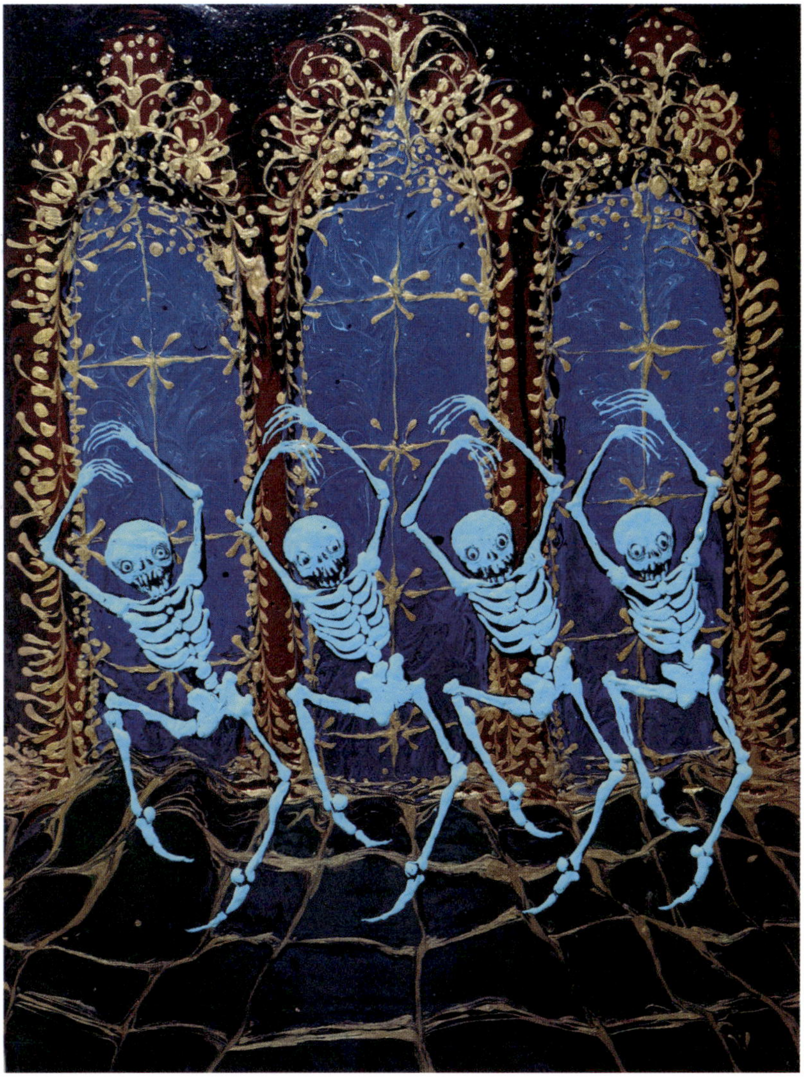

Swan Lake number 2, Anna Mond, 2024, acrylic on wood panel

Four electric turquoise skeletons strike balletic poses behind ornate arched windows, their bones glowing like radioactive stage lights, in Anna Mond's gleefully macabre take on *Swan Lake*. The artist operates in what they call 'Fantasticalizm' - a visual prism that transforms everything into something gloriously unhinged. Reality tilts and warps through Mond's filter, everyday scenes becoming stages for skeletal performers and goggle-eyed creatures who cavort in garish, gooey blobs of colour. This corps de ballet performs against swirling blues and rich reds, arms curved gracefully overhead, legs bent mid-arabesque, utterly undeterred by their complete lack of flesh. The mosaic floor beneath them pulses with dark blues and greens, while ornate golden vines frame the arched windows. Mond paints spirits who chose eternal dance rehearsal over peaceful rest - souls for whom mortality was just an inconvenient costume change, death merely an opportunity to perfect their grand jetés for all eternity.

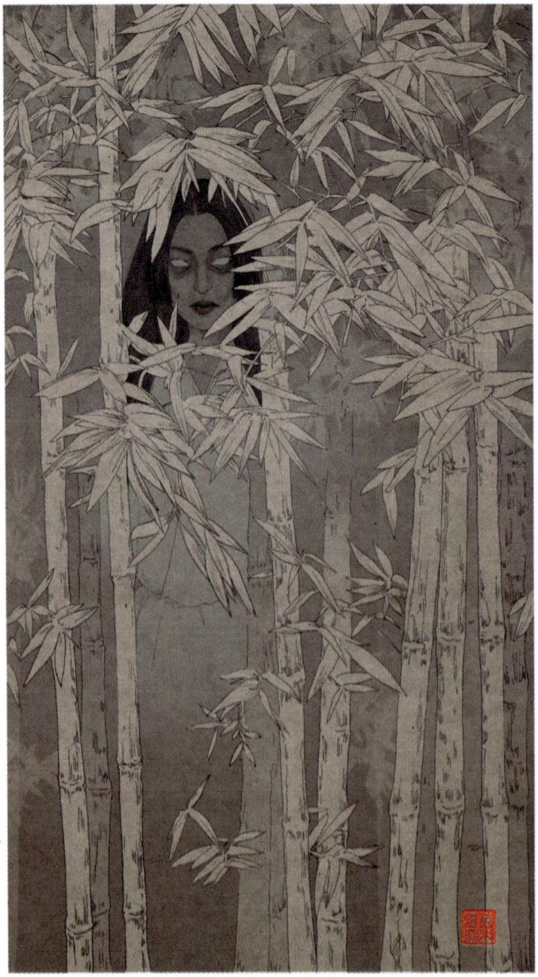

Left: 孤魂 *(The Wandering Ghost)*, Matsuyama Miyabi, 2019, digital

Bamboo stalks create an ethereal sanctuary in this composition, in which a female spectre stands among shifting patterns of light and shadow, her vacant eyes gazing out from a face partially obscured by nature. Matsuyama Miyabi's muted palette of greys and beiges transforms ordinary bamboo into something otherworldly, creating a space where this apparition seems perfectly at home. Unlike Western ghost traditions, which love their dramatic manifestations, Miyabi captures something more subtle and atmospheric, perhaps like the yūrei from Japanese folklore, or maybe just another kind of spirit that dwells within the natural world rather than barging in to disrupt it. The bamboo both reveals and conceals the ghost, creating a visual rhythm where she seems to belong among the stalks. Miyabi offers no clear story for this wandering spirit's presence, instead inviting us to simply witness this quiet moment in which the spectral and the natural worlds somehow share the same space.

Opposite: Eunice Lubovska's Ectoplasmic Apparition, 1924, Benz and Chang, 2023, watercolour on cold-pressed watercolour paper

A shadowy companion materializes from darkness in Benz and Chang's haunting composition, a hollow-eyed wraith emerging into a shared existence with its human counterpart. The phantom hovers in perfect suspense between manifestation and dissolution, its face more defined than its trailing form, as if caught in a fleeting moment of paranormal perambulation. The relationship unfolds in ambiguity - the human figure's hand rests both on their own shoulder and within the apparition's nebulous form, establishing an electric circuit of connection between worlds. Drawing from spirit photography and Victorian séance records, the artist conjures images that appear discovered rather than crafted, like forgotten evidence of supernatural encounters unearthed from some private collector's hidden archive. Through these historical aesthetics, Benz and Chang explores profound transformative moments - encounters with mortality, grief and mystical experience - where ordinary reality momentarily parts to reveal something impossible yet undeniable staring back at us through the veil.

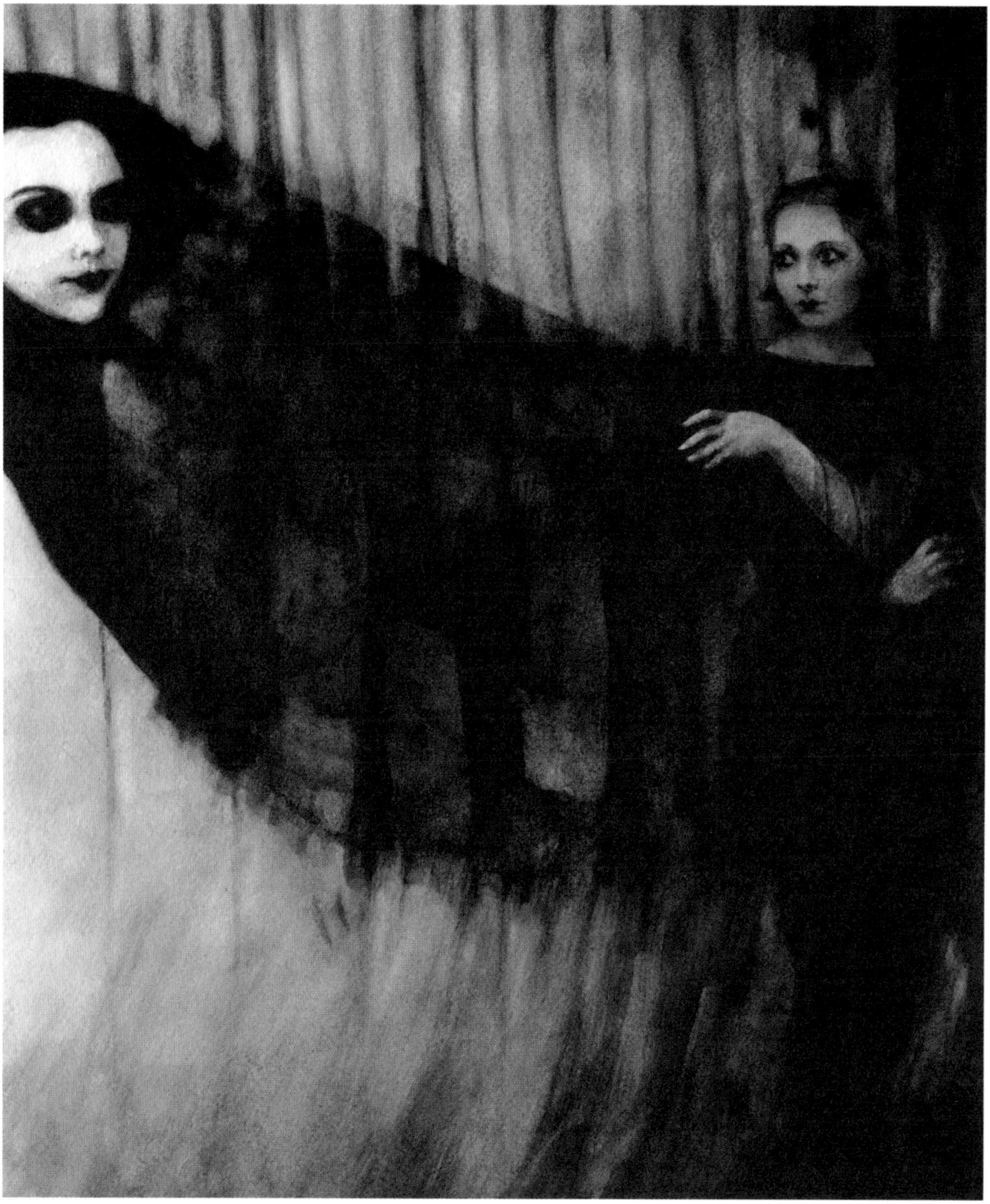

VIII

THE UNCANNY FAMILIAR

'He perfectly recognized his nocturnal visitor. The nocturnal visitor was no other than himself...'

– FYODOR DOSTOYEVSKY, *THE DOUBLE*

Stand before a mirror at midnight and watch your reflection waver in the darkened glass like a daguerreotype coming to life, as if it were contemplating untethering from its silver prison. Antique porcelain dolls sit on dusty cabinet shelves, their cracked and faded faces paradoxically insipid and sinister, their gleaming marble eyes staring with hollow intensity. Department store mannequins stand in perfect formation under flickering fluorescent lights, the sheen of their plastic skin too flawless, too smooth – identical and perfect. It's as if somewhere between the first and hundredth copy, the contract between what you're perceiving and your ability to process it becomes null and void. Even your own name, whispered 50 times in a dark room, stops making sense, becomes abstract gibberish. These are the moments when we feel betrayed by the familiar – when reflections misbehave, when repetition collapses meaning in on itself, when the home of your own body insists it never invited you inside.

This fascination with doubles permeates our culture, from *Orphan Black*'s twins and clones to the uncanny valley of deepfakes, from the shadow selves emerging from *Twin Peaks*' Black Lodge mirrors to the eerie doubles of Jordan Peele's *Us*. Traditional masked performances like Japanese Noh theatre or the Italian commedia dell'arte derive their uncanny power from the tension between the performer's living body and the mask's fixed expression.

Perfect copies unnerve us because they shouldn't exist in nature, where even identical twins carry subtle differences and no two grains of sand are alike. Folklore across cultures warns us of this truth: to meet your double is to meet your death, to glimpse your own face in an unexpected place is to see your doom foretold. Foreseen and fated, these encounters promise nothing good. Something in our primitive brain recoils from perfect duplication, as if recognizing an ontological threat to our very being, the simulacrum challenging the original's right to exist. Even our deepest stories reflect this abhorrence: 'Mirrors and copulation are abominable,' wrote Borges, 'since they multiply the numbers of men.'

Perhaps what makes these encounters so profoundly unsettling is how they challenge our own uniqueness, our very claim to existence. When faced with our double, which version is more real? What if the copy is better at being us than we are? If we are not who we think we are, who are we? And what of the mirror itself, that seemingly ordinary object that can multiply worlds, trap souls and open doorways? We're drawn to our reflections and our doubles for the same reason we're unsettled by them – they both compel and repel our attention. They smuggle in other selves we might have been, other realities pressing against the thin membrane of the familiar.

Mirrors have been bamboozling us for centuries, and artists have been documenting the evidence. Dutch painters created works where mirrors open onto impossible rooms. In Jan van Eyck's *Arnolfini Portrait*, a convex mirror reveals an additional room, capturing figures who stand just out of sight. Caravaggio caught Narcissus bent towards his reflection in dark water, the real youth and his reflection creating a perfect circle, each as solid and substantial as the other. The Surrealists took this obsession further. Dante Gabriel Rossetti's woodland lovers get ambushed by the ultimate third-wheel situation: themselves, materializing in the gloaming, turning an intimate moment into existential slapstick. Frida Kahlo split herself in two, her two exposed hearts connected by a blood vessel one self attempts to sever. Egon Schiele painted himself as warring twins locked in visible argument, while Johannes Gumpp created a mind-bending recursive loop – painting himself painting himself, in an endless hall of mirrors.

Contemporary artists continue probing these uncanny territories through vast installations in which mirrors multiply space endlessly, paintings where figures hover between being originals and copies, and photographs incorporating masks that create disturbing doubling effects. Gillian Wearing literally wears her own face as a mask. Mike Worrall's reflections multiply across rain-slicked streets, wandering independently of their source. Identity becomes performance; authenticity becomes the ultimate masquerade. Digital technology hasn't banished these anxieties but multiplied them exponentially. Every smartphone now contains a mirror that watches back. Our virtual avatars move through online spaces, versions of ourselves that might be more real to others than our physical bodies. Social media profiles function as digital twins, sometimes acting autonomously through algorithms, posting content we've forgotten creating. The persistent feeling of being doubled, copied and watched has become an inevitable part of modern existence, further intensifying our existential discomfort with these uncanny reflections of ourselves.

The Arnolfini Portrait,
Jan van Eyck, 1434,
oil on oak

Look closely enough, for long enough, at anything, and you might see it flicker and blur at the edges. You might see its shadow undulate on the wall, slither down to the carpet, unfurl its tenebrous limbs. Did you see that? No one believes you. But there, right there! That figure at the edge of your vision, turning the corner just as you look. The one wearing your face. The one who noticed you watching. The one who's already standing behind you right now, covetous breath on your neck, waiting after all these years to take on the possibly not-so-unique role of being you.

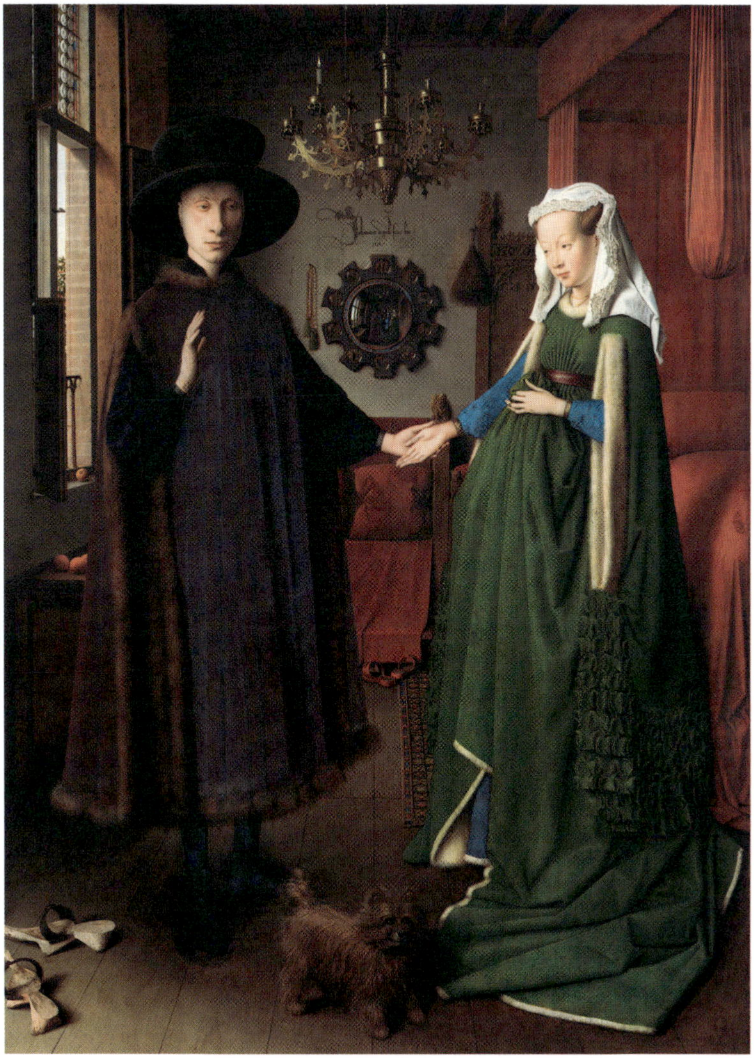

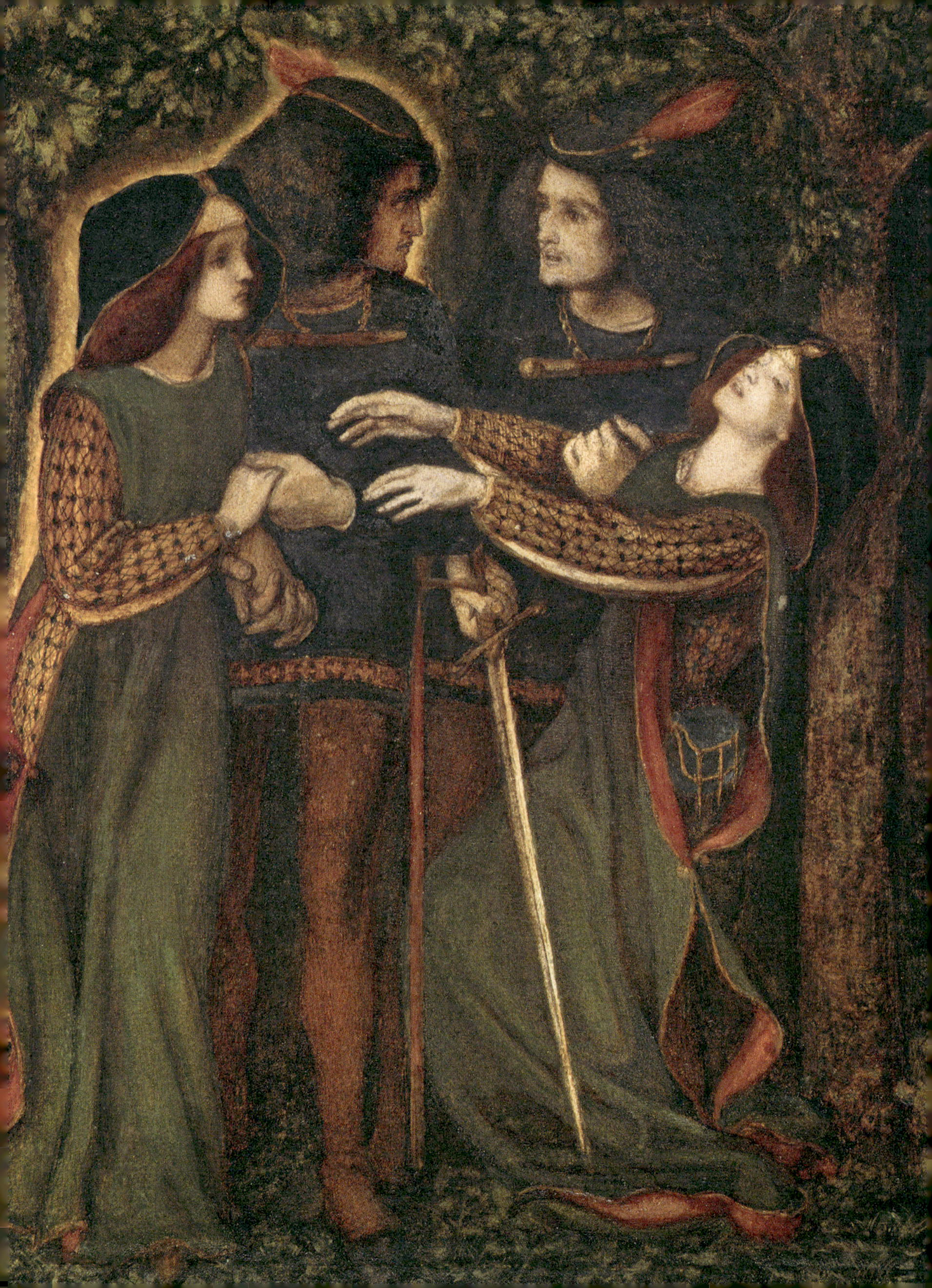

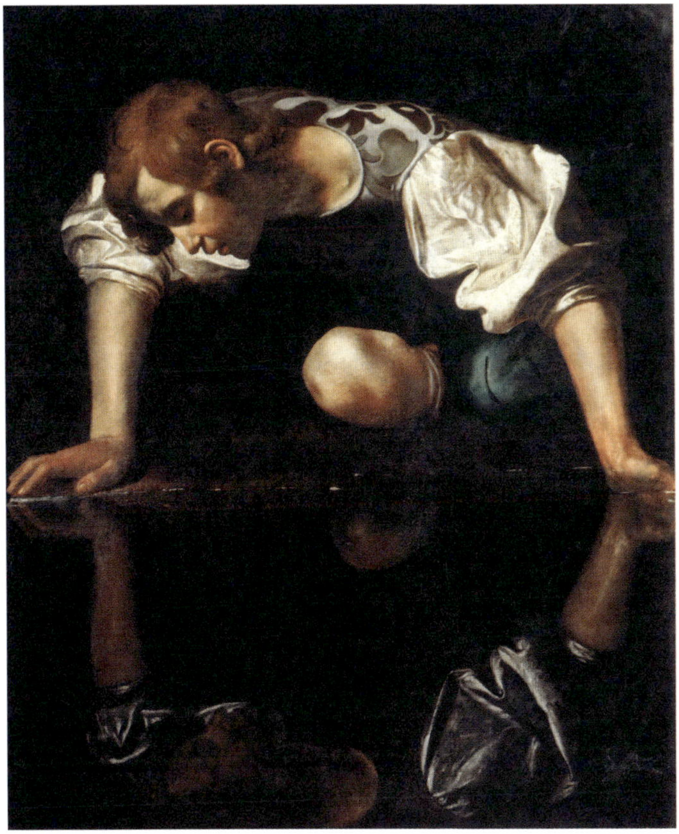

Left: Narcissus, Michelangelo Merisi da Caravaggio, *c.* 1597–99, oil on canvas

Michelangelo Merisi da Caravaggio (1571-1610) catches Narcissus at the moment of fatal recognition - bent towards his mirror image in dark water, hands outstretched in desperate yearning. The real youth and his reflection create a perfect circle, each as solid and substantial as the other. Has Narcissus recognized himself, or does he truly believe he's found another being? The inky blackness around them isolates this encounter, making it feel like a private nightmare we've accidentally witnessed. That tension between identical faces - one flesh, one water - locked in mutual fascination becomes almost unbearable to watch. Caravaggio offers no relief from this closed circuit of self-obsession. After all, who among us hasn't lingered a moment too long before our own reflection, secretly convinced we'd never be quite so obvious about it?

Opposite: How They Met Themselves, Dante Gabriel Rossetti, *c.* 1860, gouache on paper

In the gloaming of a haunted forest, Dante Gabriel Rossetti (1828-82) stages an encounter with existential terror: meeting your exact double while on a romantic stroll. ('So... come here often?' suddenly becomes a deeply unsettling question.) Two medieval lovers stumble upon their exact replicas, creating a mirrored quartet of supernatural dread. The woman on the right swoons dramatically, while her companion draws his sword against this impossible apparition. The doubled figures aren't reflections but solid presences, glowing with eerie phosphorescence against the darkening woods. Rossetti called this his 'Bogie drawing' and painted several versions over the years. Rossetti reportedly used himself and his wife, Elizabeth Siddal, as models for the imperilled couple, painting one version during their honeymoon, of all times. Folk beliefs hold that encountering one's doppelgänger portends imminent death, lending this woodland date a macabre edge. What terror might we feel, meeting ourselves in the flesh, our secret selves made manifest?

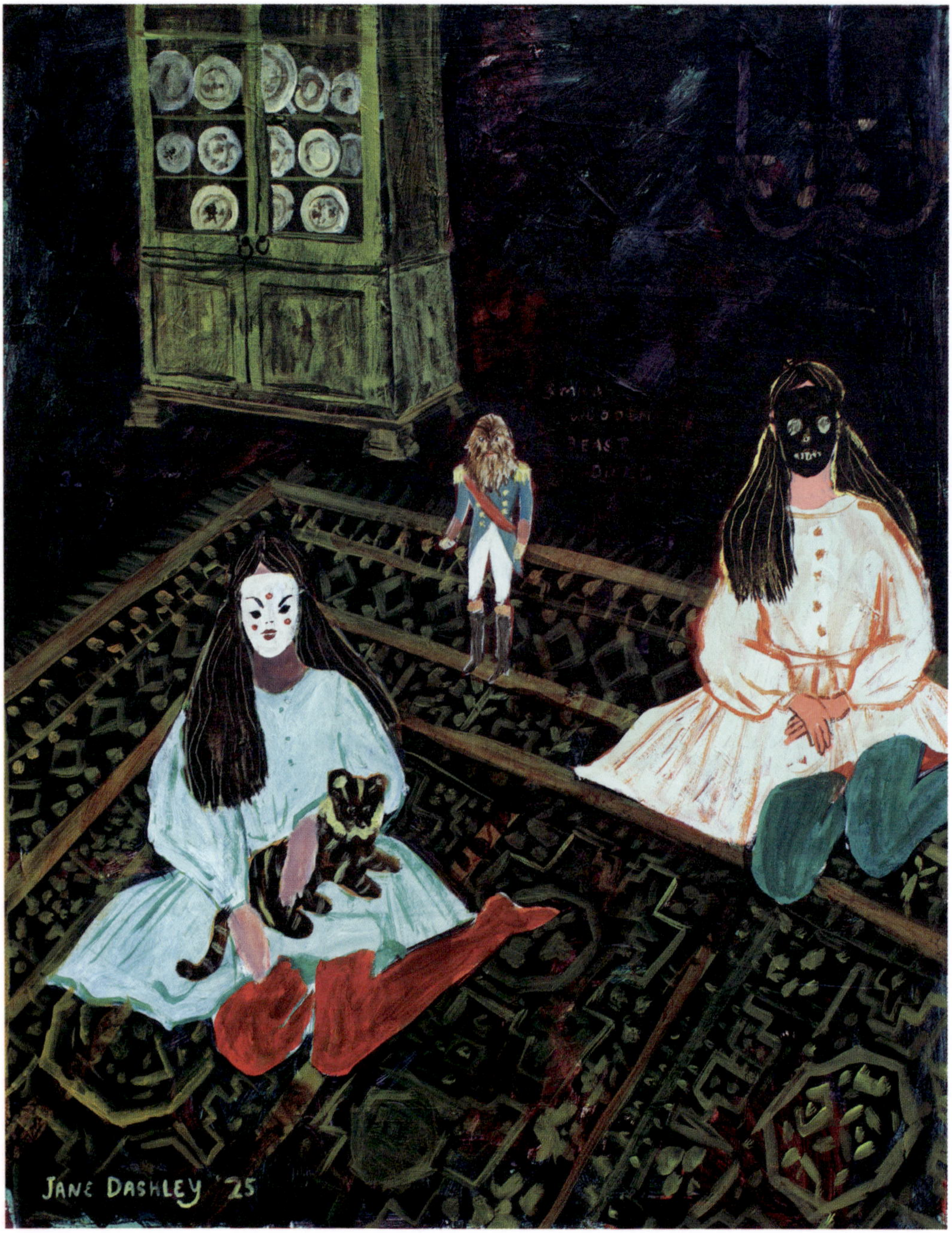
JANE DASHLEY '25

Right: Two Girls with a Doll, Léonard Tsuguharu Foujita, 1954, oil on canvas

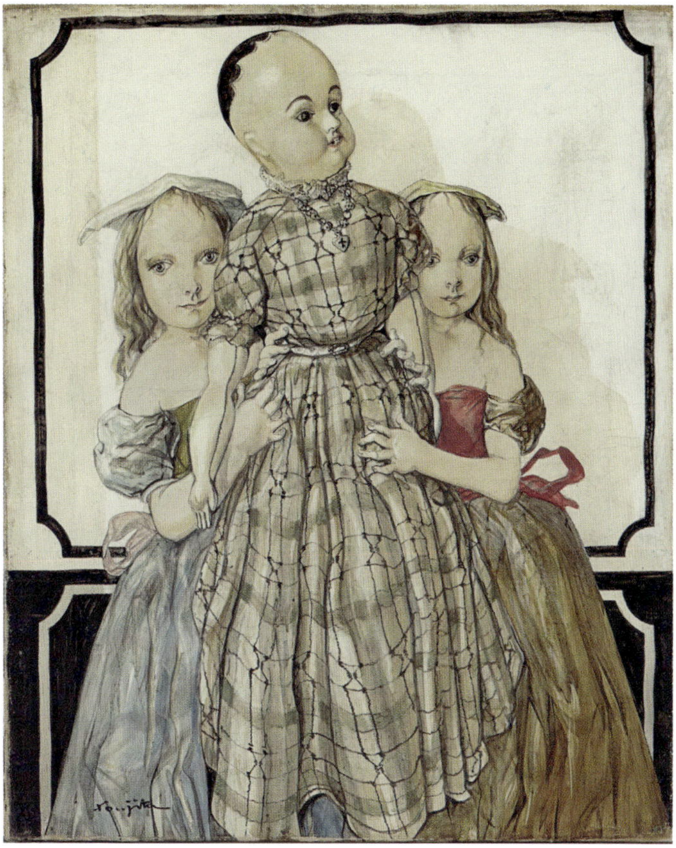

The initiation is almost complete. Léonard Tsuguharu Foujita (1886–1968) paints what appears to be two girls welcoming their doll into some private sisterhood, but look closer and you might wonder who's really orchestrating this ceremony. The 'doll' between these solemn-faced girls sports an adult's knowing smile, its mouth a precise arrangement of teeth like a Lego brick reimagined by Clive Barker, uniformly unnatural yet somehow hungry. Against Foujita's trademark milky background, the girls stand serious as pallbearers, while their peculiar companion stares out with unsettling directness, as if it has been coaching them towards this moment all along. After moving from Tokyo to Paris in 1913, Foujita developed his distinctive style merging Eastern calligraphic lines with Western portraiture, creating beings that float between cultural traditions and states of existence. Perhaps the girls think they're playing house, but their tiny companion's manipulative gaze suggests it's been playing them, guiding them step by step according to its own perfectly calculated agenda.

Opposite: Masked Twins, Jane Dashley, 2025, acrylic on canvas

Two sisters are here caught in a bizarre ritual of face-swapping! In Jane Dashley's uncanny domestic tableau, childhood games take a decidedly unsettling turn. One girl, dressed in ethereal blue, peers through a pristine white harlequin mask while clutching a small cat; her twin in white has transformed herself with a slick black leather hood that renders her features anonymous and strange. Between them stands a miniature soldier with a beast's face – neither toy nor guardian, but something that belongs to the twilight zone where nightmares go to play house. Dashley's fever-bright imagination transforms this ordinary scene into a staging ground for freaky identity theft, suggesting these sisters have graduated from ordinary make-believe to becoming their own imaginary friends – swapping identities with their shadow selves and exchanging places with their own reflections. The real question is whether they remember how to change back.

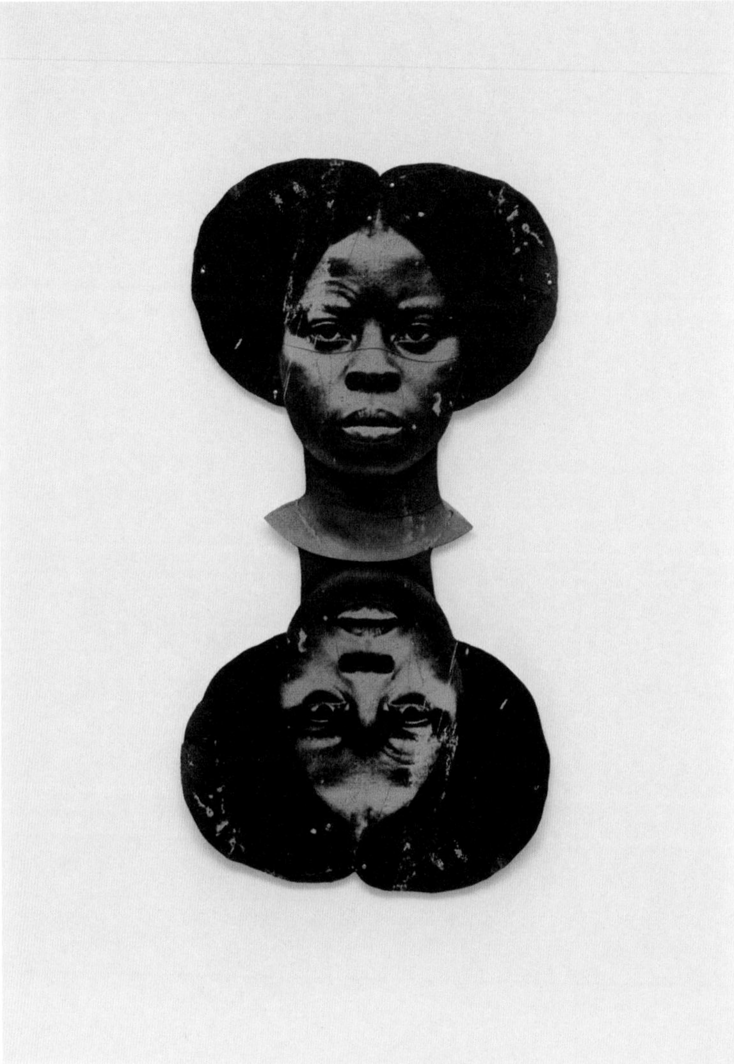

Two heads, Frida Orupabo, 2022, collage: pigment print on acid-free cotton paper, mounting tape, split pins

In Frida Orupabo's hypnotic collage, a woman's face mirrors itself - one upright, one inverted - creating a strange symmetry in which each becomes both crown and foundation for the other. The Norwegian-Nigerian artist constructs her works from archival photographs and digital libraries that have historically constrained Black identity, pinning these fragments together with visible fasteners. Here, the mirrored faces, with their calm expressions and cloud-shaped hair, create a Rorschach-like pattern that challenges our perception. Is this one woman reflected? Twins conjoined in impossible symmetry? The vintage quality of the source material, with its white speckles and uneven texture, connects to those constrained representations that Orupabo reshapes. The effect suggests that every face contains its shadow self - an inverted twin staring back at us from the other side of the mirror.

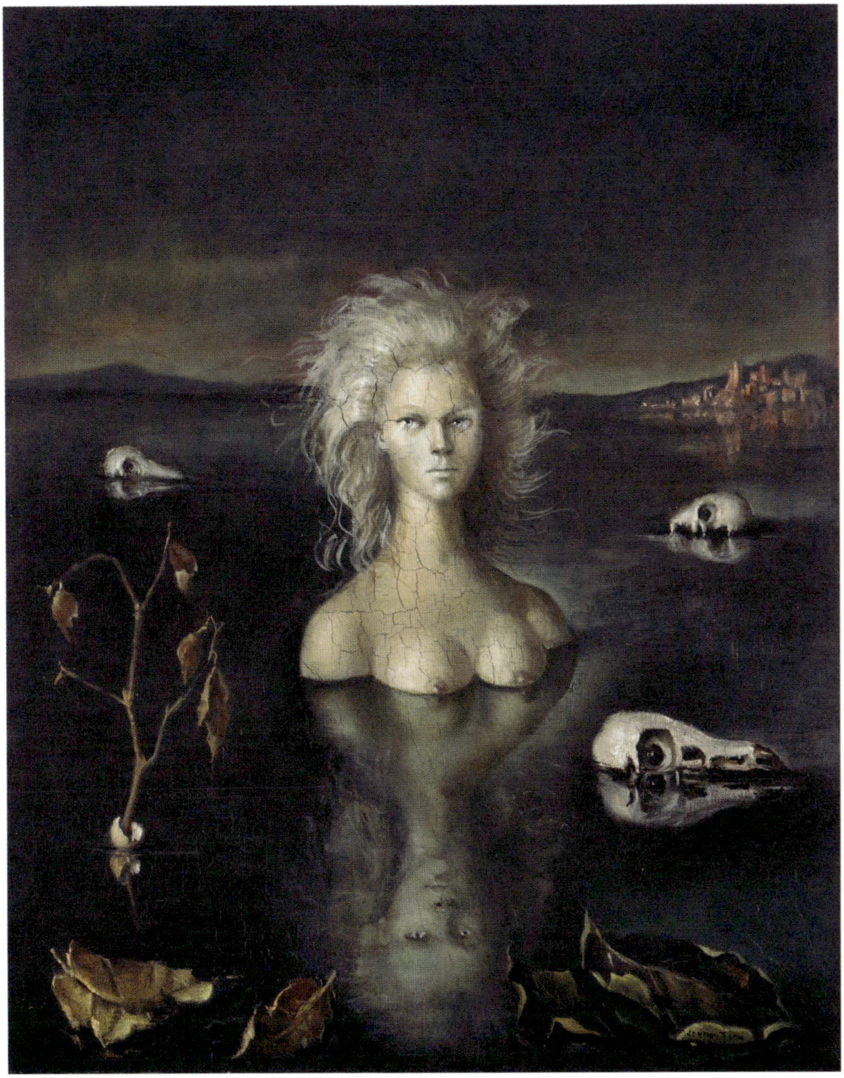

Donna del Lago or Le Bout du monde II, Leonor Fini, *c.* 1953, oil on canvas

A woman floats in dark waters, her reflection staring back with eerie ambivalence, both versions seemingly unbothered by their impossible arrangement. Leonor Fini (1908–96) paints a doubled existence where neither face claims to be the original – they simply coexist, calm as you please, while three skulls drift past and dried leaves cling to a barren branch. The Argentine-born artist gives us feminine power at the end of the world (or perhaps its beginning – the title suggests both), yet her subject appears utterly untroubled by the apocalyptic scenery. The cracked, aged texture makes the woman feel ancient, eternal, as if she's been taking this same leisurely soak since the lake first formed. In the distance, buildings huddle under a moody sky touched with orange and green – civilization reduced to a faint silhouette on the horizon. But why worry? The water's fine, the company's quiet, and there's something marvellously peaceful about having your own reflection as your only companion at the end of everything.

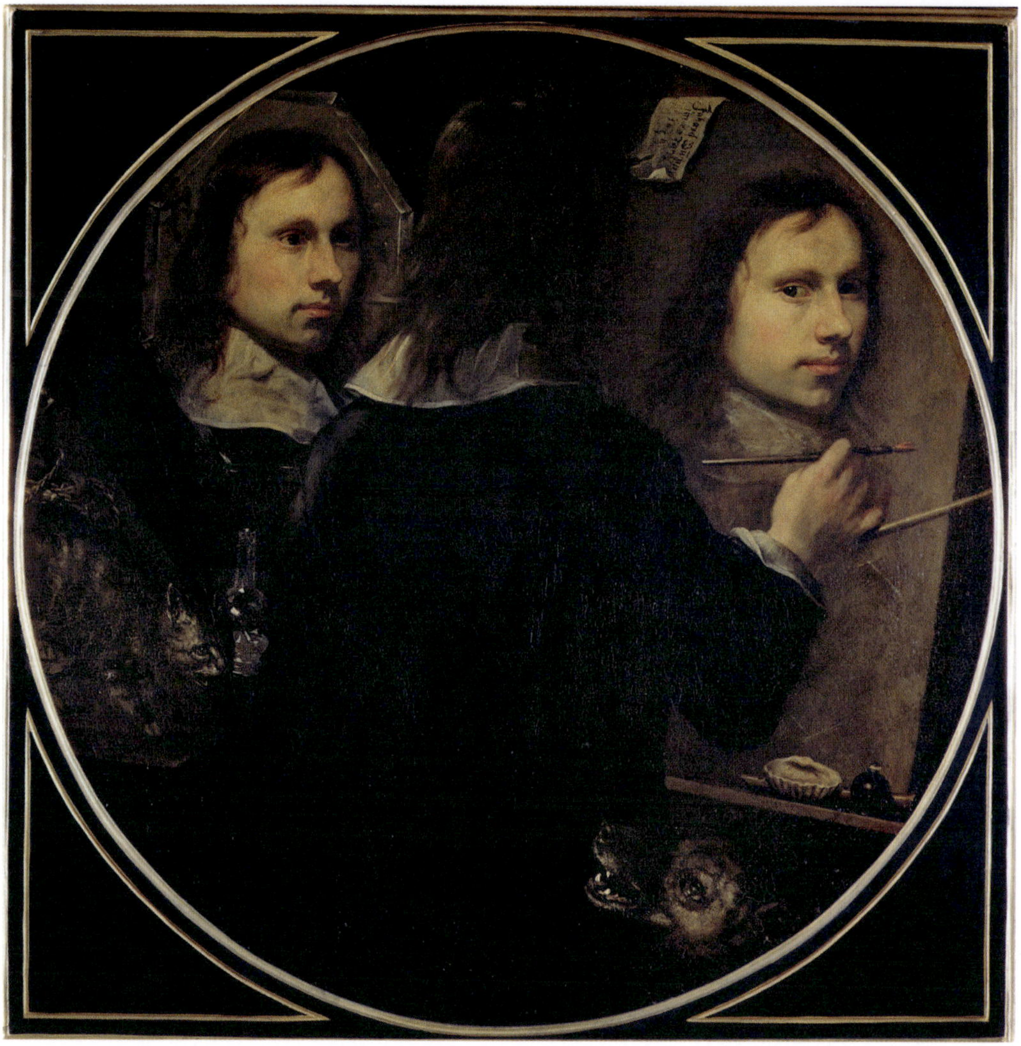

Self-Portrait, Johannes Gumpp, 1646, oil on canvas

Johannes Gumpp (1626–?) appears not once but three times in his mind-bender of a self-portrait, creating a dizzying recursive loop that predates modern art by centuries. From behind, faceless and anonymous, he gazes intently at his own reflection in the mirror, while the mirror-Gumpp stares right back at him, locked in mutual scrutiny. Meanwhile, the portrait on his easel gives them both the side-eye, completing a strange triangle of self-observation. A dog and a cat lurk at the bottom of the composition, possibly representing fidelity versus independence – or perhaps just Gumpp showing off that he could paint pets too. This visual puzzle about perception, reality and representation feels remarkably ahead of its time. Curiously, it's also Gumpp's only known painting. After creating this triple self-portrait, the artist himself seems to have vanished from the historical record, leaving us with only this single, enigmatic glimpse into his artistic vision.

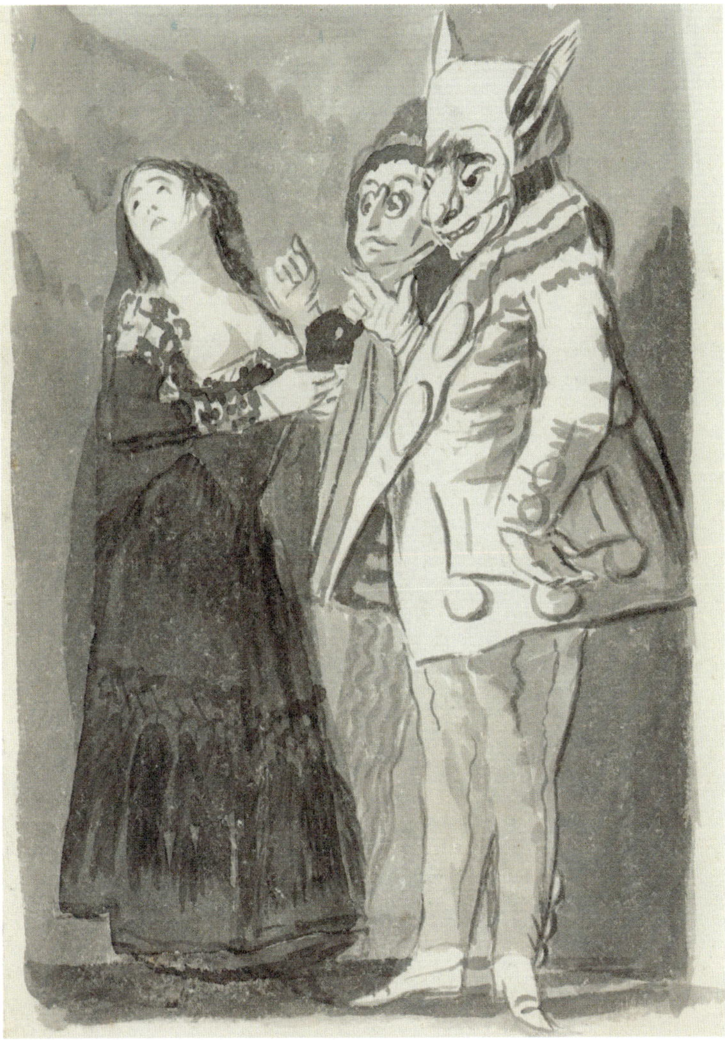

Cruel Masks, Francisco Goya, 1796/97, brush and black ink and grey wash with scraping on laid paper

Francisco Goya (1746–1828) captures the universal nightmare of being cornered by creeps at a party. A woman tilts her face skywards with the unmistakable expression of someone praying for divine intervention, while two masked figures hover beside her with predatory interest. One wears an animal mask with pointed ears that makes no pretence at humanity; the other sports a frozen leer that might be painted plaster or might be flesh – either way, deeply unsettling. This is the equivalent of 'my friend here thinks you're hot', but with actual monsters doing the talking.

The woman's body language screams trapped, while her companions radiate the particular menace of beings who've never learned to take a hint. Perhaps Goya understood that when predators drop their social masks, what you see underneath is just another mask, and behind that, probably something that was never quite human to begin with.

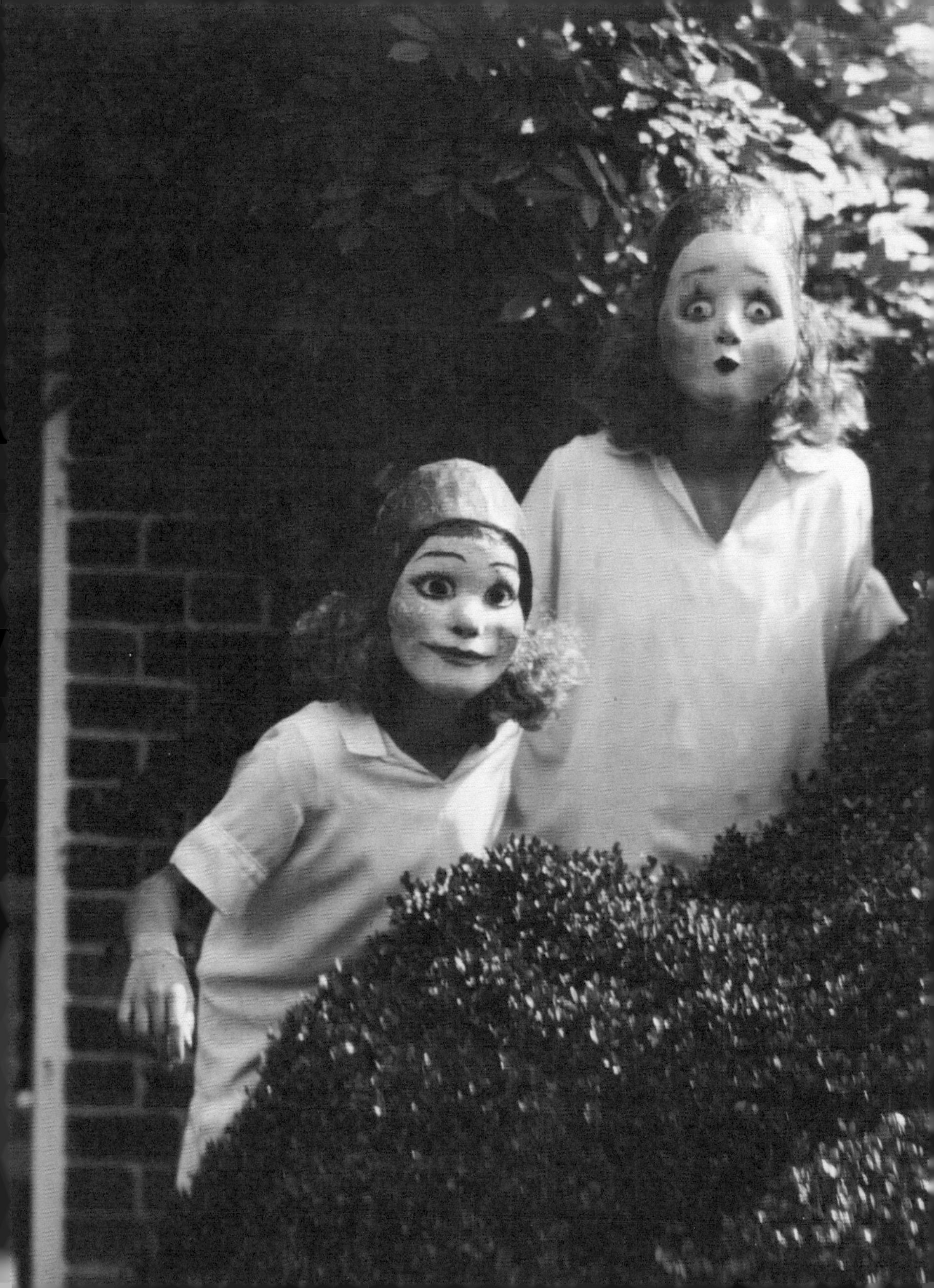

Right: Between mask and mirror, Gillian Wearing, 2017, framed c-type print

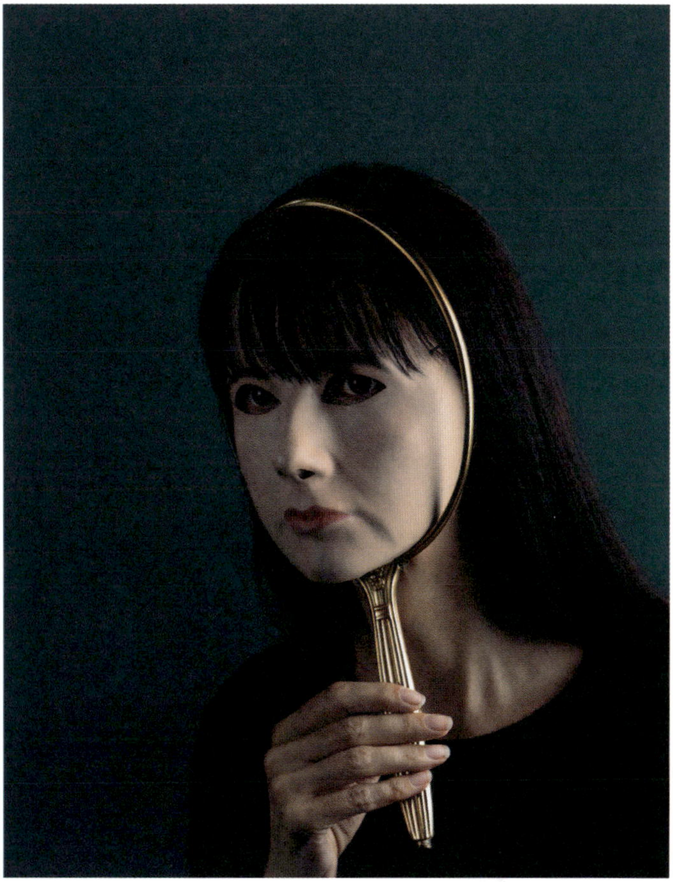

A peculiar vertigo takes hold when confronting Gillian Wearing's photograph. The uncanny sight of the artist wearing her own face as a mask feels like someone who's stolen their own identity. The silicone replica sits atop her actual features with tiny betrayals: a slight gap around the eyes, the unnatural smoothness where living skin should shift with subtle movement. This doubled visage recalls the dizzy moment from childhood nightmares when familiar things suddenly seem inexplicably strange and sinister - when Mum's face isn't quite Mum's anymore. Wearing has spent her career slipping between identities, but this feels different, more unsettling than her transformations into famous photographers or family members. She becomes her own doppelgänger, as if the gap between how we appear and who we are has suddenly become visible.

Opposite: Masks, W.T. Benda, 1925, papier-mâché, Bristol board and paint; photograph by Arnold Genthe

Peering over a hedge with faces frozen mid-emotion, these garden intruders from a 1925 Arnold Genthe (1869–1942) photograph wear W.T. Benda's (1873–1948) unsettling creations. The Polish-American illustrator layered wrapping paper over 'skull' forms, then painted and shaved repeatedly until he birthed these not-quite-human countenances - one wearing the widening smile of someone witnessing something progressively more disturbing, yet unable to stop grinning; the other caught in the desperate, wide-eyed shock of someone who's just realized a catastrophic bodily failure is imminent and unavoidable. Neighbourhood watch or nightmare vision? The hedge seems to offer inadequate protection against these suburban phantoms, with their impossibly still expressions. When these masked figures return home, do they peel away their paper faces, or has something of Benda's creations permanently fused with what lies beneath, leaving them forever stuck in their most socially mortifying moment?

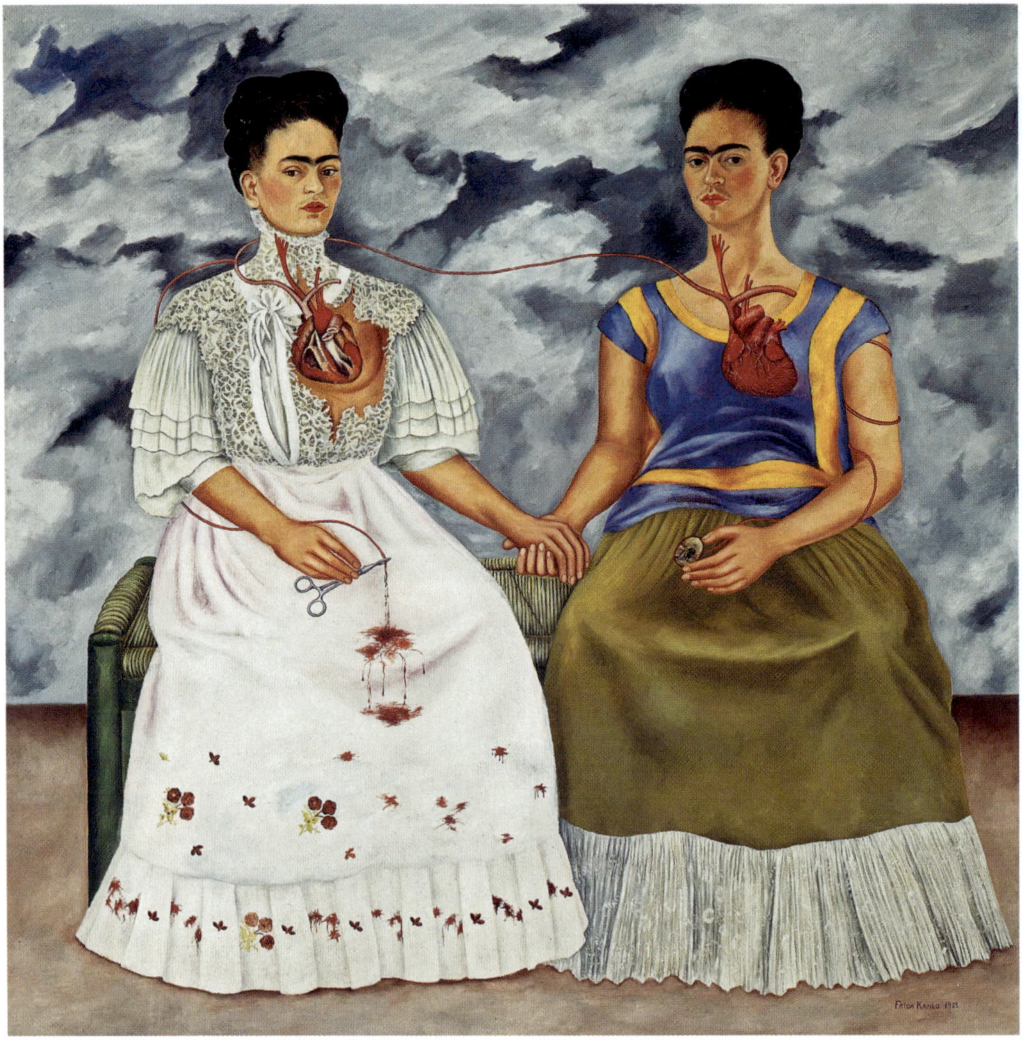

The Two Fridas, Frida Kahlo, 1939, oil on canvas

Two Fridas sit on a lonely bench against churning skies, a psychological portrait of separation from oneself. In the wake of her divorce from Diego Rivera, Frida Kahlo (1907–54) splits herself into competing identities: one in European Victorian white, the other in traditional Tehuana dress that Rivera adored. With surgical precision, the European Frida attempts to sever the blood vessel connecting their exposed hearts, while her double clutches a miniature portrait of Rivera as a child. Blood spills onto pristine fabric, yet both faces maintain identical, unnerving composure. Unlike conventional doubles in art, these twins aren't mirror images but complementary aspects, the rejected European self bleeding out while the beloved Mexican self remains intact. The paint itself seems to pulse with Kahlo's visceral emotional trauma, each brushstroke recording her divided sense of self, her doubled image asking which version of ourselves do we nurture, and which do we allow to bleed away?

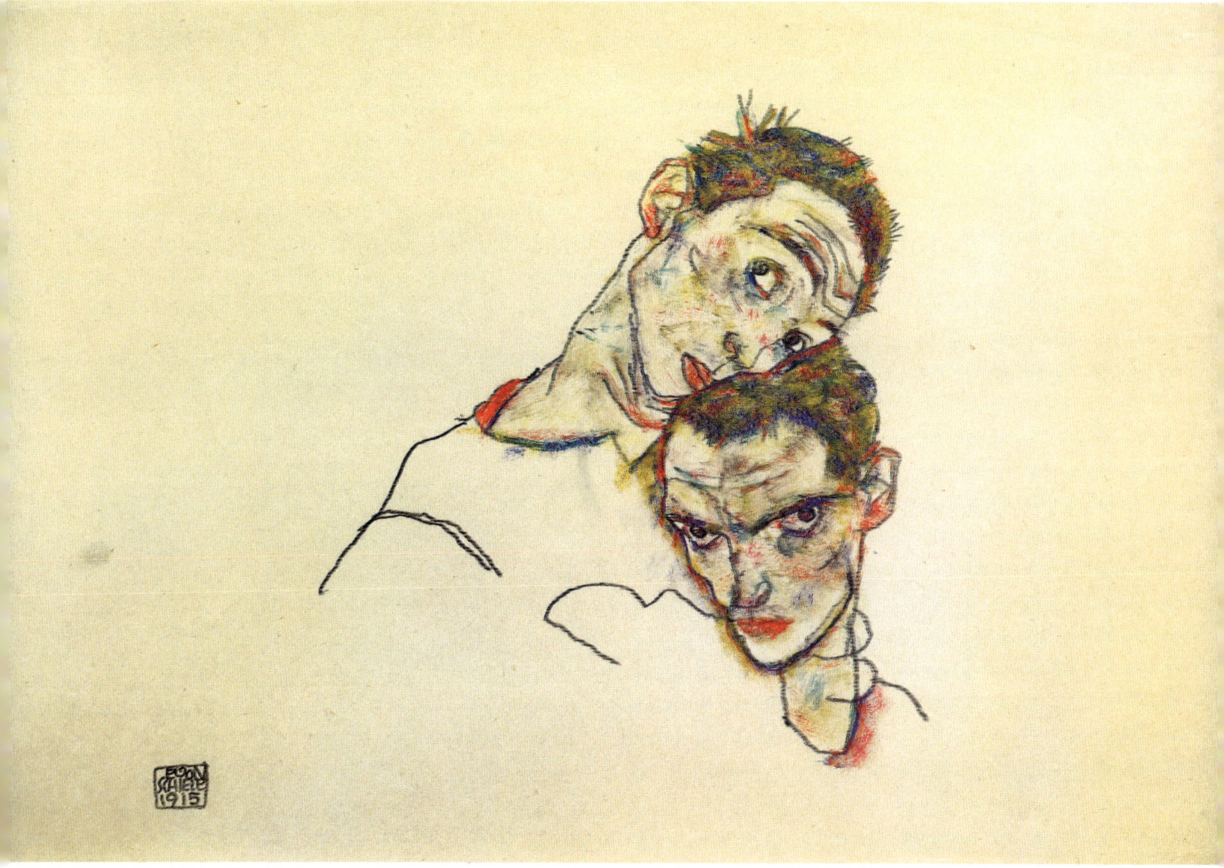

Double Self Portrait, Egon Schiele, 1915, watercolour on paper

Two versions of Egon Schiele (1890–1918) press cheek to cheek in this unnerving double self-portrait, yet they feel less like twins than opposing aspects of the same fragmented consciousness. The lower face glares with an intensity bordering on the maniacal, practically daring you to make your next move, while above, a second self tilts his head with a strange, teasing curiosity – their stark expressions creating a visual dialogue where inner argument becomes visible. Schiele was obsessed with multiplying himself on paper, creating over 240 self-portraits before his premature death at 28, including 13 doubles in which he pioneered a visual language of divided selfhood that predated psychology's later fascination with fragmented identity. The doubled face reveals a private game between competing selves, caught in a moment at which you've somehow become the object of their unsettling attention.

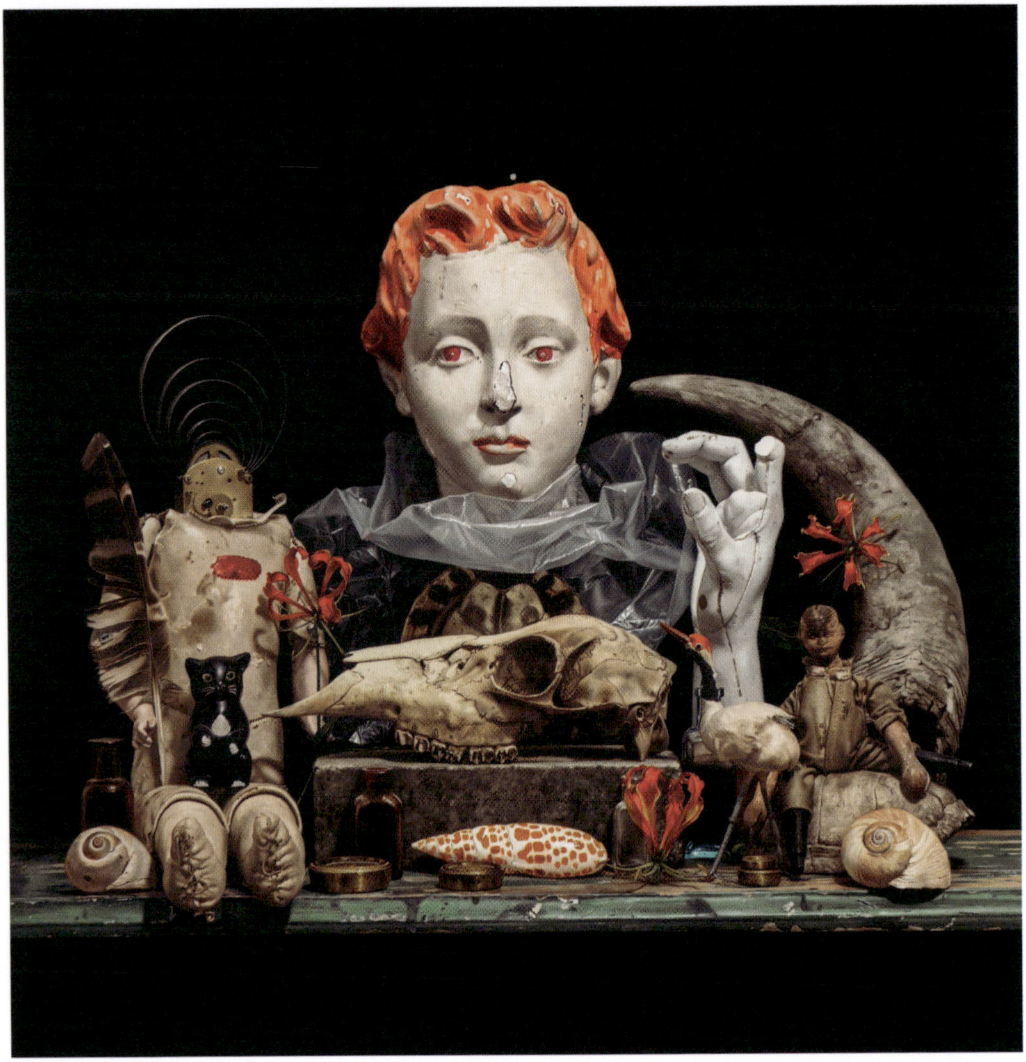

Performance 4, Matthew Bober, 2024, oil on panel

Matthew Bober casts his theatrical troupe with strange performers. A bright-haired head shrouded in plastic stares with red glass eyes, flanked by a crescent horn that curves like it fell off a mythological beast and a figure with what appears to be a wind-up toy mechanism topping a stitched leather body with teensy porcelain doll hands, one clutching a single jaunty feather. Below, an animal skull presides, while a painted black and white cat watches with the passive attention of someone who's seen this ceremony a hundred times. The nephew of fantasy illustrator Richard Bober, Bober spent countless nights watching his uncle paint, learning how to see objects as characters with their own stories. Now he gathers misfit ceramic creatures with slight chips and haunting expressions, vacant-eyed dolls asking to be noticed, his hyper-realistic technique capturing every worn edge with loving attention. Here he's assembled a cast mid-performance, frozen in the moment before something terrible or wonderful happens. It's a play that hasn't been written yet, or maybe one that's been running in empty theatres for ages, waiting for the right audience to stumble in.

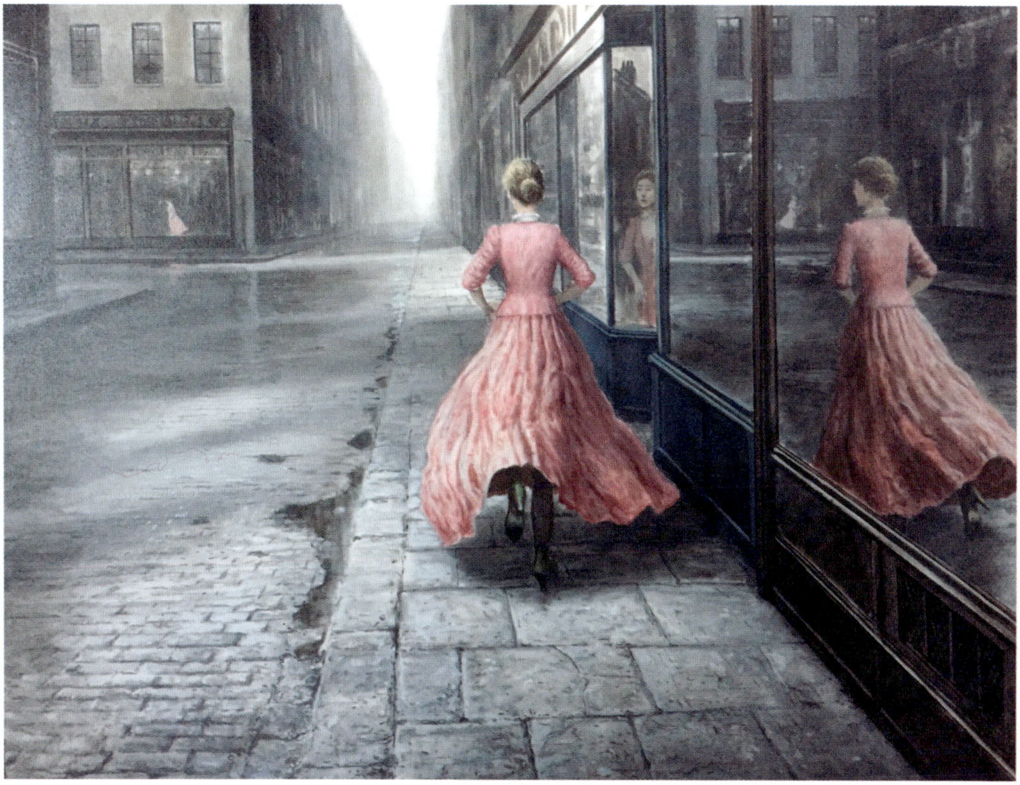

Chasing the Reflection, Mike Worrall, 2017, Windsor Newton artist oil on Belgium linen

Glancing down a quiet, rain-slicked street, we witness an impossible moment in Mike Worrall's dreamlike scene. A woman in a flowing pink dress strides confidently forwards, her back to us, but her reflections appear where they shouldn't be, in shopfronts she hasn't yet passed, perhaps on streets she'll never walk. Her mirror images multiply across glass surfaces, wandering independently of their source as if they've slipped loose from the laws that bind reflections to their owners. The woman's striking pink form against the muted architecture draws our eye, while her duplicates pull us deeper into the composition, the empty street amplifying our unease. Is she truly alone, or are these glimpses of parallel selves that have always existed, separate and sovereign? Worrall invites us to question whether reflections might harbour their own intentions, living lives that merely intersect with ours in moments of shared geography.

IX

FORGOTTEN KNOWLEDGE & MYSTERIOUS OBJECTS

'I want to be with those who know secret things or else alone.'

– RAINER MARIA RILKE

Stone circles stand sentinel across mist-shrouded landscapes, their builders' intentions as mysterious as the rituals once performed within their ancient embrace. The mechanical astrolabe gathering dust in a museum case once spoke fluently of the stars to hands now centuries dead. A cryptic codex filled with plants from no earthly garden once made perfect sense to someone, somewhere, with eyes that saw worlds we can no longer imagine. Even these words you're reading now are ghosts – remembered bones of ancient pictographs first pressed into clay when mammoths still roamed, descendants of symbols whose origins we've forgotten while using them daily.

Step into sixteenth-century Prague's legendary Kunstkammer, where Rudolf II collects narwhal tusks marketed as unicorn horns, mechanical golden ships that sail across dinner tables and intricate ivory spheres containing impossibly smaller spheres. By candlelight, you'll discover that these aren't random collections but entire cosmologies in miniature – elaborate attempts to map a world perpetually spilling over with wonders. Ancient texts rest in perpetual twilight: alchemical recipes promising transformation, coded messages between scholars, star charts mapping heavens that no longer match our skies.

The Voynich manuscript's strange diagrams and symbols resist all attempts at translation, while Roman dodecahedrons have turned up in archaeological digs with no explanation for their purpose – twelve-sided mysteries that fit perfectly in ancient hands but make no sense to modern minds. The nerd in all of us secretly hopes these are ancient monster manuals and gaming dice, proof that rolling for initiative is humanity's oldest tradition. Dungeons & Dragons aside, each artefact raises an uncomfortable possibility: we're not accumulating knowledge at all, but rediscovering fragments of wisdom repeatedly lost and found across human history, each generation convinced they're the first to stumble upon insights as old as the stones.

Artists became fascinated by this tug-of-war between the known and the unknown. Georges de La Tour's scholars bend over manuscripts by candlelight, desperate to decipher what glows before them – knowledge so close they can feel its heat, yet somehow still beyond reach. Henry Gillard Glindoni captures John Dee performing experiments for Elizabeth I and her court, his respectable face masking the occult interests that lurk beneath – forbidden knowledge painted over and sanitized by nervous patrons. The mysterious Flammarion engraving reveals a pilgrim on his knees at the boundary of everything, poking through the star-spangled curtain to discover machinery churning behind what we thought was empty sky. Jean Delville captures pure psychic intensity: a figure thrumming with occult energy, the grimoire almost incidental to the raw power she's channelling, her entire being alight with something that can't be contained in any book – it's a Whole Vibe. These artists documented the vibes of that maddening gap, between the reaching and the grasping, between the seeker and the secret.

Artists across centuries have specialized in brewing fresh enigmas. Ordinary objects become archaeological riddles under their hands. A teacup lined in fur: domestic and repulsive at once, a charming object made so unsettling it seems a small violence has been committed against gentility. Glass vessels cradle natural curiosities – bones, seeds, fragments – suspended in crystal, elevating humble scraps into precious relics. Illuminated illustrations become cryptic pronouncements, like fragments from parallel worlds, while impossible libraries hold every book

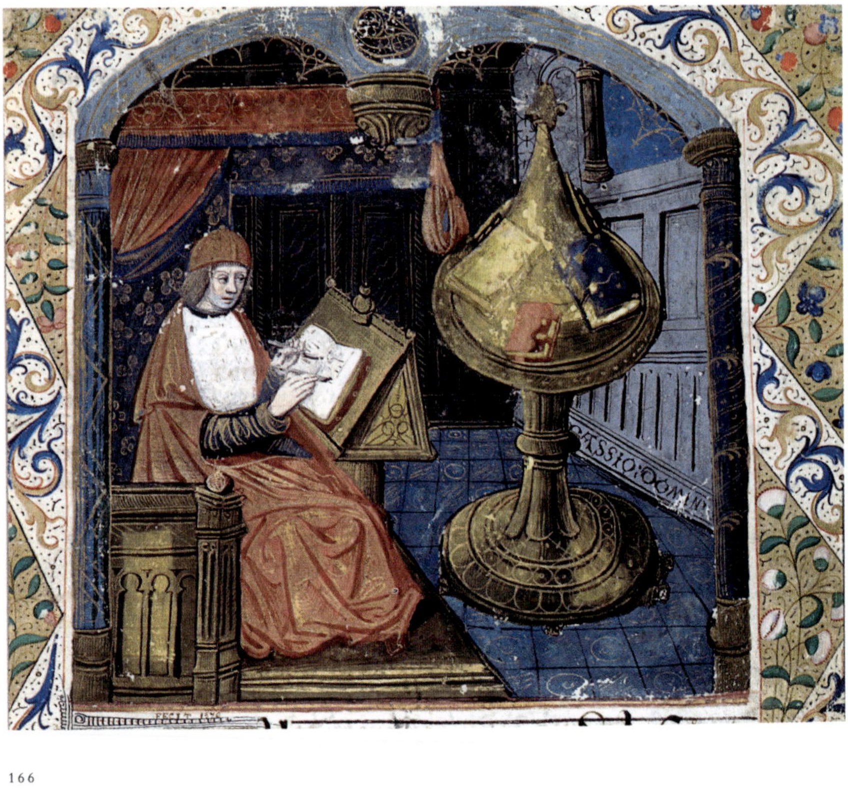

Below: A man at his writing table, Middle Ages, illuminated manuscript

Opposite: Sibyl Agrippa, Domenico Ghirlandaio, *c.* 1480, fresco, Sassetti Chapel, Basilica of Santa Trinita, Florence, Italy

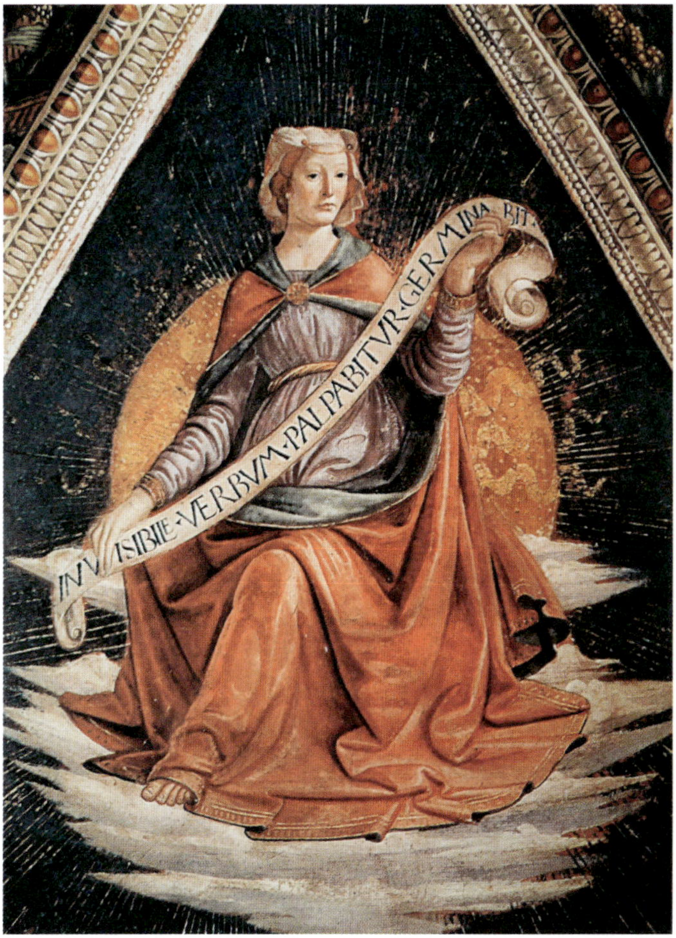

that could ever be written. Across centuries, continents, cultures, we're drawn to mystery like moths to flame. We craft it, collect it, chase it. It calls to us.

Today, we're surrounded by devices whose inner workings might as well be magic. Our phones and computers process information through mechanisms most of us couldn't begin to explain, even as they shape our understanding of reality. Yet something in us still yearns for older, stranger mysteries. Whether it's obscure manuscripts behind museum glass or clay tablets emerging from archaeological digs beside implements of unclear purpose, we feel it again: that maddening pull towards objects that defy explanation yet demand attention, like a gnawing itch in a part of your brain you can't quite reach.

Both art and craft are acts of faith – the same faith that drove ancient hands to pile up those rocks, to craft those celestial whatsits and doodads, to fill cryptic pages with impossible nonsense. Today we are both the puzzled observers of their mysteries and the mysterious creators of tomorrow's puzzles, adding our voices to humanity's endless conversation with itself across time. We have faith that someone, somewhere, will see our marks and understand, will behold our weird objects and comprehend their purpose. We're all just making stuff and hoping someone gets it.

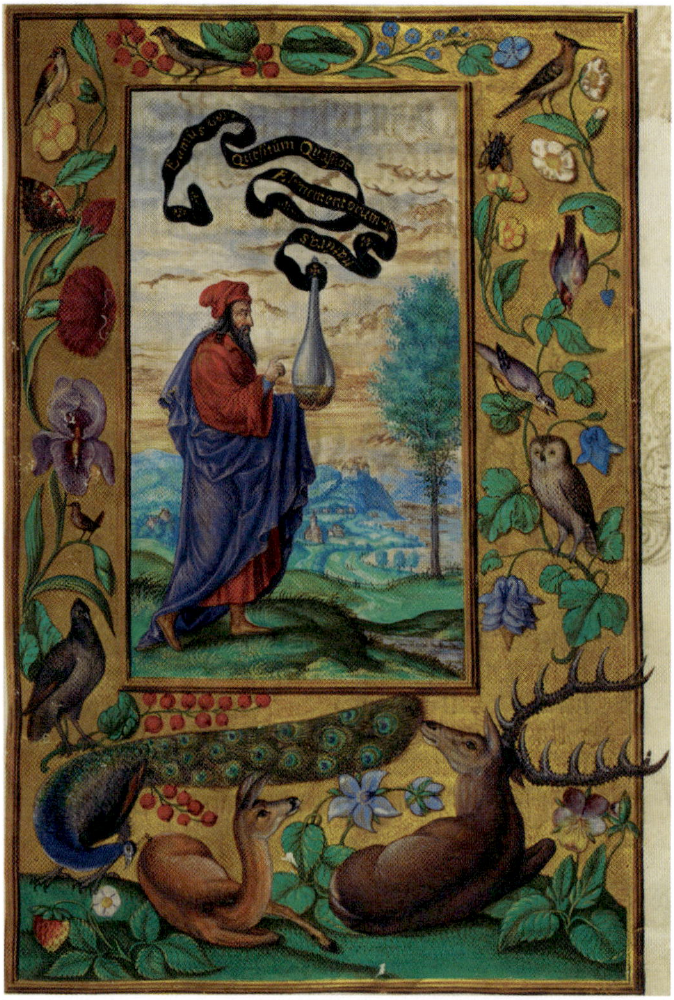

Left: The First Treatise, artist unknown, from *Splendor Solis* by Salomon Trismosin, 1582, tempera, gold leaf and ink on vellum

Meet the original mad scientist, minus the wild hair and maniacal cackle. This dignified crimson-cloaked philosopher from Salomon Trismosin's legendary *Splendor Solis* points to his golden flask with the pride of someone who has just mixed the perfect alchemical martini. That black ribbon unfurling from his alembic reads in Latin, 'Let us seek the natures of the four elements' - a bold call to mystical adventure if ever there was one. Deer, owls and peacocks crowd the ornate border, each animal hinting at its own symbolic meaning in the alchemical process. The butterfly hints at what could be the ultimate golden promise, but only if you're willing to endure the full metamorphosis. This opening scene from the First Treatise sets the stage for what many consider to be the crown jewel of alchemical texts, including 22 mind-bending illuminations that form a complex codex of forgotten wisdom.

Opposite: Melencolia I, Albrecht Dürer, 1514, engraving

Why is this winged figure so bummed amid such a bevy of intellectual treasures? Around her, the tools of measurement and creation lie untouched - a compass dangling from her hand, carpenter's implements scattered on the ground. Albrecht Dürer (1471-1528) shows us a Renaissance mind confronting the limits of human knowledge. The strange polyhedron, the magic square whose numbers equal 34 in every direction, the blazing comet and rainbow over the distant sea - these objects form a puzzle whose solution remains just out of reach. Renaissance thinkers had begun to see melancholy not as mere illness but as a condition of creative genius, where insight and frustration coexist. Dürer's angel still captivates us because we've all felt that deep funk when mastery of tools and techniques isn't enough, when that spark of deeper knowledge eludes our grasp, when we realize we're just idiot mortals forever falling short of enlightenment.

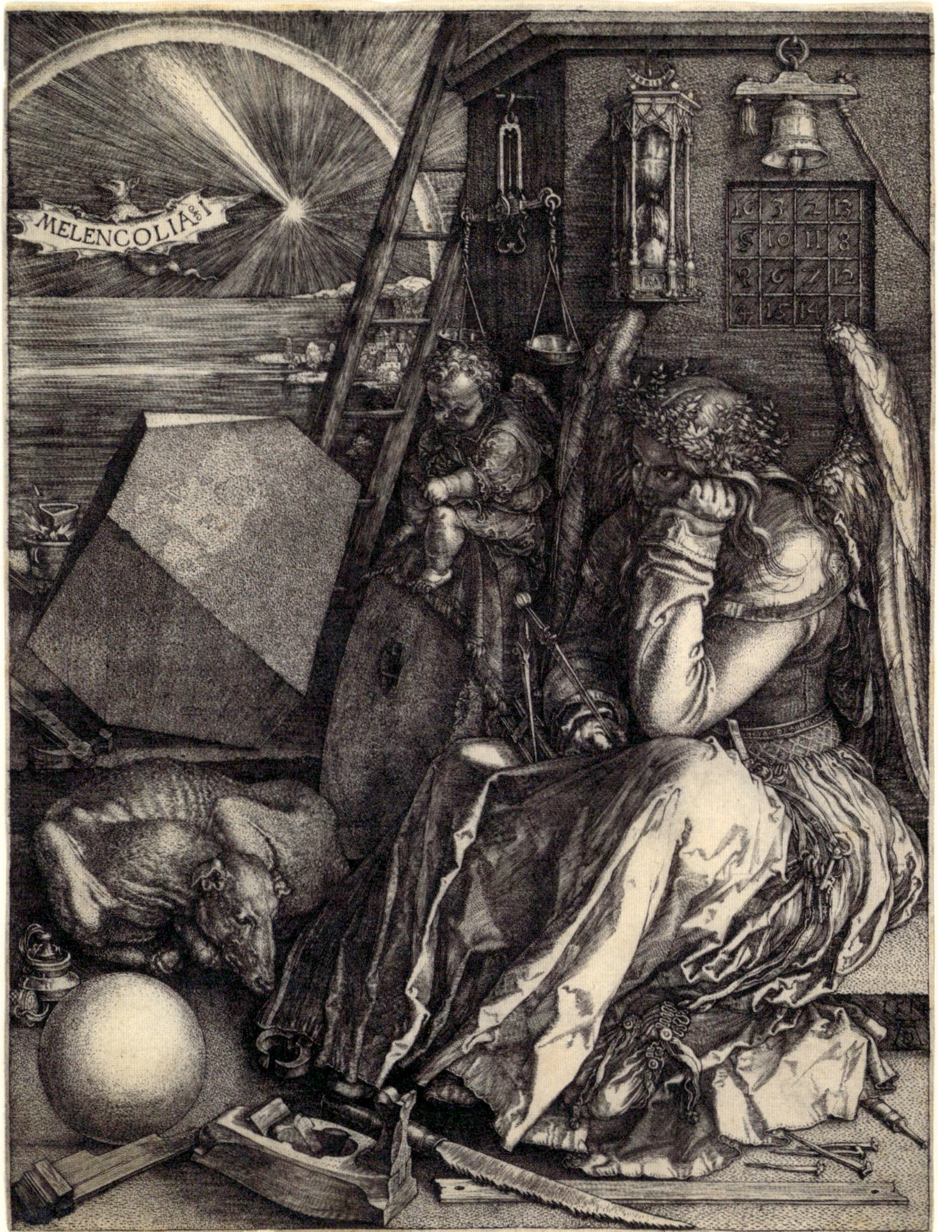
MELENCOLIA I
16 3 2 13
5 10 11 8
9 6 7 12
4 15 14 1

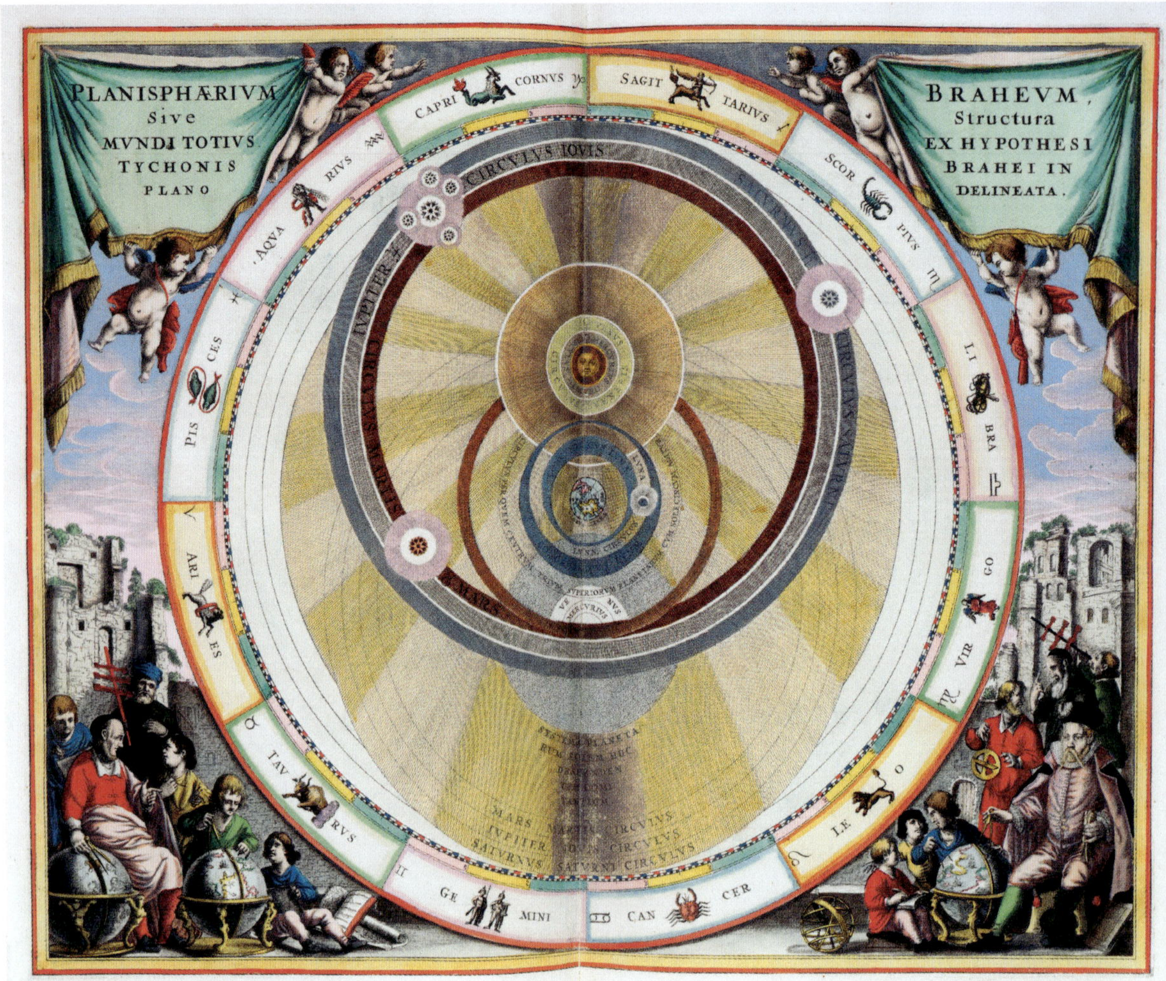

Map Showing Tycho Brahe's System of Planetary Orbits, from *The Celestial Atlas, or The Harmony of the Universe*, Andreas Cellarius, 1660–61, hand-coloured engraving

---

Behold Tycho Brahe's cosmic diplomacy in action. His geocentric-heliocentric hybrid appears here in Andreas Cellarius's (1596–1665) stunning *Harmonia Macrocosmica*. Earth stubbornly holds centre stage, while the planets cavort around the Sun, which itself politely orbits our supposedly stationary world. This celestial hedge-bet satisfied both scripture-minded scholars and observation-obsessed astronomers who couldn't quite abandon Earth's starring role. Astronomers cluster around the margins, pointing instruments skywards and debating amid ornate architectural backdrops. This was astronomy as public spectacle, when star maps looked more like festival posters than scientific diagrams. Cellarius spent decades crafting this spectacular celestial atlas of the seventeenth century – a visual feast from the golden age of Dutch mapmaking – where winged cherubs faff about trying to look useful and serious scholars argue over whether we're the centre of everything or just another rock floating in space.

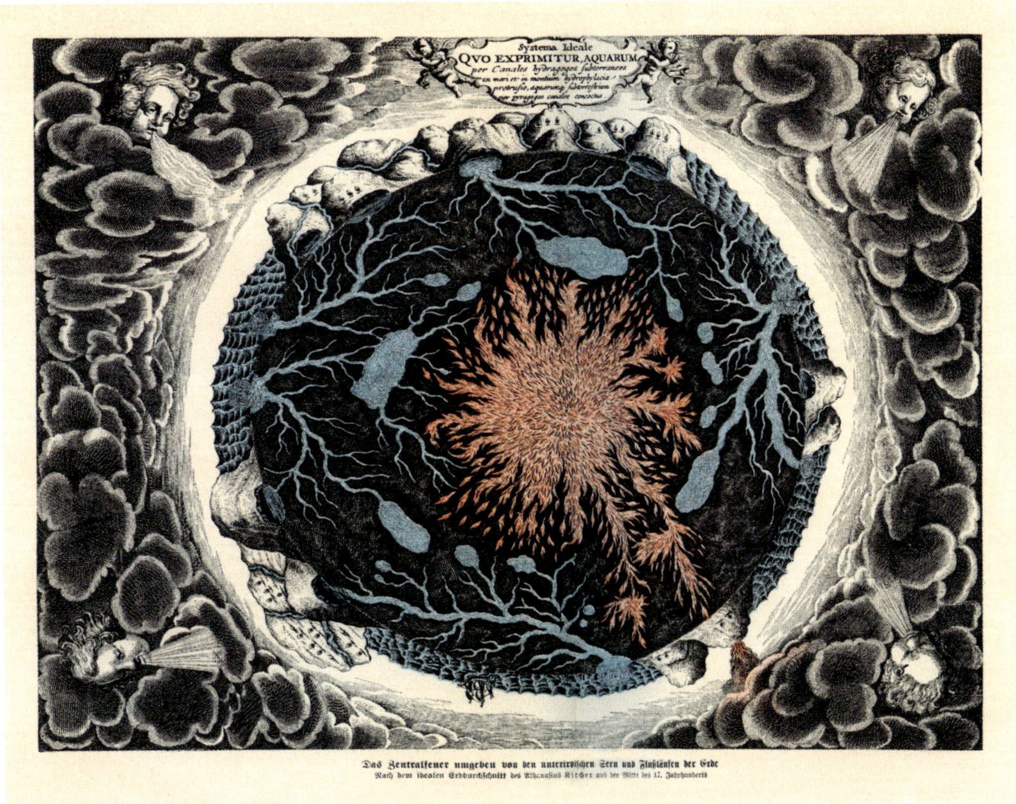

Mundus Subterraneus, Athanasius Kircher, 1664, engraving

Athanasius Kircher's (1602–80) diagram turns Earth into a cross-sectioned cosmic machine, complete with fiery channels snaking through the planet's core and underground rivers cooling everything down. His vision shows our planet as a living organism, with a molten heart pumping energy through subterranean arteries. Not content with mere theorizing, this daring Jesuit polymath actually descended into Vesuvius's smoking crater, encountering what he called 'the habitation of Hell', with 'horrible bellowings and roarings'. He was an adventurous spirit who may have later inspired Jules Verne's fictional professor in *Journey to the Centre of the Earth*. Modern geology eventually replaced Kircher's fanciful vision, but his beautiful cosmic systems capture just how mysterious the underworld once seemed to minds desperate for maps of territories they could not explore.

John Dee Performing an Experiment before Elizabeth I, Henry Gillard Glindoni, ninteenth century, oil on canvas

X-rays revealed the shocking secret hiding beneath this dignified Tudor science demonstration: a circle of human skulls around John Dee's feet. Henry Gillard Glindoni's (1852–1913) painting shows Dee, the 'Queen's Conjuror', performing what appears to be a chemistry experiment for Elizabeth I and her court at his Mortlake home. X-ray examination in 2015 revealed that Glindoni originally painted Dee standing within a ring of skulls on the floor, symbols either of anatomical study or ritual magic, depending on your scholarly leaning. The Victorian patron who commissioned this work apparently got cold feet about depicting the Tudor polymath's occult interests, preferring instead this sanitized version of history. Back then the line between 'science' and 'magic' was beautifully blurry, with Dee consulting angels through crystal balls while simultaneously advancing navigation and mathematics. Forbidden knowledge lurks beneath plenty of seemingly respectable surfaces.

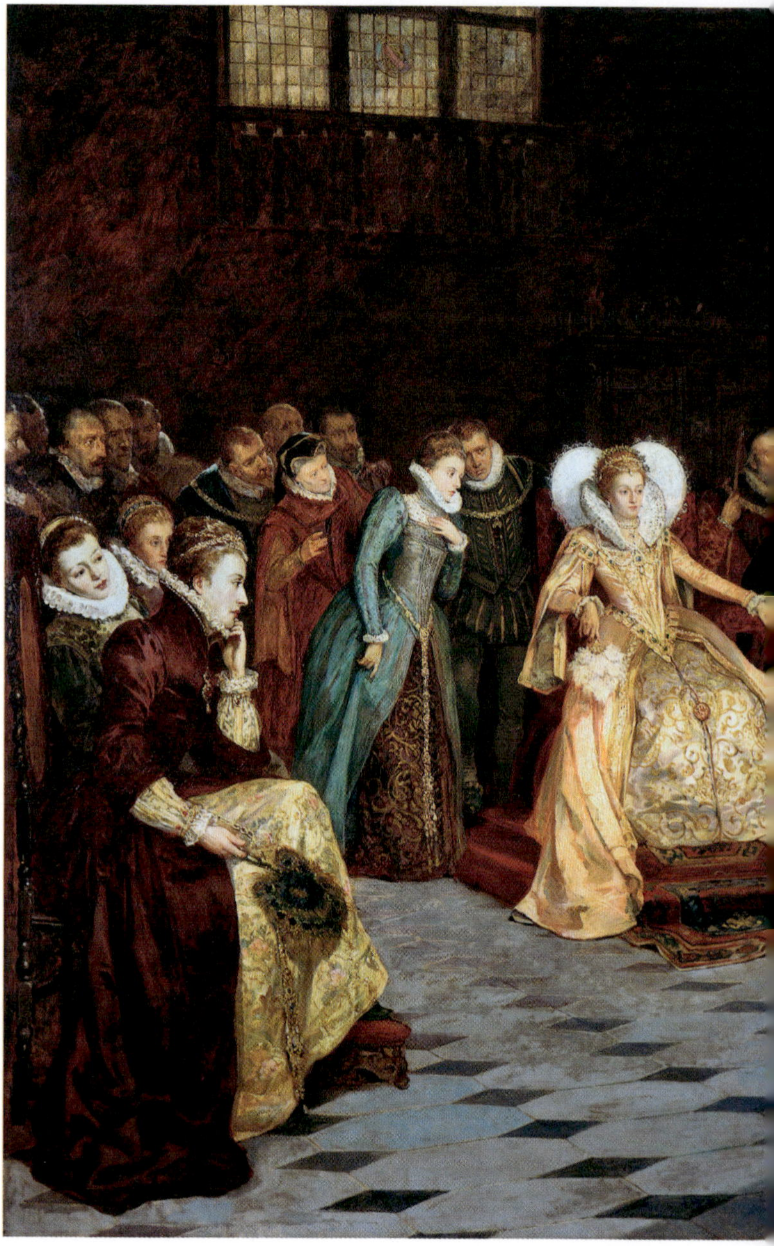

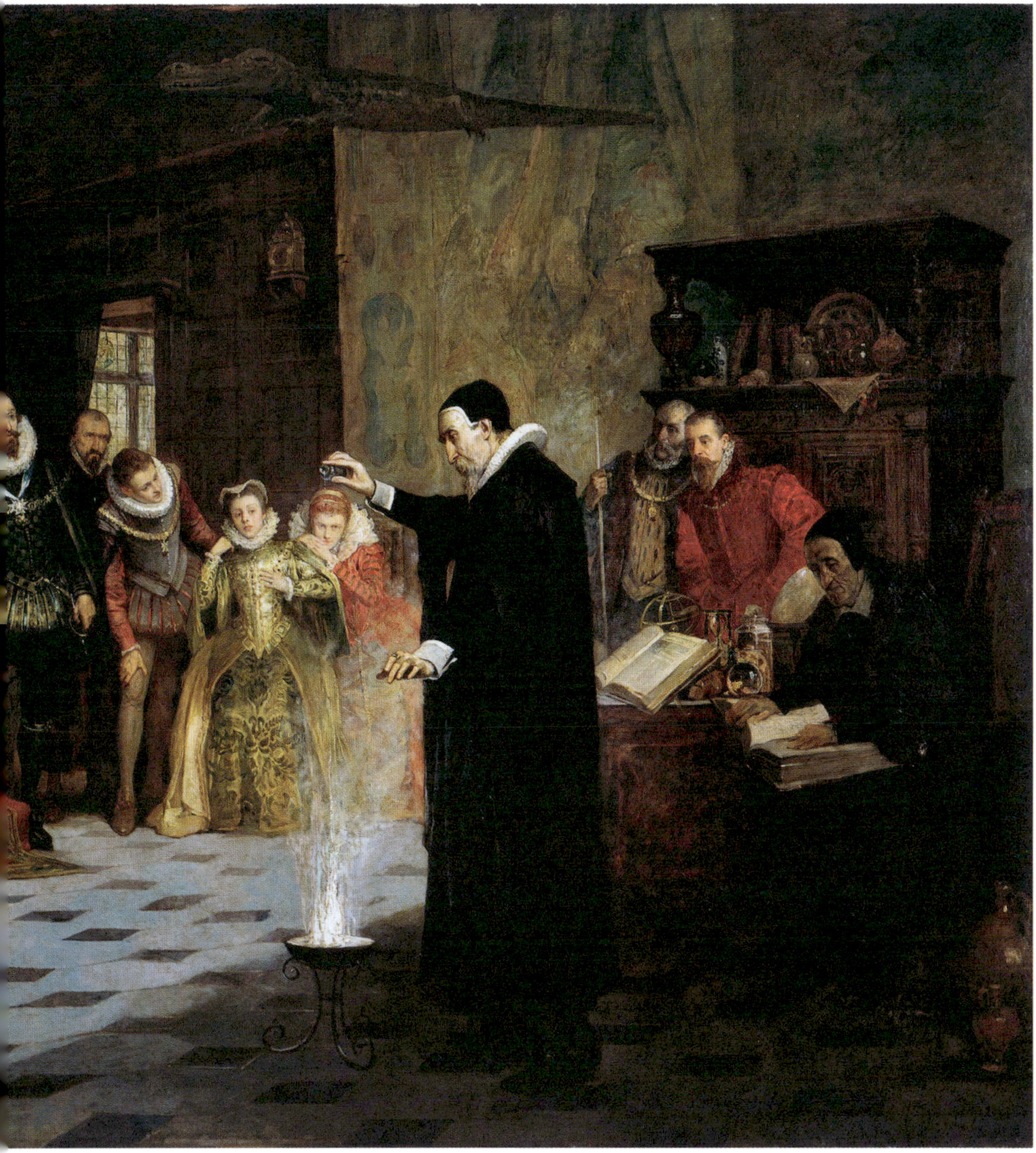

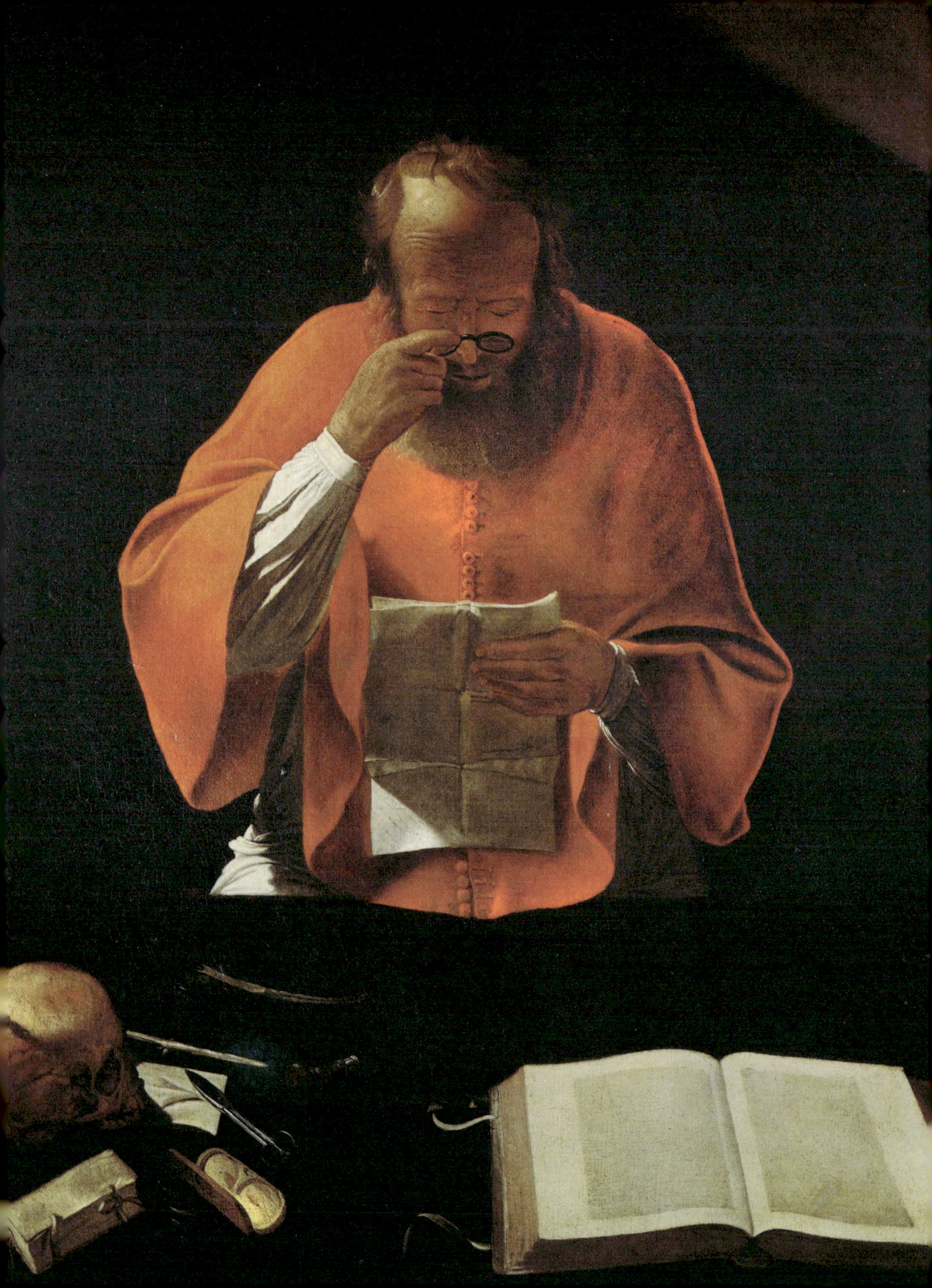

Right: Portrait of Mrs Stuart Merrill, Jean Delville, 1892, coloured pencil

Jean Delville's (1867–1953) portrait shows a woman in the throes of a mystical trance, her fiery hair crackling with psychic energy as she clutches a mysterious tome. The painting carries its own mystery: though museums date it to 1892, sculptor René Harvent insisted he watched Delville create it in 1944. This dating discrepancy adds another layer to an already enigmatic work packed with symbols of forgotten wisdom. The occult triangle represents perfect human knowledge, while the medium's spectral hands grip a grimoire we can't read. The triangle on the book's cover hints at some system of ancient wisdom once decoded by secretive Theosophists at their hushed gatherings. Delville may have returned to these mystical themes across decades, but the contested provenance itself reflects the slippery nature of occult knowledge, always appearing and vanishing when you least expect it.

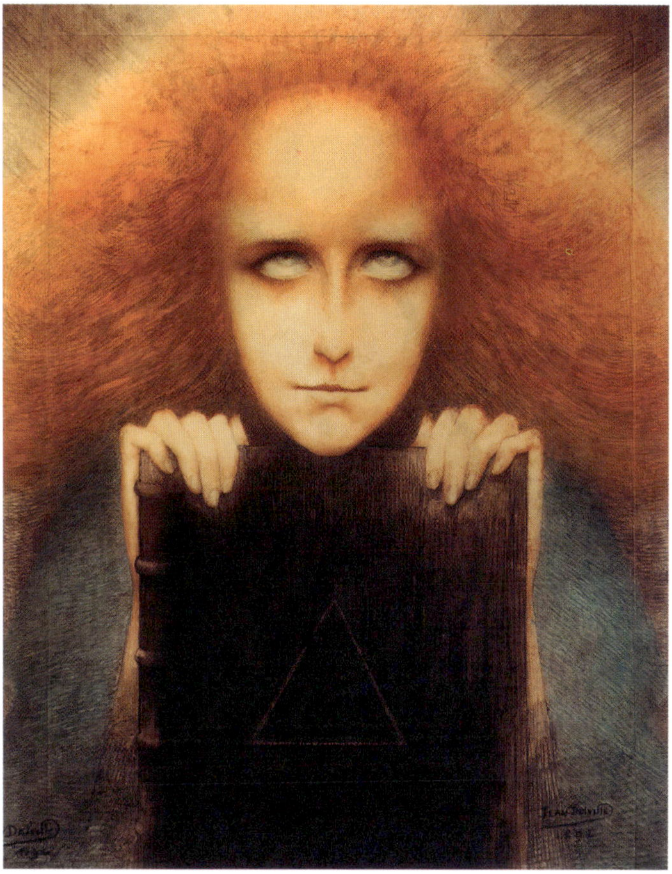

Opposite: Saint Jerome Reading, Georges de La Tour, seventeenth century, oil on canvas

History's greatest textual detective sits at work, holding knowledge so delicate that light passes right through it. Georges de La Tour's (1593–1652) painting portrays the saint who saved ancient wisdom from oblivion by translating countless manuscripts into Latin. La Tour rendered every detail with precision, from the subtly glowing page to the aged skin and faint shadows. Jerome reads with just his right eye (and left lens), his other eye having gone weak from decades squinting at tiny text by candlelight. The painting itself was completely forgotten for centuries, misattributed to Dürer and later 'Catalani', until its rediscovery in 1947. Even today, scholars continue hunting for lost La Tour works and debating attributions. Next time you're scrolling through e-books on your tablet, spare a thought for old Jerome here – preserving knowledge used to be awfully hard on the eyes.

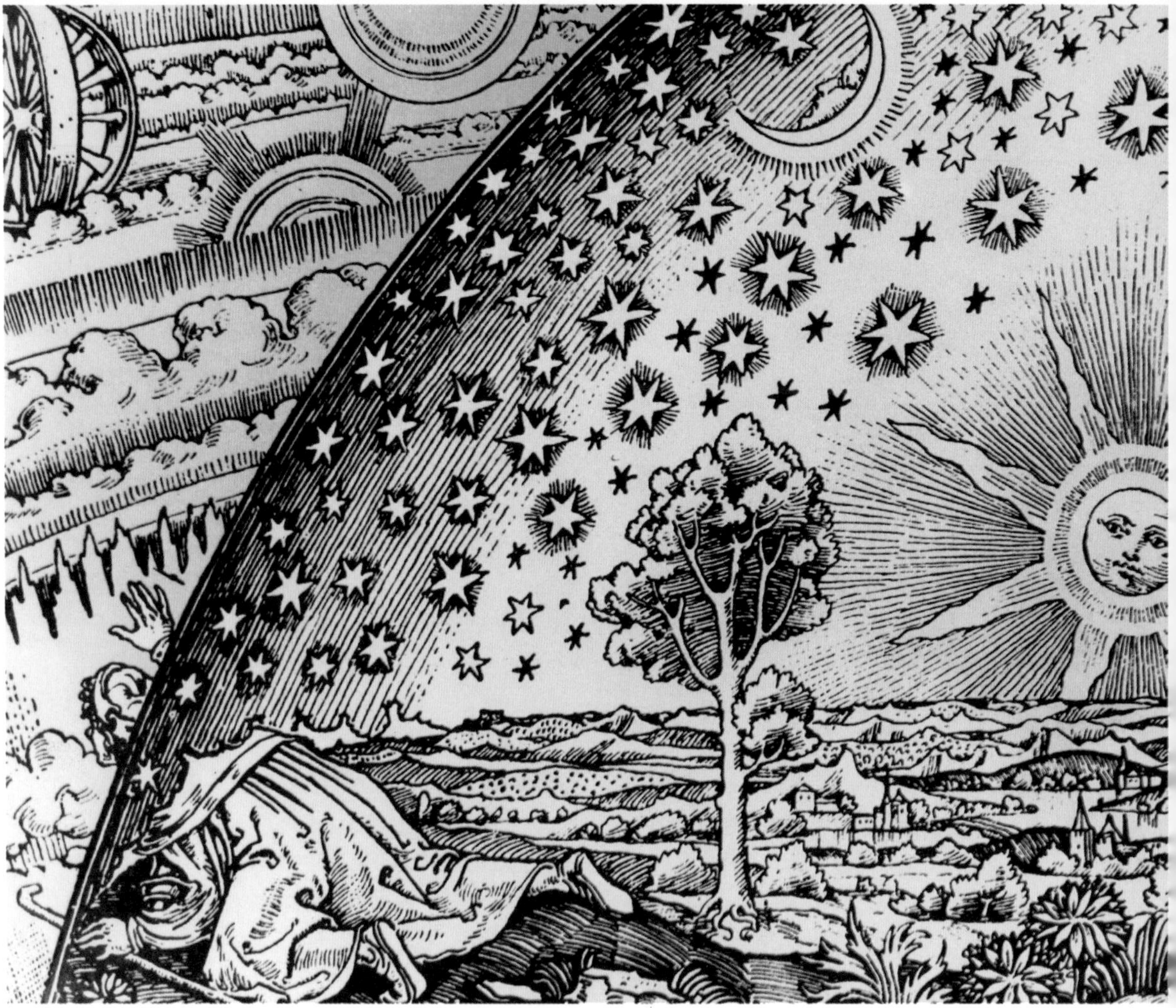

Representation of Earth and Space, artist unknown, published in *L'atmosphère: météorologie populaire*, by Camille Flammarion, 1888, wood engraving

A pilgrim kneels at the edge of the world in this haunting wood engraving first published in 1888 in Camille Flammarion's *L'atmosphère*. On hands and knees at the border of everything, he pokes his head through the star-spangled curtain of sky to discover cosmic machinery churning behind the scenes. You can almost feel his shock at finding gears and wheels of fire where he expected empty space. For centuries, scholars attributed this image to medieval or Renaissance masters, but researchers eventually uncovered its true nature as a brilliant nineteenth-century creation deliberately evoking an antiquated style, its actual creator remaining anonymous. The pilgrim's bold peek behind reality's curtain captures that universal urge to question what we're told and see what's really running the show.

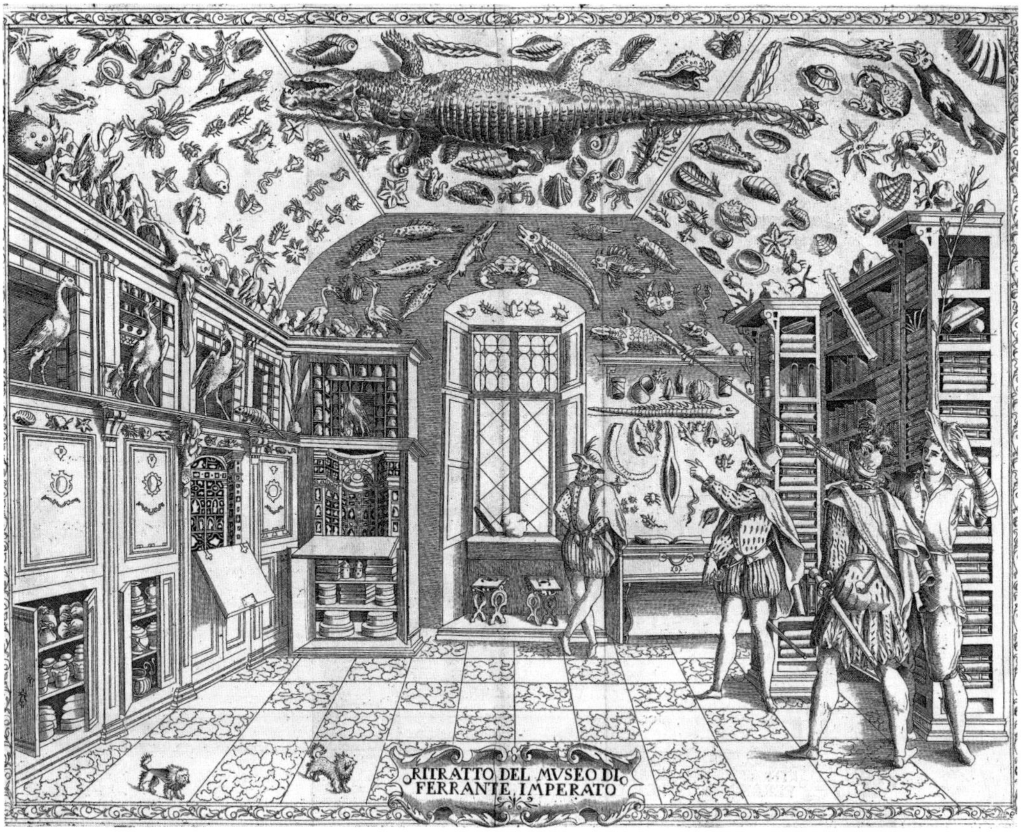

Illustration from Ferrante Imperato's *Dell'Historia Naturale*, artist unknown, 1599, engraving

Ferrante Imperato's jam-packed palace of weirdness, captured in this 1599 engraving, gives us our first glimpse into a Renaissance cabinet of wonders, where some 35,000 specimens crowded every available surface. Plants, minerals and creatures shared shelf space with books containing secrets, in a methodical attempt to organize all creation that looks like chaotic clutter to modern eyes. Early scientists used these working laboratories to understand the universe through direct observation rather than ancient texts, at a time when knowledge lived in these glorious hodgepodge rooms – before museums developed neat departments and explanatory placards. The scholarly equivalent of 'go big or go home' has never been so magnificently illustrated.

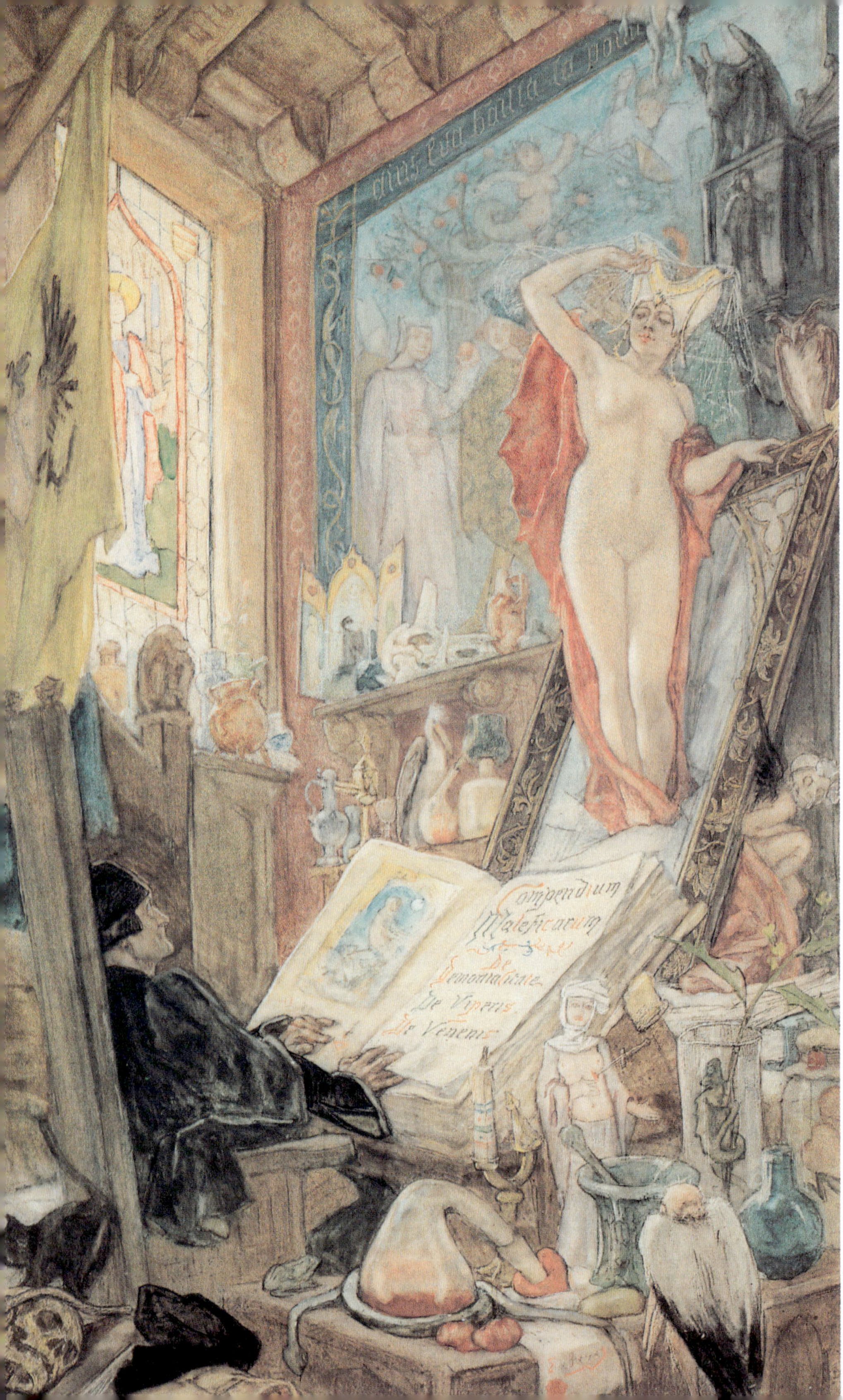
Compendium
Maleficarum
De
De Viperis

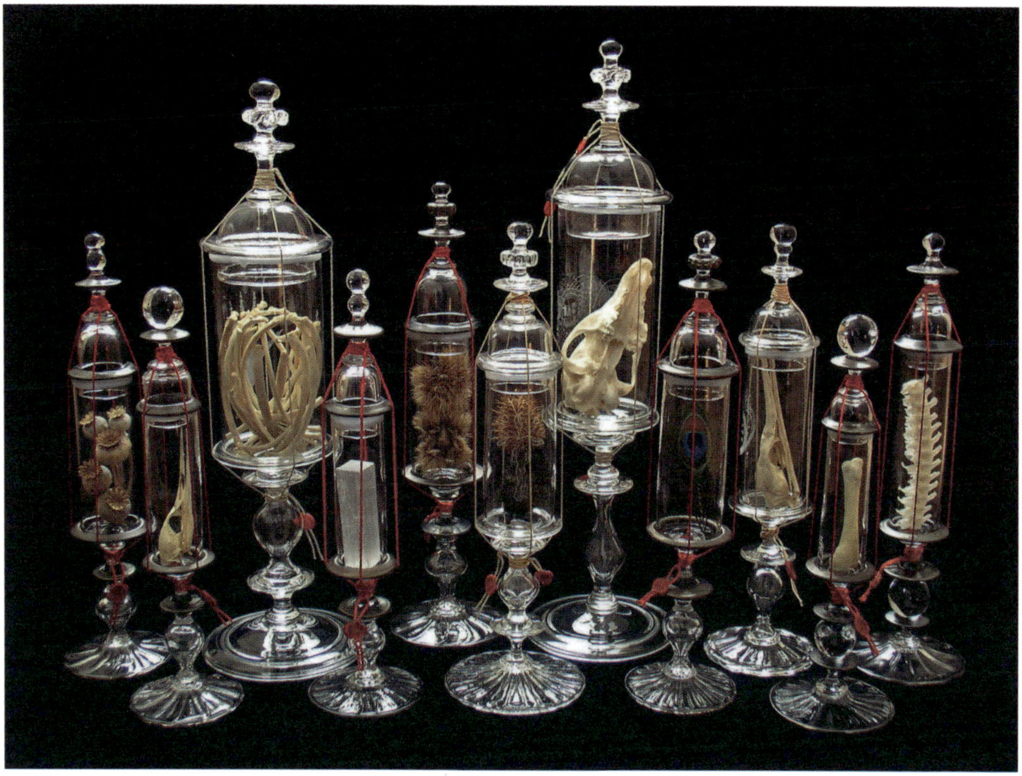

Opposite: The Incantation, Félicien Rops, 1909, coloured etching

Turning horny fantasies into magical research... what could possibly go wrong? Félicien Rops (1833–98) illustrates a scene from Octave Uzanne's story about an ageing scholar who turns to the occult when conventional pleasures fail him. Surrounded by arcane tools and specimens in jars, the alchemist pores over his *Compendium Maleficarum de Demonialitate*, while a female figure materializes from artwork into flesh, all under the disapproving gaze of a stained-glass Virgin Mary. You can almost feel the nineteenth-century anxieties about knowledge, power and gender radiating from this scene - the male intellectual armed with mystical technologies to manifest women who exist only to please him. Ancient knowledge probably never worked quite like this, but the image tells us plenty about what men like Uzanne and Rops fantasized it could accomplish. Either way, someone needs a cold shower.

Above: Reliquary Group, Andy Paiko, 2011, blown, etched and sculpted glass, selected found objects, twine, wax

Andy Paiko's 'Reliquaries' draw on the practice of enshrining sacred objects - a tradition with roots stretching back centuries, here channelled through seventeenth-century Eastern European craftsmanship. His exquisitely crafted glass vessels cradle natural curiosities--seed pods, feathers, intertwined bones and skulls - fragile treasures secured by crimson and gold thread with ceremony and care, anchored at the throat and the belly of the luminous container. The virtuosic skills required to birth these containers have nearly vanished, remnants of an age when glass-making itself was revered as sacred alchemy. Alone, each reliquary is spare and austere. Gathered together, they create an intoxicating abundance, elevating humble fragments of nature into lavish objects that compel veneration. Paiko taps into an ancient understanding: the container can eclipse its contents in power, transmuting ordinary bones and seeds into precious relics through lavish artistry. The vessel makes the treasure, not the other way around.

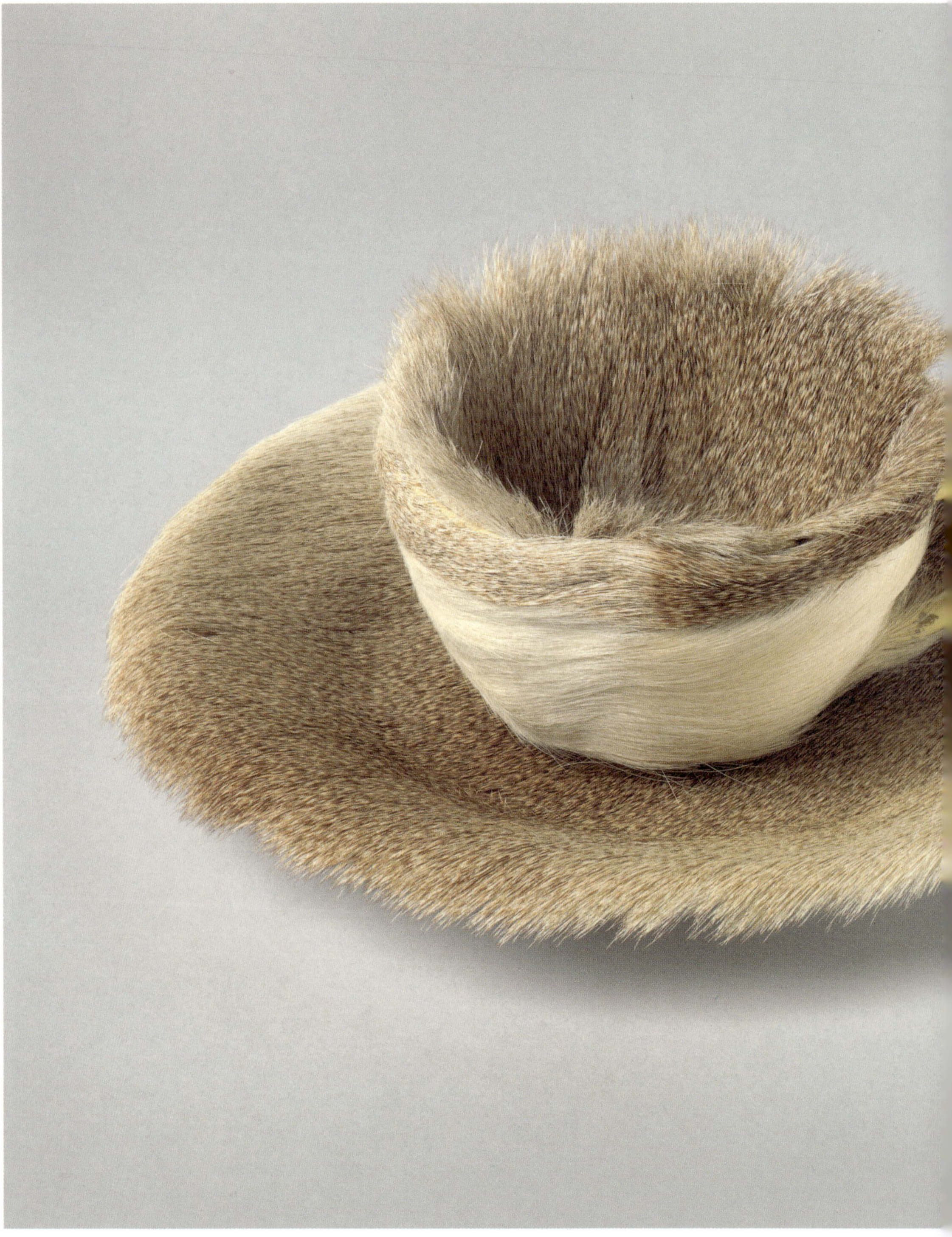

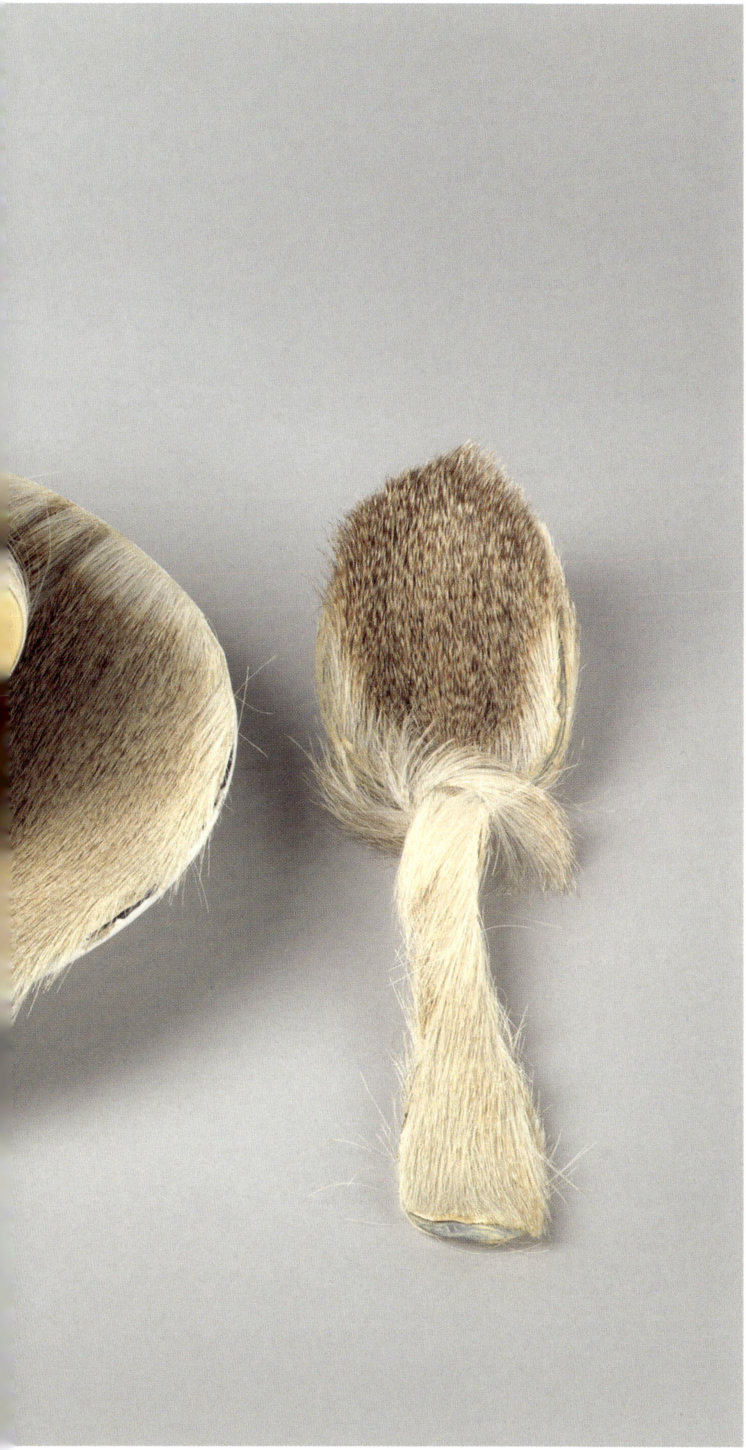

Object, Meret Oppenheim, 1936, fur-covered cup, saucer and spoon

'Oh waiter, there's fur in my teacup!' Meret Oppenheim (1913–85) turned a café joke with Picasso into art history with this simple yet audacious creation from 1936. When Picasso admired Meret's fur bracelet and suggested anything could be fur-covered, Oppenheim quipped, 'Even this cup and saucer.' She promptly bought a teacup set and wrapped it in gazelle fur, creating something both amusing and deeply mysterious. Originally displayed beneath works by male Surrealists, her furry tableware quickly became the exhibition's star. One New York viewer reportedly fainted at the sight. Initially rejected by MoMA trustees as 'ridiculous', it was eventually purchased in 1946 as their first artwork by a female artist. There's something about a fur-lined teacup that feels so viscerally, brain-revoltingly bizarre that fainting seems an entirely appropriate reaction.

PART FOUR

—

THE HUMAN MYSTERY

'If anything is sacred, the human body is sacred...'

– WALT WHITMAN

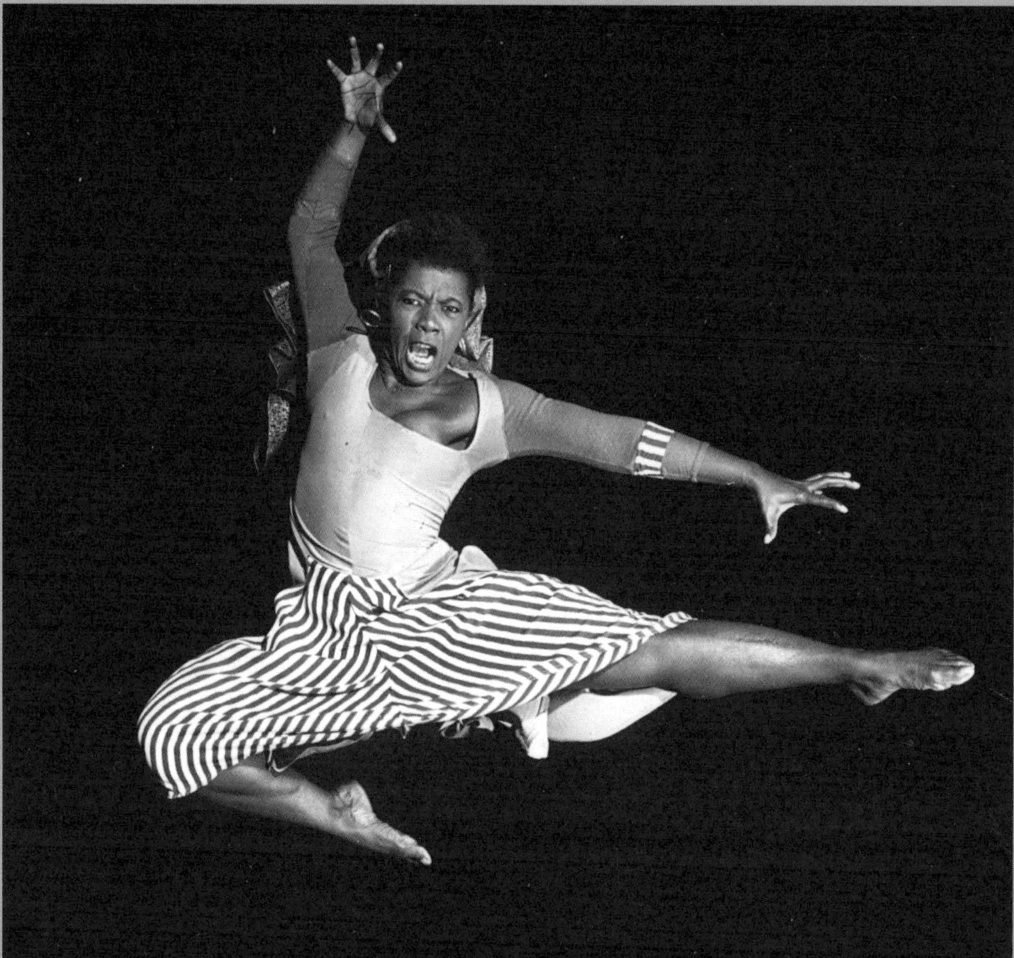

You spend a huge amount of your existence experiencing things that have never happened. Your brain builds an entire world, populates it with people you've never met and places that don't exist, and convinces you it was absolutely real nearly every night once your head hits the pillow. Or consider how your endorphin-flooded brain during a brutal workout can trick you into thinking that agony feels amazing and exhaustion equals euphoria. Or that meditative moment when you catch yourself thinking and wonder: 'Who is the "me" that's aware of thinking?' How is it that we can observe ourselves observing? How do thoughts arise from flesh? How do we inhabit these bodies that feel both utterly ours and completely unknowable, both intimate and impossible? Flesh that responds to our commands yet ages without our permission. Hearts that beat whether we're paying attention or not, then stop beating eventually, inevitably, turning these miraculous vessels that somehow once contained entire universes into empty shells and dust in the wind and all that sort of thing.

From mystic visions to modern dance to primal ritual, humans perpetually attempt to articulate the bizarre experience of consciousness inhabiting flesh. Artists have always been fascinated by moments when ordinary awareness shifts, when perception becomes distorted and disoriented, the feeling when reality is rendered unrecognizable. What happens in that space between sleeping and waking, when the mind generates entire realities from nothing? How does consciousness arise from neural firing patterns? How does wet, noodly brain matter generate the sensation of existing? When do movements transcend mechanics and become sacred?

These are the questions artists can't resist probing, driving them to push their minds and bodies to the extreme in service of reaching these extraordinary states. Joan Miró deliberately starved himself into a hallucinatory state, sitting for hours as hunger carved visions from empty air, then frantically capturing what his emptied stomach had conjured on canvas and burlap. Henri Michaux made detailed drawings while high on mescaline, documenting how chemicals rewire perception. Louise Bourgeois explored how memory and trauma live in the body, creating sculptures that gave physical form to psychological wounds. Alan Syliboy's paintings depict Mi'kmaq cycles of life, death and regeneration, utilizing traditional symbols to bridge ancient

Opposite: Pearl Primus performing her expressionistic dance piece *Strange Fruit*, based on Abel Meeropol's poem and song, 1951, photograph

knowledge with contemporary vision. Salvador Dalí explored that space between sleeping and waking, holding a key over a metal plate, jolting awake when it dropped to immediately record the visions that flickered at the edge of consciousness.

This artistic investigation of human mystery permeates everything we consume, from cinema that holds us spellbound in our theatre seats to the music that gets us up and moving, seeking transcendence through sweat and rhythm. Darren Aronofsky's *The Fountain* traces patterns of death and rebirth across centuries. Christopher Nolan's *Inception* maps layers of consciousness through dream-sharing. Music and movement chase these experiences through trance-inducing tribal drumming and the whirling dances of Sufi mystics. Buddhist monks generate internal heat so powerful that they can dry wet sheets wrapped around their bodies in freezing temperatures. Olympic athletes report 'flow states' in which they suddenly perform beyond what should be humanly possible.

These altered states of consciousness, whether accessed through fasting, meditation, movement or ritual, produce distinctive forms of artistic evidence. In gallery vaults and museum archives, we find meticulous records of prophetic dreams rendered in pigment and charcoal. Performance pieces capture moments when artists become vessels for depths within themselves that connect to something infinitely larger, channelling voices that aren't their own, moving with impossible grace, speaking words they swear they've never thought and gesturing in languages their bodies have somehow always known. Installations transform ordinary spaces into sites of ritual, where time moves in cycles rather than lines, where birth and death become stations on an endless wheel rather than beginnings and endings.

Modern science has joined this ancient quest, turning laboratories into new temples where scientists study what shamans once experienced. What once required fasting and ritual now gets measured with electrodes and brain scans, revealing fascinating patterns but leaving consciousness as enigmatic as ever. Yet artists continue pushing boundaries, venturing where flesh pulses with possibility, mortality becomes immaterial and midnight manifestations spill into daylight hours – proving that the marvel of being human remains our ultimate mystery.

Opposite: Silence, Henry Fuseli, 1799–1801, oil on canvas

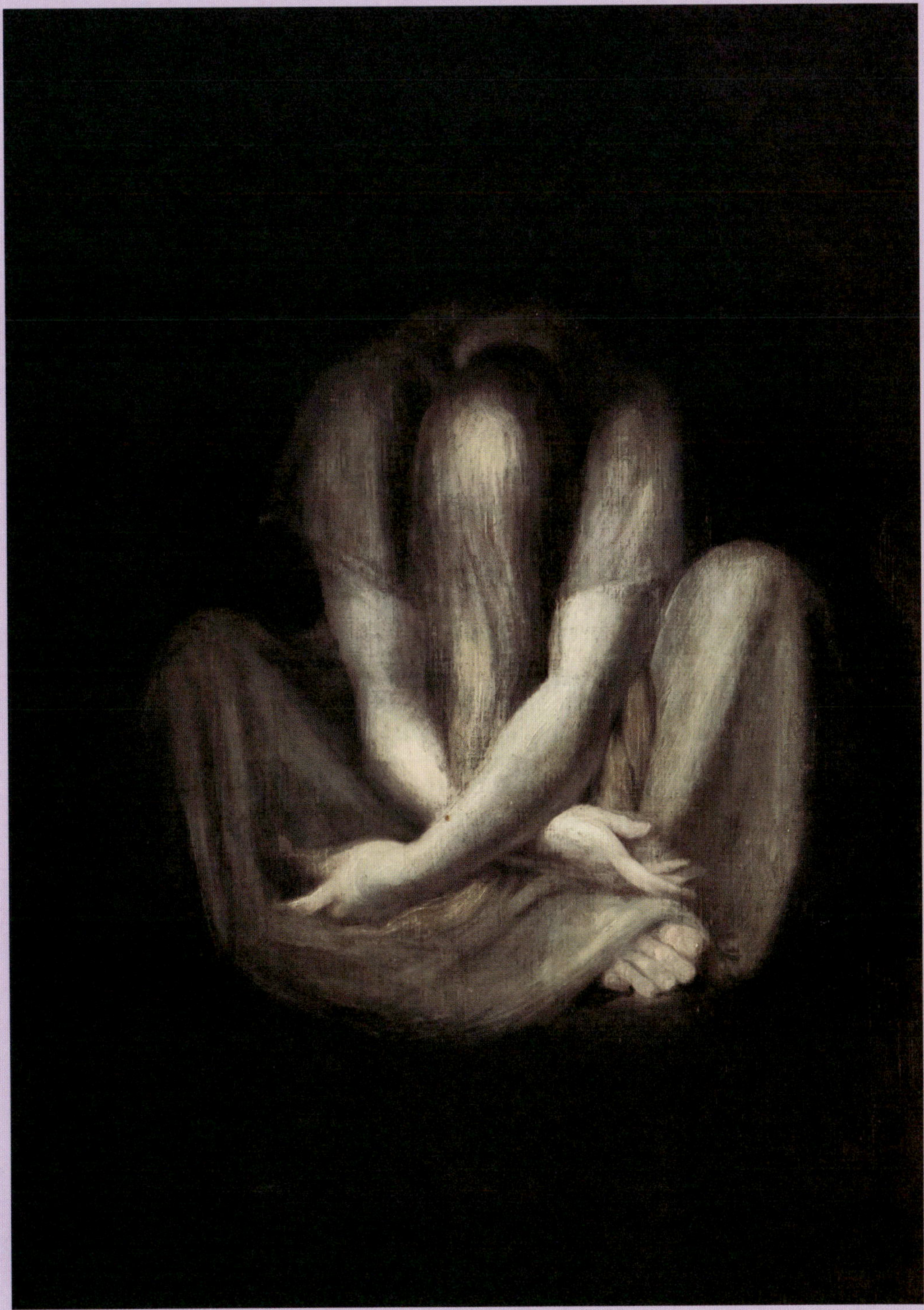

X

—

VISIONARY STATES

'We are in this life to enlarge the soul,
liberate the spirit, and light up the brain.'

– TOM ROBBINS

Imagine a museum whose galleries display not objects but states of mind. In one room, the lucid dream, where sleepers suddenly realize they're dreaming and seize control, flying through ceilings into star-filled skies, revisiting the irretrievable pasts of childhood homes or summoning deceased relatives for conversations cut short. In the basement, fevered hallucinations, in which the bedroom ceiling drips with kaleidoscopic light and the empty corner chair buzzes with the weight and noise of a thronging crowd. The east wing houses chemically altered consciousness; fungal compounds make fingertips indistinguishable from ancient bark, and laboratory synthetics fracture light into mandalas that contain entire universes in their geometry. On the top floor, bathed in impossible light, are mystical experiences, in which celestial messengers arrive leaving trails of blue fire in their wake. Each of these altered states operates according to its own physics, its own emotional temperature, its own relationship to time. And throughout history, artists have returned from these disrupted perceptions bearing visual evidence, bootleg footage from territories where consciousness strips down to its bells and pulleys – the hidden mechanisms that keep perception running.

These altered states of mind have captivated humans since we first recognized our own awareness. 'Our normal waking consciousness,' wrote William James, 'is but one special type of consciousness, whilst all about it, parted from it by the filmiest of screens, there lie potential forms of consciousness entirely different.' These other states press against that filmy screen constantly. Fever dreams turn bedrooms into urgent riddles, where solving the pattern suddenly matters more than anything in your life. Sleep paralysis conjures phantasmal watchers that perch on your chest, while practitioners of deep meditation describe watching their thoughts appear and dissolve without attachment. Fasting, sensory deprivation, rhythmic movement, extreme exertion – the human mind has countless doorways into altered awareness. Even sheer exhaustion can turn words on a page into hieroglyphs, conversations into incomprehensible noise, the world seen at a crystalline distance, as if through thick, filmy glass.

Ancient cultures turned altered states into official business, from the Oracle at Delphi inhaling vapours from geological fissures to Eleusinian initiates sipping their mysterious kykeon. Medieval visionaries like Hildegard von Bingen captured mystical experiences in illuminated manuscripts, her 'lights of heaven' blazing across parchment with an intensity that still burns through centuries, now recognized as classic migraine aura patterns, suggesting that even agony can become a doorway to vision. The monk Diebold Lauber claimed visions poured directly onto his pages, while Rupert of Deutz insisted that the Virgin Mary herself guided his hand. Once tightly contained within religious doctrine, these visions eventually broke free and became raw material for artistic exploration beyond church walls.

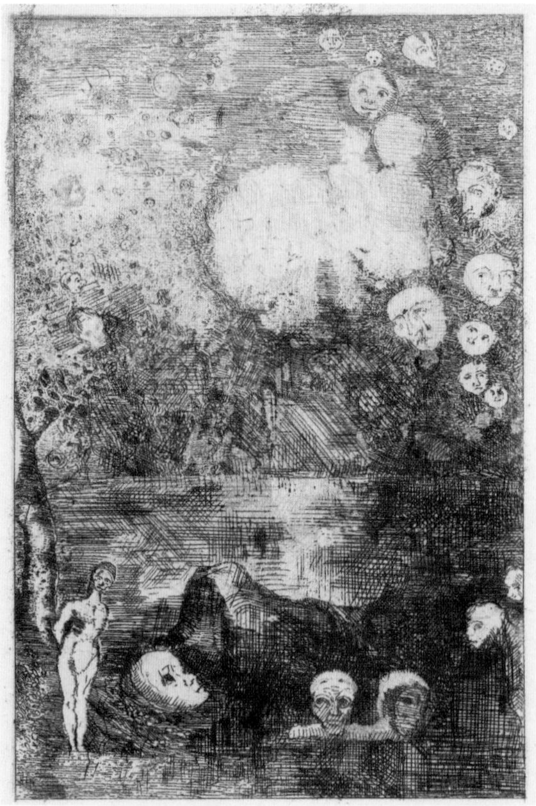

As religion's grip loosened, visionary experiences democratized. What was once claimed by saints and mystics became open territory for artists to explore. Jean Delville made meditation visible as pure radiance, Jan Toorop explored collective trance through religious devotion. Mikalojus Konstantinas Čiurlionis translated musical structures directly into cosmic landscapes. Pamela Colman Smith painted what music looked like to her through synaesthesia, unlocking doors into beautiful countries where sound became vision. Unica Zürn created phantasmagorical landscapes during her self-described 'trance states'. Frida Kahlo mapped the altered consciousness of chronic pain, while Vali Myers channelled hallucinatory visions through electric, untamed forms. Each found their own way into those same realms where saints and shamans had bridged worlds.

By the mid-twentieth century, artists were exploring chemical pathways to altered states. Salvador Dalí proclaimed, 'I don't do drugs; I am drugs,' setting the stage for more direct explorations. Ramón Medina Silva translated sacred peyote visions into vibrant yarn paintings that mapped the

Above: The Dream, Odilon Redon, 1878–82, etching

Opposite: Priestess of Delphi, John Collier, 1891, oil on canvas

Huichol cosmos, while Pablo Amaringo documented ayahuasca visions with the precision of a field researcher in his lush Amazonian tableaus. Marjorie Cameron Parsons Kimmel's mystical drawings, some influenced by her own psychedelic experiences, shocked gallery visitors and led to arrests. While mainstream culture fixated on the anarchic, chaotic qualities of the substances, these artists approached them as sacred technologies with deep cultural roots. Contemporary artists continue this ancient quest for visionary insight, each developing their own techniques to document what happens when consciousness abandons its usual post.

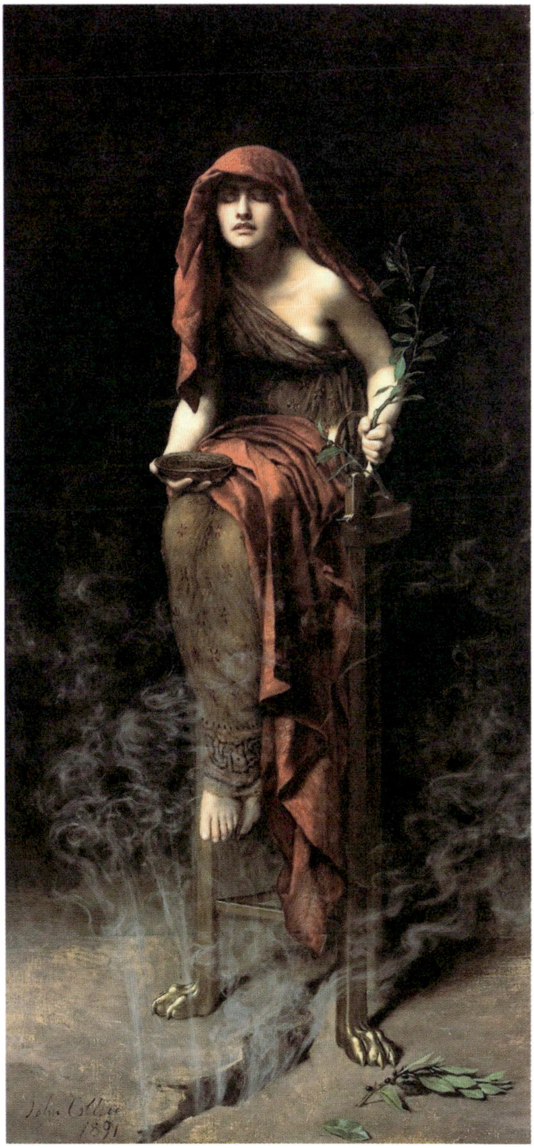

Each generation adds new wings to our museum of extraordinary consciousness, some through sacred plants, others through trance, meditation or digital exploration. The floor plan grows increasingly complex, branching like neural pathways, Smith's synaesthetic visions, connecting like Čiurlionis's cosmic notations. In this museum without walls, our default 'normal perception' becomes just another small, stuffy beige room in an infinite, expansive labyrinth of everything. The most daring artists wander its uncharted corridors, sketching maps of realms that exist between heartbeats and collecting souvenirs from the borderlands of being, where consciousness turns out to be far stranger and more spacious than we ever suspected.

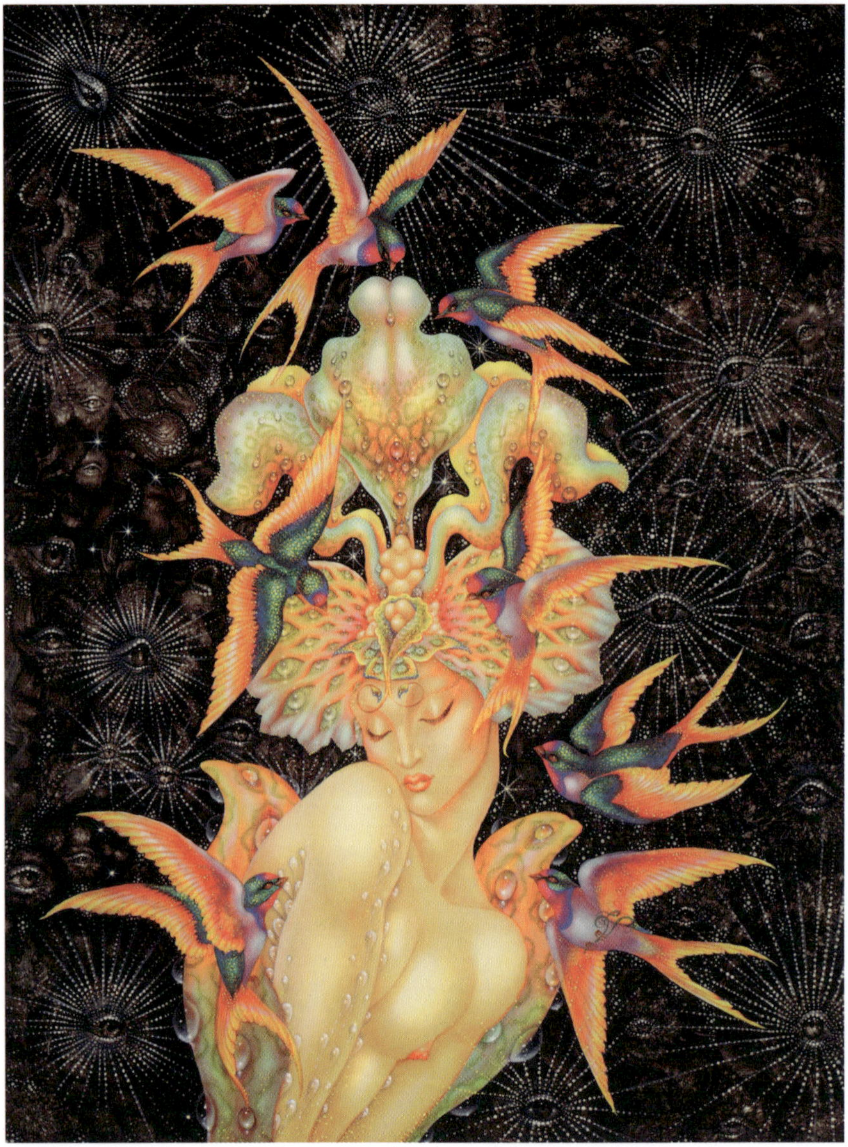

The Flower of Ecstasy (Blooming Consciousness), Virgo Paraiso, 2018, oil on wood

Sumptuous rapture, ecstatic surrender – Virgo Paraiso calls forth a vision of ecstasy in which brilliant oranges, electric blues and incandescent pinks explode across the surface. A figure with delicate features rests in bliss as their elaborate headdress of orange and pink petals bursts like an orgiastic splendour of botanical fireworks. Birds hang suspended mid-flight, dewdrops quiver on floral flesh, everything trembling with overwhelming beauty against dazzling darkness studded with watchful eyes and pulsing stars. The being's closed eyes hint at an inward journey through pleasure's infinite gardens, yet the riotous radiance around them transforms private experience into shared vision, a lush manifestation of euphoria's divine landscape.

Méditation, Jean Delville, 1929, charcoal, pen and ink, and black pencil on paper

Is that a divine figure radiating light, or light manifesting as human? Jean Delville (1867–1953) gives us a bowed head where thought appears as blazing radiance, a sunburst laser show with beams both emanating from and illuminating the meditative figure. The stark contrast between darkness and light produces a visual electricity that feels intense, almost overwhelming, maybe even forbidden, as if we are witnessing something humans aren't meant to see. During this period, Delville was steeped in Theosophy and occult practices, while confronting his profound disillusionment with Krishnamurti, whom he had championed as a spiritual teacher. This austere black and white drawing raises questions about transcendence itself: does the true seeker need to surrender completely, as suggested by that deeply bowed posture? What a strange sight to see meditation, normally hidden and internal, made visible as spectacular solar showcase.

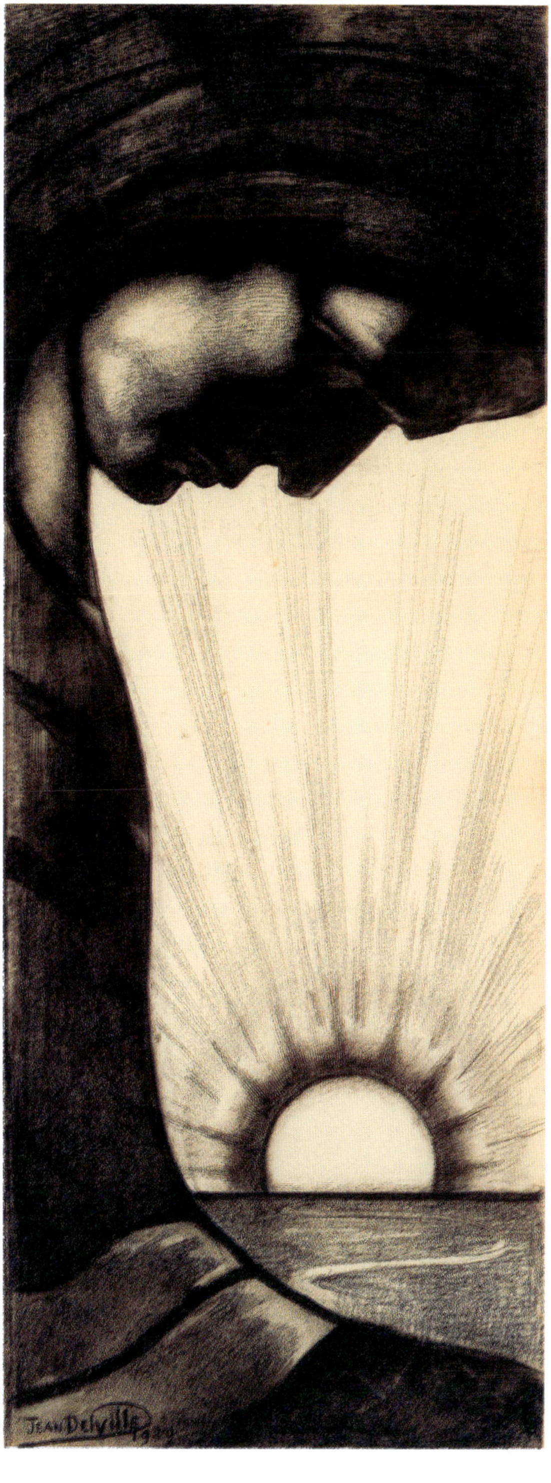

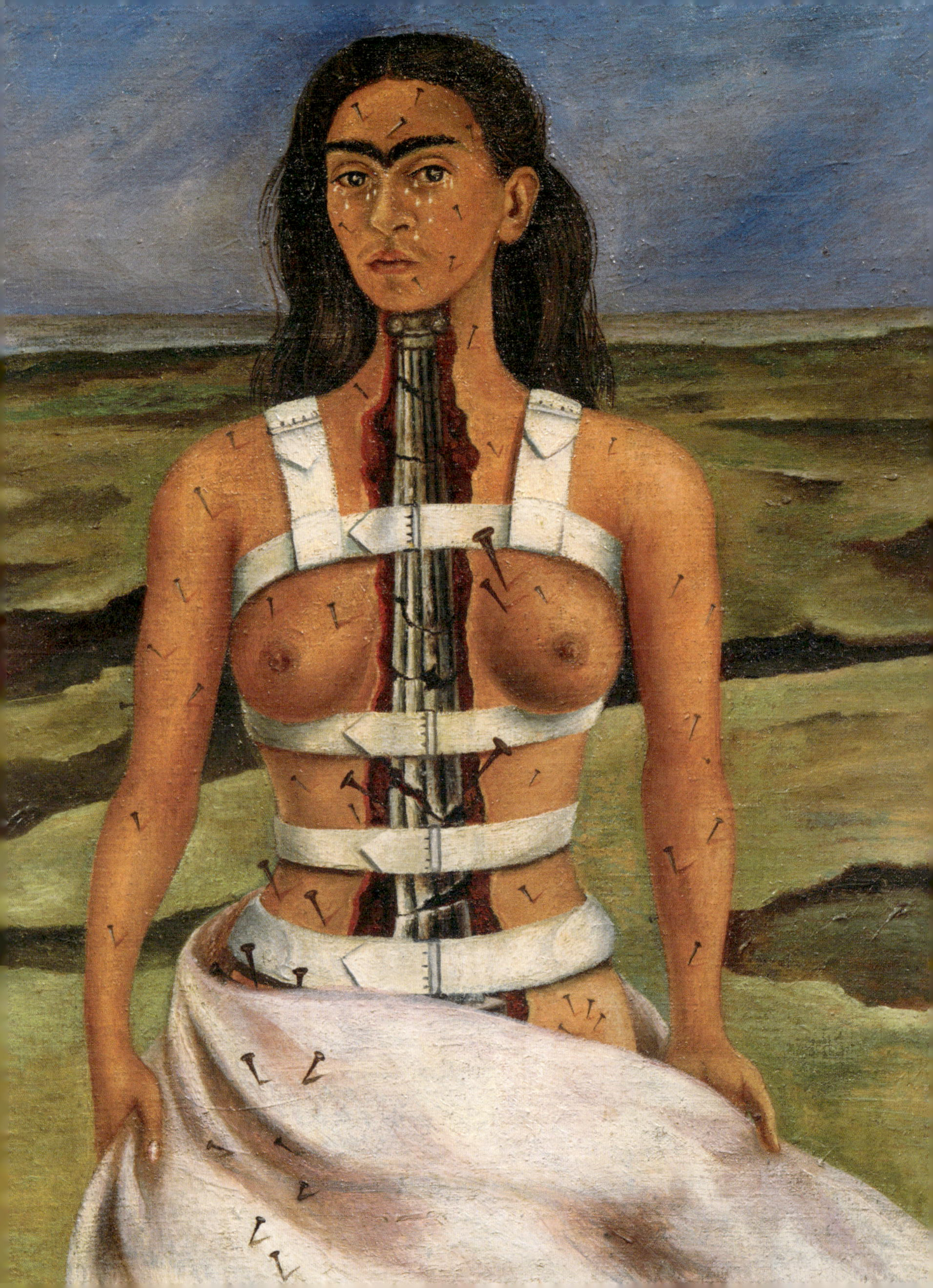

Right: Overture. "Egmont" Beethoven, Pamela Colman Smith, 1907, watercolour, brush and ink, and pencil on paper

A colossal stone face emerges from a cliff side, its dreamy gaze fixed on distant mountains, while tiny pilgrims gather at its crown in reverent communion. Pamela Colman Smith (1878–1951) painted what music looked like to her through a rare form of synaesthesia she discovered while studying at the Pratt Institute. Though now famous for creating the iconic Rider-Waite tarot deck (for which she received little recognition or payment), Smith was first celebrated for her 'music pictures', exhibited at Alfred Stieglitz's gallery in 1907. To curious viewers, she explained: 'When I take a brush in hand and the music begins, it is like unlocking the door into a beautiful country.' And what a country Smith painted! In her swirling watercolours and fluid lines, we glimpse a realm of vision that existed between her ear and eye, translated into art that still enchants us with its otherworldly beauty.

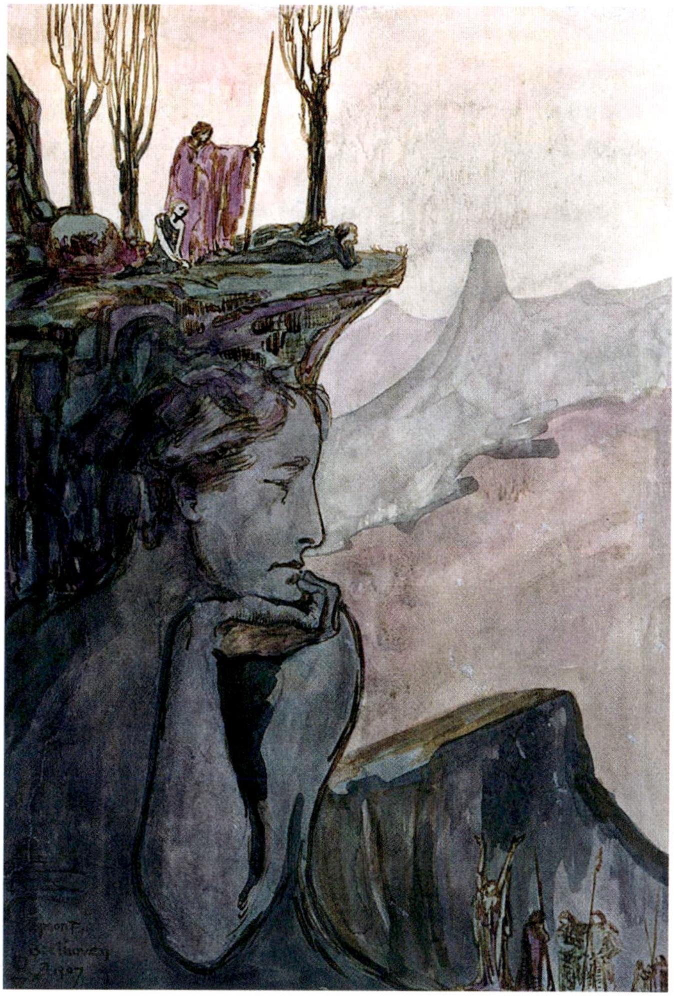

Opposite: The Broken Column, Frida Kahlo, 1944, oil on masonite

A woman stands before us, her flesh an open medical theatre in which a shattered column replaces her spine – a surreal vision born not from dreams but from the altered consciousness of chronic pain. Frida Kahlo (1907–54) created this haunting self-portrait following one of her many spinal surgeries, mapping her nervous system in nails, each one a lightning rod of sensation, while tears run down her otherwise composed face, showing that dissociative state familiar to anyone who has lived with unrelenting physical suffering. The medical corset strapping her torso suggests both imprisonment and protection, twin realities she navigated daily. Against a landscape cracked and fissured like her own body, Kahlo's self-portrait reveals that strange consciousness where pain creates its own visionary territory, a parallel reality with its own rules, revelations and strange clarities.

Dream and Premonition,
María Izquierdo, 1947,
oil on canvas

From a shadowed window, a woman extends her arm to hold her own severed head by its braided hair, while mask-like faces dangle from twisted branches against a turbulent sky. María Izquierdo (1902–55) painted this haunting vision in 1947, just before a stroke would paralyze her right side and force her to relearn painting with her left hand. Among the cross-topped graves, a headless, vaguely provocative crimson figure strides, a form that carries both freedom and doom, the complex emotions that surface in our dreaming minds. Though celebrated as the first Mexican woman to exhibit internationally, Izquierdo's career was undermined when male contemporaries blocked her from prestigious mural commissions. Unlike the overtly political art dominating post-Revolutionary Mexico, her work mixes Mexican folk traditions with European Surrealist elements without following either school's rules, creating dreamscapes from personal visions and nocturnal revelations that map the intersection of nightmares, premonitions and waking concerns.

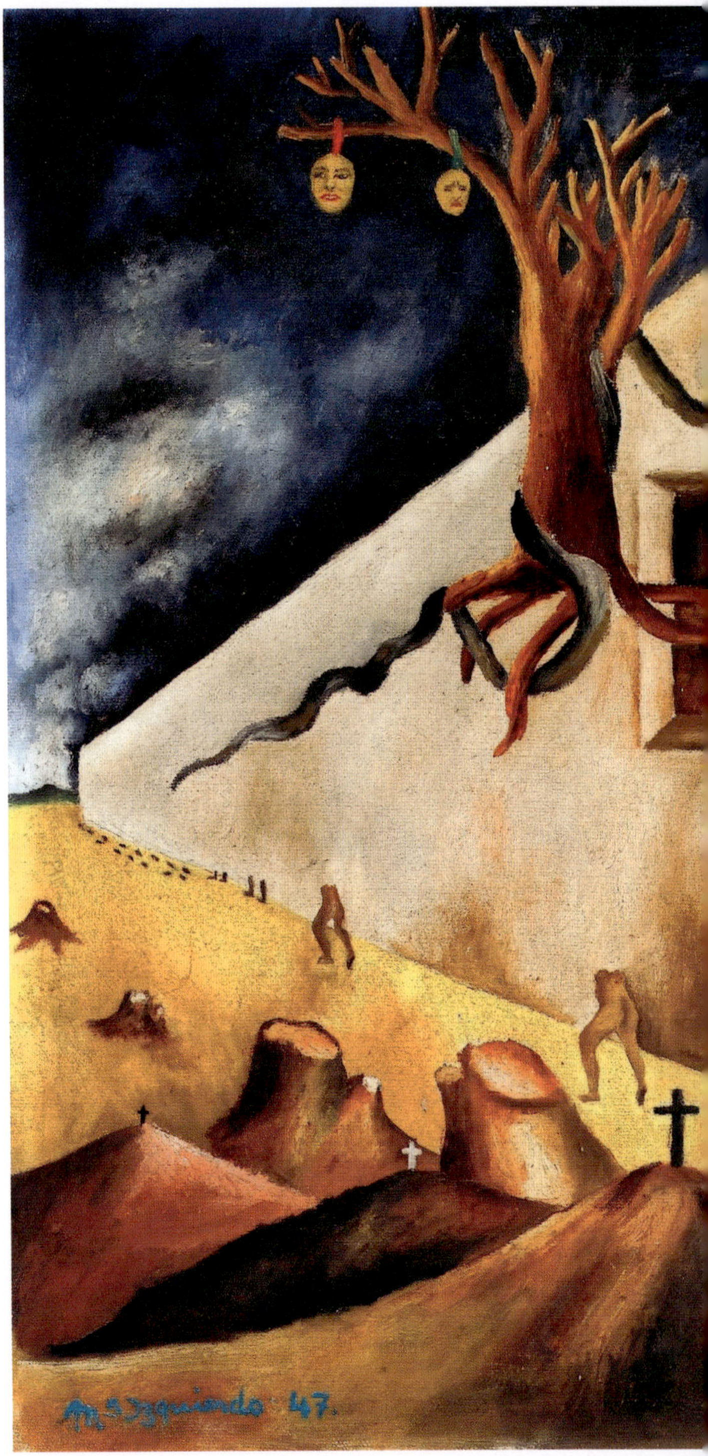

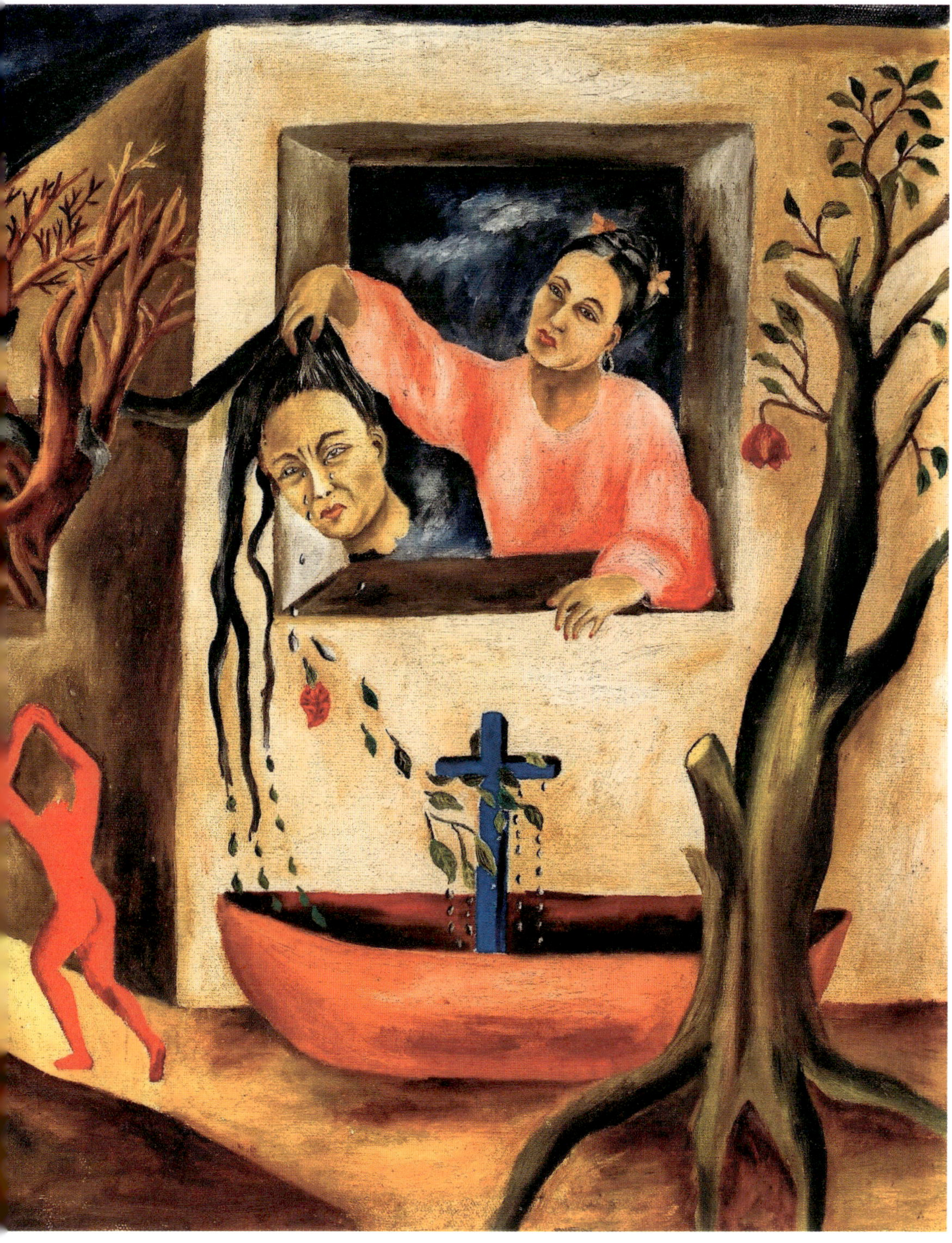

Right: Awake in a Dream, Rachael Bridge, 2024, oil on panel

A face glows electric crimson against the midnight velvet of a cloud-hazed sky, eyes tilted upwards in what might be revelation or wonder. Rachael Bridge's hyperrealistic style magnifies reality rather than mimicking it, colours pulsing with neon nightclub intensity, shadows of glossy black honey. This is how a lucid dream feels from the inside: everything too vivid, too present, as if perception and sense have been dialled up to a blazing wattage of supernatural clarity. Her haunting subjects often appear suspended in profound private moments, their luminous gazes hinting at enigmatic interior narratives playing out in secret theatres and locked rooms. This painting invites us to recognize our own experiences of dual consciousness – those rare, electric moments when we realize we're dreaming without breaking the dream's spell.

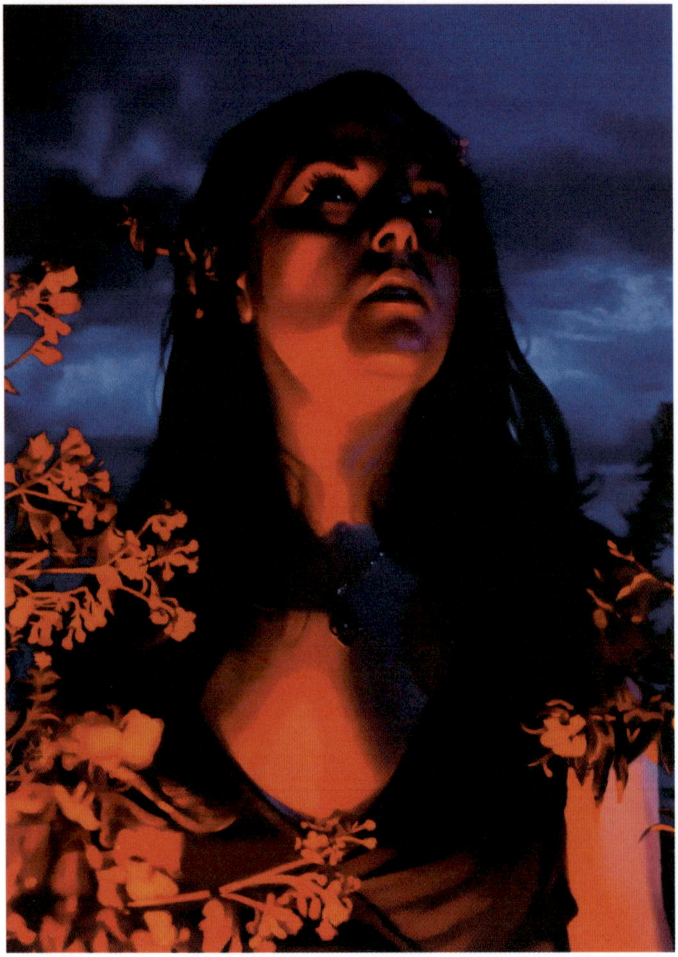

Opposite: Untitled, Unica Zürn, 1957, oil on paper mounted on wood

A tangled vision spreads across the darkness, filled with faces, eyes and tentacled forms in delicate, obsessive black ink. Unica Zürn (1916–70) created this labyrinthine phantasmagorical incantation during her intermittent hospital stays for schizophrenia. The German artist and writer moved to Paris in 1953 with Surrealist Hans Bellmer, entering a relationship in which art and mental suffering became inseparable. Working in what she called a 'trance state', Zürn produced thousands of automatic drawings in which biological forms multiply endlessly. Faces appear from cellular structures, eyes peer from twisted labyrinths and lines coil like neural pathways. 'Pairs of eyes dead full of time look earnestly across the border between being and nothingness,' she wrote, describing her art-making process. What appears chaotic actually shows precision born of necessity, desperate documents of a mind in agony, her pen following the all-consuming contours of terror, the frayed and fraught wiring and obsessive circuitry of a mind caught in an endless feedback loop.

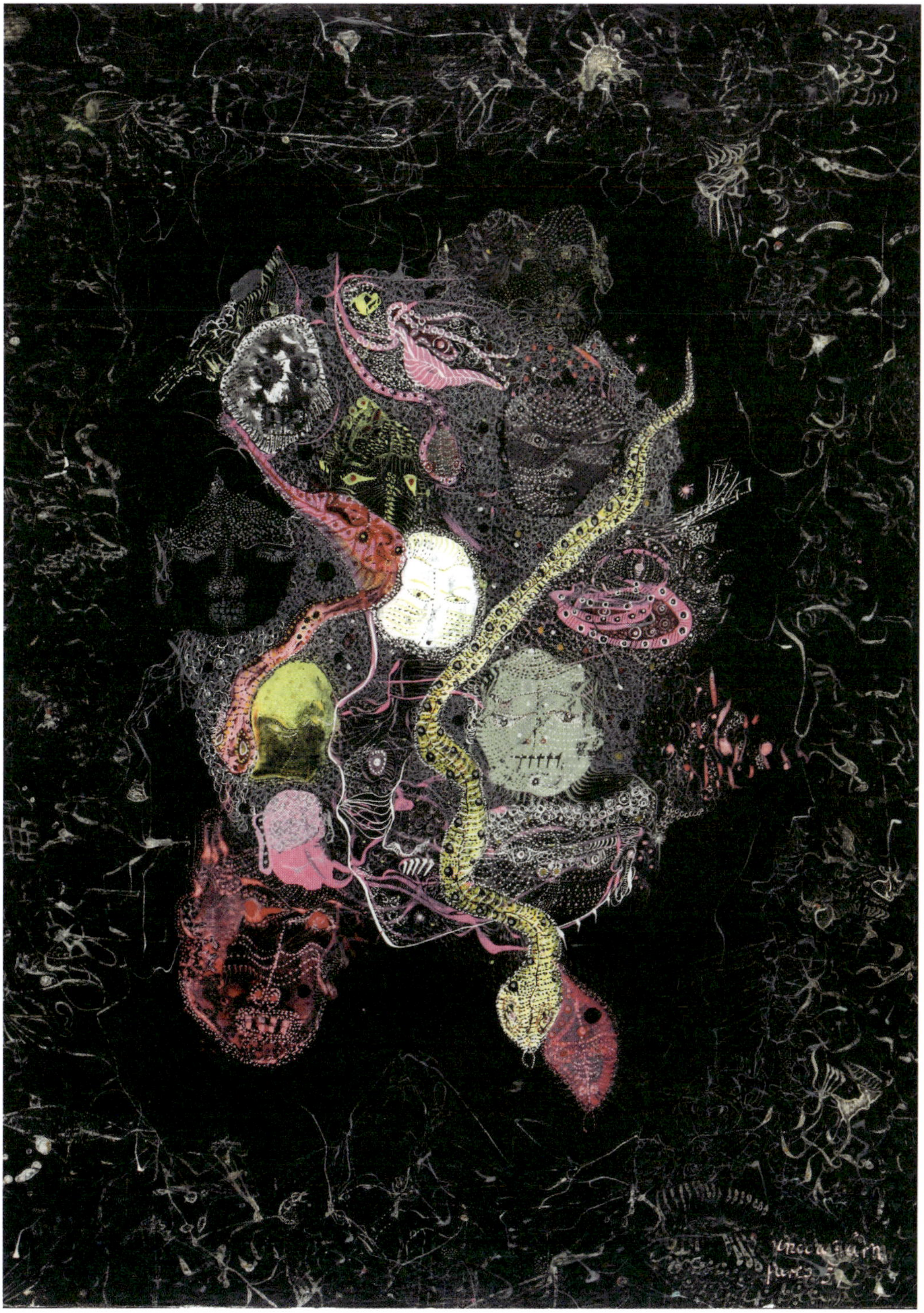

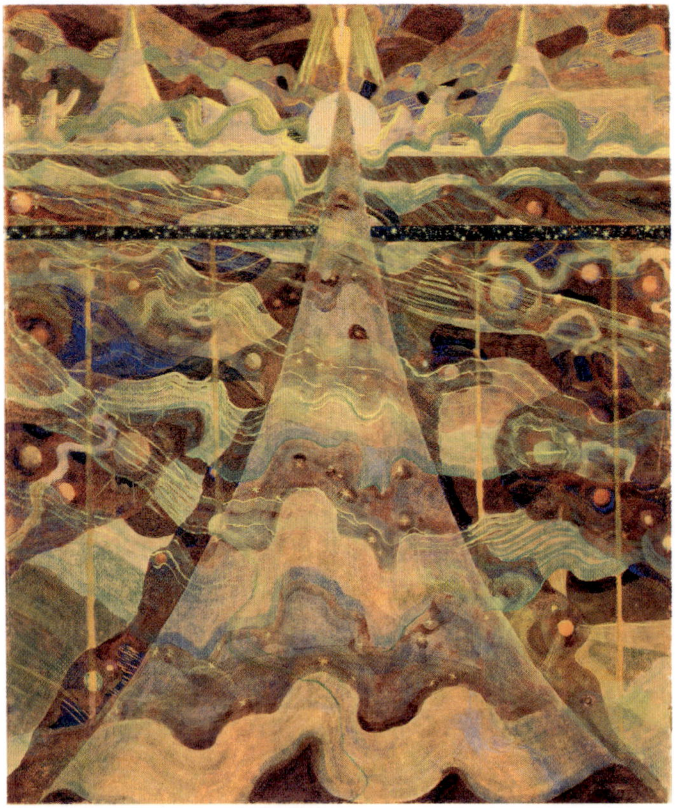

Left: Sonata No. 6 (Sonata of the Stars). Allegro, Mikalojus Konstantinas Čiurlionis, 1908, oil on canvas

Music and cosmos intertwine as Mikalojus Konstantinas Čiurlionis (1875–1911) gives sound visible form, with mountains of warm amber and bronze rising towards a central vanishing point where stellar patterns punctuate the composition like notes scattered across a celestial score. The Lithuanian composer-painter created entire 'sonata cycles', turning musical structures into visual equivalents, suggesting Čiurlionis saw the universe as an ordered polyphonic composition rather than chaotic space. Trained as both musician and painter, he spent his brief career exploring connections between sound and sight, leaving behind these strange hybrid works that merge Lithuanian folk traditions with mystical cosmology.

Opposite: Rose Moon, Rebecca Chaperon, 2022, acrylic paint on wooden panel

A magical stage is set with deliberate precision. Three candles glow against a sky washed in dusty rose, their flames steady and true; a faceted quartz crystal catches the light next to an ornate golden vase holding a single pink bloom and pale turquoise berries. That enormous moon hangs low and close, rendered in the same soft pink as the petals, as if flower and celestial body share some secret correspondence. Rebecca Chaperon arranges these elements with the intentionality of someone who knows that visionary states require preparation and the right props – what author and witch Pam Grossman calls 'enhancement accelerants' in her book *Magic Maker*, tools for focusing energy and calling in whatever forces need to be called. This is a toolkit for anyone who's ever felt that certain objects hold power beyond their physical form. You can practically smell the melted wax and rose water, and feel that peculiar quality the air takes on when ordinary objects have been set aside for extraordinary purposes. Strike a match, take a seat and see who (or what!) joins you.

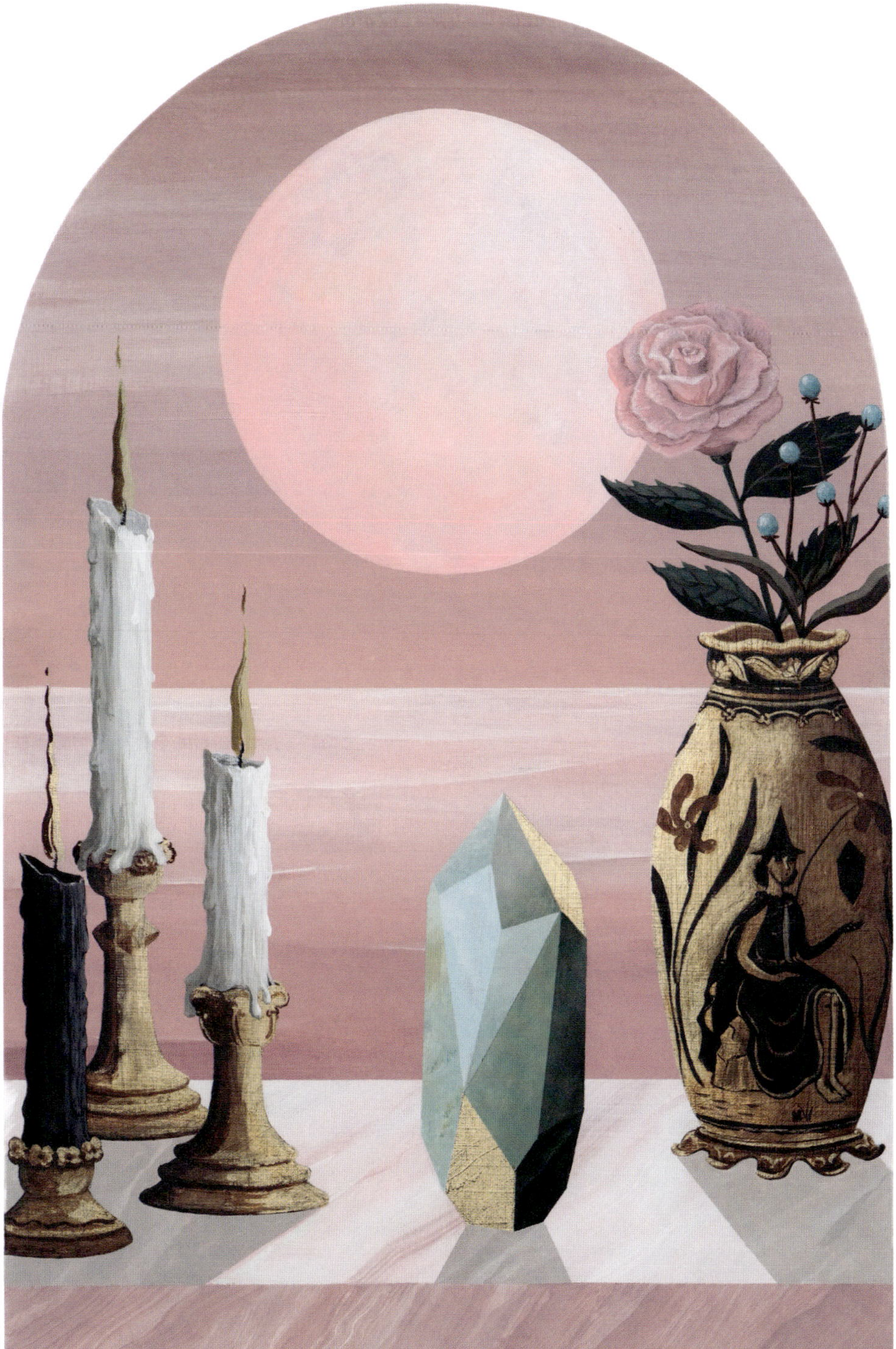

Right: On Fire, Dorothea Tanning, 1949, pencil and coloured pencil on paper

A woman flees in silent panic, her body caught in dream logic's impossible mathematics: half-clothed, half-aflame, half-swallowed by an impassive brick wall. (That's three halves if you're counting, but we mine our dreams for inspiration, not maths tutoring.) Dorothea Tanning (1910–2012) traps her figure mid-flight – fire runs down the figure's back, while her arms disappear into solid masonry that won't budge. The elongated proportions and gravity-defying posture evoke that terrifying sleep paralysis during which escape routes collapse and the body betrays itself. Is this a dream where walls turn to quicksand, or a nightmare where flesh turns to tinder? Tanning, who returned to a war-ravaged Paris in 1949, fills this fleeing figure with the urgency of genuine terror, yet maintains what she called the 'enigmatic' quality that defined her distinctive artistic legacy.

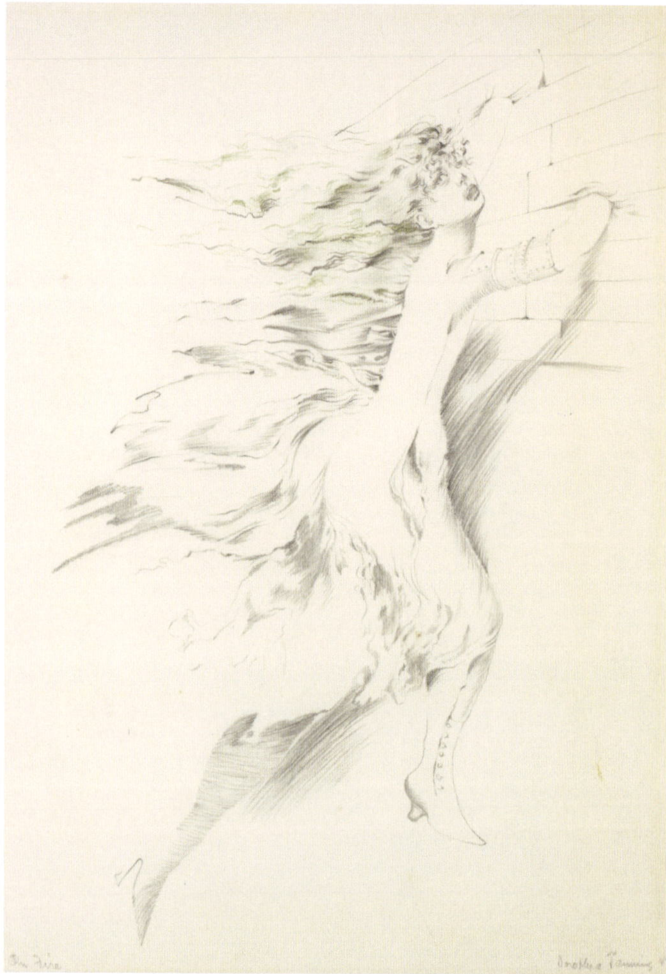

Opposite: Opium, Vali Myers, 1967, pen, black ink and watercolour

Electric and untamed, this psychedelic vision springs from the mind of Vali Myers (1930–2003). Her hallucinatory tableau explodes with vibrant forms, centred around a hypnotic face with blue-orbed eyes, while artful spirits and phantoms observe. Below, a pink-haired figure reclines on a chequered cushion, inhaling from a pipe that recalls Myers' own hazy Paris years. Self-taught and fiercely independent, the flame-haired dancer fled Melbourne at 19 to dance in Parisian jazz clubs, drawing the attention of Jean Cocteau before tattooing Patti Smith's knee at the Chelsea Hotel decades later. Between these worlds, she established a wildlife sanctuary in an Italian valley, where she wrote of wanting life and death to be 'hard and clean', like an animal's. In these swirling visions, you can almost see what lurked behind her kohl-lined eyes when the opium smoke cleared and her heart beat wild with the creatures she loved.

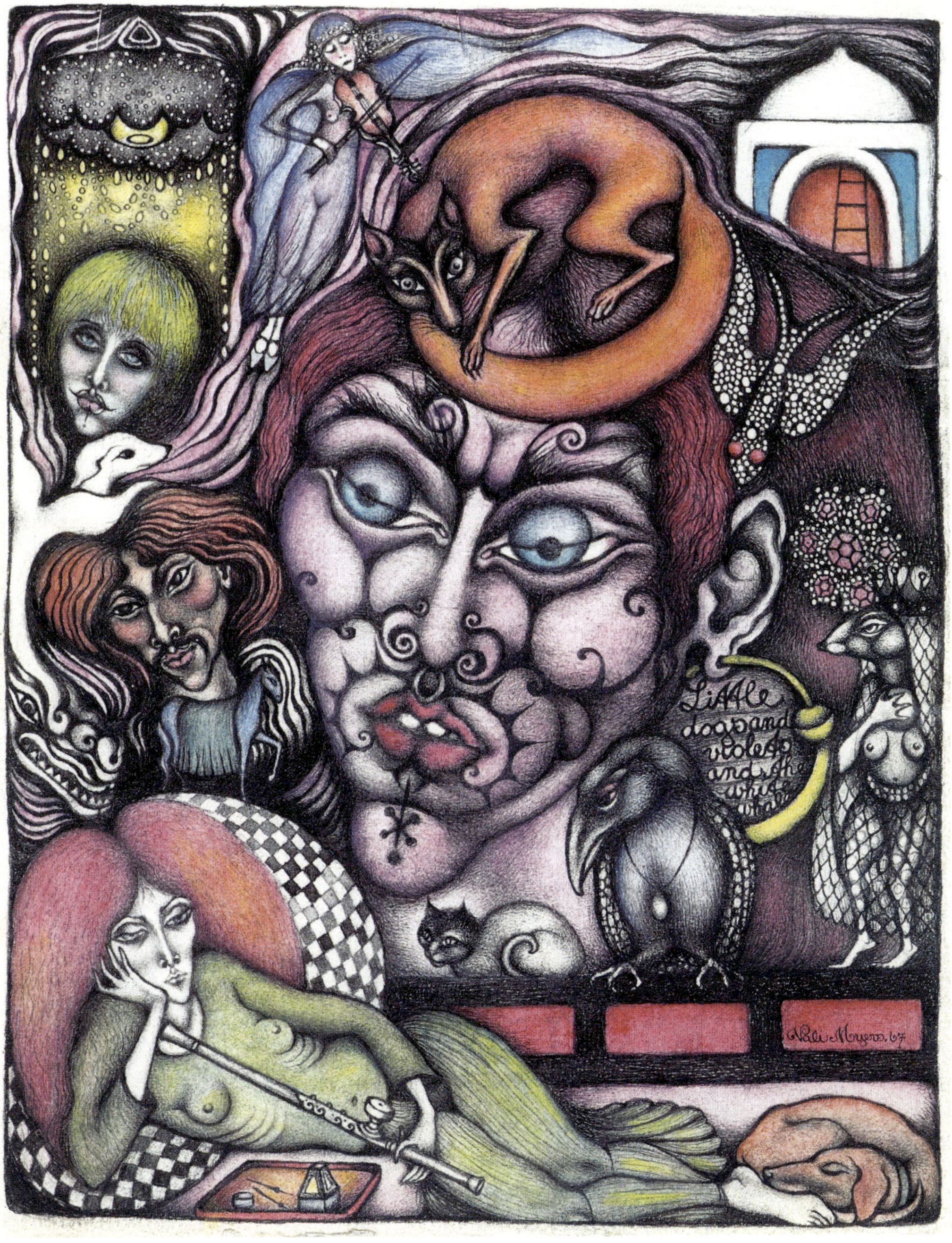
Little
dogs and
violets
and the
Vali Myers. 67

XI

—

CORPOREAL ENERGIES

'There is more wisdom in your body than in your deepest philosophy.'

– FRIEDRICH NIETZSCHE, *THUS SPOKE ZARATHUSTRA*

Your mind isn't just in your brain. It's in the clenched fist that's ready to punch someone's lights out, the heart hammering when you hit that jump scare in the horror movie, the dancer's legs that seem to move to the beat of your favourite song before you even hear it. We like to imagine consciousness as a tidy little command centre trapped inside our skull; that is, until we notice where it actually shows up. Fingers tapping, knees knocking, bellies butterflying – your body's just a big consciousness antenna tuned to whatever frequency your brain refuses to admit it's picking up. The plot thickens when you factor in other humans. Ever watch a crowd from above and notice how humans move like schools of fish, unconsciously syncing their steps in mysterious patterns? Or catch yourself mirroring someone's gestures during an intense conversation? Bodies have their own secret wireless network, sharing signals below the threshold of conscious awareness.

Artists throughout history have made it their business to explore these strange corporeal frequencies, from the earliest cave painters capturing the galloping energy of charging animals and handprints that turned body parts into permanent signatures, to the maenads who spun themselves into altered states through wild movement alone, no Instagram tutorial or app store wellness subscription purchase required, just pure primal impulse and physical frenzy. Greek artists captured these ecstatic dances in pottery that still throbs with kinetic energy. Medieval mystics would fast for weeks, believing hunger could open doorways to the divine, creating art where bodies bent like rubber, rear ends sprouted tiny faces that tooted on trumpets, and martyred saints' stab wounds bloomed into ecstatic smiles. They depicted these hallucinations in manuscripts and marginalia, documenting what happens when the body is pushed to its breaking point – consciousness becomes weird, and weird consciousness produces weird art. Renaissance artists approached anatomy like detectives hunting for evidence: where exactly does mind meet muscle? Where does thought become gesture? Where does spirit slip into flesh? Their drawings documented the physical machinery of consciousness, every sinew, every nerve pathway a clue to the mind–body puzzle.

By the eighteenth century, artists were pushing further into uncharted territory with bodies. Rococo painters depicted flesh mid-gesture: the momentum of a swing, the tension in a glance.

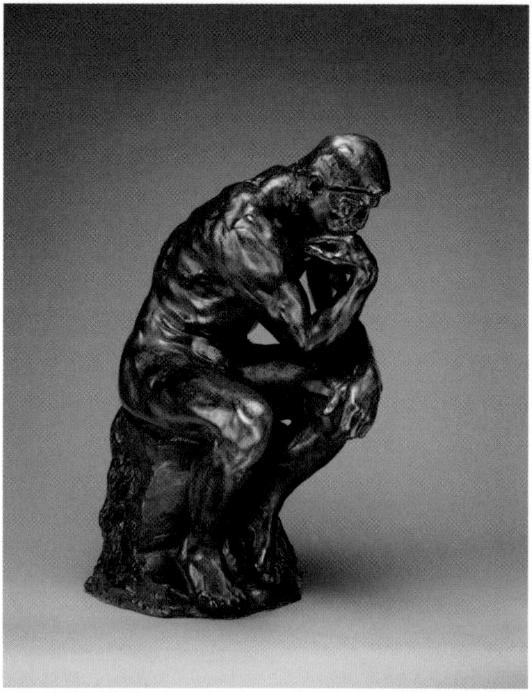

Romantic painters like Théodore Géricault painted flesh pushed to its breaking point, raw desperation made visible in every stretched sinew. The nineteenth century explored how consciousness inhabits movement. Auguste Rodin's sculptures caught bodies mid-movement, mid-thought, mid-everything. Paul Cézanne began mapping how psychological states manifest as physical tension, paving the way for Marcel Duchamp's radical *Nude Descending a Staircase*, which captured an entire movement sequence in a single frame, like a glitchy time-lapse photograph.

The early twentieth century exploded with kinetic experiments. Giacomo Balla's *Dynamism of a Dog on a Leash* proved that corporeal energy transcends human boundaries. (Yes, it's a dog, but look at those little legs go!) The Expressionists revealed what happens when inner turmoil rewires the body. Edvard Munch painted bodies bent by invisible pressures, their wretched contortions echoing torments that only they can hear, seemingly piped directly into their poor, anguished skulls. Egon Schiele's contortions express psychological states through twisted limbs and sharp angles, his figures bent into origami made of bone and neurosis. Willem de Kooning painted bodies that looked like they'd been put through a blender, flesh scrambled and churned into violent abstractions that still pulse with disturbing life.

Post-war, Francis Bacon showed us the visceral horrors of flesh under siege. His figures writhe with consciousness trapped inside melting, distorting forms with screaming, blurred faces. Meanwhile, the Surrealists were developing their own twisted body language. Max Ernst's feathered women, Man Ray's instrumental torsos, Salvador Dalí's melted forms – bodies that had clearly been reading kooky manifestos instead of anatomy textbooks. Andrew Wyeth found power in stillness. *Christina's World* depicts a woman frozen mid-crawl, her body radiating tension despite absolute stillness, demonstrating that embodied energy can be about potential just as much as movement.

Opposite: The Thinker, Auguste Rodin, 1904, bronze

Below: The Raft of the Medusa, Théodore Géricault, 1818–19, oil on canvas

'The body knows things about which the mind is ignorant,' Louise Bourgeois once observed, and, in recent decades, artists have found wildly different ways to decode this psychic physicality. Jenny Saville's massive canvases show flesh as defiant and noncompliant; her presences exist on their own terms, spilling beyond every boundary. Bill Viola's bodies move like prayers in slow motion, luminous figures caught somewhere between flesh and shimmering light, and Michaël Borremans's quietly unsettling paintings feel like screenshots of interpretive dance from an art-house horror film. They all remind us that embodiment itself might be the most bewildering mystery we face.

Think about it: you're a brain in a jar piloting a flesh mecha powered by sugar and electricity; coordinating throbbing pulses, twitching muscles and gyrating joints; broadcasting on frequencies you don't even know exist; tuning into signals from every other consciousness antenna around you; and pretending it's all perfectly normal. Artists just remind us how deeply bonkers that actually is.

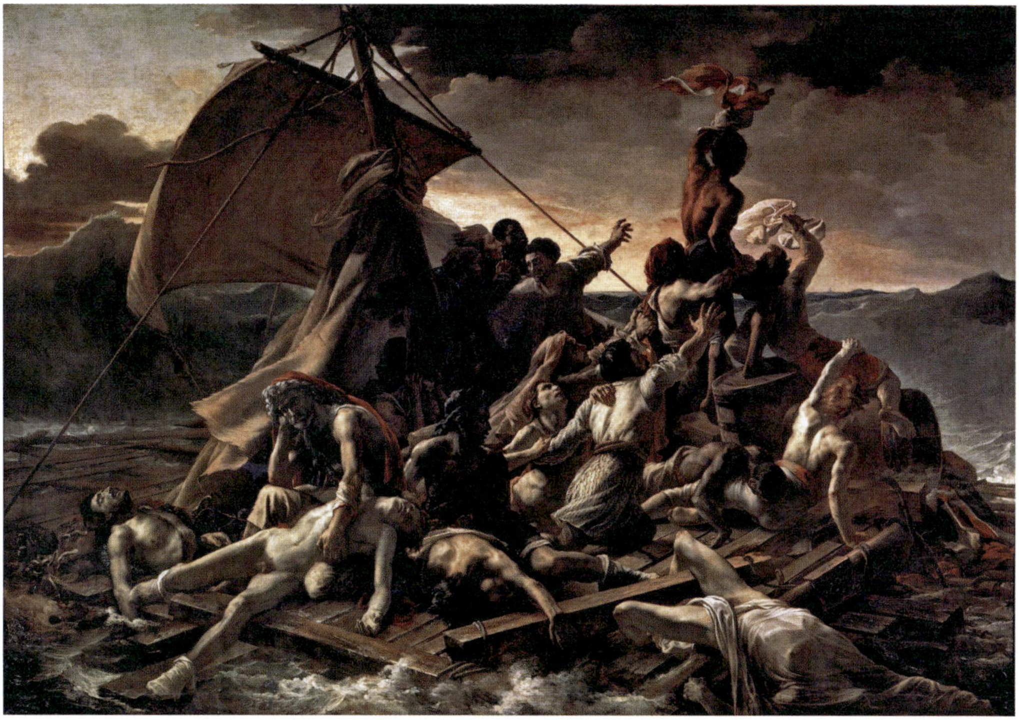

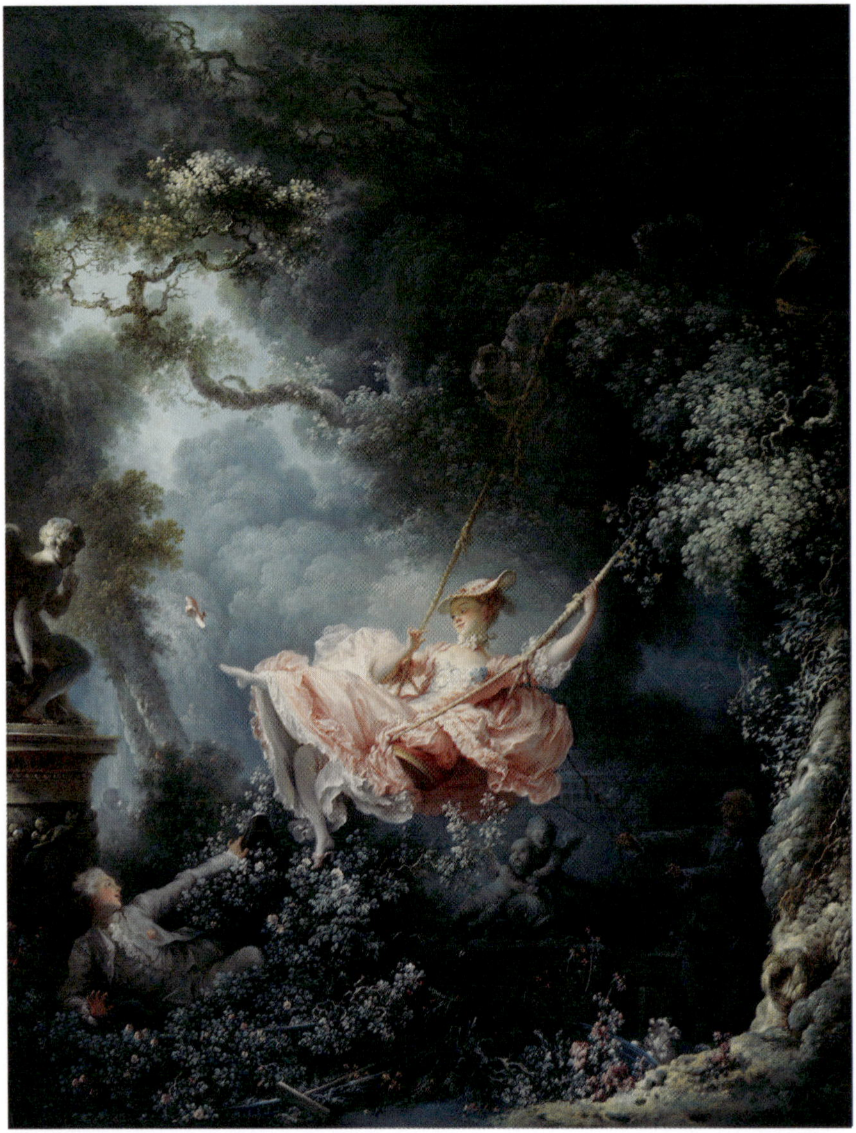

The Swing, Jean-Honoré Fragonard, 1767, oil on canvas

A young woman in billowing pink silk soars through dappled sunlight, her body arcing upwards as momentum carries her frothingly skywards. Jean-Honoré Fragonard (1732-1806) orchestrates this seemingly innocent garden scene in which three bodies operate on entirely different frequencies. The swinging lady broadcasts pure physical joy, her slipper sailing off in gleeful abandon. Below, her lover receives every signal she transmits, sprawled artfully in the undergrowth while enjoying an excellent view of the proceedings. Meanwhile, the older gentleman pushing the swing remains completely tuned out, obliviously powering the very mechanism of his own betrayal. Fragonard reveals how bodies communicate through movement, gesture and proximity, the swing's rhythmic motion creating a kind of corporeal Morse code between the conspirators. Same garden, same moment, three wildly different experiences.

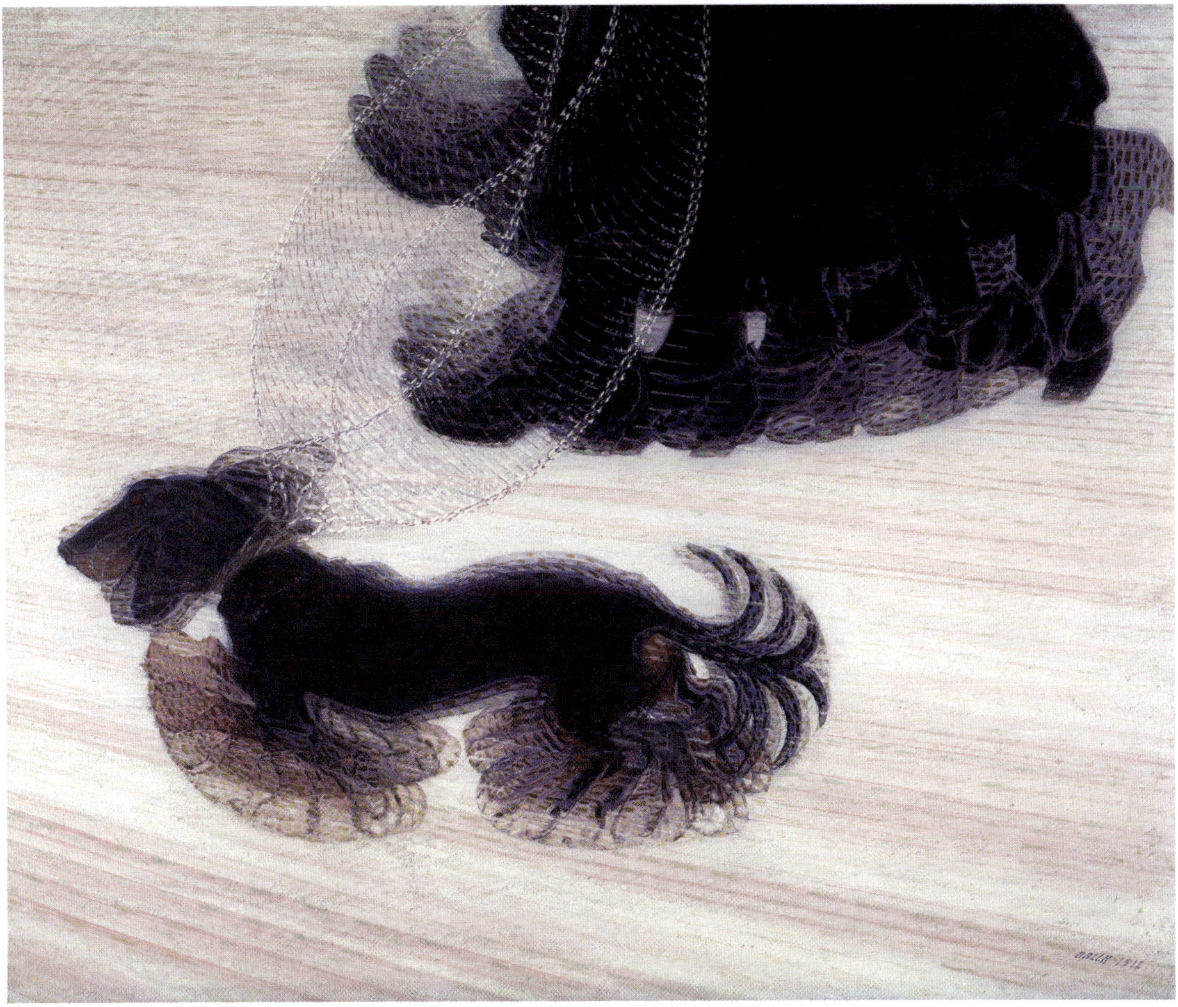

Dynamism of a Dog on a Leash, Giacomo Balla, 1912, oil on canvas

A dachshund explodes across the canvas in a frenzy of multiplied legs, paws and tail, creating one seriously enthusiastic blur. Giacomo Balla (1871–1958) painted this delightfully frantic scene while visiting a student in Tuscany, capturing his subject with the fervour of someone documenting a minor miracle. The little dog's legs whir like tiny pistons, each paw repeated eight or ten times in ghostly succession, while its tail wags with such vigour it resembles a bottle brush dancing an ecstatic jig. Above this canine chaos, the owner's feet tap out their own staccato rhythm, boots multiplied in motion while her dark skirts flutter like curtains in a breeze. The leash swings in lazy parabolas between them, connecting these two figures in their shared forward momentum. Balla was riding the Futurist wave that championed speed and multiplied motion, and here he proves that even the most ordinary afternoon dog walk can become a testament to the sheer manic joy of modern life.

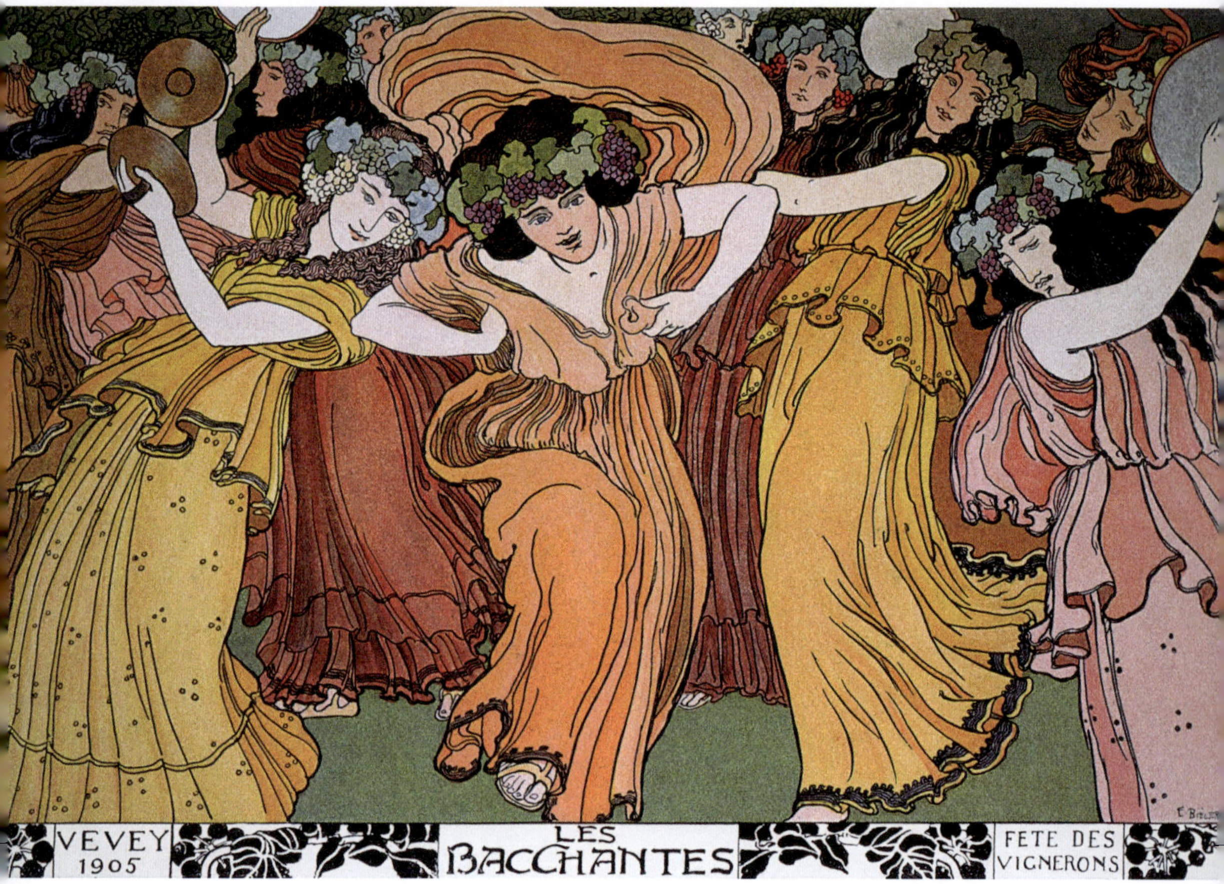

Les Bacchantes, Ernest Biéler, 1905, watercolour and ink on paper

A feverish spiral of ecstatic women whirl across the canvas, their saffron and flame-coloured dresses creating a vortex of holy madness. Ernest Biéler (1863–1948) captures the Ancient Greek followers of Dionysus mid-trance, their flower-crowned heads tilted skywards, tambourines and cymbals raised like offerings to the god of wine and frenzy. The Swiss painter, renowned for blending Art Nouveau decoration with folkloric themes, focuses on the moment these devotees cross the razor's edge between civilization and wilderness, where, as Donna Tartt's fictional professor Julian might lecture, 'terrible things become beautiful'. Against a muted green background suggesting sacred groves, the dancers' ruffled garments swirl with kinetic energy, their expressions somewhere between rapture and abandon, ecstasy and savagery. These are women who might tear a passing stranger limb from limb, yet Biéler renders their ritual with such decorative precision that violence and beauty dance together – the same paradox that has fascinated artists and writers from Euripides to Tartt.

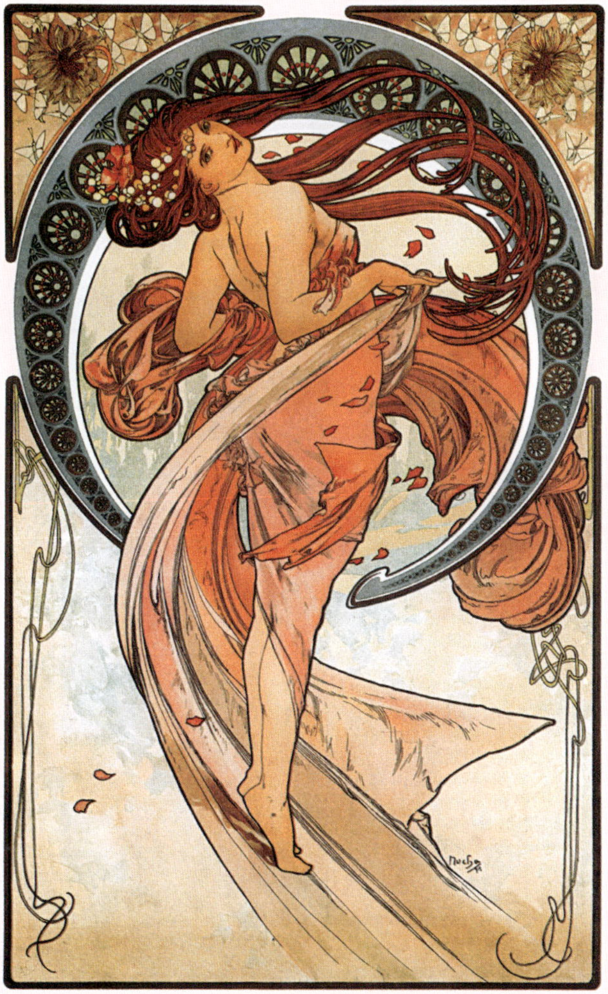

The Arts: Dance, Alphonse Mucha, 1898, colour lithograph

She twirls in perpetual return, always glancing back as if she's just remembered something beloved and irreplaceable she left behind. Alphonse Mucha (1860–1939) enshrines the coexistence of momentum and pause – the dancer's hair still flying forwards while her face turns back, fabric both embracing and abandoning her form. That backwards glance feels wonderfully human, a consciousness that exists within the dance rather than surrendering to it. The real Mucha magic happens where the woman's body meets the background: her curves continuing the visual melody established by the seashell spirals, her flowing lines harmonizing with the ornamental border, russet leaves and auburn waves merging into a single decorative symphony. The woman's body and the ornamental border speak the same visual language, the dancer and decorative embellishments frilling and thrilling to secret choreography.

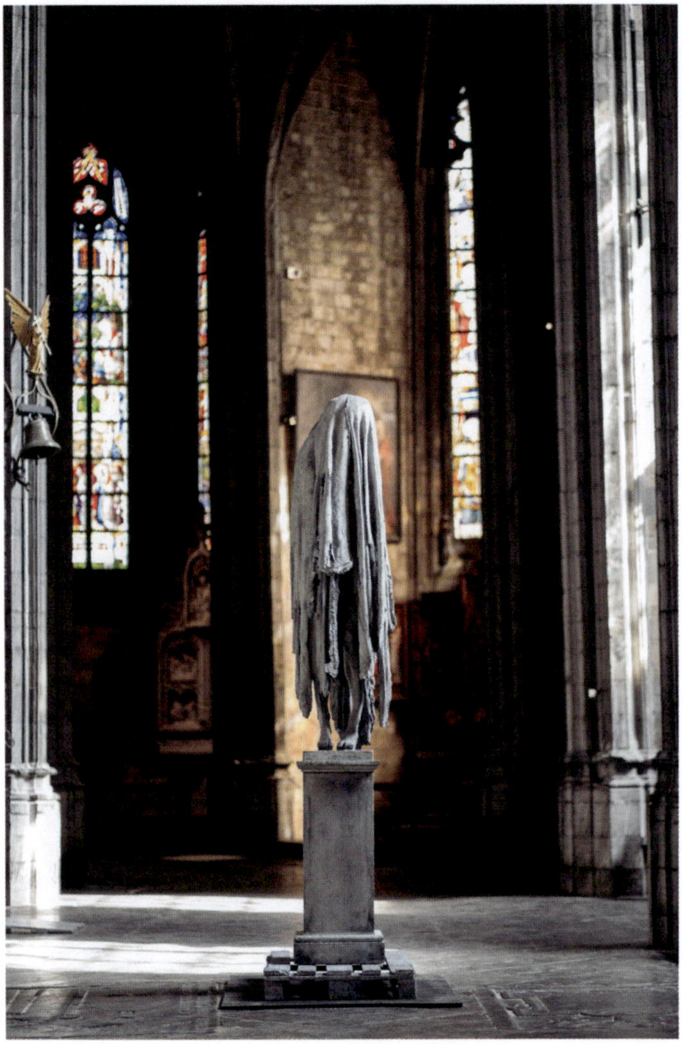

Right: Arcangelo I, 2022–2023, Berlinde De Bruyckere, 2023, bronze, lead and chrome steel; photograph by Kévin Rinclin.

Installation view, Sainte-Waudru Collegiate Church, Mons, Belgium, 2024. Exhibited as part of the exhibition 'Rodin. A Modern Renaissance. In dialogue with Berlinde De Bruyckere', organized by CAP/Mons, 2024.

This angel carries no halo, no beatific smile, just a faceless form leaning forwards in precarious balance. Berlinde De Bruyckere casts this 'Arcangelo' in bronze and lead, materials whose permanence contrasts with the fragility they evoke. The cast of a draped animal hide flows around precisely rendered human feet while creating wing-like shapes at the shoulders, a protective cloak that speaks of both shelter and weariness. Created as a tribute to healthcare workers during the pandemic, the sculpture presents divinity stripped of heavenly perfection. This guardian figure stands elevated on its plinth, offering protection while bearing the visible weight of its calling, a reminder that those who care for us often carry more than we realize.

Opposite: The Anatomical Angel, or Dissection of a Woman's Back, Jacques Fabien Gautier d'Agoty, 1746, colour mezzotint on laid paper

Skin peels away from a woman's back like unfurling celestial petals, muscles exposed in rosy detail while she peeps over her shoulder - a dead woman's corpse, likely a criminal sold after execution, posed coquettishly for male observers. Jacques Fabien Gautier d'Agoty (1716–85) painted this for his 1746 anatomy book *Myologie Complete*, using a four-colour mezzotint process that made dead flesh look alarmingly alive, the images existing somewhere between medical textbook and art gallery. Deeply uncomfortable, bordering on profoundly wrong and absolutely impossible to ignore, this is the visual language Bryan Fuller's *Hannibal* would perfect centuries later: flesh as both canvas and violation, beauty extracted from brutality, the same aesthetic that the extreme pleasure/pain-seeking Cenobites from Clive Barker's *Hellraiser* understand instinctively. d'Agoty's contemporaries criticized him as a sensationalist showman lacking proper anatomical rigour, his work too artistic for science, too morbid for art. But that's surely what makes this image endure! Whether intentionally or not, he revealed that bodies resist reduction; they're simultaneously meat and meaning, mechanics and metaphor, clinical specimen and cultural artefact.

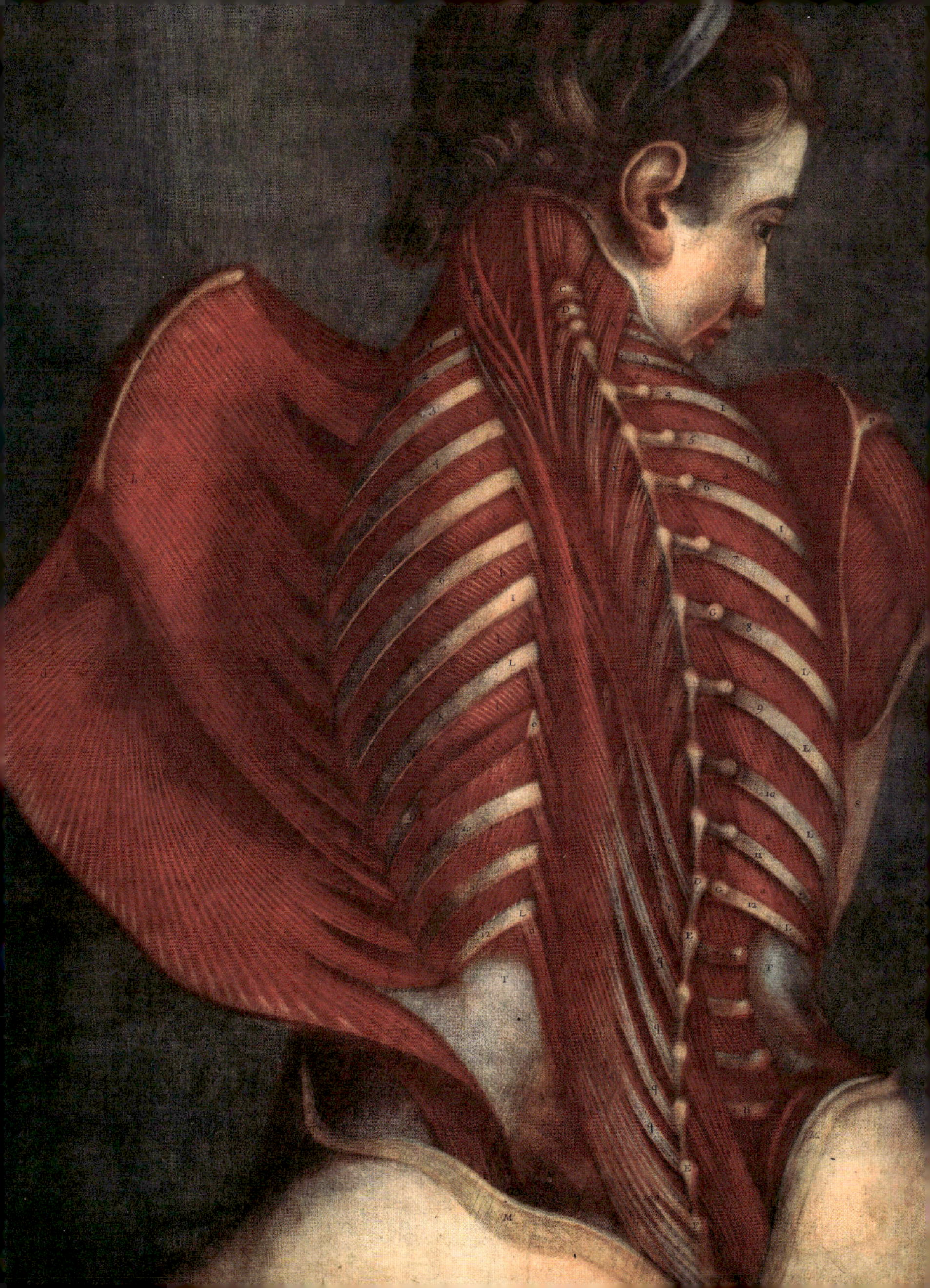

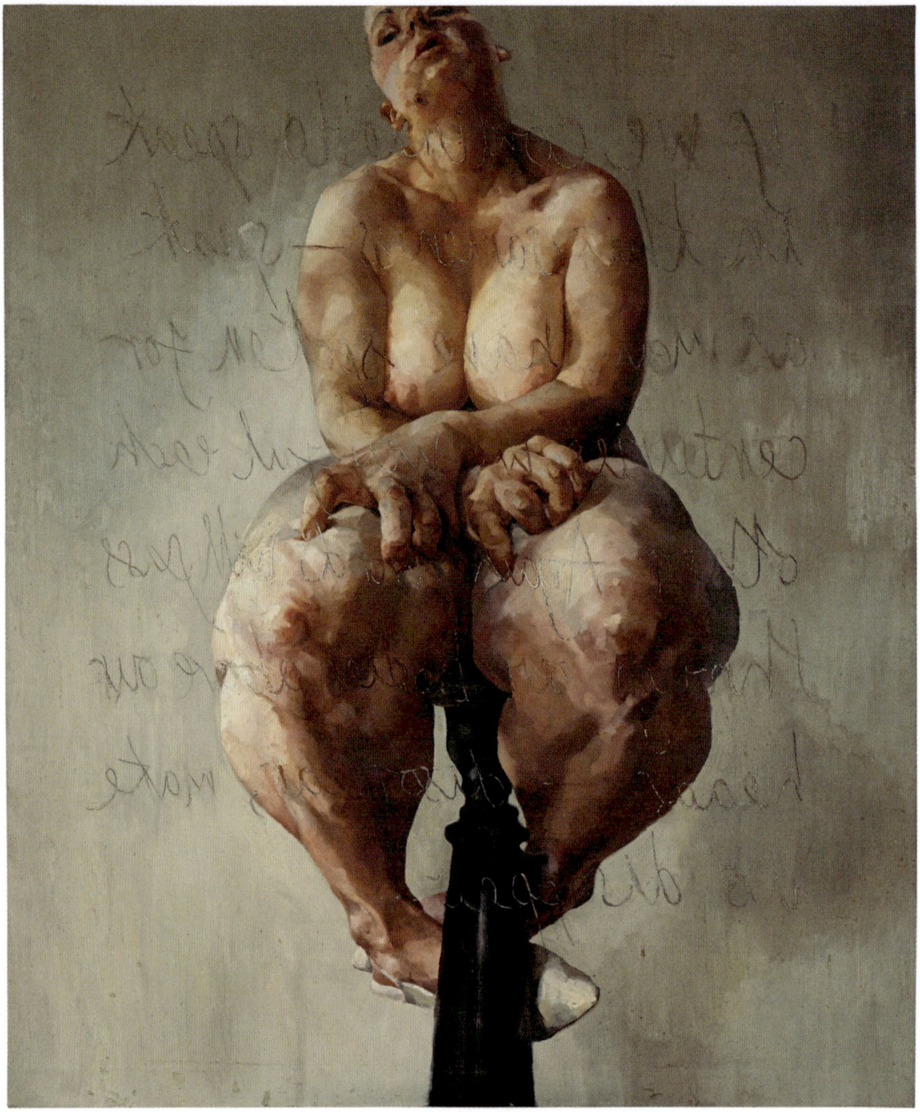

Propped, Jenny Saville, 1992, oil on canvas

Jenny Saville builds flesh from thick swirls of paint, each richly textured brushstroke adding weight and presence to this monumental self-portrait. The figure fills the canvas completely, hands resting on knees while her head tilts upwards in the frame, as if to say, 'Oh yeah? So what?' Reversed text from feminist philosopher Luce Irigaray gets etched right into the paint: 'If we continue to speak this sameness, speak as men have spoken for centuries, we will fail each other.' Paint layers build up surfaces that seem almost sculptural, flesh rendered with startling immediacy. The precarious pedestal looks ready to tip, but the figure's solid pose anchors the composition. It occupies space on its own terms rather than conforming to traditional ideals. Her downward gaze meets yours, and she doesn't give a fart for your approval.

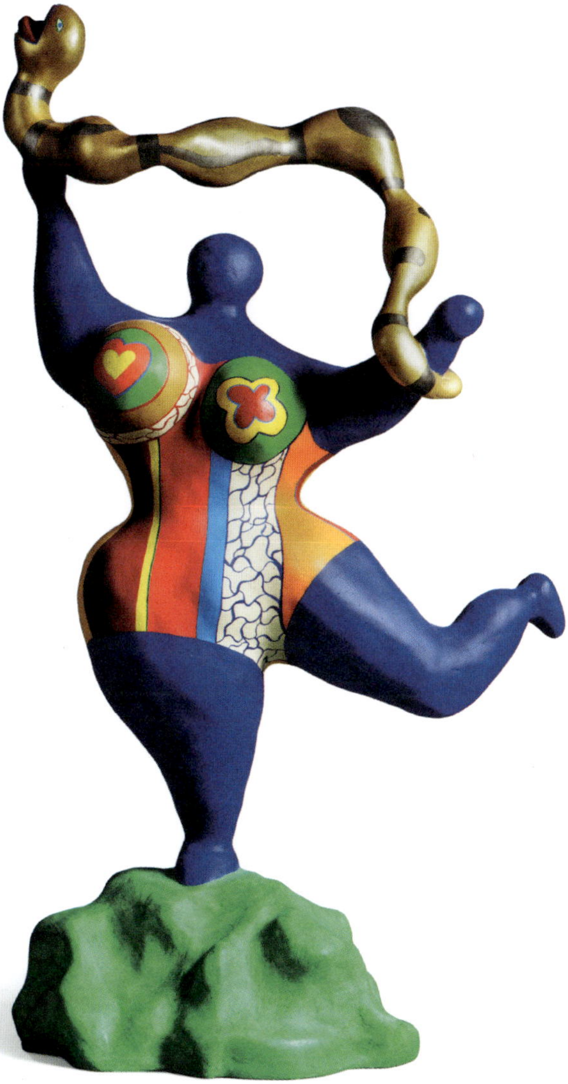

Nana Boa (Petite), Niki de Saint Phalle, 1984, painted resin with gold leaf

A voluptuous blue goddess twirls with spectacular abandon, holding aloft a golden serpent as her fabulous ophidian dance partner. Here, Niki de Saint Phalle (1930–2002) gives us her signature Nana figure at full power. These jubilant, full-bodied feminine totems became her artistic hallmark, and this one reaches peak mythic celebration. The figure's torso is festooned with vibrant patterns in red, orange, yellow and green, combining bold stripes with mosaic-type sections reminiscent of Murano glasswork, all topped with a stylized flower-like sunburst that practically blooms towards the sun. She dances with arms flung outwards, her body frozen mid-twirl yet somehow still in ecstatic motion. Like all of De Saint Phalle's Nanas, this figure celebrates the female form as dazzling power and uncontainable energy, pulsing with zeal - woman as cosmic force, dancing through the universe with serpentine wisdom and technicolour exuberance!

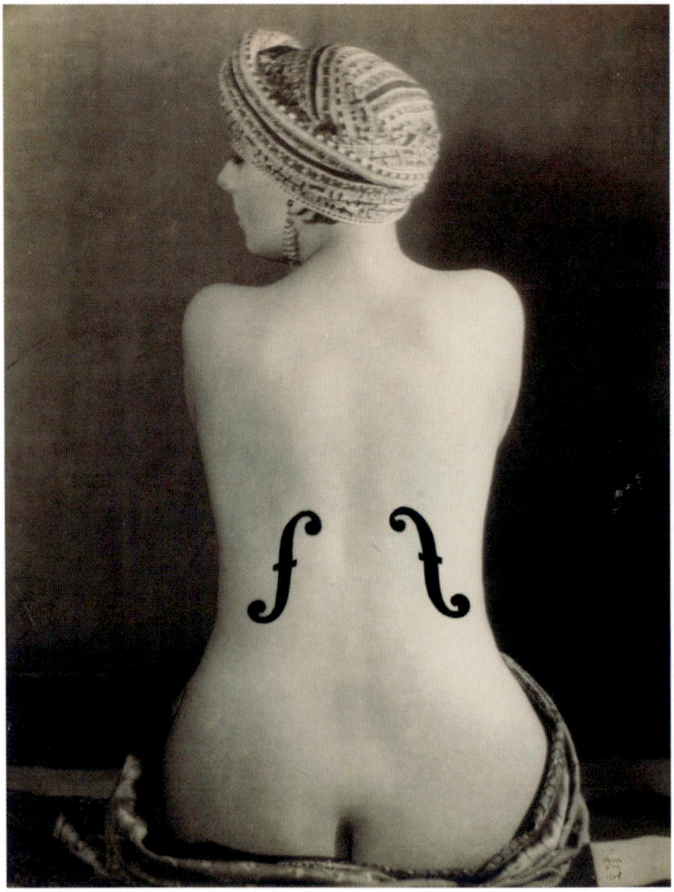

Le Violon d'Ingres (Ingres's Violin), Man Ray, negative 1924, print probably 1950s–60s, gelatin silver print

Two f-holes painted onto a woman's back, and suddenly flesh becomes fiddle. Man Ray (1890–1976) added those violin sound holes in his darkroom, but Kiki de Montparnasse was already living as her own walking symphony. She painted self-portraits that sold out gallery shows, wrote scandalous memoirs that made front-page news, and got banned in America for obscenity. She sang in packed Montparnasse cabarets where audiences came specifically to watch her perform folk songs and crack wise between sets. Man Ray's trick transforms her into an instrument, but the joke's on him: Kiki was already making music with every gesture, every laugh, every performance. That straight-backed posture radiates the confidence of a woman who turned her entire existence into a dazzling, unrepentant work of art. The violin holes are his addition, but everything else - the poise, the presence, the sheer magnetic pull - belongs entirely to Kiki.

Opposite: Nude Descending a Staircase, No. 2, Marcel Duchamp, 1912, oil on canvas

When Bill Watterson drops your painting into his Calvin and Hobbes comic not once but twice, a little boy and his tiger making jokes about it in the funny pages, you've officially made it from art world scandal to six-year-old philosopher territory. Marcel Duchamp (1887–1968) earned his reputation as an artistic provocateur with this tumbling, fragmented figure that resembles a person who has been put through a paper shredder and reassembled mid-fall. This brown and ochre blur of intersecting planes and fractured forms caused such uproar at the 1913 Armory Show that critics dubbed it 'an explosion in a shingle factory', and Teddy Roosevelt compared it to his bathroom rug. Duchamp's brothers even tried to censor it! But the artist was thrilled by the controversy. Duchamp strips the human body of everything recognizable except riotous kinetic energy - muscle memory and bodily rhythm scattered across 20 different positions, movement made visible, flesh as mechanics and momentum.

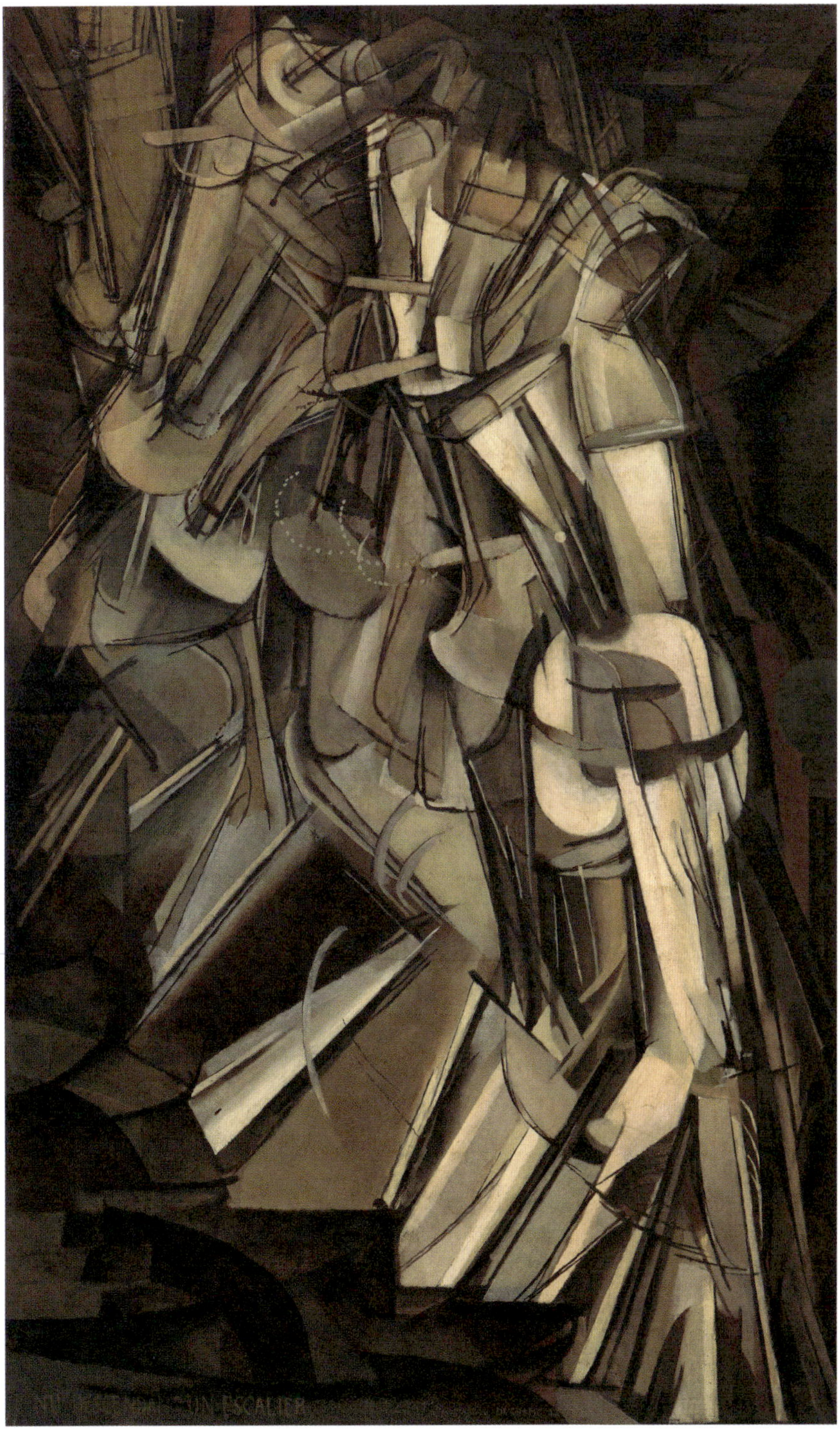

XII

—

SACRED CYCLES

'The crickets felt it was their duty to warn everybody that summertime cannot last forever.'

– E.B. WHITE, *CHARLOTTE'S WEB*

Every January, people make resolutions they'll abandon by February, but somehow we still believe that *this time* will be different. We're hooked on cycles, convinced we can game the system, that we can break free from patterns while simultaneously creating new ones. Right now, your heart beats in the same rhythm that has pulsed through human chests for millennia, a tiny drum echoing the vast cycles turning overhead. We're pattern-seekers and ritual-makers, marking time through ceremony, trying to make sense of the ancient clockwork of sun and stars that has measured out our days since we first looked up in wonder. We can't help but see meaning in these cycles – it's written into our DNA, encoded in our art, embedded in our stories.

'Ritual and ceremony in their due times kept the world under the sky and the stars in their courses,' wrote Terry Pratchett. This keen observer of human society had a particular fondness for humanity's foibles and understood that we've always used ceremony to convince ourselves that we have some control over eternal patterns. Ancient artists documented the afterlife journey, rich with symbols of renewal, creating guidebooks for the soul's passage between worlds. Medieval illuminators created Fortune's wheel in gold and ultramarine – crowned heads turning to dust, beggars rising to glory. Buddhist monks pour their mandalas grain by grain, then sweep them away, careful destruction as sacred as the creation. Across myriad cultures, ancient serpents devour their own tails in endless cycles of death and rebirth. Renaissance painters incorporated hints of resurrection into their memento mori: flowers sprouting from empty skulls, butterflies emerging from split chrysalises, eggs hatching to reveal new life.

These eternal cycles fascinate us not because we can't predict them – we know spring follows winter, dawn follows night – but because each instance is unique and full of unknowns, never fully surrendering its full cache of secrets. We can map every angle of sunrise, decode the chemistry of decay and document each cell of a butterfly's metamorphosis. Yet their inherent ineffabilities remain untouchable; the more desperately we grasp at them, the more elusive they become. Artists gravitate towards these patterns because they're endlessly surprising, each cycle offering infinite variations, each repetition showing something new. Every dawn catches us off guard, even though we've seen it 10,000 times before. The pattern is the same, but our place within it has shifted, and everything looks different from this new angle of understanding.

For all our technological sophistication, we still plant gardens every spring with the same hope that maybe this year the tomatoes won't die. We still gather around fires in winter, even if they're gas fire pits on restaurant patios. We are still governed by the same rhythms that drove ancient harvest festivals and spring planting ceremonies, by those ancient human urges to find meaning in the great wheel's turning and to understand our place in cycles larger than ourselves. We exist as both observer and participant, breathing in rhythm with tides we'll never see, our cells replacing themselves in patterns older than civilization, our brief lives intersecting with forces that began long before we arrived and will continue long after we're gone. It's precisely at this intersection, amid all this vast machinery of time and moment, where individual experience meets eternal pattern, that mystery finds its home.

Here in this corner of our warehouse tour, among these corridors devoted to sacred cycles, we'll encounter artists who map the eternal rhythms: birth, death, renewal, the seasons of soul and flesh.

Below: Page from *One Hundred Views of Mount Fuji*, Katsushika Hokusai, *c.* 1849, woodblock printed book, ink on paper

Opposite: Starry Messenger, with drawings of the phases and surface of the Moon, manuscript by Galileo Galilei, 1610, pen and ink on paper

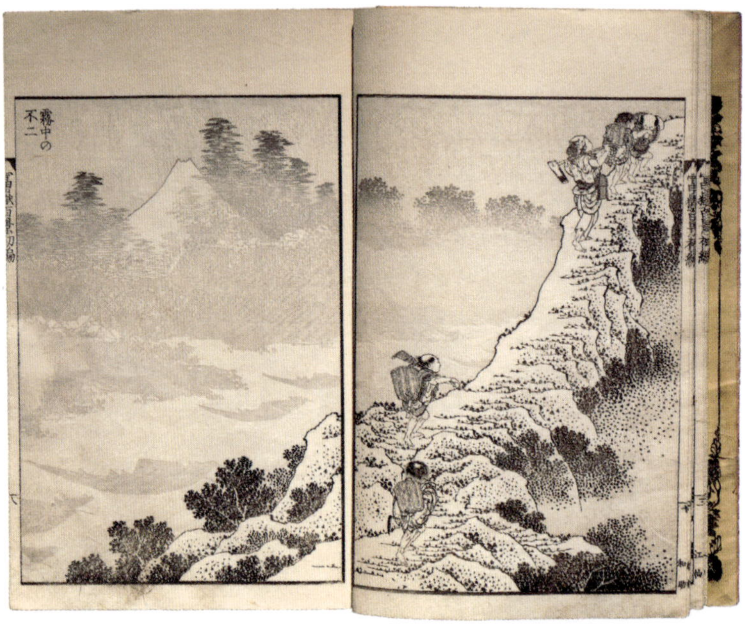

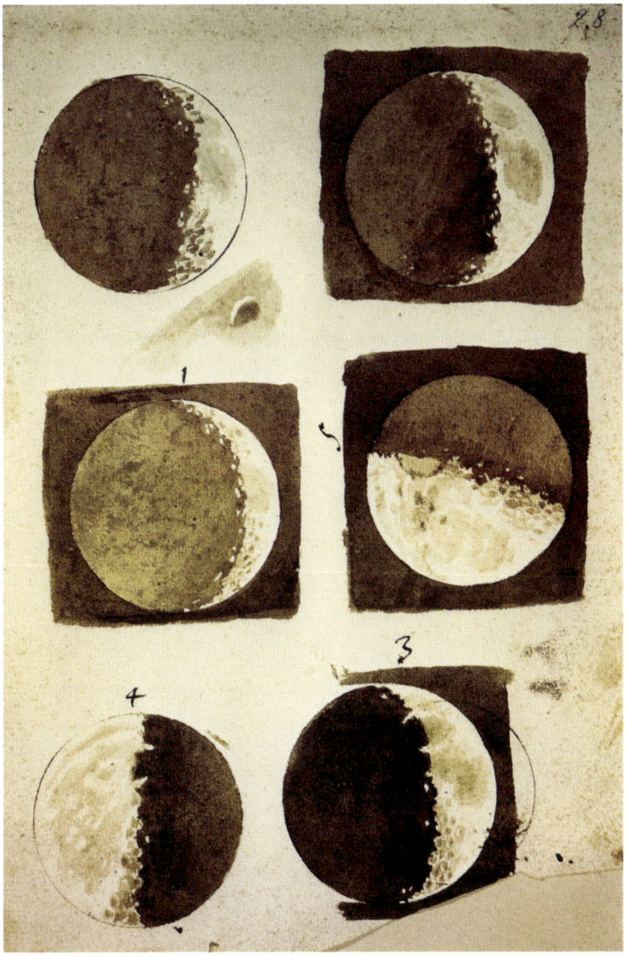

In his seventies, Katsushika Hokusai signed his works 'Old Man Crazy to Paint', insisting that everything he had done before the age of 70 was merely practice. His late masterwork *One Hundred Views of Mount Fuji* tracked nature's cycles through endless variations of the same peak, each drawing finding something new in the familiar silhouette. Giuseppe Arcimboldo built faces from seasonal fruits, while Dora Maar understood how time weaves invisible nets around us, trapping us in patterns we don't notice until it's too late. Käthe Kollwitz carved loss into woodblocks, revealing grief so primal it transcends time and culture. Tyler Thrasher collaborates with chemistry as his creative partner, allowing molecular forces to determine how death receives its makeover. Katie Paterson grinds extinction into pigment, making the planet's lost species visible through the very substance of that which we've lost.

The warehouse stretches on, its inventory of mysteries vast and inexhaustible. Each turn of the great wheel reveals new rooms to explore, new questions to call into the void. What returns isn't an echo but a voice you've never heard before, an invitation to keep wondering. This is why mystery matters. It challenges and sustains us – not with answers, but with more provocations, puzzles and paradoxes; not solid conclusions, but urgent calls to dig deeper, to question harder, to find the endless doors swinging open into forever. Standing at the threshold of the unknowable, we find ourselves speaking the three words that open every door to wonder: 'I don't know.'

And thus, the cycle continues.

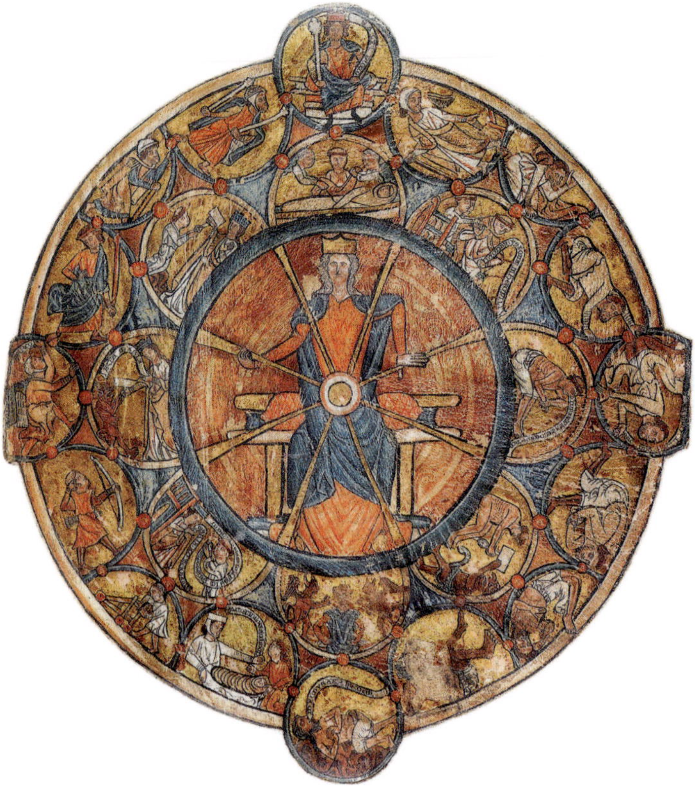

Left: An early wheel of fortune, William de Brailes, *c.* 1240, illuminated psalter

Fortuna spins her wheel with the casual indifference of someone shuffling a deck of cards, watching mortals ride her cosmic carnival attraction from glory to gutter and back again. William de Brailes (active *c.* 1230–*c.* 1260) painted this medieval game show - in which contestants have no choice but to participate - around 1240. 'I am borne again to the stars!' shouts the ascending youth, drunk on possibility, while the king at the top smugly declares, 'I exalt on high!', evidently having forgotten that wheels, by their very definition, keep turning. Gravity delivers its inevitable verdict: down crashes the formerly fortunate, wailing, 'Reduced, I descend,' before hitting rock bottom with a final wheeze of, 'Lowest, I am ground by the wheel.' Three rings of scenes spin around this cosmic roulette: the ages of man from babbling infant to doddering corpse, plus the cautionary tale of Saint Theophilus, who learned that deals with devils come with terrible interest rates.

Opposite: The Bhavachakra – Wheel of Life, artist unknown, *c.* 4th–5th century, wall painting from a Buddhist temple, Ladakh, India

A monstrous red demon clutches the wheel of existence in his claws, ready to devour the whole cosmic carousel, while Buddha points serenely towards escape at the painting's edge. This Buddhist wall painting charts every possible way to be born, live, suffer and die again - gods partying in heaven until their karma runs out, hungry ghosts with needle throats and balloon bellies, humans stumbling through familiar desire and disappointment. At the wheel's centre, three animals chase each other's tails: a pig, a snake and a rooster, representing the poisons that keep this show spinning. What's curious is how comforting this vision of cosmic entrapment feels - every realm mapped, every suffering categorized. The Buddha's outstretched finger suggests escape, but wouldn't enlightenment feel lonely without all this beautiful, terrible company?

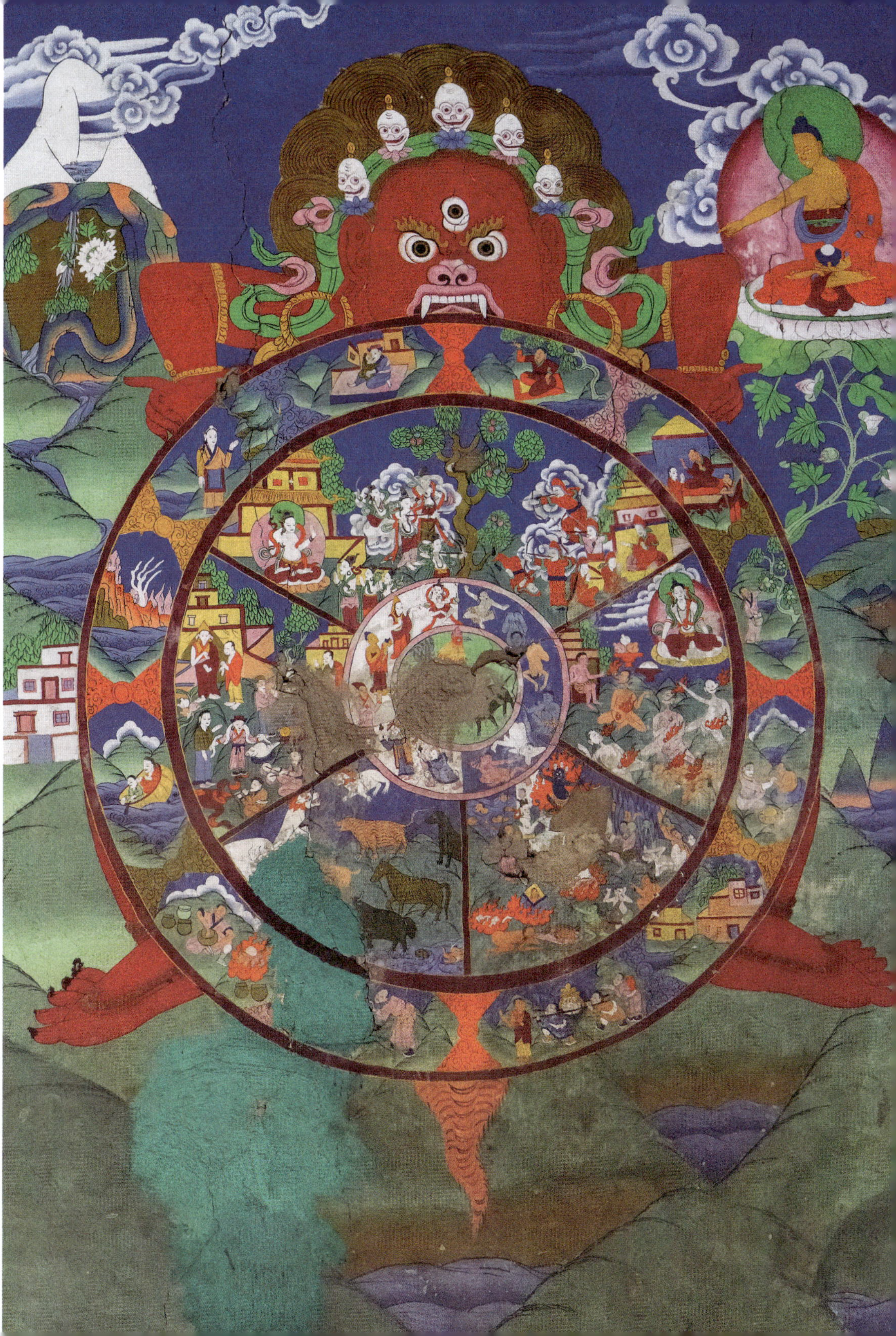

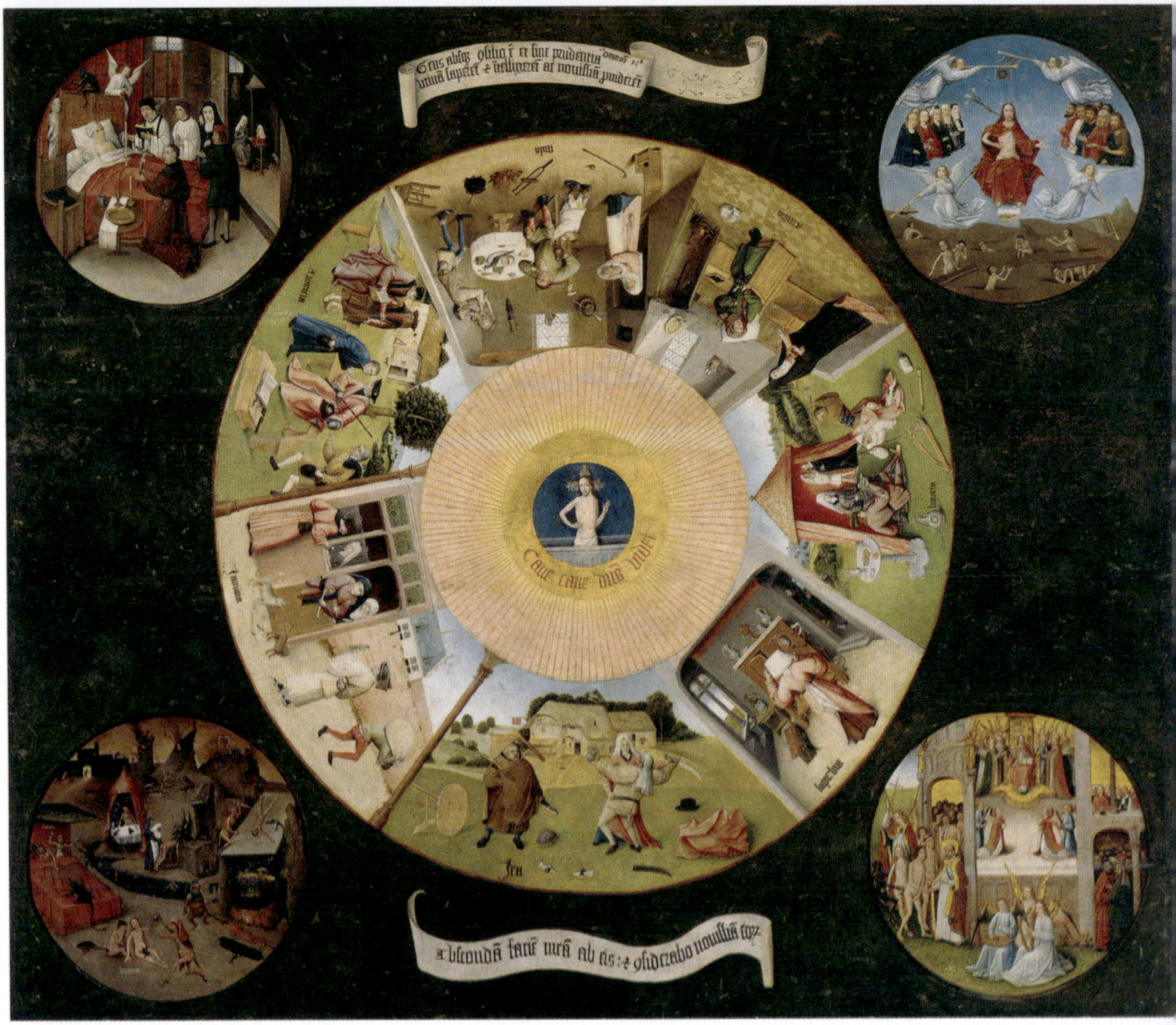

The Seven Deadly Sins and the Four Last Things, Hieronymus Bosch (disputed), *c.* 1500, oil on wood

God's all-seeing eye peers from the centre of this cosmic game board, watching humans fail spectacularly at basic morality, while Christ warns, 'Beware, beware, the Lord is watching.' Maybe Hieronymus Bosch (*c.* 1450–1516) painted this around 1500; maybe one of his followers did – art historians have been arguing about it for centuries and, frankly, the jury's still out. King Philip II didn't care about attribution debates; he loved this painting so much he kept it in his private rooms like a dreadfully judgemental coffee table. Seven wedges radiate outwards, showing humanity's greatest hits: drunken brawls outside taverns, gluttonous families gorging themselves silly, corrupt judges pocketing bribes, lustful couples canoodling in luxurious tents while jesters mock them from outside. The four corner circles lay out your post-death options: deathbed last rites, final judgement, heavenly gates or hellish punishment, where sinners get exactly what they dished out in life. Whether authentic Bosch or brilliant imitator, this artist understood that humans are endlessly entertaining in their determination to choose the wrong path.

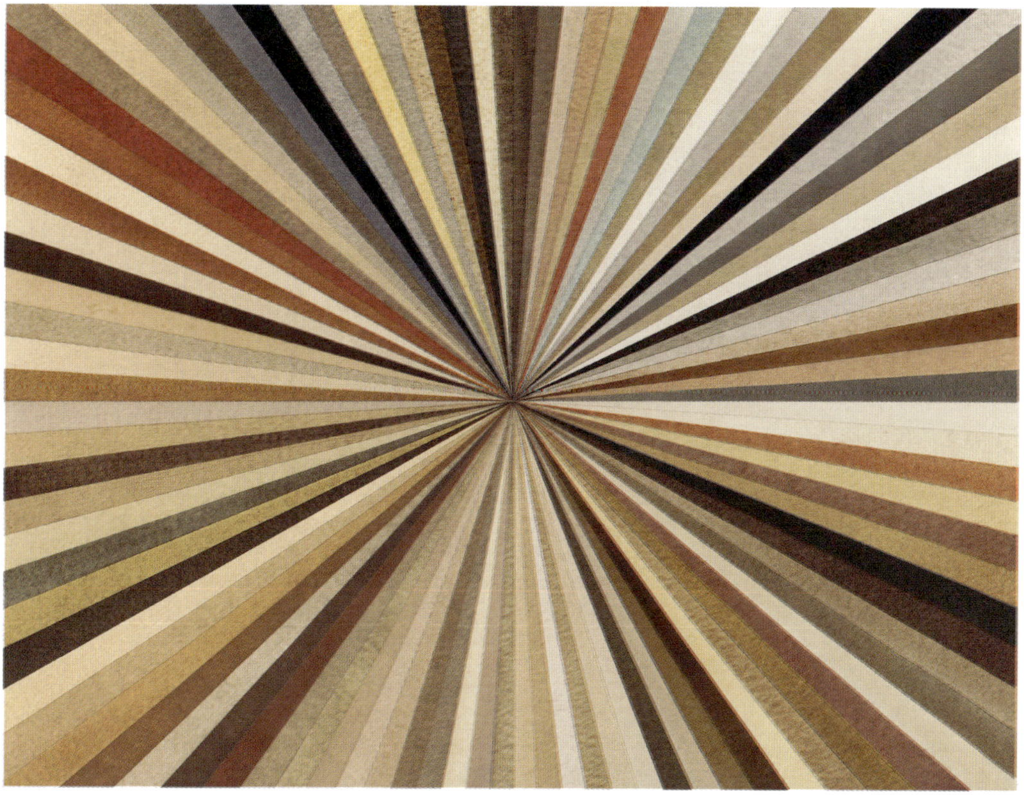

Endling (detail), Katie Paterson, 2022, mixed media in 100 pigments made from the pre-solar dust of 5 billion years ago to the ginkgo trees of Himakujumo

A wheel of extinction spins through 4.5 billion years, each wedge painted with pigments ground from the actual remains of vanished worlds. Katie Paterson crushed fossilized remnants from every era of life on Earth – from pre-solar dust to atomic bomb survivor trees – then mixed them into watercolours that tell the story of planetary mortality. Starting at 12 o'clock with the earliest microbes, this timeline spirals through mass extinctions and evolutionary explosions, each painted section literally containing the creatures it represents. The Scottish artist renders deep time visible in a single gaze, compressing billions of years into one circle. 'Endling' refers to the last individual of a species, the final passenger pigeon, the last Tasmanian tiger. You're looking at Earth's death certificate written in the bones of its former inhabitants, a memorial in which every brushstroke contains actual evidence of what we've lost.

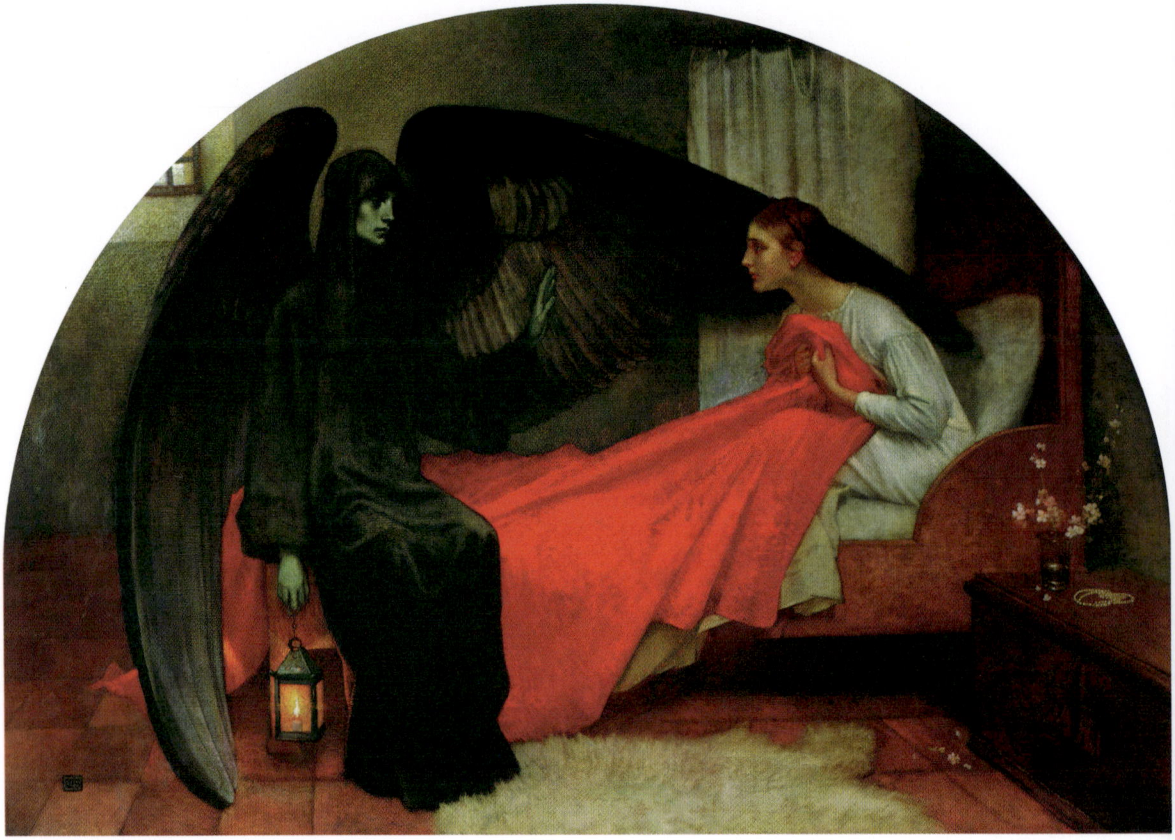

Death and the Maiden, Marianne Stokes, 1908, oil on canvas

Death arrives as a woman in black wings, holding up one hand in a gesture that seems to say, 'Be not afraid, babe' – although the young woman clutching her red bedcover clearly disagrees. Marianne Stokes (1855–1927) painted this unusual take on the classic 'Death and the Maiden' theme in 1908, softening centuries of skeletal menace into something almost maternal. The Austrian-born artist, who settled in Victorian England and championed women's causes, presents Death not as an aggressive predator but as a gentle escort. Unlike the typically threatening Death figures of German Renaissance art, this dark angel seems genuinely sorry to interrupt such a young life. Her lantern casts just enough light to reveal compassion where terror usually reigns, making an ancient allegory of mortality surprisingly tender.

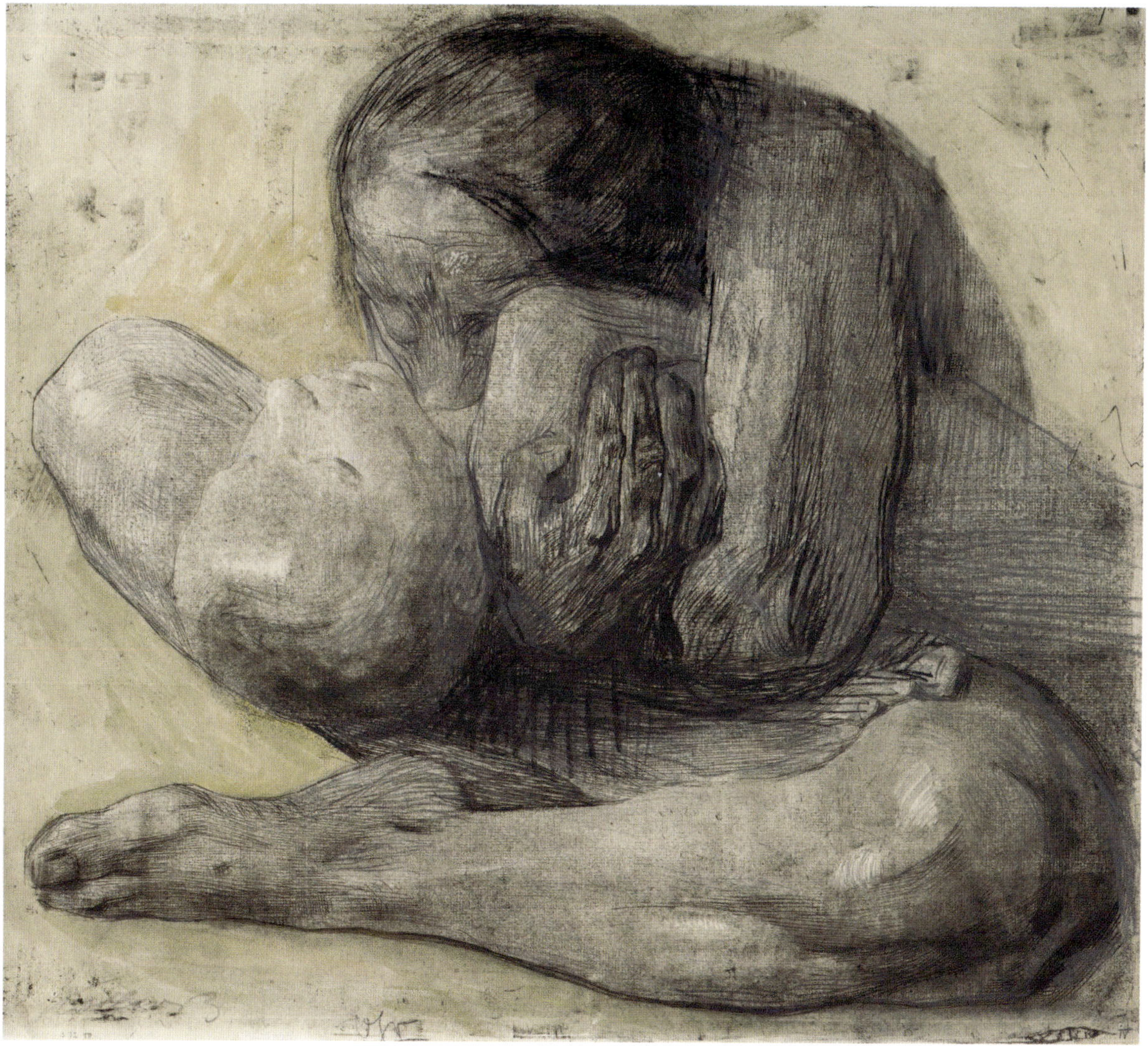

Woman with Dead Child, state VIII/X, Käthe Kollwitz, 1903, line etching, drypoint, sandpaper and soft-ground etching with the imprint of laid paper and Ziegler's transfer paper on chine collé

A mother's body wraps around her child's lifeless form, her naked torso becoming a cocoon of grief that cannot resurrect what it holds. Käthe Kollwitz (1867–1945) etched this pietà in 1903 using herself and her seven-year-old son Peter as models, though she couldn't have known she was rehearsing for a devastation that would consume her eleven years later when Peter fell in the First World War. Every line Kollwitz carved into the copper plate throbs with primal desperation – the mother's hand gripping the child's shoulder with such force you can feel her knuckles turn white against the impossible task of holding on. The natural order collapses when those meant to bury us lie cradled in our arms instead, when the generational rhythm breaks and leaves us clutching what should have outlived us. We recognize this posture from every war photograph, every hospital corridor, every moment when love proves both boundless and utterly helpless – the body's desperate attempt to shelter what can no longer be saved.

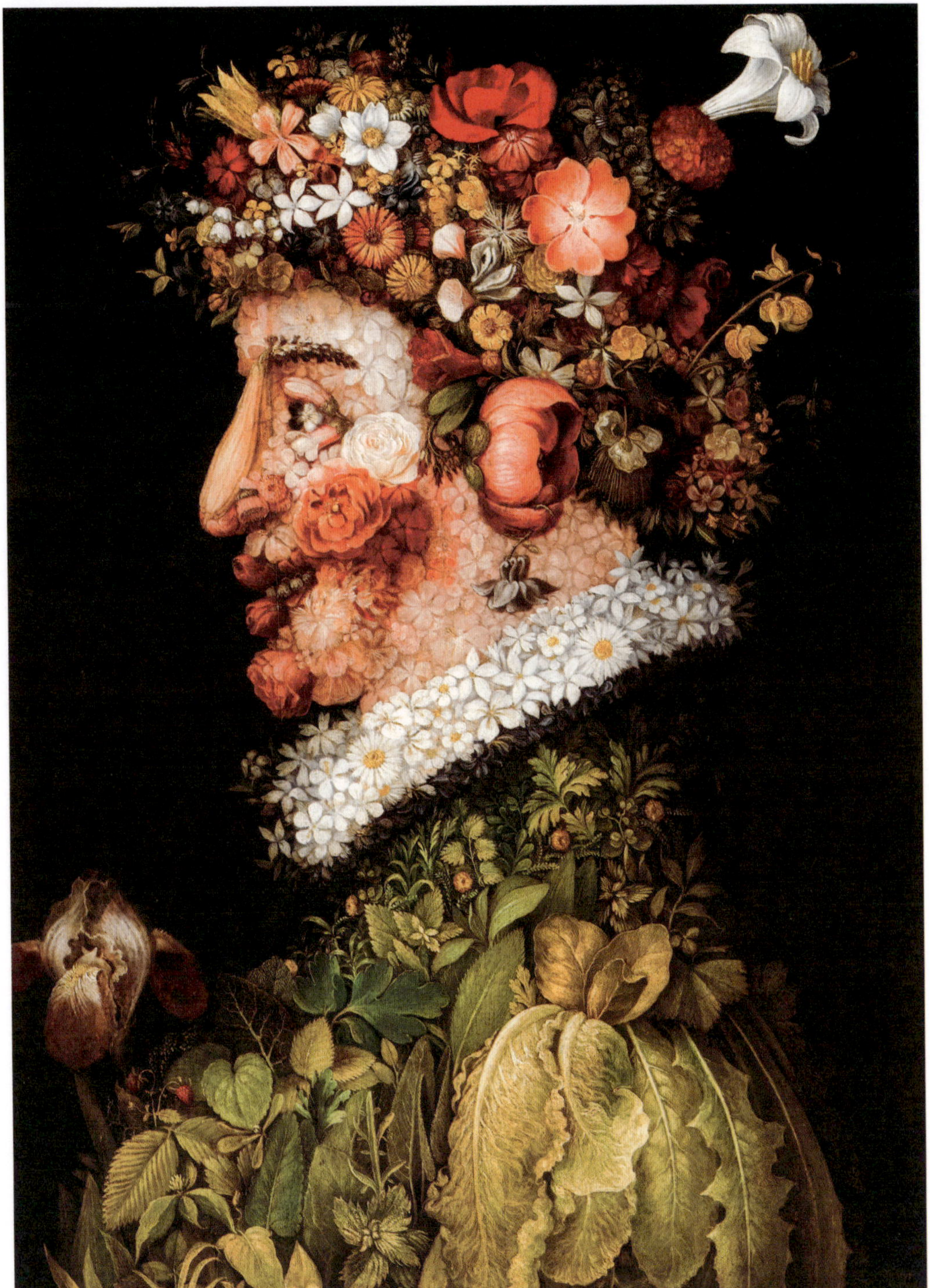

Right: Flora, Hannah Flowers, 2022, oil on poplar wood

A disembodied visage is crowned in a profusion of blooms: scarlet poppies, ivory roses, delicate blues and vivid yellows clustered and cascading against dim shadows. A snail inches up the jaw while a butterfly pauses at the temple, admiring the view. Hannah Flowers paints almost perversely beautiful surfaces for such a seemingly macabre tableau, and this severed head floating serenely among its opulent floral abundance feels less like tragedy and more like rapturous transformation. The Tasmanian-born, Scotland-based artist works genuine vermillion and lapis lazuli onto Belgian linen, rendering each dewy petal with such luscious attention that the paint feels edible, wearable, kissable. The flora glows jewelled against the void with intoxicating intensity. Every surface drips with swooning beauty – the heavy, heady gravitas of death and decay, but rich, ripe and deliriously decadent.

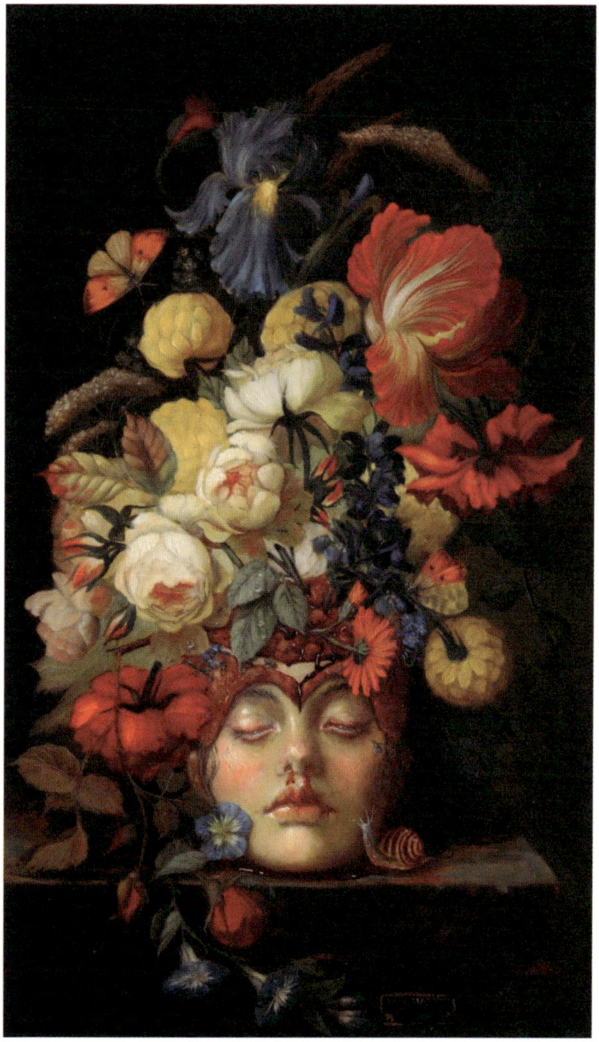

Opposite: Spring, Giuseppe Arcimboldo, 1563, oil on oak panel

A woman's profile blooms from the canvas, her entire being crafted from nature's spring prêt-à-porter collection: roses for flushed cheeks, lily-of-the-valley teeth flashing in a gentle smile, tulips and daisies cascading as hair, while strawberry leaves and dandelion greens compose her leafy couture. (In the words of Miranda Priestly from *The Devil Wears Prada*: 'Florals? For spring? Groundbreaking.') Giuseppe Arcimboldo (1526–93) painted this botanical portrait in 1563 for Emperor Maximilian II, creating what amounts to a visual manifesto from a botanical atelier: we are nature, nature is us, and spring's arrival happens as much inside our bodies as outside our windows. You can almost smell the earth-rich perfume drifting from this figure, her serene expression capturing that particular spring contentment of growth finally unleashed after months of dormancy. This is spring's haute couture incarnate, reminding you that the same force currently pushing green shoots through pavement cracks is pulsing through your own bloodstream, awakening appetites and ambitions that have been dormant since the last leaf fell.

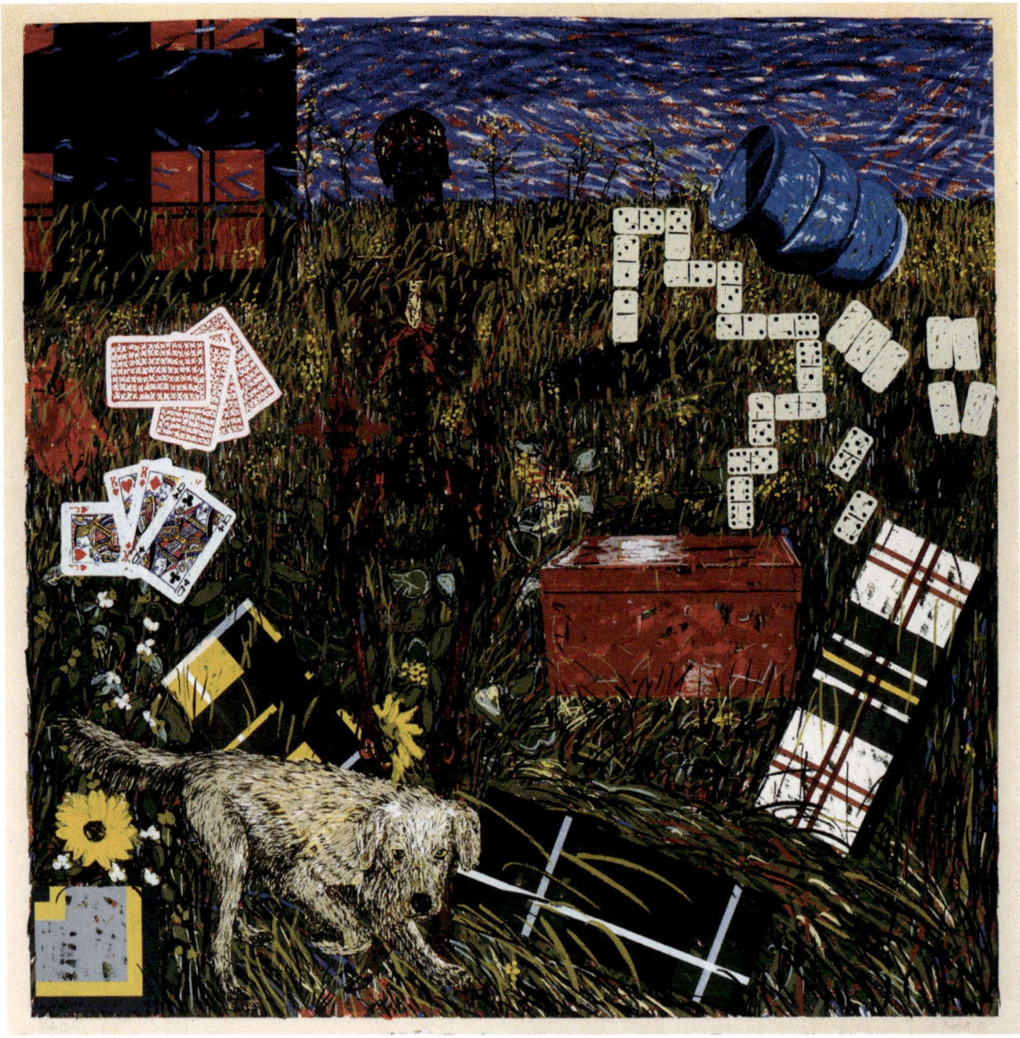

Autumn, Jennifer Bartlett, 1993, colour screenprint on Japanese handmade Kurotani Hosho paper

A skeleton occupies a field of wildflowers while dominoes scatter through grass and playing cards lie abandoned near ghostly translucent quilts – comforting patterns that hover like the memory of domesticity rather than actual textiles. A shaggy dog trots through sunflowers, the only living creature, and seemingly unbothered by the skeleton's presence. Jennifer Bartlett (1941–2022) turns her garden into a surreal inventory of endings, where death mingles casually with games and toolboxes and other remnants of human pastimes. Part of her 'Four Seasons' series, the painting captures autumn's essential paradox: the season of harvest is also the season of decay, when summer's abundance turns into winter's preparation. Autumn's strange mixture of melancholy and liberation permeates this scene – an annual reminder that letting go is just another form of gathering, that death is simply life shuffling the deck for the next round of play.

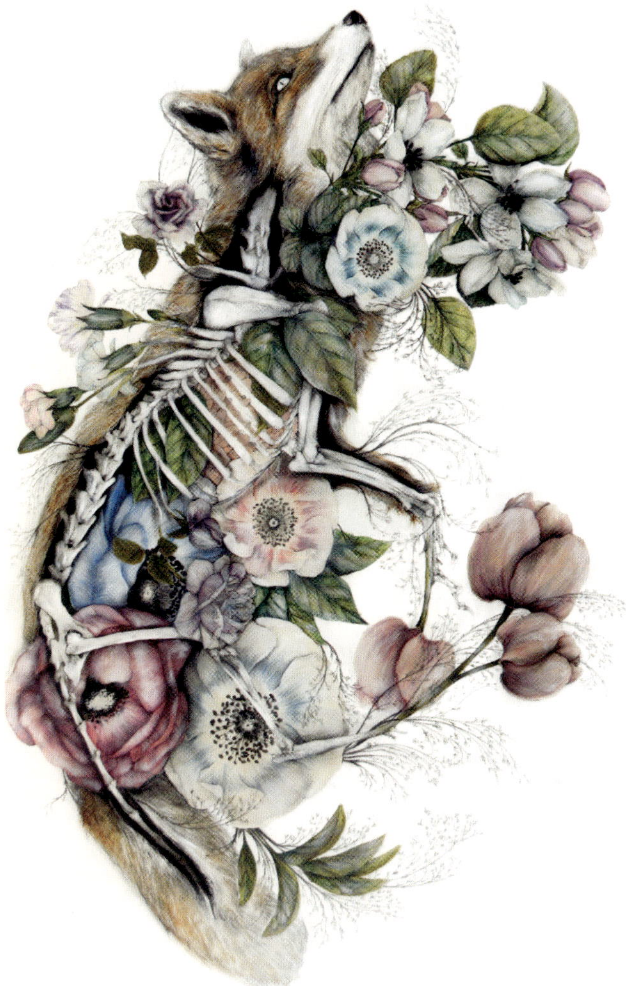

Taxidermy Garden, Nunzio Paci, 2017, graphite, pastels, acrylic and oil on canvas

A fox lies on its side, ribcage split to reveal a gathering of delicate flowers spiralling through its flesh, claiming the corpse as genteel nursery. Nunzio Paci fills the cavity where organs once lived with pink, white and blue blossoms, their stems winding through bone as naturally as blood once flowed through veins. The Bologna-based artist renders fur in earthy oranges and whites, while delicate ferns spiral around the fox's head, its gaze lifted as though idly watching snow melt, seeds drift past, moss creep across stone – slow seasonal studies. Working in graphite, pastels, acrylic and oil, Paci builds scenes in which flesh becomes soil and bones become trellises, each body repurposed, transformed, a nursery for cultivating new life. He calls his work a meditation on 'how all is slowly dying', noting that even a new sprout has already begun its decline. Here is his meditation made visible: the dying and the growing happen in the same breath, the same body, the same beautiful rot.

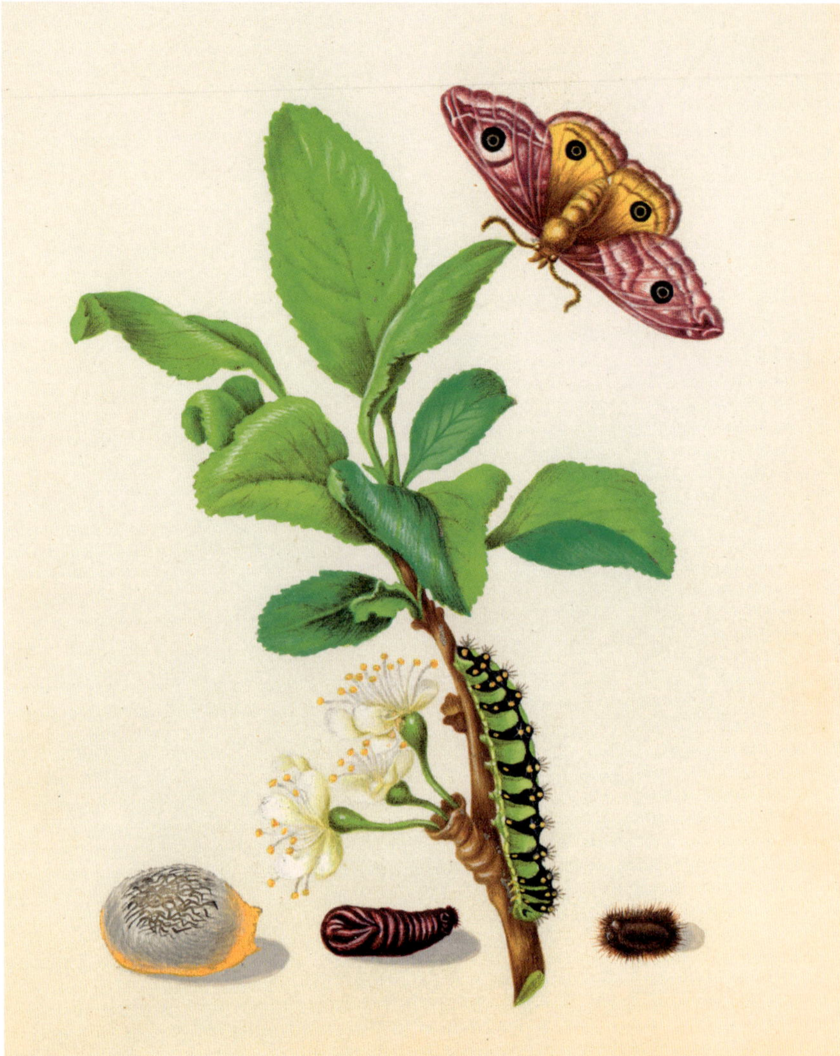

Metamorphosis of a Small Emperor Moth on a Damson Plum, Maria Sibylla Merian, 1679, watercolour over counterproof print on parchment

Here is nature's most outrageous magic trick performed on a single branch: caterpillars gorge themselves silly, wrap up in silk sleeping bags, then emerge as completely different creatures with wings and reproductive urges. Maria Sibylla Merian (1647–1717) painted this jaw-dropping transformation in 1679, while male scientists were still insisting that insects popped out of mud like popcorn. The German naturalist had been secretly breeding bugs in her garden for decades, watching the whole show unfold from egg to caterpillar to pupa to moth, then starting all over again with ruthless efficiency. Her neighbours probably thought she'd lost her mind, obsessing over creepy-crawlies while ignoring proper feminine pursuits. But Merian knew that she was documenting something revolutionary: proof that nature follows patterns more reliable than clockwork, more intricate than any human invention. This single branch contains everything: birth, growth, death, renewal. It's the eternal wheel scaled down to fit on a damson plum.

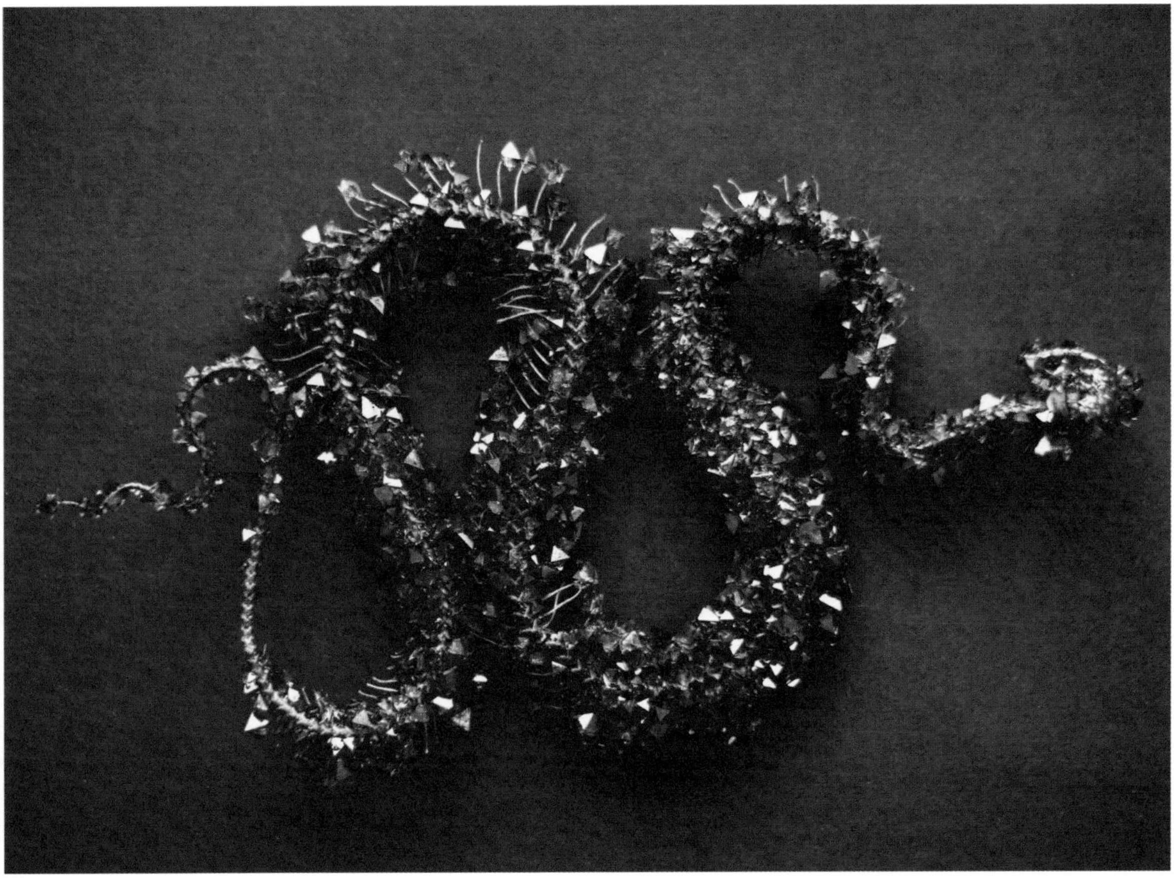

Crystallized Snake Skeleton,
Tyler Thrasher, *c.* 2020,
chromium potassium sulfate

A crystallized snake coils in a dazzling posthumous makeover, its skeletal form now encrusted with geometric jewels that shimmer purple and green like a disco ball designed by Mother Nature via her fairy godmother side-hustle. Tyler Thrasher performs modern alchemy in his mad scientist lab, conducting resurrection ceremonies where dead creatures become sparkling mineral beings. The artist stumbled onto this process by sheer abundance of scientific curiosity mixed with a healthy dose of 'fuck around and find out', wondering what would happen if he stuck a cicada shell in a crystal bath. Thrasher works in collaborative alchemical relationship with the natural process - he sets up the ritual conditions and lets molecular forces decide how this serpent's next incarnation will unfold. This echoes every funeral that becomes a celebration, every compost pile that feeds next season's riotous garden, except here death literally turns into eternal beauty, asking questions about what magic might be possible if we just pay attention to the cycles already spinning around us.

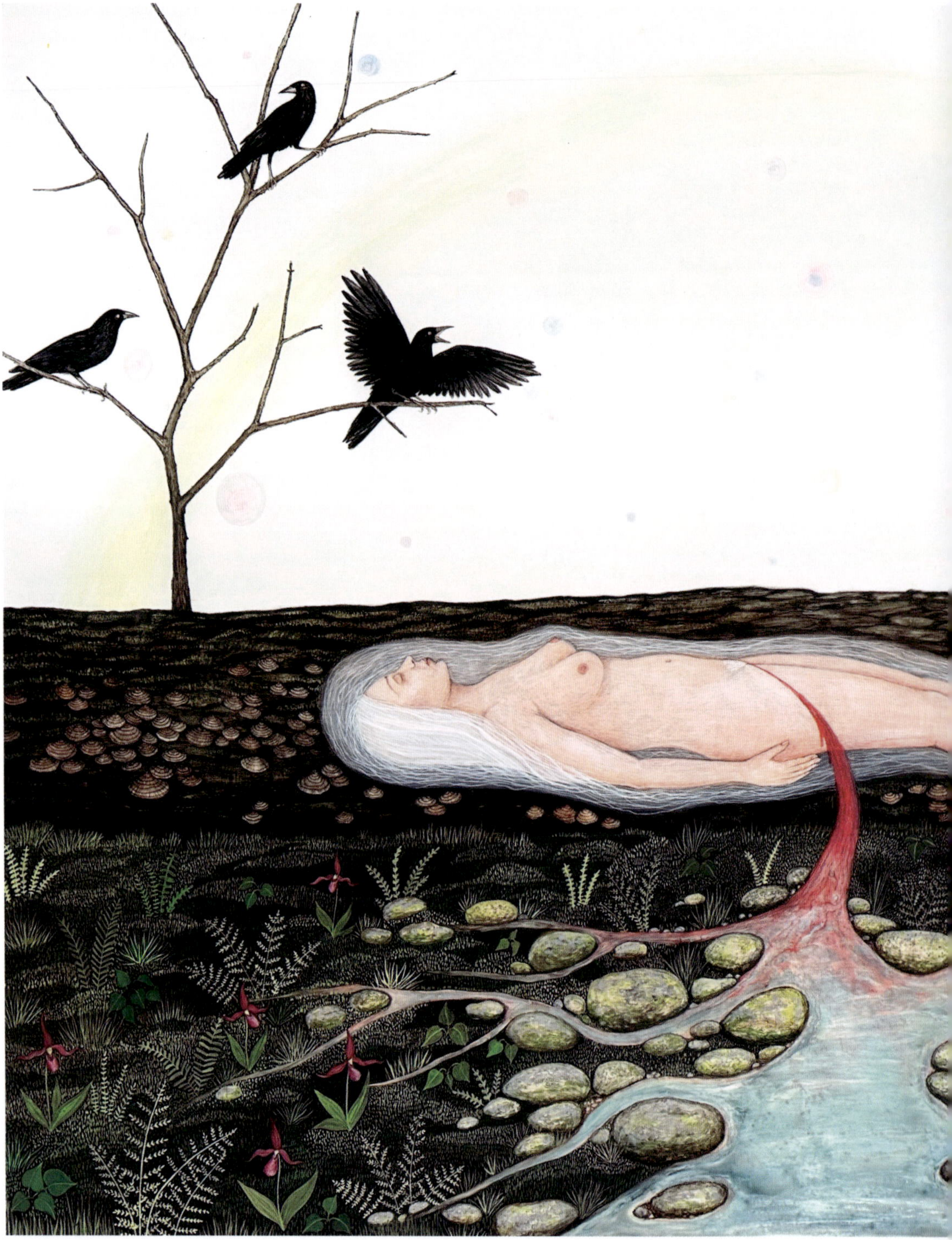

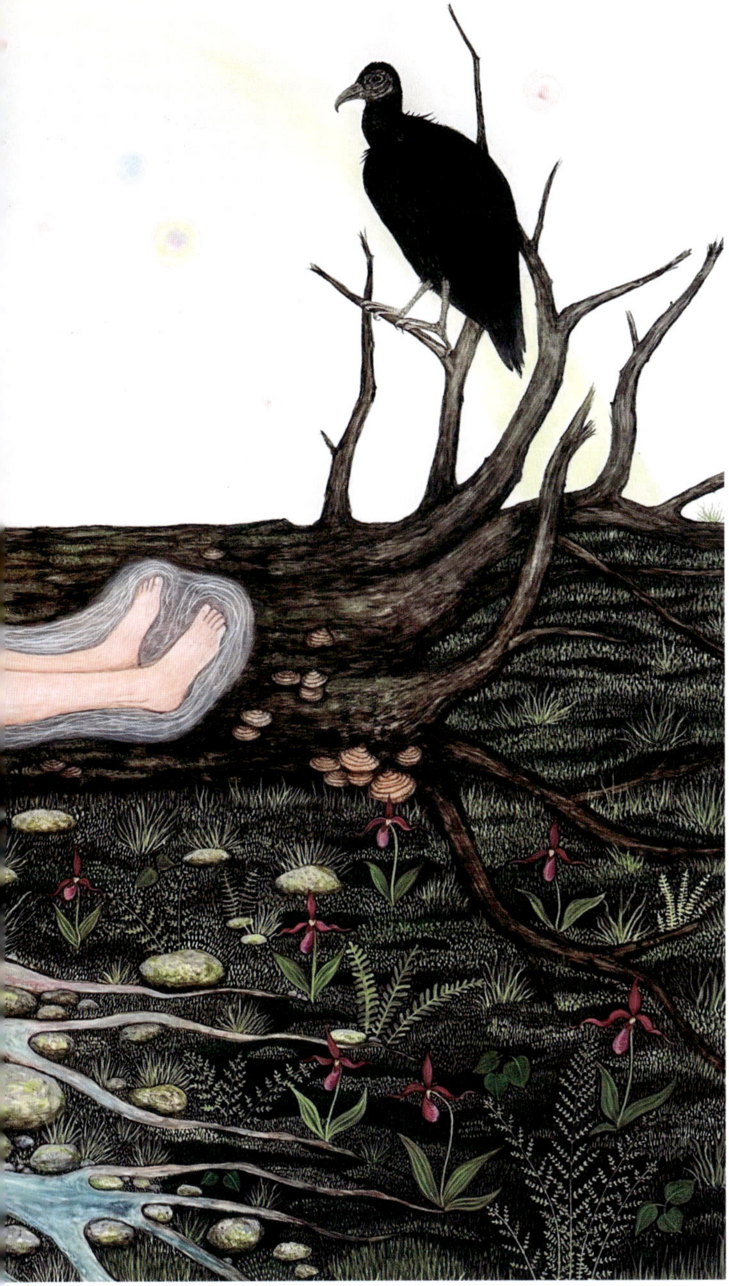

The Mothership, Susan Jamison, 2025, egg tempera on panel

A nude figure with long white hair lies cradled within the hollow of a fallen tree, her body serving as both womb and tomb in this cycle of eternal return. Susan Jamison discovered inspiration for this painting during a mountain residency, where she encountered a decaying log that had become a thriving ecosystem in death. From the figure's pelvis flows a red stream that turns into pale blue water, irrigating the forest floor, where pink wildflowers push through moss and stone. Four black birds witness this metamorphosis from their perches, silent observers of the ancient contract between death and regeneration. This scene echoes every fairy tale in which protagonists sleep in enchanted forests, every myth in which earth mothers birth rivers and mountains, every moment when you've felt the pull of soil calling your bones home. The fallen trunk serves as a birthing chamber, where decomposition and creation flow together in one continuous cycle, reminding you that every ending seeds a beginning, every death feeds new life. We are part of this ancient machinery, simultaneously observer and participant in something infinitely larger than ourselves, inhaling and exhaling in rhythms older than language, our brief lives intersecting with forces that will outlast us. What becomes of us, at the end of everything? Who knows! We can only hope that what we create endures.

Further Reading

Here's the thing about writing a book about the unknowable: you end up reading anything and everything and all bits and bobs and odds and ends in between. The following is a haphazard assemblage of books that either directly informed these pages, smuggled their way into my thinking or frolicked like freaky little gremlins in my brain while I was writing. Some you'll recognize quoted or referenced. Others shaped the research, informed the mood and rewired how I think about mystery, art and the slippery, shadowy spheres of the unknowable. The rest are just books that felt necessary while I was putting this together: they infused the thinking even if they didn't make it onto the page. Consider this less a formal bibliography and more a tour of all the stuff rattling around in my skull while I wrote this.

An Alchemy of Mind, Diane Ackerman, 2004

The Anthropocene Reviewed: Essays on a Human-Centered Planet, John Green, 2021

Area X, Jeff VanderMeer, 2014

Atlas of Improbable Places: A Journey to the World's Most Unusual Corners, Travis Elborough, 2016

Beloved, Toni Morrison, 1987

Bird by Bird, Anne Lamott, 1994

Catching The Big Fish, David Lynch, 2006

Charles Fort: The Man Who Invented the Supernatural, Jim Steinmeyer, 2008

The Chronicles of Narnia, C.S. Lewis, 1950-56

Dictionary of Obscure Sorrows, John Koenig, 2021

The Doors of Perception, Aldous Huxley, 1954

An Exorcism, Penny Slinger, 2024

Ficciones, Jorge Luis Borges, 1944

The Hero with a Thousand Faces, Joseph Campbell, 1949

Hilma af Klint: A Biography, Julia Voss, 2022

The Hocus-Pocus of the Universe, Laura Gilpin, 1977

How to Restore a Timeline: On Violence and Memory, Peter Counter, 2023

Lapidarium: The Secret Lives of Stones, Hettie Judah, 2022

Little Hidden Doors: A Guided Journal for Deep Dreamers, Naomi Sangreal, 2023

Magic Maker, Pam Grossman, 2025

The Nineties: A Book, Chuck Klosterman, 2022

The Old Ways: A Journey on Foot, Robert Macfarlane, 2012

The Other Side: A Journey into Women, Art and the Spirit World, Jennifer Higgie, 2023

Pamela Colman Smith: The Untold Story, Stuart R. Kaplan, 2018

Psychonauts: Drugs and the Making of the Modern Mind, Mike Jay, 2023

Remedios Varo: Science Fictions, editor Caitlin Haskell, 2023

Room to Dream, David Lynch and Kristine McKenna, 2018

The Secret History, Donna Tartt, 1992

Sick Houses: Haunted Homes and the Architecture of Dread, Leila Taylor, 2025

The Sphinx and the Milky Way: Selections from the Journals of Charles Burchfield, editor Ben Estes, 2023

Spiritus Mundi: Writings Borne from the Occult, editor Elizabeth Kim, 2022

Surreal Spaces: The Life and Art of Leonora Carrington, Joanna Moorhead, 2023

Symbolorum: The Secret Wisdom of Emblems, Mandy Aftel, 2025

Time-Life The Enchanted World series, editor Ellen Phillips, Tristram Potter Coffin, et al., 1984-87

The Transcendent Brain, Allan Lightman, 2023

The Universe in 100 Colors: Weird and Wondrous Colors from Science and Nature, Tyler Thrasher, 2024

Wanderings and Wonderings through the British Ritual Year, Weird Walk, 2023

The Way of Zen, Alan Watts, 1957

Ways of Seeing, John Berger, 1972

The Weird and the Eerie, Mark Fisher, 2016

What Art Does: An Unfinished Theory, Brian Eno, 2025

Women and Art: Contested Territory, Judy Chicago and Edward Lucie-Smith, 1999

Worlds Beyond Time: Sci-Fi Art of the 1970s, Adam Rowe, 2023

Index

Page numbers in *italics* indicate illustration captions.

Picture Credits

4 Getty Museum (CC0 1.0); **7** PiercingEyes (public domain); **8** Artvee; **12** Artepics/Alamy; **14** Getty Museum (CC0 1.0); **15** Album/Alamy; **18** Heritage Images//Getty; **19** Metropolitan Museum of Art, New York (public domain); **20** incamerastock/Alamy; **21** Bafuncius (public domain); **22** Trzęsacz (public domain); **23** Peter Palladino/The Agnes Pelton Society/Bridgeman Images; **24-25** Penta Springs Limited/Alamy; **26** Album/Alamy; **27** © Watts Gallery/© Trustees of Watts Gallery/Bridgeman Images; **28-29** PantheraLeo1359531 (public domain); **30** © Kysa Johnson; **31** © Pablo Carlos Budassi; **34** Heritage Art/Heritzage Images via Getty Images; **35** Universal History Archive/Getty Images; **36** © Valerie Hammond; **37** Ashmolean Museum/Heritage Images/Getty Images; **38** Historic Images/Alamy; **39** Fine Art Images/Heritage Images/Getty Images; **40** Fine Art Images/Heritage Images/Getty Images; **41** © Luciana Lupe Vasconcelos; **42** Gobonobo (public domain); **43** The Cleveland Museum of Art (public domain); **44** Heritage Art/Heritage Images via Getty Images; **45** Bridgeman Images; **46-47** © David Huggins; **48** Courtesy Andrew Edlin Gallery, New York; **49** © 2026 The Easton Foundation/VAGA at ARS, NY and DACS, London. Digital image, The Museum of Modern Art, New York/Scala, Florence; **51** From the British Library archive/Bridgeman Images; **52** Wellcome Collection. (public domain); **53** From the British Library archive/Bridgeman Images; **54** Metropolitan Museum of Art, New York (public domain); **55** Imagno/Getty Images; **56** © The Estate of Elda Cerrato Courtesy Galerie Lelong, New York. Colección Museo de Arte Moderno de Buenos Aires; **57** © 2026 Bharti Kher. All Rights Reserved, DACS. Photo by Jeetin Sharma, copyright Bharti Kher Studio; **58** © Agostino Arrivabene; **59** © Tino Rodríguez; **60** © Ann McCoy; **61** © Benjamin A. Vierling. Image originally appears on the cover of *Veneficium*, by Daniel Schulke, published by Three Hands Press, 2012.; **62-63** The Picture Art Collection/Alamy; **64** © Tate; **65** © Daniel Martin Diaz; **68** Владислав Резвый (public domain); **71** Fine Art Images/Heritage Images via Getty Images; **74** incamerastock/Alamy; **75** Kobac (public domain); **76** Photo © The Maas Gallery, London/Bridgeman Images; **77** Hallaluja (public domain); **78-79** Alric (public domain); **80** © Richard Bober Studios; **81** © Fairy Art Museum/Bridgeman Images; **82** © 2026 ADAGP, Paris and DACS, London. Photo: James Goodman Gallery, New York, USA/Bridgeman Images; **83** Album/Alamy; **84** Heritage Image Partnership Ltd/Alamy; **85** © Alex Eckman-Lawn; **88** © 2026 Heirs of Josephine Hopper/Licensed by Artists Rights Society (ARS) NY/DACS, London. © NPL - DeA Picture Library/Bridgeman Images; **89** Artepics/Alamy; **90** Artepics/Alamy; **91** © Aron Wiesenfeld; **92** Surajr7 (public domain); **93** © 2026 Foundation Paul Delvaux, Brussels - SABAM Belgium/DACS. Photo: Album/Alamy; **94-95** Dcoetzee (public domain); **96** incamerastock/Alamy; **97** Artvee; **98** © Tristan Elwell 2005; **99** © Todd Hido; **100** © 2026 Candida Höfer/VG Bild-Kunst, Bonn and DACS, London.; **101** Vintage Archives/ Alamy; **102** © Erich Lessing/Bridgeman Images; **103** © 2026 Estate of Kay Sage/DACS, London and ARS, NY. Digital image, The Museum of Modern Art, New York/Scala, Florence; **106-07** Painters/Alamy; **108** © Sally Mann. Courtesy Gagosian; **109** Bridgeman Images; **110** Bridgeman Images; **111** © Adam Lee. Image: Christo Crocker. Courtesy of the artist and STATION, Australia; **112** Bridgeman Images; **113** The Most Comfortable Chair (public domain); **114** ARTGEN/Alamy; **115** Heritage Art/Heritage Images via Getty Images; **116** Bridgeman Images; **117** Photo © Peter Nahum at The Leicester Galleries, London/ Bridgeman Images; **118** Archivart/Alamy; **119** © Andy Goldsworthy Courtesy Galerie Lelong; **120** Wmpearl (public domain); **121** © Linda Westin, 2019. Used by permission; **124** © 2026 ADAGP, Paris and DACS, London. Image copyright The Metropolitan Museum of Art/Art Resource/Scala, Florence; **127** FA2010 (public domain); **131** incamerastock/ Alamy; **132** Bridgeman Images; **133** © Chris Beetles Ltd, London/Bridgeman Images; **134** Bridgeman Images; **135** Tremendo (public domain); **136** Art Institute Chicago (CC0); **137** Model: Michele Delving; photograph © Nona Limmen; **138** DcoetzeeBot (public domain); **139** © Becky Munich; **140** © 2026 Penny Slinger. All Rights Reserved, DACS.; **141** piemags/Alamy; **142** National Trust Photographic Library/Paul Highnam/Bridgeman Images; **143** © Anna Mond; **144** © matsuyama miyabi; **145** © 2026, Benz and Chang; **149** Gennadii Saus i Segura (public domain); **150** © Fitzwilliam Museum/Bridgeman Images; **151** Fine Art Images/Heritage Images/Getty Images; **152** © Jane Dashley; **153** © 2026 Fondation Foujita/ADAGP, Paris and DACS, London. Photo: Christie's Images/Bridgeman Images; **154** Courtesy The Artist and Galerie Nordenhake Berlin/Stockholm/Mexico City. Photo: Carl Henrik Tillberg; **155** © 2026 ADAGP, Paris and DACS, London. Image courtesy of Sotheby's; **156** Fine Art Images/Heritage Images/Getty Images; **157** National Gallery of Art, Washington (public domain); **158** Heritage Art/Heritage Images via Getty Images; **159** © Gillian Wearing. All rights reserved, DACS Images. Image Courtesy Maureen Paley, London; **160** © Fine Art Images/Heritage Images via Getty Images; **161** Photo Austrian Archives/Scala Florence; **162** © Matthew Bober; **163** © Mike Worrall; **166** © Leonard de Selva/Bridgeman Images; **167** The Picture Art Collection/Alamy; **168** Bari' bin Farangi (public domain); **169** Metropolitan Museum of Art, New York (public domain); **170** Historica Graphica Collection/Heritage Images/Getty Images; **171** Quagga Media/Alamy; **172-73** Wellcome Collection (CC BY-NC 4.0); **174** © Erich Lessing/ Bridgeman Images; **175** Artepics/Alamy; **176** Sueddeutsche Zeitung Photo/Alamy; **177** Magnus Manske (public domain); **178** Artefact/ Alamy; **179** © Andy Paiko. Artist photo.; **180-81** © 2026 DACS. Digital image, The Museum of Modern Art, New York/Scala, Florence; **184** Baron/Hulton Archive/Getty Images; **187** Peter Barritt/Alamy; **191** steeve-x-art/Alamy; **190** Sepia Times/Universal Images Group via Getty Images; **192** © Virgo Paraiso; **193** Bonhams; **194** © Erich Lessing/Bridgeman Images; **195** steeve-x-art/Alamy; **196-97** Album/Alamy; **198** © Rachael Bridge. IG: @ RachaelBridge; **199** © Verlag Brinkmann & Bose Berlin. Photo courtesy Ubu Gallery, New York; **200** Villy Fink Isaksen (public domain); **201** © Rebecca Chaperon; **202** © 2026 ADAGP, Paris and DACS, London. Photo Smithsonian American Art Museum/Art Resource/Scala, Florence; **203** © Vali Myers. Photo courtesy The Vali Myers Art Gallery Trust; **206** Metropolitan Museum of Art, New York (public domain); **207** Yann (public domain); **208** Ajc994 (CC BY-SA 4.0); **209** © 2026 DACS. Photo: Buffalo AKG Art Museum/Art Resource, NY/Scala, Florence; **210** © Archives Charmet/Bridgeman Images; **211** Buyenlarge/Getty Images; **212** © Berlinde De Bruyckere. Courtesy the artist and Hauser & Wirth. Photo: Kévin Rinclin; **213** Historical image collection by Bildagentur-online/Alamy; **214** © 2026 Jenny Saville. All rights reserved, DACS. Photo: Bridgeman Images; **215** © 2026 Niki de Saint Phalle Charitable Art Foundation/ADAGP, Paris and DACS, London. Photo courtesy Sotheby's; **216** © 2026 Man Ray 2015 Trust/DACS, London. Photo: Dom Slike/Alamy; **217** © 2026 Association Marcel Duchamp/ADAGP, Paris and DACS, London. Photo: Philadelphia Museum of Art/The Louise and Walter Arensberg Collection, 1950/Bridgeman Images; **220** Metropolitan Museum of Art, New York (public domain); **221** DeAgostini/Getty Images; **222** Michael Hurst (public domain); **223** iStock Editorial/ Getty Images Plus; **224** Artepics/Alamy; **225** © Katie Paterson; **226** Bridgeman Images; **227** Primaler (public domain); **228** incamerastock/Alamy; **229** © Hannah Flowers; **230** © Jennifer Bartlett 2013 Trust. Courtesy Marianne Boesky Gallery, New York and Aspen and Paula Cooper Gallery, New York. Photo © Mead Art Museum/Purchase with Acquisition Fund/Bridgeman Images; **231** © Nunzio Paci - courtesy of the artist; **232** incamerastock/Alamy; **233** © Tyler Thrasher; **234-35** © Susan Jamison.

Acknowledgements

In addition to my beloved companions and incredible support system that make it into every acknowledgement section for every book I write (Yvan, Mary, Melissa, Violet, Maika, Sonya, here you are again!) I also want to thank Amory Sivertson and Ben Brock Johnson of Endless Thread Podcast for their enthusiasm and persistence regarding the Wrinkle In Time Mystery, which is partly what inspired the idea for this book; John Coulthart, who was among the first to offer suggestions and ideas as to that mystery; Adam Rowe, whose friendship evolved out of that very mystery, and whose camaraderie has been a gift I didn't know to ask for; and Matt Bober, whose generosity in sharing both his uncle Richard Bober's iconic work and his own transformed this book into the one I'd been dreaming of. And in that vein, a million heartfelt thanks to all of the incredible artists who have allowed me to include their works in these pages. To my lovely and knowledgeable editors at Quarto – thanks again for wrangling my nonsense into a beautiful tome! To all my readers, thanks for your continued support of my writing and for making another weird art book possible. And to all the folks on Reddit who have ever read one of my perfume reviews and said, 'Wow, you should be a writer!' Thanks for the validation! I hope this book finds its way into your hands.